The Frontier in British India

Thomas Simpson provides an innovative account of how distinctive forms of colonial power and knowledge developed at the territorial fringes of colonial India during the nineteenth century. Through critical interventions in a wide range of theoretical and historiographical fields, he speaks to historians of empire and science, anthropologists, and geographers alike. *The Frontier in British India* provides the first connected and comparative analysis of frontiers in northwest and northeast India and draws on visual and written materials from an array of archives across the subcontinent and the United Kingdom. Colonial interventions in frontier spaces and populations were, it shows, enormously destructive but also prone to confusion and failure on their own terms. British frontier administrators did not merely suffer 'turbulent' frontiers, but actively worked to generate and uphold these regions as spaces of governmental and scientific exception. Accordingly, India's frontiers became crucial spaces of imperial practice and imagination throughout the nineteenth century.

THOMAS SIMPSON is a research fellow at Gonville and Caius College, University of Cambridge.

T0364219

The Frontier in British India

Space, Science, and Power in the Nineteenth Century

Thomas Simpson

University of Cambridge

CAMBRIDGE
UNIVERSITY PRESS

Shaftesbury Road, Cambridge CB2 8EA, United Kingdom

One Liberty Plaza, 20th Floor, New York, NY 10006, USA

477 Williamstown Road, Port Melbourne, VIC 3207, Australia

314–321, 3rd Floor, Plot 3, Splendor Forum, Jasola District Centre, New Delhi – 110025, India

103 Penang Road, #05–06/07, Visioncrest Commercial, Singapore 238467

Cambridge University Press is part of Cambridge University Press & Assessment, a department of the University of Cambridge.

We share the University's mission to contribute to society through the pursuit of education, learning and research at the highest international levels of excellence.

www.cambridge.org
Information on this title: www.cambridge.org/9781108794121

DOI: 10.1017/9781108879156

First published 2021
First paperback edition 2022

A catalogue record for this publication is available from the British Library

ISBN   978-1-108-84019-4   Hardback
ISBN   978-1-108-79412-1   Paperback

For my Nan and Grandad

The joy that scatters all things in the dust,
Which no last word has ever quite expressed

Rabindranath Tagore

Contents

Figures

Acknowledgements

For all the hours of solitude spent poring over crumbling, barely legible documents in hushed and dimmed rooms, this book is really made up of collaborations, conversations, and friendships. Without such generous colleagues, I could not have researched and written it. Without such supportive friends and family, I would not have enjoyed the process half as much as I have. I am truly grateful to you all.

My greatest academic debt in writing this book is to Sujit Sivasundaram. From overseeing my undergraduate thesis at the London School of Economics in 2008 to reading recently revised chapters, Sujit's unwavering support and perceptive guidance have made him the ideal supervisor and mentor. I'm sure that he is as delighted as I am to see the back of British India's nineteenth-century frontiers after putting up with my thoughts on them for nearly a decade. Thank you, Sujit.

The other steadfast supporter I especially want to thank is Ben Hopkins. Without Ben's captivating teaching on colonial India at the London School of Economics in 2007–8, my academic trajectory would have been very different. More recently, he has gone above and beyond in supporting my research and being an invaluable sounding board for all things frontier-related. Ben is also part of a wonderful group of fellow frontier scholars – along with Magnus Marsden (who was an excellent PhD examiner), Bérénice Guyot-Rechard, Elisabeth Leake, Dan Haines, Martin Bayly, Mark Condos, Francesca Fuoli, Zak Leonard, and Kyle Gardner – who have shown admirable perseverance with my jetlagged ramblings at conferences and on archival trips, and given me invaluable intellectual input at various stages.

During my PhD I was fortunate to receive advice and feedback from a thriving community of world historians and South Asianists in Cambridge, and would particularly like to thank Kate Boehme, Devyani Gupta, Vikram Visana, Patrick Clibbens, Teresa Segura-Garcia, Annamaria Motrescu-Mayes, Shruti Kapila, David Washbrook, and Joya Chatterji. I have, no doubt, taxed the patience of members of Sujit's reading group with unruly drafts of portions of this book over the past eight years. Their advice has always been invaluable, as has their company afterwards in 'The Granta'. Thanks, then, to Hatice Yıldız

Yaman, Naomi Parkinson, James Wilson, Jake Richards, Meg Foster, Jagjeet Lally, Sim Koole, Tom Smith, Dwayne Menezes, Steph Mawson, Callie Wilkinson, Kate Stevens, Alix Chartrand, Taushif Kara, Tamara Fernando, Scott Connors, Kate Stevens, Mattia Pessina, Mishka Sinha, Shinjini Das, and Catarina Madruga. For a variety of conference invitations, critical readings, and stimulating conversations, I'm also grateful to Felix Driver, Gavin Rand, Shah Mahmoud Hanifi, Marcus Banks, Edward Boyle, Edward Moon-Little, Efram Sera-Shriar, Jan Seifert, Lipokmar Dzüvichü, Pratik Chakrabarti, Branwyn Poleykett, Michael Bravo, Min Jung Kim, and Freddy Foks.

During the latter stages of my PhD and throughout my postdoc, I have gradually found myself becoming a historian of science. This was primarily a result of some fascinating conversations with members of the History and Philosophy of Science community in Cambridge, which made me realise that history of science is where many of the questions that I want to answer are being discussed. I am especially grateful to Simon Schaffer for providing invaluable advice as my PhD examiner and giving insights that have shaped how I think about science and colonialism. Jim Secord and Richard Staley have been approachable and helpful, and I particularly appreciate Josh Nall's efforts to show me how a nineteenth-century theodolite works. Thanks also to Rohan Deb Roy, Seb Kroupa, and Eóin Phillips for enlightening chats in Delhi, Cambridge, and London.

Special thanks go to six people variously connected to the history of science who have been generous colleagues and great friends. For generously sharing her huge stock of cartographic expertise over coffees, beers, and dosas (not all at the same time), I am very grateful to Meg Barford. For guiding me through some of the foothills of the history of science – including, appropriately, on a train journey from Delhi to Simla – many thanks to James Hall. For helping me understand what my work is actually all about on more than a few occasions, always interspersed with a good amount of chatting about sport, thanks to James Poskett. For her unfailingly insightful feedback on my work and discussions of life inside and outside academia during the past couple of years, thank you Charu Singh. For enlightening discussions of frontiers, maps, and frontier maps, thanks to Marie de Rugy. And for being a steadfast companion into mountainous terrain while remaining rooted in the flatlands of Cambridge, I'm extremely grateful to Lachlan Fleetwood.

I was very fortunate to end up at Gonville and Caius College as a PhD student, and luckier still to have been given the time to complete this book alongside other projects during my time as a research fellow. The college community – fellows, librarians, catering and cleaning staff, and porters – have provided a friendly and stimulating environment in which to do my work. In particular, I'd like to thank the historians at Caius, especially Melissa Calaresu, Peter Mandler, and Emma Hunter, for their advice and for offering teaching opportunities. The company and conversation of my fellow research fellows over the past five years, and the friendships I developed over the preceding four years of PhD research, have also been crucial to staying interested and happy. There are too many people to thank from my stint at Caius, but some friends have been too important to me not to mention by name: Roeland Verhallen, Dan Peat, Dan Costelloe, Anna Osnato, Lala Haris Sheikh, Ben Folit-Weinberg, Mike Price, Ani Mukkavilli, Marius Somveille, Robin Thompson, and Matthieu Palayret.

Although I put work on this book largely on hold during my time there, a teaching fellowship at Royal Holloway in 2016–17 offered welcome time away from research along with opportunities to consider elements of this project more broadly. I'd especially like to thank Sarah Ansari, Markus Daechsel, and Mike Horswell for prompting new ways of thinking and for providing support during and since that year.

This book was made possible by generous funding from the Arts and Humanities Research Council, Gonville and Caius College, and the Cambridge University History Faculty. I would like to thank the editors and anonymous referees of *The Historical Journal* and *History of Science* for polishing and publishing earlier versions of parts of this book. The editorial and production teams at Cambridge University Press have been attentive and helpful throughout the publication process, and I would especially like to thank my commissioning editor Lucy Rhymer for her enthusiasm and guidance.

I am indebted to the assistance I received from wonderful staff at numerous archives and libraries: the British Library, Royal Anthropological Institute, Royal Geographical Society, Cambridge University Library, Centre for South Asian Studies in Cambridge, National Archives of India in New Delhi, Punjab State Archives in Chandigarh, and Maharashtra State Archives in Mumbai. I am extremely grateful to Philip Grover at the Pitt Rivers Museum for his assistance on numerous visits over the past six years; and to Arnab Kashyap and Jishnu Barua at the Assam State Archives in Dispur for providing wonderful service and hospitality in 2014.

Time spent in India was a personal highlight of this project, made memorable by some exceptional hosts and friends. My thanks to Mrinal and Krishna Talukdar in Guwahati, Partha Borgohain in Sivasagar, Mahesh Mehta in Mumbai, the staff and residents of Moonlighting and Bed and Chai, and Vinod and Vandana Mohindra in Delhi. For their companionship in happy and challenging times alike, special thanks to Auke Douma, Luna Sabastian, Jameson Karns, and Mingma Lhamu.

The unequivocal support of close friends and family has made the tougher parts of life as a PhD candidate and early career scholar bearable. They are the most important people in my life. I hope that this book can go some way to living up to the love they have given me over not only the past decade but the decades before that too. Thank you to my godfather, Brian, and my parents-in-law, Charles and Diana, for your emotional and practical support. Dad, Toni, Ros, and Piers – thank you for understanding what studying and researching means to me and for backing me throughout. Mum and Adrian – thank you for being my most loyal and steadfast supporters and for always being there.

This book is dedicated to my Nan and Grandad, with two lines from Rabindranath Tagore's *Gitanjali*.[1] As I wrote these words I thought back to when I first read them, on my final research trip to Delhi for this book. Then, they helped me comprehend what my grandparents mean to me as I grappled with the grief of losing one of them. My Nan and Grandad have been the people who have taught me about those inexpressible things that matter most – starting with the value of family. Now, to think of my grandparents and read these same words by Tagore helps me grasp what it means to be a husband and a dad. That I am lucky enough to start my own family with someone who understands me so perfectly is the great joy of my life. Jude, thank you for everything, and especially for Lyra.

---

[1] Rabindranath Tagore, *Gitanjali*, trans. William Radice (Gurgaon: Penguin, 2011), p. 113.

Map 1 Northwestern frontier regions

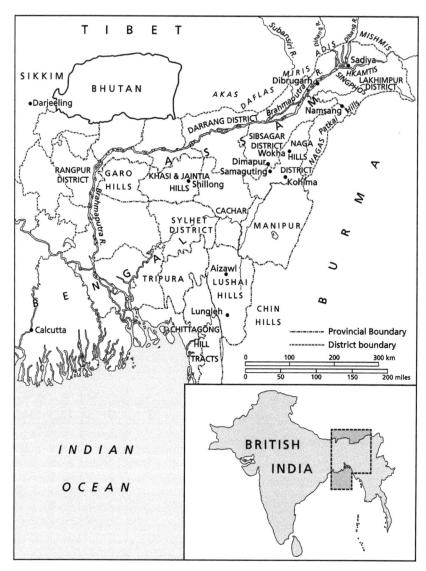

Map 2 Northeastern frontier regions

Introduction

Of Flies and Ants

Hurbut Tongloyn, Thangliena, and Thomas Herbert Lewin were some of the names of a man renowned in British circles and, supposedly, among frontier inhabitants for his escapades beyond the eastern edge of Bengal from the 1860s to 1880s.[1] He was given to outbursts of maniacal ambition, as when he confided to his diary 'I am now founding a new colony here – among the Lushai'.[2] His first forays into the uplands resulted from a determination to gather information on the Lushai people, coupled with imagined journeys through frontier space. 'I had arrived at the conclusion', he later recalled, 'that by going some distance southwards and then striking east I should get to Burmah, perhaps, if I went far enough, to China'.[3] This mixture of scientific-observational motives with fantastical schemes was a key constituent of high imperial frontiers, areas in which neat delineations between knowing and desiring did not hold. Frontiers disrupted conventions not only at the grandiose level of legal frameworks and scientific techniques but also at intimate scales: interpersonal encounters, the body, and the self. By the later nineteenth century, when normalised processes of knowing and governing seemed to have spread across most of Britain's imperial possessions, agents of empire widely construed India's frontiers as what Michel Foucault termed 'spiritual' spaces.[4] Comprehending and acting in these spaces seemed to demand not a masterful and removed subject-position, but rather that frontier officials became other than they were before and elsewhere. In short, British agents of empire conceived of frontiers as productively strange.

---

[1] J. Shakespear, *The Lushei Kuki Clans* (London: Macmillan and Co., 1912), frontispiece. See also John Whitehead, *Thangliena: The Life of T.H. Lewin* (Gartmore: Kiscadale, 1992).

[2] Senate House Library, University of London (hereafter 'SHL'), Lewin Collection, MS 811/II/27, f. 53, xxv.

[3] T. H. Lewin, *A Fly on the Wheel, or How I Helped to Govern India* (London: W.H. Allen & Co., 1885), pp. 221–6.

[4] Michel Foucault, *The Hermeneutics of the Subject: Lectures at the College de France, 1981–1982*, ed. Frédéric Gros, trans. Graham Burchell (New York, NY: Picador, 2005), pp. 15–9.

In the event, on this journey Lewin did not reach China, nor anywhere near Burma. Shot by one of his guides (whether accidentally or not remained a mystery), he laboured back from the first village that he reached beyond administered colonial territory.[5] During the following years, however, he persistently pierced the formal limits of British rule, developing a conceptual apparatus to justify his activities to others and to himself. He praised the hill dwellers in primitivist terms while critiquing 'civilization' for its fixation on luxury.[6] Yet he could not bring himself to extol the frontier communities' existing state in its entirety: to do so would not only remove his role but would obliterate the self that the uplanders allowed him to be – the 'Hurbut Tognloyn' or 'Thangliena' that he apparently came to consider no more affected than 'T. H. Lewin'. He accordingly proposed something between 'civilization' and the 'simple people like our hill men' – and that something was, implicitly, his own self. 'If', he mused in 1869, 'these people could be taught to live according to Nature in its higher sense, to rise above all gross and base indulgences, mindful of those higher laws of which only self-denial and self-command can render observance possible, I am not prepared to say but this be the wisest and the grandest ideal'.[7] Such tuition would come from 'not measures but a man . . . an officer gifted with the power of rule; not a mere cog in the great wheel of government'.[8] He felt that this approach held out the promise of a double flourishing. Guided by someone aware of the pitfalls as well as the promises of civilisation, frontier communities would become 'not debased and miniature epitomes of Englishmen, but a new and noble type of God's creatures'.[9] This was a case of a British imperialist self-deifying as an awesome agent of reform; but it was also something more. Lewin believed that he too would benefit through immersion among frontier communities that 'live according to Nature as the old Stoic philosophers taught'.[10] Here, then, was a scheme in which the colonising self and the colonised frontier were inseparable, with changes in one implying and requiring shifts to the other.

Lewin did not unquestioningly adhere to this entwined ideal of frontier and self. In January 1871 he wrote a poem entitled 'Change', the sentiment of which evidently lasted or returned, as he transcribed the words into his diary once again in early 1873.

> Cast away these phantasmatic aimless wanderings erratic
> And forswearing moods prismatic cease to roam
> Pleasure seek not in things strange, true love only knows no change
> There's true pleasure, true variety at Home.[11]

---

[5] Lewin, *Fly*, pp. 255–77.
[6] T.H. Lewin, *The Hill Tracts of Chittagong and the Dwellers Therein; with Comparative Vocabularies of the Hill Dialects* (Calcutta: Bengal Printing Company, 1869), pp. 115–16.
[7] Ibid., p. 115.   [8] Ibid., p. 118.   [9] Ibid., p. 118.   [10] Ibid., p. 115.
[11] SHL, Lewin Collection, MS 811/II/27, f. 53, xxvii.

The struggle against his frontier-self and all it represented – casting off the normality and stasis of Home in favour of wanderings erratic and things strange – was one that Lewin wanted to lose. He was seemingly unable to be content with the unchanging, favouring instead the fragmentation of his personality, scattering differing selves like light shone through a prism. Yet his efforts to maintain these multiple selves were also destined to seem forlorn.

Lewin's memoirs, published in 1885, attest to a man still unconvinced by the merits of cultivated civilisation and prone to seeing in Lushai society another world, one of 'contentment and well-being', set against 'the feverish anxieties of civilized life'.[12] By this stage, however, he acknowledged that this other world was one that he could never fully enter. He referred to the dream-like moods that the frontier had inspired, which at their most extreme expressed an urge to disappear completely and merge with the upland landscape. '[The mist] gave one an impulse to spring out into the soft white fleece . . . [I] watched the rushing torrent cast its masses of topaz-coloured water over the dark rocks, foaming, raging, and tumbling headlong down, with such an uproarious sympathy with the wild water'.[13] But he became increasingly convinced that being enveloped by Lushai society and landscape was simply not possible. As early as 1873, he related to his diary the exotic and erotic allure of 'the girls in the country . . . almost a gold colour, they are like statues of transparent gold through [which] shines out the life light'. No sooner had he projected his domineering, desiring gaze outwards than it reflected back, as if he imagined the eyes of Lushais on his own body and experienced a sharp apprehension of his entrapment in a pallor that signified, at least momentarily, not power but self-disgust.[14] 'I feel almost ashamed of my dead white skin – it looks leprous & unhealthy among these gun metal beauties'.[15]

By 1885, Lewin felt, with evident misgivings, that his Thangliena persona could not mediate all racial and civilisational differences. The Lushais, he insisted, were 'happy' with their materially limited lot. 'We English people' – the first-person pronoun is notable – were mistaken in promoting 'civilization as the antidote for all earthly ills' in the manner of 'some good old country dame with a turn for doctoring'.[16] Gone was any sign of faith in Thangliena's ability to perfect the Lushais as archetypes of a community living in accordance with Nature. Lewin instead quietly admitted that he could not be Thangliena. The final paragraph of *A Fly on the Wheel* contained the final repudiation of his claim sixteen years earlier that the Lushais needed 'not measures but a man' and of his efforts to be that man:

---

[12] Lewin, *Fly*, p. 428.   [13] Ibid., pp. 457–9.

[14] On the recursive quality of the imperial gaze, especially in frontier environs, see Erik Mueggler, *The Paper Road: Archive and Experience in the Botanical Expedition of West China and Tibet* (Berkeley, CA: University of California Press, 2011), p. 60.

[15] SHL, Lewin Collection, MS 811/II/27, f. 53, xxv.   [16] Lewin, *Fly*, p. 428.

I knew and loved my hill people. I lived among them and was their friend . . . But, after all, I was only 'a fly on the wheel'; they were not *my* people. I did but represent and make known to them the impartial justice, the perfect tolerance, and the respect for personal freedom which characterise the British rule in India.[17]

The elegiac 'after all' acts as a pivot between the dream of Thangliena's fluid frontier identity and Lewin's realisation that he had been nothing more than a conduit of imperial ideals in which he had little faith.

In this light we can see that Lewin all along conceived of salvation as a two-way track: saving the Lushais was always an attempt to save himself as well. In November 1871, Lewin had journeyed off from Chittagong into the hills as part of a colonial force sent to enact violence against Lushai villages. Despite the pressures of his official role with the expedition – and notwithstanding his admission a couple of years later that his 'head becomes silly' when reading Descartes and Kant[18] – his diary entry that day consisted mainly of musings on the fallibility and limitation of human senses. He then turned to consider the animal kingdom. 'Can it be that ants have some other new sense or some variation of sense more refined and delicate than ours that leads them to find their food – else how do they find a fly on a pot of jam?' A note to the side of this train of thought abruptly halted the tone of scientific investigation, stating that 'No data are obtainable by which to estimate the powers of scent of these creatures'.[19]

The importance of sensory intensity and inadequacy to British dealings in frontier environs suggests that we should read this entry as more than a mere oddity. Still more significance emerges if we take seriously the apparently arbitrary example of the ants and the fly. In his memoirs published fourteen years later, Lewin denoted his insignificance and the limitations of his Thangliena self with a nod to Aesop's fable of the fly on the wheel: he was the fly that believes for a time that he kicked up all that dust from the track. Narrating in that book the final stages of the 1871 expedition, when the colonial party came across the last band holding out against it, Lewin wrote: '[there] surged myriads of Lushais; the jungle was like an ants' nest. As I was led forward by my white-bearded conductor, there was a cry from the crowd of "Thangliena! Thangliena!"' Here was something more than merely a dismissive rendering of frontier inhabitants as insects, the irritating yet ultimately crushable animalistic mass that many of Lewin's administrative contemporaries invoked when describing communities at the edge of empire. It was the ants that called into being Thangliena, the frontiersman. Among members of the expeditionary force, he was simply T. H. Lewin, stuck with executing measures that seemed farcical and feeble in comparison to the rich, 'magical' Lushai culture.[20] Lewin was the fly mired in the jam, trusting that the ants, with their delicate and unknowable

[17] Ibid., pp. 465–66.   [18] SHL, Lewin Collection, MS 811/II/27, f. 53, xxxiii.
[19] SHL, Lewin Collection, MS 811/II/27, f. 53, xxiii.   [20] Lewin, *Fly*, p. 407.

means of negotiating frontier environs, would find, change, and save him. That this did not happen was a crushing blow.

Many of his contemporaries shared both Lewin's insistence on India's frontiers as an invaluable margin for self-fashioning and his sense of being complicit in the narrowing of this space of freedom and play.[21] Looked at from established imperial hubs, the later nineteenth century was an era of confidence in the technologies and ideologies of European global supremacy. Viewed from the frontiers, these things seemed simultaneously fragile and threatening, and high empire appeared to be not just an age of progress but one of belatedness and shortcomings. British frontiersmen were troubled as much by the extension of conventional forms of imperial power as by the excessive challenges that frontiers often presented. Staving off these twin threats and maintaining frontiers as spaces of productive difficulties entailed sustaining a host of laborious discursive and material strategies. This was difficult, perilous work – and for Lewin and many others, it proved impossible.

The State of Power and Knowledge

India's frontiers were spaces in which the colonial state was both dramatically present and frequently ineffective. There was no essential contradiction here but rather symbiosis between the spectacular and the chaotic. British power at frontiers was only occasionally predicated on categorising and codifying, emanating more often from indeterminacy and upheaval. Decades before the likes of Lewin conceived of them as ambiguous counterpoints to core features of high empire, the British were already construing India's frontiers as sources of productive difficulties. The annexations of Assam (1826), Sind (1843), and Punjab (1849) brought agents of empire into sustained contact with the areas that became frontiers until the British quit the subcontinent in 1947. Early dealings with these regions did much to set the tone and agenda for the significance of frontiers in the era of high empire. From the outset, the supposed unruliness of upland and desert-bound regions beyond the formal administration of the Company-State was prized as well as feared. Frontier communities and terrain threatened to overwhelm the state's resources by impacting prestige and income alike, not to mention the danger they presented to the life and limb of British personnel and colonised subjects. But for these very reasons frontiers became celebrated as proving grounds for individual men and for colonial rule.

---

[21] On the importance of 'play' to British men in another fringe space of the Indian empire, the Andaman Islands, see Satadru Sen, *Savagery and Colonialism in the Indian Ocean: Power, Pleasure and the Andaman Islanders* (Abingdon: Routledge, 2010), p. 11. Hannah Arendt also comments on 'crimes committed in the spirit of play' as a hallmark of colonial activity: Hannah Arendt, *The Origins of Totalitarianism*, 3rd ed. (London: George Allen & Unwin, 1967), p. 190.

The ideas and practices established during the initial flurries of activity following annexations were vital influences on, and resources for, the intensified burst of theorising and fashioning frontiers from the late 1860s onwards. India's fringes could only become peculiarly significant to imperial personnel towards the close of the nineteenth century because of theories and materials that had accumulated during the preceding decades.

High imperial frontiers did not emerge from the development of stable governmental logics and the cumulative acquisition and dissemination of information as the nineteenth century progressed. Instead, the colonial state developed ways of comprehending and working in these regions that relied on strategies of forgetting, overlooking, and occluding. Just as Ann Laura Stoler has shown in the case of the Dutch East Indies, colonial statecraft in India's frontiers was as much about disconnecting events to render them 'insignificant or unintelligible' as it was about gathering them together and making them 'legible'.[22] Even in those instances in which information on frontiers accumulated, its meaning often remained indeterminate. The concept of the frontier as a space of openness and exception was a prime example of the power of vague categories. It allowed agents of the colonial state to act in ways that contravened notions of what was viable or acceptable elsewhere and to ignore similar undertakings in the past that had conspicuously failed. Frontier forgetting was sometimes bound up in the state's shortcomings and quotidian cases of information blockages and interpretative confusions, but in many cases it was a deliberate strategy. Imperial personnel perceived that their status as frontier experts depended on limiting the spread of certain types of knowledge and wilfully disregarding others. They engaged in activities that Stoler assigns to what she terms 'aphasia' in postcolonial French attitudes to empire, including 'active dissociation' and the 'occlusion of knowledge'.[23] In significant ways, British men at India's frontiers sought to avoid becoming enmeshed in bureaucracy and abstraction, instead exhibiting 'no will to know'.[24]

This characteristic of colonial engagements with frontiers compels us to rethink the motives and logics of British power in India and of modern states more widely. Postcolonialist accounts, most notably those emanating from the Subaltern Studies tradition, suggest that colonial domination in the subcontinent was premised on epistemic projects of defining and taxonomising. The

---

[22] Ann Laura Stoler, *Along the Archival Grain: Epistemic Anxieties and Colonial Common Sense* (Princeton, NJ: Princeton University Press, 2009), p. 29.

[23] Ann Laura Stoler, 'Colonial Aphasia: Race and Disabled Histories in France', *Public Culture*, 23, 1 (2011), pp. 121–56, here p. 125.

[24] Keith Breckenridge, 'No Will to Know: The Rise and Fall of African Civil Registration in Twentieth-Century South Africa', *Proceedings of the British Academy*, 182 (2012), pp. 357–83; see also Keith Breckenridge, *Biometric State: The Global Politics of Identification and Surveillance in South Africa, 1850 to the Present* (Cambridge: Cambridge University Press, 2014).

unflinchingly confident projection of Western rationality provided the epistemic and moral sovereignty that simultaneously enabled and justified the subjugation of India to British rule and logics of capital.[25] According to this interpretation, substantial opposition to empire's tyrannical imposition of supposedly universal categories came from what Partha Chatterjee termed 'the fragmentary, the local, and the subjugated', through which colonised people created a 'spiritual' domain beyond the sovereignty of the colonial state.[26] Focusing on frontiers suggests a related but distinct story, which pays attention to the importance of the fragmentary and the local to British colonial power. At India's frontiers, the categories supposedly foundational to modern empire – spatial and intellectual delineations, notions of representational truth, and the investment of uniform sovereignty in a unitary state – frayed at the edges. These regions called into question the notion that all people and spaces could be subsumed within a single field of analysis, the field of 'historicism' that Dipesh Chakrabarty identifies as integral to European imperial thought and practice.[27] Helen Tilley's assessment of early to mid-twentieth-century colonial Africa applies to many agents of empire engaged at India's frontiers: 'the very people engaged in creating and maintaining structures of imperial domination ... were, ironically, among those who shared with postcolonial scholars a desire to "provincialize Europe" ... challenging truth claims that accepted European examples and standards as the norm'.[28] The men who imagined and enacted colonial frontiers often made the 'assumption that historical time is out of joint with itself'.[29] Practices derided as barbaric were co-opted into supposedly civilised projections of state power, while the divine and fantastical inhered within ostensibly disenchanted schemes to know subject peoples and spaces.

The very different perspective on colonial power from India's fringes can be understood by revisiting Michel Foucault's theories on power and recasting the way in which they have been put to work in accounts of British India. Frontiers were a kind of reverse 'heterotopia', inverting Foucault's notion of a 'space as perfect, as meticulous, as well arranged as ours is messy, ill constructed, and jumbled'.[30] They came to be constituted precisely as the 'messy' spaces that enabled escape from the 'meticulous' structures that supposedly bound ruled

---

[25] Partha Chatterjee, *The Nation and Its Fragments: Colonial and Postcolonial Histories* (Princeton, NJ: Princeton University Press, 1993), xi.

[26] Ibid., xi; pp. 6–13.

[27] Dipesh Chakrabarty, *Provincializing Europe: Postcolonial Thought and Historical Difference*, 2nd ed. (Princeton, NJ: Princeton University Press, 2008), xiv; pp. 6–9.

[28] Helen Tilley, *Africa as a Living Laboratory: Empire, Development, and the Problem of Scientific Knowledge, 1870–1950* (Chicago, IL: University of Chicago Press, 2011), pp. 314–15.

[29] Chakrabarty, *Provincializing*, pp. 15–16.

[30] Michel Foucault, 'Of Other Spaces', trans. Jay Miskowiec, *Diacritics*, 16, 1 (1986), pp. 22–7, here p. 27.

and ruler elsewhere in India. It was no coincidence that these land frontiers far from the shores of the Indian Ocean developed at a time when the challenges offered to the early colonial state by an 'unruly' maritime frontier had drawn to a close.[31] Faced with the prospect of becoming, in Foucault's terms, a 'civilisation without boats, where dreams dry up, espionage takes the place of adventure, and the police take the place of pirates', colonial agents strived to construct and maintain the productive tensions and freedom of action derived from partially unsubjugated spaces.[32]

Even when frontier administrators attempted to impose what James C. Scott terms 'state simplifications',[33] they tended to be disrupted both by contact with the would-be objects of power/knowledge and by disputes and misunderstandings within the state itself. The colonial state was not a unitary entity but, in the words of Aradhana Sharma and Akhil Gupta, 'a multilayered, pluri-centred, and fluid ... ensemble that congeals different contradictions'.[34] And British interventions at India's frontiers did not necessarily fail as Scott (intermittently) has it, but nor did they straightforwardly succeed.[35] Born of varying intentions, their effects were more variable still, often seeming unclear even to their initiators and looking very different from distinct vantage points. As Nayanika Mathur has shown in the case of contemporary upland India, agents of the state are in many cases as befuddled as subjects regarding governmental projects and direct their energies to make it appear '*as if*' these projects were functioning as much as to actually implement the substance of the projects.[36] And, to quote Matthew Hull, 'state control can be extended not only through specification, but through ambiguity, by leaving matters undocumented'.[37] One vital element of bureaucratic confusion and the emphasis on spectacle at India's high imperial frontiers was the colonial state's engagement in open-ended cycles of violence.[38]

---

[31] S.H. Layton, 'Hydras and Leviathans in the Indian Ocean World', *International Journal of Maritime History*, 25 (2013), pp. 213–25, here p. 221.

[32] Foucault, 'Other Spaces', p. 27.

[33] James C. Scott, *Seeing Like A State: How Certain Scheme to Improve the Human Condition Have Failed* (New Haven, CT: Yale University Press, 1998), pp. 2–3.

[34] Aradhana Sharma and Akhil Gupta, 'Introduction: Rethinking Theories of the State in an Age of Globalization', in id (eds.), *The Anthropology of the State: A Reader* (Oxford: Blackwell, 2006), pp. 1–41, here pp. 9–10.

[35] Scott, *Seeing*, p. 6; elsewhere, Scott instead supposes the crushing effectiveness of state schemes: for example, p. 83.

[36] Nayanika Mathur, *Paper Tiger: Law, Bureaucracy and the Developmental State in Himalayan India* (Cambridge: Cambridge University Press, 2015), quotation on p. 3.

[37] Matthew S. Hull, *Government of Paper: The Materiality of Bureaucracy in Urban Pakistan* (Berkeley, CA: University of California Press, 2012), p. 248.

[38] On the need for historians of modern empire to focus on physical violence rather than epistemic violence, see Richard Drayton, 'Where Does the World Historian Write from? Objectivity, Moral Conscience and the Past and Present of Imperialism', *Journal of Contemporary History*, 46, 3 (2011), pp. 671–85, here pp. 679–81. On the limitations of interpretations of British rule in India that prioritise 'epistemic violence', see Jon Wilson, *The Domination of Strangers: Modern Governance in Eastern India, 1780–1835* (Basingstoke: Palgrave Macmillan, 2008);

Egregious destruction and farcical ineffectiveness were not at distant ends of a linear spectrum but resided in proximity to each other – a proximity that was devastating to many frontier people, perplexing for some colonial officials, and difficult for scholars of empire to account for.

The fragmented quality of India's colonial frontiers can be engaged through recent theories that go beyond assumptions that modern states necessarily seek to create uniform sovereign territories. Political geographers such as Stuart Elden and John Agnew have argued that territory is not 'a static terrain' but 'a vibrant entity' and 'a process, made and remade, shaped and shaping, active and reactive'.[39] Sovereignty, meanwhile, is not an innate capacity 'pooled up neatly in territorial spaces' but a set of practices exercised by multiple agents prone to substantial variations across time and space.[40] As Lauren Benton's work has shown, such insights are well suited to understanding modern empires, which 'did not cover space evenly but composed a fabric that was full of holes, stitched together out of pieces, a tangle of strings'.[41] Just as these analytical tools shed light on the quirks of administrative space at colonial India's frontiers, so focusing on these regions allows us to further develop understandings of sovereignty and territory in empire. Frontiers push against the lingering notion that the era of high empire saw the global spread of uniform and comprehensive sovereign space.[42] Contrary to the established analysis centred on North America and settler colonies, the period around the turn of the twentieth century did not see the collapse of locally mediated borderlands into state-imposed borderlines in British India.[43] Instead, unusual sovereign arrangements and territorial vagueness were pushed to imperial fringes,

---

Jon Wilson, 'How Modernity Arrived to Godavari', *Modern Asian Studies*, 51, 2 (2017), pp. 399–431.

[39] Quotations from Stuart Elden, 'Land, Terrain, Territory', *Progress in Human Geography*, 34, 6 (2010), pp. 799–817, here p. 810; Stuart Elden, *The Birth of Territory* (Chicago, IL: University of Chicago Press, 2013), p. 17.

[40] Quotation from John Agnew, 'The Hobbesian Excuse: Where Is Sovereignty and Why Does It Matter?', in Saul Takahashi (ed.), *Human Rights, Human Security, and State Security: The Intersection* (Santa Barbara, CA: Praeger, 2014), pp. 119–36, p. 119.

[41] Lauren Benton, *A Search for Sovereignty: Law and Geography in European Empires, 1400–1900* (Cambridge: Cambridge University Press, 2010), p. 1.

[42] For example, Charles S. Maier, 'Transformations of Territoriality: 1600-2000', in Gunilla Budde, Sebastian Conrad and Oliver Janz (eds.), *Transnationale Geschichte: Themen, Tendenzen und Theorien* (Göttingen: Vandenhoeck & Ruprecht, 2006), pp. 32–55.

[43] On North America, see Jeremy Adelman and Stephen Aron, 'From Borderlands to Borders: Empires, Nation-States, and the Peoples in between in North American History', *American Historical Review*, 104, 3 (1999), pp. 814–41; Pekka Hämäläinen, *The Comanche Empire* (New Haven, CT: Yale University Press, 2008), pp. 321–41; Pekka Hämäläinen, 'What's in a Concept? The Kinetic Empire of the Comanches', *History and Theory*, 52 (2013), pp. 81–90, here p. 90. On settler colonies, see James Belich, *Replenishing the Earth: The Settler Revolution and the Rise of the Anglo-World, 1783–1939* (Oxford: Oxford University Press, 2009). On nineteenth-century borderlands in general, see Paul Readman, Cynthia Radding, and Chad Bryant, 'Introduction: Borderlands in a Global Perspective', in id (eds.), *Borderlands in World History, 1700–1914* (Basingstoke: Palgrave Macmillan, 2014), pp. 1–23.

where they continued to thrive. India's frontiers also give invaluable insights into how indeterminate spaces of government were not only outcomes of states' limitations but also the product of the ways in which states functioned. Many imperial agents and institutions saw distinct advantages in ensuring that the territories in which they acted were not smooth but patchy, and went to great lengths to ensure that this was the case. Taking a bottom-up approach to territory and sovereignty builds on recent work by foregrounding the deliberate and often laborious nature of constructing and sustaining uneven state spaces.

As scholars of British India pursuing otherwise diverse approaches such as Bernard Cohn and C. A. Bayly have recognised for some time, forms of colonial power were thoroughly entwined with forms of colonial knowledge.[44] The partially wilful rendering of frontiers as spaces beyond the means of normal government and conventional sovereign arrangements was mirrored by, and reliant upon, the conviction that methods and forms of knowledge had to be adapted to function in these areas. Teasing out the epistemic peculiarity and significance of British India's frontiers requires engagement with recent work on the history and geography of 'colonial' and 'global' sciences. Work in the past two decades has made clear that sciences did not simply spread from Europe or the West to the rest of the world during the modern era.[45] Colonies were not mere scientific peripheries, mined for data that could then be implanted into rigid, predetermined frameworks: they impacted sciences in multiple ways.[46] Generating knowledge and putting it to work over long distances involved the amalgamation of diverse material, necessitating long-distance connections that were delicate and often prone to failure.[47] What Felix Driver has termed 'disturbance' was widespread: people, instruments, and terrains alike inflected what could be known and how it could be known.[48] Strategies for occluding and overcoming the 'states of disrepair' that afflicted sciences and their components were similarly prevalent.[49] Making knowledge

---

[44] C. A. Bayly, *Empire and Information: Intelligence Gathering and Social Communication in India, 1780–1870* (Cambridge: Cambridge University Press, 1996); Cohn, *Colonialism*. See also William Pinch, 'Same Difference in India and Europe', *History and Theory*, 38, 3 (1999), pp. 389–407.

[45] This work is often posited against George Basalla's 'diffusion' model: George Basalla, 'The Spread of Western Science', *Science*, 156, 3775 (1967), pp. 611–22.

[46] For example, Gyan Prakash, *Another Reason: Science and the Imagination of Modern India* (Princeton, NJ: Princeton University Press, 1999); Pratik Chakrabarti, *Western Science in Modern India: Metropolitan Methods, Colonial Practices* (New Delhi: Permanent Black, 2004); Marwa Elshakry, 'When Science Became Western: Historiographical Reflections', *Isis*, 101, 1 (2010), pp. 98–109.

[47] For example, James A. Secord, 'Knowledge in Transit', *Isis*, 95, 4 (2004), pp. 654–72; Mark Harrison, 'Science and the British Empire', *Isis*, 96, 1 (2005), pp. 56–63.

[48] Felix Driver, 'Distance and Disturbance: Travel, Exploration and Knowledge in the Nineteenth Century', *Transactions of the Royal Historical Society*, Sixth Series, 14 (2004), pp. 73–92.

[49] Simon Schaffer, 'Easily Cracked: Scientific Instruments in States of Disrepair', *Isis*, 102, 4 (2011), pp. 706–17.

work – by making it seem to the right audiences that it did – was an unstable business, all the more so when the fractious dynamics of colonial situations were involved.

Assuming a singular category of 'colonial science' only takes us so far.[50] While imperatives of European domination and attitudes of racialised and gendered difference influenced practices of generating and spreading knowledge, they did not definitively structure these activities. Colonial encounters intermingled diverse knowledge traditions, generating 'new forms' of science, imperial rule, and modes of resistance and reworking.[51] Far from agreeing on or even having individually clear conceptions of what should be known and how it could be known, agents of imperial frontiers frequently operated near or beyond the fringes of epistemic consensus. As Martin Jay has said of imperial visual regimes, colonisers were 'haunted by fractures' internal to their communities, such that 'rather than speaking of Euro-centrism, it may well be better to speak of "Euro-eccentrism"'.[52] Many imperial agents' attempts to disseminate information had to be paired with contestable justifications of the significance of that information and of the techniques employed to gather it. Sciences at the fringes of the British subcontinent did not simply work with already-established categories and methods. They were as much about keeping certain things beyond the bounds of the conventionally known as they were concerned with subsuming spaces and people into regionally and globally extensive schemes.[53] The evidence from India's frontiers suggests that, as well as being 'disturbed' by intransigent peoples and spaces and by the exigencies of long-distance 'transit', imperial knowledge was also constrained by internal fractures and by wilful efforts to occlude.

Connected and Fragmented Frontiers

Throughout the nineteenth century, colonial officials imagined and enacted frontier regions at the northwestern and northeastern outskirts of India in part through connections and comparisons to other frontiers and exceptional spaces. These points of reference could be located in the past or the present (and in

---

[50] Sujit Sivasundaram, 'Sciences and the Global: On Methods, Questions, and Theory', *Isis*, 101, 1 (2010), pp. 146–58, here pp. 154–55; Neil Safier, *Measuring the New World: Enlightenment Science and South America* (Chicago, IL: University of Chicago Press, 2008), pp. 14–15.

[51] Sivasundaram, 'Sciences', p. 155; on the complex and entangled nature of 'resistance' and 'power', see Sherry B. Ortner, 'Resistance and the Problem of Ethnographic Refusal', *Comparative Studies in Society and History*, 37, 1 (1995), pp. 173–93.

[52] Martin Jay, 'Conclusion. A Parting Glance: Empire and Visuality', in id and Sumathi Ramaswamy (eds.), *Empires of Vision: A Reader* (Durham, NC: Duke University Press, 2014), pp. 609–20, here p. 610.

[53] On 'opacity' and 'non-knowledge' in Western global scientific practices, see Daniel Rood, 'Toward a Global Labor History of Science', in Patrick Manning and Daniel Rood (eds.), *Global Scientific Practice in an Age of Revolution, 1750–1850* (Pittsburgh, PA: University of Pittsburgh Press, 2016), pp. 255–74, here pp. 263–6.

some cases imagined the future). They were sometimes located in the subcontinent and sometimes in another colony, nation, or empire. In certain instances, they were informed by extensive personal experiences; in others, by fleeting and half-remembered fragments of reading or conversation and a good deal of assumption and speculation. Materials mattered as well as ideas, or rather the two were inseparable: the transit of books, images, instruments, and people enabled the development of related conceptions of 'the frontier' across spatially disparate portions of the subcontinent. The connected and comparative frameworks within which colonial India's frontiers took shape have only just begun to receive attention in scholarship on these regions.[54] Work to date has largely overlooked the related fact that major changes in frontier practices, especially the intensification of certain forms of intervention from the later 1860s onwards, occurred more-or-less synchronously across portions of the northwest and northeast. This book seeks to substantiate and specify David Ludden's identification of a generalised increase in British involvement at India's frontiers in the decades following the Rebellion of 1857.[55] To understand the significance of spatially peripheral regions to British agents of empire, we must follow the links they formulated and tapped into almost every time they invoked 'the frontier' and associated notions such as 'tribes' and 'hills'.

Despite these limitations, in recent times there has been a welcome glut of scholarship on portions of British India's frontiers. Some of the most insightful work on both the northwest and northeast has focused on the variegated quality of frontier spaces. Magnus Marsden and Benjamin Hopkins describe the northwest frontier as composed of 'fragments', 'a collage of interlinked and overlapped spaces'.[56] Dealing with the opposite side of the colonial subcontinent – northeastern India and northern Burma – Mandy Sadan writes of the 'fractal' quality of communities and spaces.[57] This is a vital point, but there remains a tendency to slightly misconstrue the colonial state's role in rendering frontiers as fragmentary spaces. Marsden and Hopkins and Sadan share the assumption that the British treated, and thereby partially constituted, the frontier and its communities as 'a unitary whole', deploying ethnic

---

[54] For example, Mark Condos, '"Fanaticism" and the Politics of Resistance along the North-West Frontier of British India', *Comparative Studies in Society and History*, 58, 3 (2016), pp. 717–45; Benjamin D. Hopkins, 'The Frontier Crimes Regulation and Frontier Governmentality', *Journal of Asian Studies*, 74, 2 (2015), pp. 369–89.

[55] David Ludden, 'The Process of Empire: Frontiers and Borderlands', in P. F. Bang and C. A. Bayly (eds.), *Tributary Empires in Global History* (London: Palgrave Macmillan, 2011), pp. 132–50, here p. 139.

[56] Magnus Marsden and Benjamin D. Hopkins, *Fragments of the Afghan Frontier* (London: Hurst, 2011), pp. 4–5

[57] Mandy Sadan, *Being and Becoming Kachin: Histories Beyond the State in the Borderworlds of Burma* (Oxford: Oxford University Press, 2013), pp. 20–4.

and spatial categories the 'simplicity' of which 'developed largely to efface ... hyper-complexity'.[58] While they are right to show that frontiers were not simply *sui generis* creations of colonial power, they do not pursue the ways in which elements within the colonial state – itself a fragmented entity – worked with and fostered complexity.

To adapt Eric Lewis Beverley's formulation referring to the boundary between Bombay Presidency and Hyderabad, the frontier was a 'resource' for agents of empire every bit as much as subcontinental subjects and semi-subjects. British officials shared with these groups a common – if differently expressed – desire to 'manipulate the contradictions of colonial sovereignty'.[59] Against John S. Galbraith's famous 1960 argument that the 'turbulent frontier' 'pulled ... clear-headed' colonial administrators into expansion across the subcontinent, it should instead be understood that frontier officials were sources and beneficiaries of turbulence.[60] The notion that colonialists were unwitting and unwilling victims of anarchic circumstances in India has long been debunked. Some recent work nonetheless continues to conceive of frontier functionaries as men uniformly wedded to principles of legibility and certainty who struggled against frontiers' instability. This has been especially evident in scholarship focusing on frontier terrain and border-making in the northeast (a topic hitherto under-explored in the northwest). Gunnel Cederlöf argues that the period of an 'open-ended' colonial frontier in the northeast concluded when 'universal principles of administration began to influence governmental practice from the 1830s onwards'.[61] David Vumlallian Zou and M. Satish Kumar suggest that British surveyors 'reduced India's Northeast borderlands to thin boundary lines' and that any residual 'indeterminacy of boundaries in the colonial Northeast did not reflect the inconsistency of British policy, but the existence of "political volatilities in the region"'.[62] Such formulations overstate the homogeneity of colonial intentions in delineating frontier spaces. When examining borders and terrain in the northwest as well as the northeast, we should instead follow Bodhisattva Kar in acknowledging that 'too much attention to the rhetoric of fixity' can obscure the informality and mobility of colonial borders and internal divisions and

[58] Marsden and Hopkins, *Fragments*, p. 6; Sadan, *Kachin*, p. 24.
[59] Eric Lewis Beverley, 'Frontier as Resource: Law, Crime, and Sovereignty on the Margins of Empire', *Comparative Studies in Society and History*, 55, 2 (2013), pp. 241–72, here p. 269.
[60] John S. Galbraith, 'The "Turbulent Frontier" as a Factor in British Expansion', *Comparative Studies in History and Society*, 2, 2 (1960), pp. 150–68, here pp. 150, 168.
[61] Gunnel Cederlöf, *Founding an Empire on India's North-Eastern Frontiers, 1790–1840: Climate, Commerce, Polity* (New Delhi: Oxford University Press, 2014), p. 6.
[62] David Vumlallian Zou and M. Satish Kumar, 'Mapping a Colonial Borderland: Objectifying the Geo-Body of India's Northeast', *The Journal of Asian Studies*, 70, 1 (2011), pp. 141–170, here pp. 144, 159 (the latter quotes Peter Robb's words).

incoherence within the British Indian state.[63] Agents of empire generated and saw opportunities in spatial chaos; they did not merely suffer it.

Understanding frontiers as spaces fashioned by multiple spatial and human encounters involving diverse colonial agents extends the recent scholarly turn away from grand strategy – especially rivalries with Russia and China – as the driver of frontier policies.[64] Martin Bayly's work on the northwest frontier and Afghanistan highlights the importance of focusing not on distant imperatives of high politics but on 'men on the spot' as key actors of frontier making.[65] I develop this insight by emphasising how administrators sought to constitute their epistemic and administrative authority in relation not just to frontier communities but also to others in the colonial state and imperial knowledge apparatuses. It was through these fraught interactions that the concept of the frontier specialist emerged and took on significance in various settings during the nineteenth century. In the later decades of the century, it is also notable that in some fields, especially surveying, frontier expertise was both attained and applied through activities that linked locales in the northwest and the northeast.

Recent scholarship on the northwest frontier has focused attention on the colonial imposition of legal categories in dealing with populations in the region.[66] Benjamin D. Hopkins outlines how the Frontier Crimes Regulation, introduced in 1872, emanated from the colonial state's search for ways to 'manage' frontier populations rather than to 'govern' them.[67] The Regulation, he argues, positioned tribal people as 'imperial objects' as opposed to colonial subjects: 'people who were acted upon'.[68] Elizabeth Kolsky and Mark Condos suggest that the Murderous Outrages Act, first implemented in 1867, was an act of 'lawfare' – state violence and coercion legitimated by and perpetrated through legal reforms.[69] Collectively, these works make the

---

[63] Bodhisattva Kar, 'When Was the Postcolonial? A History of Policing Impossible Lines', in Sanjib Baruah (ed.), *Beyond Counter-Insurgency: Breaking the Impasse in Northeast India* (New Delhi: Oxford University Press, 2009), pp. 49–77, here p. 54.

[64] Two notable exceptions identify strategic imperatives as central to frontier-making activities: Elizabeth Kolsky, 'The Colonial Rule of Law and the Legal Regime of Exception: Frontier "Fanaticism" and State Violence in British India', *American Historical Review*, 120, 4 (2015), pp. 1218–46, here p. 1221; Christian Tripodi, *Edge of Empire: The British Political Officer and Tribal Administration on the North-West Frontier 1877–1947* (London: Ashgate, 2011), pp. 17–18. The classic work on strategy in and beyond the northwest frontier is Malcolm Yapp, *Strategies of British India: Britain, Iran, and Afghanistan, 1798–1850* (Oxford: Clarendon Press, 1980).

[65] Martin Bayly, *Taming the Imperial Imagination: Colonial Knowledge, International Relations, and the Anglo-Afghan Encounter, 1808–1878* (Cambridge: Cambridge University Press, 2016).

[66] Among the earliest of these was Robert Nichols, *Settling the Frontier: Land, Law, and Society in the Peshawar Valley, 1500–1900* (Karachi: Oxford University Press, 2001).

[67] Hopkins, 'Frontier Crimes Regulation', p. 375.   [68] Ibid., p. 381.

[69] Kolsky, 'Colonial', pp. 1244–45; Mark Condos, 'Licence to Kill: The Murderous Outrages Act and the Rule of Law in Colonial India, 1867-1925', *Modern Asian Studies*, 50, 2 (2016), pp. 479–517, here p. 488.

important point that frontier laws tended to be less about normalising than enshrining exceptions.[70] This insight should be extended beyond the Punjab frontier, since it was in the northeast and Balochistan that many features of the late-nineteenth-century version of 'frontier governmentality' first developed.[71] Contrary to Peter Robb's claim that British expansion and legislation in the northeast sought to incorporate and standardise upland fringes, in this region every bit as much as at the northwest frontier law worked in tandem with state violence.[72] This book also looks beyond interventions in the legal sphere, building on recent work on the advent of wider administrative schemes in portions of the northeast frontier.[73] Just as knowledge of frontiers always entailed maintaining margins of the overlooked and unknown, so administration in these regions entailed leaving much beyond their remit and granting substantial discretion to the 'man on the spot'.[74] Such interventions at the edges of empire sought – paradoxically – to fix and codify exceptions.

Overview of the Book

The fringes of colonial control were crucial to the cultural and political development of the British East India Company-State in the period prior to 'paramountcy', attained with the defeat of the Marathas in 1818, which removed the Company's last hostile internal frontier.[75] The subsequent four decades, up to the outbreak of the Indian Rebellion of 1857, saw further major additions to colonial territory. These included the annexation of three areas – Assam, Sind, and Punjab – that brought the colonial state into proximate

---

[70] On the notion of law enshrining exceptions, see the work of Carl Schmitt: Carl Schmitt, *The Concept of the Political*, trans. George Schwab (Chicago, IL: University of Chicago Press, 2007 [1932]); Carl Schmitt, *The Nomos of the Earth in the International Law of the* Jus Publicum Europaeum, trans. G.L. Ulmen (New York, NY: Telos Press, 2003 [1950]).

[71] Marsden and Hopkins, *Fragments*, pp. 49–73.

[72] Peter Robb, 'The Colonial State and Constructions of Indian Identity: An Example on the Northeast Frontier in the 1880s', *Modern Asian Studies*, 31, 2 (1997), pp. 245–83.

[73] Lipokmar Dzuvichu, 'Roads and the Raj: The politics of road building in colonial Naga Hills, 1860s-1910s', *The Indian Economic and Social History Review*, 50, 4 (2013), pp. 473–94; Sanghamitra Misra, 'The Sovereignty of Political Economy: The Garos in a Pre-Conquest and Early Conquest Era', *The Indian Economic and Social History Review*, 55, 3 (2018), pp. 345–87.

[74] Benjamin D. Hopkins, 'A History of the "Hindustani Fanatics" on the Frontier', in id and Magnus Marsden (eds.), *Beyond Swat: History, Society and Economy along the Afghanistan-Pakistan Frontier* (New York, NY: Columbia University Press, 2013), pp. 39–49, here p. 49.

[75] Maya Jasanoff, *Edge of Empire: Lives, Culture, and Conquest in the East, 1750–1850* (London: Vintage, 2006); Gunnel Cederlöf, 'Fixed Boundaries, Fluid Landscapes: British Expansion into Northern East Bengal in the 1820s', *Indian Economic and Social History Review*, 46, 4 (2009), pp. 513–40. On maritime frontiers in western India, see Layton, 'Hydras'. For frontiers under the Mughal state, see Gautam Bhadra, 'Two Frontier Uprisings in Mughal India', in Ranajit Guha (ed.), *Subaltern Studies II: Writings on South Asian History and Society* (Delhi: Oxford University Press, 1983, pp. 43–59.

contact with the regions that became designated as 'frontiers'. With these bursts of expansion, 'normally' governed British India assumed what would essentially remain its extent until India and Pakistan gained independence in 1947.[76] Of course, colonial power, strategic interests, trade, and violence did not stop at the often hazy and variable limits of fully governed territory. The regions beyond were zones of persistent British interference and fascination. In this book, I show that colonial actions in, and imaginings of, frontiers were diverse even at the most localised levels: between one valley and the next, one community and another, and one administrator and his neighbour, successor, or superior. Complexity did not resolve into stability even at the most granular scale; tensions and contradictions were central features of British India's frontiers.

Yet alongside the agglomeration of chaotic low-level circumstances, there are discernible trends in colonial frontier making across the nineteenth century. In both northeast and northwest, spurts of activity in frontier areas followed the annexation of contiguous regions to colonial India. These relatively brief bursts consisted especially of episodes of violence and far-fetched projects masterminded by small coteries of men operating with limited oversight from distant administrative superiors. Following a period of retrenchment, what can be thought of as an intensification of frontier making began in the northwest and northeast from the late 1860s. This shift was not spatially uniform, nor was it part of a centrally orchestrated plan: it instead emanated primarily from agents of empire based at the fringes. Although it entailed deeper interventions in frontier regions, it remained bound up with ideas of frontiers as spaces of self-fashioning, risk, and play. It was in this era of high empire that India's frontiers came to assume a peculiar significance as spaces of productive difficulties. And it was the notion of frontiers as regions of exception that came to be enshrined through the creation of designated administrative units around the turn of the twentieth century: British Baluchistan and the Naga Hills, Garo Hills, and Lushai Hills from the late 1860s to the 1890s, North-West Frontier Province in 1901, and North-East Frontier Tracts in 1912.

While periodisation matters, this book does not have a chronological structure. Instead each chapter deals with a distinct mode of colonial frontier making. Although there is no ideal way of organising a study of this temporal and spatial breadth, this approach has a number of advantages. First, it enables the distinctive qualities and tempos of different colonial activities to be considered in relation to relevant historiographies and theories. Second, the vital connections and comparisons that existed between spatially and temporally

---

[76] The notable addition to British possessions in South Asia after the Rebellion was the annexation of Upper Burma in 1885: see Thant Myint-U, *The Making of Modern Burma* (Cambridge: Cambridge University Press, 2001).

diverse frontier locales can be foregrounded, helping us follow the people, materials, and methods that made frontiers. Third, it emphasises that, despite changes over time, this is not a straightforwardly teleological story of the growing power of state institutions and technologies or particular modes of information gathering and representation. It is a story in which people and things matter, and in which forgetting and overlooking were as vital as selective invocations of other times and spaces as resources for particular purposes. A structure that does not prioritise chronology is intended to allow greater prominence to themes of cyclicality, irresolution, and strangeness, which were essential to British engagements with India's frontiers. As David Ludden perceptively comments, 'on imperial margins, the complexity and ambiguity of imperial time and space appear more clearly'.[77] These regions and their inhabitants disturbed many preconceptions of agents of empire; perhaps they should do something similar to us.

In the first chapter, 'Borders', I explore the gulf that existed between theories of linear boundaries and unitary sovereign territory on the one hand, and myriad localised and precarious practices of bordering on the other. I suggest that three distinct periods of bordering common to the northwest and northeast can be discerned. The decades immediately following the annexation of adjacent lowland regions were marked by a concern among officials to instantiate partially porous borders that would provide security while allowing themselves freedom of action in frontier regions. The limitations of these schemes led to a widespread flurry of bordering in the 1860s and 1870s led by administrators 'on the spot'. Much of this activity directly contradicted orders from superiors in the colonial state hierarchy and took the form of breaking existing boundaries as well as instantiating new ones. A third period, around the turn of the twentieth century, was distinguished by heightened attention to international boundaries. But these borders remained fragmented and limited, bedevilled by similar shortcomings and tensions to earlier projects. They also had disruptive effects on internal boundaries, reopening questions over where fully governed colonial territory ended and the frontier began. I argue that the universalising projects of imperial strategists were relatively insignificant influences on many of the borders that made and remade India's frontiers. By the era of high empire frontiers had become spaces of myriad mutable sub-divisions. This was partly a result of intractable terrain and resisting frontier populations, both of which impacted borders in substantial and lasting ways. This lack of fixity also resulted, however, from confusion and deliberate subversion on the part of colonial officials.

In the second chapter, 'Surveys and Maps', I show how frontiers became increasingly central to colonial spatial sciences as the nineteenth century

---

[77] Ludden, 'Process', p. 148.

progressed. Examining surveyors' activities in the field along with the material processes by which maps were produced and circulated, I identify and analyse three broad junctures of frontier surveying based on distinct techniques of seeing and representing space. Route surveys of the 1820s to 1840s mostly gave way to trigonometrical surveying from the 1850s on, and trigonometrical survey parties increasingly ventured into frontier regions from the later 1860s rather than viewing prominent topographical features from a distance. By this later period, there was a distinct designation of 'frontier surveying', and surveyors and 'men of science' in metropole and colony alike deemed comprehending inaccessible and spectacular frontier locales as a key goal of imperial science. Agents of empire considered these regions as providing not only unparalleled opportunities but also substantial challenges to established modes of spatial knowledge and representation. The chapter shows how this ambiguity reached a peculiar resolution, as many surveyors and geographers came to celebrate and to uphold the elusive and unknowable quality of India's frontiers. Focusing on the particularities of surveying and mapping India's frontiers, I argue, tells a very different story about colonial spatial knowledge than that established in existing histories of cartography. Far from assuming that their techniques and technologies held out the promise of accurately representing terrestrial space,[78] frontier surveyors engaged in their own critical assessments of cartography. They acknowledged, and even revelled in, the shortcomings of their high imperial science. And they saw frontiers as spaces in which standard methods went awry and, therefore, romanticism and mysticism could commingle with quantification and empiricism.

India's frontiers were areas of extraordinary human interest for agents of empire and men of science throughout the nineteenth century. In the third chapter, 'Ethnography', I investigate the production, dissemination, and reception of British knowledge of frontier inhabitants. I show that widespread recognition among British personnel in colony and metropole alike that frontier people were important did not, however, emanate from or lead to settled knowledge of their origins or significant characteristics. Doubts over the validity of particular informants and modes of representation, disputes over competing theoretical frameworks, and controversies over the nature of frontier communities were at the heart of colonial ethnography. The production of greater quantities of ethnographic data from India's frontiers and the emergence of anthropology as a discipline as the

---

[78] Matthew H. Edney, *Mapping an Empire: The Geographical Construction of British India, 1765–1843* (Chicago, IL: University of Chicago Press, 1997); Matthew H. Edney, 'Bringing India to Hand: Mapping an Empire, Denying Space', in Felicity Nussbaum (ed.), *The Global Eighteenth Century* (Baltimore, MD: John Hopkins University Press, 2003), pp. 65–78; Matthew H. Edney, 'The Irony of Imperial Mapping', in James R. Akerman (ed.), *The Imperial Map: Cartography and the Mastery of Empire* (Chicago, IL: University of Chicago Press, 2009), pp. 11–45.

nineteenth century progressed in fact led to ever sharper disputes between competing methodologies and theories of human diversity. Fleshing out these contentions through a series of chronologically ordered case studies, this chapter shows
that frontier ethnography was a diverse field with complex relations to state power.
Examining sketches and photographs as well as written material, it demonstrates
how processes of reproduction, adaptation, and circulation generated influential
but highly unstable ethnographic knowledge.

The fourth chapter, 'Violence', focuses on colonial military ventures against
frontier communities, which were widely deployed throughout the nineteenth
century. It foregrounds previously overlooked debates between administrators
and soldiers on dynamics of state and tribal violence in Balochistan, the Naga
Hills, and along the Punjab frontier. Despite environmental and social differences that gave rise to distinctive forms of violence between these regions,
there were substantial overlaps in colonial rationales and tactics of military
engagement across India's frontiers. In northeast and northwest alike, administrators frequently argued that violence could be an effective method of communication and education for ostensibly refractory tribes, which could be
punished legitimately as a corporate body. They also often employed frontier
inhabitants as agents of colonial violence, figuring that the predilection for
violence in frontier environments that warranted punishment also rendered
these people uniquely adept at meting it out. Following Ricardo Roque's
work on Portuguese Timor,[79] I conceptualise the colonial state's use of violence
as 'atavistic' – that is, deriving an unstable form of power from the very
methods it derided as barbaric. The chapter shows that this was just one of
many tensions within colonial frontier violence. Many administrators viewed it
as ineffective and believed that it threatened the moral basis of imperial rule.
They also often contested who could legitimately be punished, advancing
contradictory conceptions of the collective tribal subject. Despite growing
colonial capacities for violence in the late nineteenth century, military ventures
against frontier peoples continued to belie administrators' intentions and
instead perpetuate cycles of destructive hostility.

The fifth chapter, 'Administration', centres on case studies from portions of
the Assam frontier and Balochistan, arguing that key logics of colonial frontier
administration originated in these regions rather than along the Punjab frontier.
I identify two distinct moments and forms of British administrative intervention in frontier regions. The earlier mode of 'frontier governmentality' involved
the relocation of entire frontier communities to fully governed state territory.
This policy tended to be preceded and facilitated by the forms of state violence
discussed in the previous chapter. Drawing on relatively scant traces in colonial

---

[79] Ricardo Roque, *Headhunting and Colonialism: Anthropology and the Circulation of Human Skulls in the Portuguese Empire, 1870–1930* (Basingstoke: Palgrave Macmillan, 2010).

archives, in this chapter I reconstruct the main features of these displacements, demonstrating that they intermingled ideas of 'improvement' with logics of punishment and incarceration. They were also notably unsuccessful on their own terms, generating substantial resistance from their subjects and either collapsing or dwindling shortly after their creation. The second set of case studies examines the types of administration implemented with the colonial state's permanent expansion from the late 1860s onwards into Balochistan and uplands to the south of Assam. Government in these regions took on exceptional forms, with state sovereignty rooted in the discretionary authority of individual administrators. Legal codes, taxation, and subjecthood remained hazily defined, contributing to a distinct later-nineteenth-century mode of 'frontier governmentality' shared across the colonial subcontinent rather than arising in the northwest alone. This final chapter, then, proposes a new way of thinking about the geography, chronology, and characteristics of frontier administration in colonial India.

1 Borders

By the early 1870s, some of the tea gardens that rendered the region the most heavily capitalised fringe of India had spread beyond the administered limits of Assam.[1] Inhabitants of the areas in question orchestrated a series of attacks on British-claimed territory. Having previously let the tea companies operate what Bodhisattva Kar terms 'a vast, paralegal empire' with fleeting oversight,[2] the Government of India now set a new boundary – the 'Inner Line' – beyond which its subjects required a licence to travel or settle. Despite its apparently straightforward rationale and decisive declaration, the Inner Line proved a fragmented border that varied across space and time.[3] The Government of Bengal, then in charge of the administration of Assam, considered that governmental intervention would continue beyond the Line in 'indefinite fashion'.[4] Subordinate officials based in Assam initially assumed otherwise, understanding that the Line instead marked the outer limits of state authority.[5] Furthermore, the Commissioner of Assam remained sceptical of the possible effect of any bordering project in the vicinity of 'wholly savage tribes', fearing that the survey and demarcation parties necessary to lay down the border would be attacked. He continued to associate the Inner Line with a definite limit on governmental authority, which went against his desire to retain an indeterminate zone in which the state could deal with inhabitants 'in the simple and summary manner applicable to their rude

---

[1] Bodhisattva Kar, 'Nomadic Capital and Speculative Tribes: A Culture of Contracts in the Northeastern Frontier of British India', *The Indian Economic and Social History Review*, 53, 1 (2016), pp. 41–67, here pp. 42–43. See also Jayeeta Sharma, *Empire's Garden: Assam and the Making of India* (Durham and London: Duke University Press, 2011).

[2] Kar, 'Nomadic Capital', p. 43.

[3] Alexander Mackenzie, *History of the Relations of the Government with the Hill Tribes of the North-East Frontier of Bengal* (Calcutta: Home Department Press, 1884), pp. 55–56; Kar, 'When Was the Postcolonial?'.

[4] National Archives of India (hereafter 'NAI') Foreign Department, Political Consultations (hereafter 'Foreign Political') A, December 1873, No. 42: Bengal Government to Assam Chief Commissioner, 29 October 1873, ff. 1–2.

[5] NAI Foreign Political A, April 1874, No. 269: Government of India to Assam Chief Commissioner, 2 April 1874, f. 2.

condition'.[6] At many points over the decades to come, the roles would be reversed: frontier officials in Assam repeatedly ventured beyond the Line without authorisation from distant – and generally displeased – superiors.[7] Mutable and conflicting definitions of what the Line meant, where it was, and its proper material manifestation persisted for as long as the British remained in India.[8] The toxic combination of variable borderlines and prejudicial notions of difference between hills and plains continues to manifest in violence at the fringes of Assam.[9] The Inner Line was, then, one of many bordering efforts at its hazy fringes that generated confusion rather than clarity for the British Indian state and people on the outskirts of its empire.

The complexities that marked colonial modernity were especially apparent in the processes by which British India's frontiers were spatially defined during the nineteenth century. Linear boundaries and unitary territory under singular sovereignty began to be asserted in this era as key distinguishing elements of modern states. Some scholars continue to assume that these more confident statements of intent regarding state space became an incontrovertible logic that was largely realised on the ground.[10] At first glance, the British Indian state appears to have been no exception. Especially in the metropole, a great deal of ink was spilled following Russian expansion into Central Asia in the mid-1860s debating if, where, how, and at what financial cost, a 'scientific frontier' that 'unites natural and strategical strength' might be implemented in India's northwest (a concept notably absent from discussions of the northeast).[11] Administrators often described bordering in India as part of the larger European attempt in the late nineteenth century, including most famously the 'Scramble for Africa', to configure global space

---

[6] NAI Foreign Political A, March 1876, No. 505: Assam Chief Commissioner to Government of India, 17 May 1875, f. 4.

[7] Bérénice Guyot-Rechard, *Shadow States: India, China and the Himalayas, 1910–1962* (Cambridge: Cambridge University Press, 2017), pp. 36–37.

[8] Ibid., pp. 89–90.

[9] 'Behali Killings: Assam Registers Case Against 12', *Times of India*, 14 February 2014. http://timesofindia.indiatimes.com/city/guwahati/Behali-killings-Assam-registers-cases-against-12/articleshow/30369083.cms (accessed 10 March 2014).

[10] For example, Maier, 'Transformations'. For a classic counter-example, see Peter Sahlins, *Boundaries: The Making of France and Spain in the Pyrenees* (Berkeley, CA: University of California Press, 1989).

[11] Quotation from Lord Curzon of Kedleston, *The Romanes Lecture 1907: Frontiers* (Oxford: Clarendon, 1907), p. 19. See also W. P. Andrew, *Our Scientific Frontier* (London: W.H. Allen & Co., 1880); George N. Curzon, 'The "Scientific Frontier": an Accomplished Fact', *The Nineteenth Century: A Monthly Review*, 136 (1888), pp. 901–17; John Dacosta, *A Scientific Frontier: or, the Danger of a Russian Invasion of India* (London: W.H. Allen & Co., 1891); H. B. Hanna, *India's Scientific Frontier: Where Is It? What Is It?* (London, Westminster: Archibald Constable and Company, 1895). On these debates, see Bayly, *Taming*, pp. 252–9; Kyle Gardner, 'Moving Watersheds, Borderless Maps, and Imperial Geography in India's Northwestern Frontier', *The Historical Journal*, 62, 1 (2019), pp. 149–70.

'scientifically'.[12] In fact, a vast gulf separated such confident global claims from the myriad localised practices of bordering, which indicate the precariousness and limitations of centralised control.[13] Christoph Bergmann is right to suggest that 'confluent territories and overlapping sovereignties are key to understanding imperial frontiers', with British colonial agents often obliged to 'work with what and whom they [found] on the ground'.[14] The Inner Line was not unique – nor even unusual – among processes of bordering in the subcontinent in remaining piecemeal and provisional throughout and beyond the colonial period.[15]

As the case studies later in this chapter show, this was especially – and perhaps surprisingly – true of international boundaries (Sections 1.6 and 1.7). But setting definitive limits with other states was rarely the primary bordering concern of British India until the closing decades of the nineteenth century.[16] Furthermore, the universalising projects of imperial strategists were relatively insignificant in many of the bordering projects that made and remade India's frontiers. Even as political imperatives at the imperial level became more clearly communicated to those on the ground in the later nineteenth century, lower-level officials and local communities continued to hold the key to the substantive realisation of these projects. Colonial agents worked on multiple and sometimes contradictory projects of internal variegation within the fluctuating areas over which the state claimed at least nominal sovereignty. Assumptions of clear, 'natural' limits to colonial rule that followed the annexations of Assam, Punjab, and Sind were quickly shown to be radically over-optimistic. Complex, often violent, interactions with frontier inhabitants intensified as tea cultivation spread rapidly in the northeast. While the northwest had no equivalent concentration of European capital, agricultural expansion undergirded by state-backed irrigation gave rise to similar, if more sporadic, pressures.[17] As a result, by the era of high empire frontiers in northeast and northwest became spaces of myriad mutable subdivisions.

---

[12] John Agnew, *Geopolitics: Re-visioning World Politics*, 2nd ed. (London: Routledge, 2003), pp. 5–6; Curzon, *Frontiers*, pp. 51–4.

[13] On the importance of global spatial claims to high imperialism, see C. A. Bayly, *The Birth of the Modern World: 1870–1914* (Oxford: Blackwell, 2004), ch. 7.

[14] Christoph Bergmann, 'Confluent Territories and Overlapping Sovereignties: Britain's Nineteenth-Century Indian Empire in the Kumaon Himalaya', *Journal of Historical Geography*, 51 (2016), pp. 88–98, here pp. 91–92.

[15] On postcolonial manifestations, see Reece Jones, 'Spaces of Refusal: Rethinking Sovereign Power and Resistance at the Border', *Annals of the Association of American Geographers*, 102, 3 (2011), pp. 685–99.

[16] On British efforts in the 1870s to broker the northwestern boundary of Afghanistan with Russia, see Benjamin D. Hopkins, 'The Bounds of Identity: The Goldsmid Mission and the Delineation of the Perso-Afghan Border in the Nineteenth Century', *Journal of Global History*, 2 (2007), pp. 233–54.

[17] David Gilmartin, *Blood and Water: The Indus River Basin in Modern History* (Oakland, CA: University of California Press, 2015).

The general trend in bordering at the fringes of British India as the nineteenth century progressed was not the elimination of nebulous 'frontiers' in favour of precise 'borders'.[18] Especially telling in this respect was the persistent lack of any clear-cut lexical distinction between the term for a peripheral zone and that for a linear boundary: into the twentieth century, 'frontier' commonly denoted both.

Slippages between areas and lines derived substantially from the tendency for officials in northeast and northwest India alike to be ambivalent towards imposing and maintaining fixed boundaries. These men may have been prepared to play their part in the cartographic-discursive fiction of fixed and precise imperial boundaries by drawing lines on maps in bold scarlet ink and drafting lengthy musings on the merits of different principles and material forms of bordering. When it came to making a border real – performing it in the territory instead of just depicting it on the map – officials could be as prone to subversion as the most resolutely state-opposing frontier communities.[19] As well as being inimical to the practices that sustained the livelihoods of many communities at the fringes of British India, clear and precise borders were equally misaligned with practices foundational to the 'heroic' identities of frontier officials. 'Turbulent frontiers' were to a significant extent products of the colonial state's own agents breaking boundaries as well as making them.[20] The response of higher-ranking administrators in provincial governments, the Government of India, and the India Office to what I term 'official subversion' varied between vexation, acquiescence, and explicit approval. Although principles of spatial fixity and exactitude became more prominent as the nineteenth century progressed, in British India they served mainly to throw a veil over the reality of the colonial government's preparedness to authorise – or at least inability to prevent – the indeterminacies generated in significant part by its own officials in outlying regions.

Recent literature in political geography on boundaries and territory emphasises that even the most apparently immutable spatial categories are best understood as processes that exist only through the interactions of various human and non-human agents.[21] As John Agnew highlights, the lived realities

---

[18] On this argument, see also Andrew Walker's work on the French colonial boundary with Laos: Andrew Walker, 'Borders in Motion on the Upper-Mekong: Siam and France in the 1890s', in Yves Goudineau and Michel Lorrillard (eds.), *Recherches nouvelles sur le Laos* (Vientiane, Paris: École française d'Extrême-Orient, 2008), pp. 183–208; Andrew Walker, 'Conclusion: Are the Mekong Frontiers Sites of Exception?', in Martin Gainsborough (ed.), *On the Borders of State Power: Frontiers in the Greater Mekong Sub-Region* (London, New York: Routledge, 2009), pp. 101–11; Andrew Walker, *The Legend of the Golden Boat: Regulation, Trade and Traders in the Borderlands of Laos, Thailand, China and Burma* (Richmond: Curzon, 1999).

[19] The concept of 'making a border real' draws on Nayanika Mathur's notion of 'making a law real': Mathur, *Paper Tiger*, p. 2.

[20] Galbraith, 'Turbulent Frontier'.

[21] See Elden, 'Land'; John Agnew, 'Borders on the Mind: Re-framing Border Thinking', *Ethics & Global Politics*, 1, 4 (2008), pp. 175–91; Noel Parker, Nick Vaughan-Williams, et al.,'Lines in

concerning borders belie their conventional status as 'facts on the ground' that exist for practical reasons and have broadly consistent effects. Instead, all boundaries are 'equivocal' and 'open to question, if not to all who would cross them'.[22] The questionable nature of borders makes them multivalent: in the words of Thomas M. Wilson and Hastings Donnan, any 'border, far from being the same phenomenon for all for whom it is significant, is a focus for many different and often competing meanings'.[23] Borders and the spaces they enclose are, like any attempted project of power, proposals that subjects may renegotiate. Despite the use of material strategies from physical violence to posts and pillars used to embed boundaries, considering borders as fixed and singular lines omits the diverse ways in which they emerge through – and are subsequently changed by – the involvement of various individuals and groups. These ideas can do much to aid our understanding of India's colonial frontier regions as spatial objects, and can help in a broader reassessment of how space across the globe came to be reconfigured during the era of modern empires. Borders had very real effects for colonised and colonisers, but rarely of the colonisers' exact choosing. The lines and areas that comprised British India's frontiers can, in turn, enhance theoretical understandings of the creation and operation of borders. In particular, evidence from these regions shows the need to acknowledge the impact on spatial schemes of the internally fragmented nature of states, manifested as disputes and misunderstandings between officials and discrepant attitudes over time. Agents within those 'modern' states that claim fixed and clear boundaries can be among the leading drivers of shifting and opaque borders.

The case studies in this chapter show that the bundles of borders and territories that constituted frontier spaces in nineteenth-century British India were contested and confused, less a coherent exercise in spatial rationality than a jumble of tangled lines. The analysis shuttles between various locales, allowing continuities and disparities between bordering processes across the subcontinent's frontiers to be drawn out. The chapter is structured around what I argue were three distinct periods of bordering common to the northwest and northeast. The first was the decade or so immediately following the British annexation of provinces contiguous to what became long-term frontiers: the 1820s to 1830s in Assam (Section 1.1), and the 1840s to 1850s in Sind and Punjab (Section 1.2). This era was marked by a concern to instantiate partially porous borders that would simultaneously secure colonial revenue and capital

the Sand? Towards an Agenda for Critical Border Studies', *Geopolitics*, 14, 3 (2009), pp. 582–87; E. Berg and H. van Houtum (eds.), *Routing Borders between Territories, Discourses and Practices* (Aldershot: Ashgate, 2003); Thomas M. Wilson and Hastings Donnan (eds.). *Border Identities: Nation and State at International Frontiers* (Cambridge: Cambridge University Press, 1998).

[22] Agnew, 'Borders', pp. 175–83.

[23] Wilson and Donnan, 'Nation, State and Identity at International Borders', in *Border Identities*, pp. 1–30, here p. 24.

in fully governed 'plains' while allowing frontier officials some freedom of action in the 'hill' and 'desert' areas beyond. It also saw the frustration of attempts to achieve such borders in the face of limited resources, material and human resistance, and incomprehension between various colonial agents. The second period, a widespread flurry of bordering activity, began in the later 1860s and was most pronounced in the 1870s (Sections 1.3, 1.4, and 1.5). It was primarily a bottom-up phenomenon, driven by official subversion – frontier administrators persistently superseding their formal remit and breaking boundaries as much as making them. It was not simply a straightforward shift from a 'close border' to a 'forward policy' as analyses of the northwest have often supposed. Instead, various bordering projects arose from restlessness among frontier officials about their lack of sway over communities beyond fully governed British India. The third period was during the decades either side of the turn of the twentieth century (Sections 1.6 and 1.7). It was distinguished by heightened attention to international boundaries and, as such, involved more explicit direction from London, Simla, and Calcutta. But these borders remained fragmented and limited, bedevilled by similar shortcomings and tensions to earlier projects. They also had disruptive effects on internal boundaries, reopening questions that had either seemed resolved or had sat in abeyance over where normally governed colonial territory ended and where 'the frontier' began. Taken as a whole, the case studies in this chapter show that borders at the fringes of British India were not instruments of spatial legibility that were fixed by a unitary state with a clear purpose. They were, rather, expressions of colonial power's basis in diverse and inconsistent agents, its tendency to be remoulded in local settings by material and human interventions, and, consequently, its patchiness across time and space.

1.1   'Rude and Complicated': The *Posa* Boundary in Northern Assam

The British Indian state did not simply create the partially and irregularly governed 'frontiers' at the outskirts of its territories from scratch. These areas had been zones of variable and indeterminate state penetration and control prior to the expansion of the colonial state. Sikh rulers in Punjab had mixed aloofness with violent reprisals in their dealings with the inhabitants of the mountains beyond the River Indus during the early nineteenth century.[24] The Kingdom of Kabul also had a fraught, albeit more intimate, set of relationships with the Pashtuns of this region, stretching back to the sixteenth century.[25] Many of the

---

[24] J. S. Grewal, *The Sikhs of Punjab*, 2nd ed. (Cambridge: Cambridge University Press, 2008), pp. 99–127.

[25] Christine Noelle, *State and Tribe in Nineteenth-Century Afghanistan: The Reign of Amir Dost Muhammad Khan (1826–1863)* (Richmond: Curzon, 1997).

Balochs to the west and north of Sind retained a significant degree of independence from surrounding states including the Khanate of Kalat, which during the seventeenth and eighteenth centuries expanded to claim authority over an area of 30,000 square miles.[26] Along with other regional powers, the Ahom kingdom in Assam had long exercised a combination of discretion and occasional violent forays in dealing with the residents of the hilly regions to the north, east, and south of the Brahmaputra Valley.[27] The stated British border policy upon annexation was to retain the clear spatial divide colonial administrators claimed had existed between largely ungoverned uplands and deserts and settled administered areas. Continuities between British India's frontier spaces and those of its predecessors resulted not only from colonial intentions but also from the 'friction' of terrain and hostility of some of the inhabitants of these regions.[28] These were variable and contingent rather than immutable factors, but nonetheless they made lasting penetration by revenue-extracting states exceptionally difficult.

The colonial state's bordering and territory-making activities also featured significant breaks from previous spatial arrangements. For example, British officials had been posted to the outskirts of Punjab during the three years prior to formal annexation in 1849 and had attempted various measures, including regularising revenue demands in administered areas, which served to sharpen the divide between assessed plains and non-assessed hill regions. In many areas the colonial state simply lacked the means of obtaining an accurate understanding of the relations that had previously existed between frontier communities and lowland states.[29] In addition, colonial conceptions of state space in the mid-nineteenth century were in certain respects more unyielding than those of the states that preceded them.[30] While Sanghamitra Misra's claim that 'the master oppositional binary' of the colonial state was a rigidly enforced dichotomy between hills and plains did not always hold true, the transition to British rule in outlying regions entailed significant shifts in the form of boundaries.[31] Prior to its conquest of Assam, the Company-State had already engaged in ambivalent border-making at what was then its northeastern limits in the Khasi Hills, imposing what on paper was a definitive

---

[26] Nina Swidler, 'Kalat: The Political Economy of a Tribal Chiefdom', *American Ethnologist*, 19, 3 (1992), pp. 553–70, here p. 555.

[27] For a summary of the complex dynamics of this region in the era immediately prior to the advent of British rule, see Cederlöf, *Founding*, pp. 6–10.

[28] On the 'friction' of terrain in upland areas, see James C. Scott, *The Art of Not Being Governed: An Anarchist History of Upland Southeast Asia* (New Haven: Yale University Press, 2009).

[29] C. A. Bayly's concept of 'information famines' at South Asian colonial frontiers is useful in this respect: *Empire and Information*, especially pp. 97–133.

[30] On Ahom conceptions of state space, see Sadan, *Kachin*, pp. 43–53.

[31] Sanghamitra Misra, *Becoming a Borderland: The Politics of Space and Identity in Colonial Northeastern India* (New Delhi: Routledge, 2011), pp. 81–82.

boundary but, in reality, one crossed with impunity by upland inhabitants and colonial subjects alike.[32]

A prime example of the significant but limited changes to borders between administered and unadministered territory that followed the advent of colonial rule in many areas was the *posa* system in northern Assam. *Posa* referred to economic arrangements in which inhabitants of the *duars*, outlying portions of the Brahmaputra Valley, gave goods to upland communities on an annual basis. The Ahom state had acquiesced to this system, which existed on the outskirts of their effective power. It was part of an intricate and flexible set of relations between various groups with a share in the dynamic and dispersed set of power relations that existed in the foothills of the eastern Himalaya.[33] Although some British officials later in the nineteenth century admitted *posa*'s merits, in the years immediately following the annexation of Assam the newly minted provincial government looked on the practice with suspicion and contempt.[34] Its attitudes towards monetising and codifying exchange relationships that were prone to localised fluctuations closely followed British initiatives elsewhere in the subcontinent to regularise revenue collection and bring it under unitary colonial control.[35] But like the most famous of these schemes, the Permanent Settlement introduced in Bengal in 1793, the British version of *posa* was incompletely realised and often ineffective.[36]

In 1834, the first extensive report on *posa* reached the Government of India. It showed little agreement between colonial officials over the nature of the hills–plains divide in northern Assam and over the coercion involved in the process. Some administrators said that the inhabitants of the *duars* were simply giving goods to neighbouring communities without complaint; others described aggressive border crossings during which materials were grabbed with 'conduct ... such as is most naturally to be expected from a rude people invested with so singular a power over the inhabitants of another country'.[37] Thomas Robertson, the Governor-General's Agent in Assam, insisted that the practice should be commuted to a money payment administered by the colonial state, since 'it seems to me quite impossible for Government long to tolerate so

---

[32] Cederlöf, *Founding*, pp. 51–52; Thomas Simpson, 'Forgetting Like a State in Colonial North-east India', in Shah Mahmoud Hanifi (ed.), *Mountstuart Elphinstone in South Asia: Pioneer of British Colonial Rule* (London: Hurst, 2019), pp. 223–47.

[33] Guyot-Rechard, *Shadow States*, pp. 10–11.

[34] For example, Mackenzie, *History*, p. 21; *Frontier and Overseas Expeditions from India. Vol. IV: North and North-Eastern Frontier Tribes* (Simla: Government Monotype Press, 1907), pp. 160–61.

[35] On *posa* reform as an intervention in political economy, see Kar, 'Nomadic Capital'.

[36] On Permanent Settlement, see Ranajit Guha, *A Rule of Property for Bengal*, 2nd ed. (New Delhi: Orient Longman, 1981); Eric Stokes, *The Peasant and the Raj: Studies in Agrarian Society and Peasant Rebellion in Colonial India* (Cambridge: Cambridge University Press, 1978).

[37] NAI Foreign Political, 20 February 1834, No. 23: Robertson to Government of India, 3 February 1834, ff. 4–5.

barbarous an interference with its own territory'.[38] The Government of India agreed that the practice constituted 'blackmail' and was 'rude and complicated', criticisms that administrators still repeated fifty years later.[39]

Following the initial uncertainties, colonial actors involved in *posa* reform came to concur on two key spatial ideas: that the Company-State had sole sovereignty over territory in the Brahmaputra Valley; and that *posa* consisted of barbaric oppressions by upland outsiders. However, the Government of India agreed to Robertson's suggestion with clear misgivings. It felt ill-equipped to coerce upland communities to accept the revised terms of *posa* and, embarrassingly, evidence came to light that Robertson's predecessor, David Scott, had in the 1820s formally recognised the practice as legitimate.[40] In addition, the mismatch of colonial intentions with the extant structure of *posa* generated substantial problems. Captain Matthie, who led efforts to monetise *posa*, reported his confusion over the proper collection methods or value of existing transactions. 'There is', he said, 'no ancient document extant that I can find out detailing these circumstances ... I have taken several statements of the Articles, said to have originally fixed, to be collected from each house, but no two agree ... aris[ing] from the circumstance of the hill tribes not taking the same articles every year'.[41] This indicates that a major limitation of colonial meddling in *posa* arrangements was officials' inability to properly conceive of socio-economic relations that were not codified in writing. To an even greater degree than efforts in late eighteenth century to unearth 'ancient constitutions' upon which to base Hindu and Muslim legal codes in Bengal, the colonial search for a documentary basis for interactions at the outskirts of northern Assam thoroughly failed to comprehend the fluidity and nuance of existing socio-spatial relations between communities around the *duars*.[42] A further source of trouble for the colonial state was inconsistency between various layers of administration. In 1837, Robertson's successor, Francis Jenkins, voiced suspicions that 'the misrepresentations of our own [Assamese] subordinate officers, who had an interest in upholding the ancient system' were a contributing factor to the ongoing struggle to implement the new form of *posa*.[43] These shortcomings

---

[38] Ibid., ff. 6–7.

[39] NAI Foreign External A, March 1885, No. 256: Assam Chief Commissioner to Lakhimpur Deputy Commissioner, 4 December 1884.

[40] NAI Foreign Political, 20 February 1834, No. 24: Government of India to Robertson, 20 February 1834.

[41] NAI Foreign Political, 18 July 1836, No. 77: J. Matthie, Officiating Magistrate, Durrung District, to Jenkins, 13 June 1836, ff. 35–36.

[42] On the 'ancient constitution' concept in early colonial rule, see Tony Ballantyne, *Orientalism and Race: Aryanism in the British Empire* (Basingstoke: Palgrave Macmillan, 2002), pp. 21–3; Thomas R. Metcalf, *Ideologies of the Raj* (Cambridge: Cambridge University Press, 1998), pp. 9–10; Robert Travers, *Ideology and Empire in Eighteenth-Century India: The British in Bengal* (Cambridge: Cambridge University Press, 2007).

[43] NAI Foreign Political, 15 May 1837, No. 10: Jenkins to Government of India, 15 May 1837, f. 11.

within the colonial state partly explain the limited implementation of *posa* reform, but equally significant was the reception of the new system by its subjects.

Colonial actions connected to *posa* were an act of bordering. In attempting to stop what they understood to be threatening annual incursions by upland inhabitants into colonial sovereign territory, officials in Assam instantiated a new type of border between the valley and the hills. By monetising *posa* and placing it under their control, colonial agents instituted a new form of border crossing and tied 'unadministered' communities into state-controlled socio-economic relations, as also occurred through systems of payments in Balochistan three decades later (see Section 1.4). But when enacted, *posa* reform provoked from some communities the very type of violent crossings it sought to counteract. When members of the Dafla community were first prevented from taking *posa* in 'traditional' fashion in 1835, they responded by taking goods by force. Officials only felt able to conclude written agreements on the new form of *posa* with some Dafla potentates after the colonial state responded with violence of its own. Following Walter Benjamin's claim that law is instantiated through state violence, this was one instance of many at British India's fringes of what might be termed border-making violence.[44] Even then, the border remained incomplete: some communities did not sign up to the adapted form of *posa* and collected goods without the mediation of a state representative in what Jenkins termed the 'traditional' manner.[45] As Bodhisattva Kar has suggested, the *posa* border proved to be an 'impossible' one for the colonial state.[46]

Frontier officials were troubled not only by uplanders' spectacular incursions across the border but also by their refusal to participate in authorised rituals of border crossing. An impermeable border seemed as problematic as a fully open one. The importance of the adjusted *posa* boundary as a form of oversight and limited control over ostensibly 'independent' communities is apparent from officials' assumption that the periodic failures of chiefs to cross the border in this authorised fashion were expressions of discontent. In 1872, one administrator noted that although various sections of the 'Abor' (now Adi) community had come in to collect their *posa* from him, one that had previously come in did not on this occasion: 'they seem to be tired of coming down to take the subsidy'.[47] This concerned him because the *posa* collection constituted the only regular contact

---

[44] Walter Benjamin, 'Critique of Violence', in M. Bullock and M. W, Jennings (eds.), *Selected Writings* (Cambridge, MA: Harvard University Press, 1996), p. 248.

[45] NAI Foreign Political, 18 January 1850, No. 73: Jenkins to Government of India, Foreign Department, 8 December 1849, f. 9.

[46] Kar, 'When Was the Postcolonial?', pp. 63–9.

[47] NAI Foreign Political A, August 1872, No. 141: W. S. Clarke, Lakhimpur Deputy Commissioner, to Assam Commissioner, 9 May 1872, ff. 1–2.

between the state and this community, and therefore the only means of exerting influence over them.

Posa reform is indicative of the centrality of performance to acts of bordering and the fact that boundaries do not simply exclude those on the other side but seek to instantiate a particular relationship with them. The *posa* boundary was intended to be porous – to allow certain flows while blocking others. A British map of Assam produced in the mid-1830s, the time that interference in *posa* began in earnest, effectively represented what colonial officials intended the northern Assam border to mean and do.[48] Despite pretensions to precision and scale in the agrarian regions of the Valley, the map represents the boundary between plains and hills with a series of scalloped lines, giving the approximate effect of a cartoon cloud. This apparent lack of precision represented the significance of the border to officials in Assam at the time, as primarily defined by actions and movements across it rather than specific spatial positioning or linearity. Gunnel Cederlöf has claimed that a profound shift towards precise demarcation took place in colonial space making in the northeast during the 1830s. In fact, her characterisation of the previous decades of expansion from northeastern Bengal, when 'marking out territorial claims meant fortifying strategic strongholds such as heights or river bifurcations, or exercising authority by taxing market places', continued to be the case at the northern fringes of Assam.[49] British interference with *posa* did not change the indistinct location of the border but instead altered the set of practices that could legitimately take place across it. What emerged was a changed – and much contested – boundary in the same approximate place.

1.2   'Making Outside Barbarians': The Administrative Border in Early Colonial Punjab

In northern Assam, local responses clearly inflected the meaning of the border even as colonial actions produced a distinct shift in the practices that constituted this boundary. Turning to the period of the advent of colonial power at the trans-Indus fringes of Punjab in the late 1840s, it is clear that pressures and confusions between administrators and local communities rendered the boundary between administered and 'independent' regions at the colonial state's northwestern limits a similarly unsettled object. Armed with preconceptions from earlier travelogues (see Sections 3.2 and 3.3), British officials first came into prolonged contact with the inhabitants of territory to the west of the River

---

[48] NAI Foreign Political, 16 May 1838, No. 53: Jenkins to Government of India, 3 April 1838.
[49] Cederlöf, *Founding*, p. 49.

Indus following the 1846 Treaty of Bhairowal.[50] In his newly expanded role as Regent to the child Maharaja Duleep Singh, the British Resident at Lahore Henry Lawrence deputed a number of Assistants to serve at the outer limits of the Sikh kingdom in Punjab. While Lawrence and the Government of India debated the amount of interference these men should be allowed to exercise, the Assistants themselves swiftly set about exceeding the advisory functions with which they were officially invested, fashioning governmental roles which combined judicial, executive, and revenue-collecting powers.[51] Before and after formal annexation of the Punjab in 1849, the British explicitly stated that they retained the Sikh boundary between administered territory, where inhabitants were required to pay revenue to government, and unadministered territory. The dividing line was said to be where the plains gave way to the foothills of the mountain ranges beyond which lay the possessions of the Amir of Kabul.

Beneath this apparent continuity, the forms of administration that the Assistants sought to implement imposed a sharper divide between the plains and the hills than had existed under Sikh officials, whose focus had been more or less confined to collecting revenue and curbing serious incursions from upland communities.[52] Reynell Taylor, the Deputy Commissioner stationed at Dera Ismail Khan, claimed that:

We ... strive and intend to make all good ryots [cultivators] ... In this way, our method of managing a frontier province is diametrically different from that practised by our predecessors, the Sikhs, who, when they occupied a district even on a border, merely looked to the requisite facilities for collecting their own revenue, without the slightest reference to the safety of the villages from external aggression, except on a grand scale.[53]

Although Taylor's juxtaposition of the carelessness of the Sikhs with his own government's beneficence was part of a broader effort to downplay colonial

[50] Bikrama Jit Hasrat (ed.), The Punjab Papers: Selections from the Private Papers of Lord Auckland, Lord Ellenborough, Viscount Hardinge, and the Marquis of Dalhousie, 1836–1849, on the Sikhs (Hoshiarpur: V.V. Research Institute, 1970), pp. 107–9. On the impact of the 'Elphinstonian episteme' on subsequent British imaginings of Afghanistan and the northwest frontier, see Benjamin D. Hopkins, The Making of Modern Afghanistan (Basingstoke: Palgrave Macmillan, 2008); Bayly, Taming.

[51] British Library, Oriental and India Office, European Manuscripts Collections (hereafter 'MSS Eur') F171/70: Henry Lawrence to Government of India, 21 June 1847; Government of India to Henry Lawrence, 3 July 1847, pp. 16, 18–19. The most famous account of the Assistants' role is Herbert Edwardes, A Year on the Punjab Frontier, in 1848–49 (London: Richard Bentley, 1851).

[52] However, the Sikh kingdom's frontier personnel, especially Paolo Avitabile, the European governor of Peshawar from 1834 to 1843, had a reputation for severe punishment of infractions: MSS Eur F171/70: George Lawrence to Henry Lawrence, 19/04/1847, p. 3; General Report on the Administration of the Punjab for the Years 1849–50 and 1850–51 (Lahore: Punjab Government Press, 1851), pp. 7, 11.

[53] IOR/V/27/273/1: Reynell Taylor to John Nicholson, 'District Memorandum: Derah Ismael Khan', 1852, pp. 113–14.

violence, the advent of British rule in Punjab undoubtedly entailed a shift in what the administrative border meant. In some areas, officials sought to give the boundary a newly material form. James Abbott, the Assistant stationed at Hazara, levelled existing forts built by local potentates and constructed boundary pillars from 1847 onwards, indicating British assumptions of unitary sovereign territory here as in northern Assam during the 1830s.[54]

Colonial intentions did not, however, translate into a completely different type of border. Adjustments in the location of the boundary continued after pillars had been erected. A disparity persisted between formally administered areas and areas in which the state interfered, showing that the impact of the Assistants' actions was insufficient to impose a coherent space of government. The policy they pursued of attempting to fashion inhabitants of the administered plains into settled agriculturalists – and thereby governable subjects – was a gradual and fraught process, which did not create a definitive distinction between independent 'hill tribes' and administered plains people.[55] Officials were also far from unanimously agreed on whether the border should be completely closed. Taylor pronounced himself 'a decided advocate for allowing the men of the hills to mix freely with all classes in the plains, cultivate land in the plain district wherever they possess them, attend our markets, &c.' His call for a porous border was not rooted in confidence of the 'civilising' effects that border crossing might have, but on the practical impossibility of enforcing a strict boundary. 'It will be very long,' he wrote, 'before we shall establish a frontier line that could not be passed by individuals or small parties night or day, and an attempt to make outside barbarians of the mass of men inhabiting the hills would make literally thousands of men who now pursue peaceful avocations our active enemies'.[56]

Whether British officials accepted it or not, the largely unenforced and undemarcated boundary between independent territory in the hills and the administered plains continued to be crossed with impunity. Even in the few areas in which the British materially demarcated the boundary, such as Hazara, transgressions continued largely unchecked.[57] Many communities also inhabited areas bisected by the boundary, causing officials uncertainty when dealing with violence in administered areas. These confusions were apparent in the British response to a large-scale attack in 1849 on revenue-paying agriculturalists by a section of Waziris straddling a portion of the administrative border in southern Punjab. Officials in the area suggested that 'the difficulty of

---

[54] MSS Eur F171/25: James Abbott, 'Narrative of Events in Huzara', ff. 2–14; MSS Eur F171/70: Henry Lawrence to Government of India, 3 July 1847, p. 24.
[55] For example, MSS Eur F171/70: George Lawrence to John Lawrence, 1 October 1847, pp. 72–80.
[56] IOR/V/27/273/1: Taylor, 'District Memorandum', pp. 125–26.
[57] MSS Eur F171/70: Abbott to Henry Lawrence, 5 August 1847, pp. 54–55.

ascertaining the real offenders and punishing them without causing a decided breach between Government and the Wuzeeree [*sic*] tribes is so great as to amount to an impossibility'.[58] In the face of their inability to dispense 'justice' against individuals, some officials suggested directing violence against all Waziris who resided within the administered limits of British India. The tendency to criminalise entire frontier communities (see Section 4.3) was both symptom of and contributor to the indeterminate administrative boundary in Punjab.

In the early years of colonial rule in the region, frontier officials broke borders first and gained superior approval later. Henry Lawrence's authorisation of the military occupation of Hazara in 1847 followed an unsanctioned and unsuccessful pursuit into the hills of the perpetrators of a crime in governed territory.[59] The first generation of the Punjab frontier cadre developed various rationales for assuming discretionary powers beyond the proclaimed administrative boundary in Punjab. Reynell Taylor warned of 'the error of visiting the offence committed by the Majority of the tribe upon individuals of it living within the Government limits' and insisted that he should be allowed to cross the border at will.[60] His successor in Hazara argued, successfully, that a force should be stationed under his command must be allowed 'at a moment's warning, and at any hour of the night or day, [to go] up the mountains, without giving notice of the movement to a living creature', as 'the mountains are scarcely assailable, if [the] Enemy are allowed time to find their posts'.[61] During the early years of British involvement at the Punjab frontier, those who resided beyond the border were deemed liable to the same punishment as inhabitants of fully governed territory. Border transgressions were, then, a two-way phenomenon, a cycle that involved officials who proclaimed to establish boundaries every bit as much as communities arrayed across the division of plains and hills. As in northern Assam, administrators claimed that the movements and characteristics of local inhabitants compelled them to adopt transgressive tactics and a fluid definition of the limits of state territory and subject populations.

1.3   'Absurd and Impossible': Bordering the Naga Hills District, 1866–1905

In 1866, interventions began that fundamentally reshaped two borderlands of British India. The regions, Balochistan and the Naga Hills, were separated by the full longitudinal width of the colonial subcontinent, but the processes of colonial interference shared notable features. Frontier officials initiated and provided ongoing impetus for both. In doing so, these men embraced, and at least some of their superiors came to acknowledge, a principle of perennially unsettled

---

[58] MSS Eur E417/5: Taylor to George Pearse, 7 December 1849, f. 5.
[59] MSS Eur F171/70: Henry Lawrence to Government of India, 14 August 1847, p. 55.
[60] MSS Eur E417/5: Taylor to George Pearse, 7 December 1849, f. 7.
[61] NAI Foreign Secret, 26 May 1849, No. 63: Abbott to Henry Lawrence, 29 March 1849, ff. 9–10.

borders and the corollary of territory that was, in Lauren Benton's words, 'full of holes'.[62] After a lull from the early 1850s, a combination of occasional Naga infractions into British Assam and colonial officials' desire to interfere in episodes of violence between Naga villages tipped debates over the proper extent of British sovereignty and responsibility back in favour of expanding colonial authority into the hills (see Section 4.2). Although its title may have suggested the imposition of uniform authority over a clearly bounded area, the Naga Hills District was initially little more than a set of proclaimed intentions. In 1866, a British officer, Lieutenant Gregory, and a party of troops were established in the Angami Naga village of Samaguting. They were tenuously linked to the nearest major outpost in Assam by a thirteen-mile road that the soldiers constructed as they marched, and a further sixty miles' journey by river. Despite the colonial state's claim to hold territorial sovereignty over a large swathe of the uplands, Gregory was initially instructed not to exercise 'direct control' over Nagas except those residing in Samaguting, although he was allowed summary punitive powers against 'any village proved to have been concerned in any gross outrage'.[63] In this initial form, the Naga Hills District was not a clear territory delineated by a border: its limits were explicitly amorphous, ebbing, and flowing seasonally and with intermittent journeys of military parties to enact violence, and of survey parties to map the hills.

Perceived difficulties of terrain, limits on effective knowledge gathering, and tactics of flight and avoidance by local inhabitants all severely circumscribed colonial territorial power. Partly because of these limitations, the British Indian state's power to define territory in the Naga Hills District consisted more of destructive interludes than entrenched and lasting structures. Probably the most significant spatial intervention in the years immediately after the foundation of the District was the destruction of the village of Razepemah following an attack on colonial subjects, and subsequent prohibition on villagers rebuilding on the same site. The Commissioner of Assam ordered that 'not a hoe must be raised anywhere on the Razepemah lands, not a hut built, not a grave dug there, but they must remain a desert, unless, or until at some future period, we may think fit to re-occupy the locality with our own Naga subjects under a new name'.[64] At this stage, the colonial state's appearance in the hills was generally limited to spectacular shows of force rather than consistent efforts to construct stable administrative space.

From the mid-1870s a creeping expansion of formal British authority took place, with the colonial official on the spot intermittently taking villages under

[62] Benton, *Search*, p. 2.
[63] NAI Foreign Political A, July 1866, No. 16: Bengal Government to Government of India, 27 June 1866, f. 1; NAI Foreign Political A, December 1866, No. 137: Henry Hopkinson, Commissioner of Assam, to Bengal Government, 14 September 1866, ff. 4–5.
[64] NAI Foreign Political A, April 1868, No. 261: Hopkinson to Bengal Government, 4 March 1868, f. 1.

formal British protection in return for securing villagers' assent to pay a house tax (see Section 5.3). Commenting on the first two villages taken into British 'protection' through this process, the Government of India explicitly stated that there was no need for a general principle to be laid down to dictate similar events in the future. Instead, what it termed a 'rough and indefinite' process of expansion was assumed sufficient to fulfil the primary purpose of 'keeping order on the frontier' – with 'frontier' in this instance referring to the boundary between Naga villages and the tea gardens and agricultural fields of Assam.[65] As had been the case at the Punjab frontier immediately following annexation, officials at various levels of the colonial state agreed that upholding the limits of Assam required interference beyond those limits. Permeable borders were, once more, the order of the day.

Despite the amorphous nature of the Naga Hills District, the location of its nominal boundaries still greatly exorcised officials in the area. Gregory's successor as the Deputy Commissioner in the region John Butler claimed that the 'theoretical boundaries of this district' laid down in 1867 were 'absurd and impossible', being in many places 'utterly wrong, or so extraordinarily defined as to be quite impossible of identification'.[66] Although his superiors accepted Butler's alternative border, this too quickly became provisional. Ever more villages continued to be incorporated within the colonial pale and an intensified series of military and survey expeditions performed territory in ways that differed substantially from its relatively fixed representation in maps and official diktats. The cumulative effect of these various space-making practices was, as one member of the Government of India put it, 'a perpetually disturbed frontier line'.[67] Another acknowledged that the territorial and border confusions arose in significant part because the mainspring of actions by local colonial officials was 'no longer ... protecting our own frontier or our settled districts ... [but] extending our authority, village by village, over the whole tract of country ... The Naga Hills District ... is a geographical expression, not an administrative fact'. He admitted that 'consequently, the present boundary has no special or intelligible meaning from an administrative point of view'.[68]

The deliberately indeterminate limits of the Naga Hills District continued long after the bloody suppression of a major rebellion at the British post at Kohima in 1879, which has often been seen as a major turning point in the normalisation of British authority in the region.[69] All that was normalised was the principle of persistent, creeping expansion primarily at the behest of

---

[65] NAI Foreign Political A, July 1874, No. 45: Government of India to Bengal Government, 30 June 1874, f. 1.

[66] NAI Foreign Political A, December 1875, No. 87: Butler to Assam Chief Commissioner, 26 June 1875, ff. 1–2.

[67] NAI Foreign Political A, October 1878, No. 7–51, Keep-With, f. 4.   [68] Ibid., f. 8.

[69] Julian Jacobs with Alan Macfarlane, Sarah Harrison and Anita Herle, *The Nagas: Society, Culture and the Colonial Encounter*, 2nd ed. (London: Edition Hansjörg Mayer, 2012), pp. 21–22; Robb, 'The Colonial State'.

officials stationed at the frontier. During the 1880s, officials in Assam creatively interpreted prior instructions from the Government of India and instituted a hazy area beyond the gradually advancing eastern boundary of the
District under what it termed 'political control'. The communities within this
region were subject to annual visits, known as 'promenades', by the Deputy
Commissioner of the Naga Hills District and his armed retinue.[70] That the lure
of boundary crossing for officials was the key element of the border's continued
provisional and flimsy status was acknowledged even by a member of the
Government of India, who stated in 1888, 'the political control system seems
particularly adapted to force our hand in extending territory'.[71]

Although controversial and subject to periodic interruptions from more senior
and distant administrators, the system of 'political control' and the sporadic
eastward extension of the Naga Hills District continued into the twentieth
century.[72] In missives to superiors and on maps (see Figure 1.1), frontier
officials disavowed any form of border that might close off further expansion.
The Deputy Commissioner pronounced in 1903 that he was 'not prepared to
recommend either a natural or a tribal boundary', and instead suggested 'a
mixture of the two, the principle to be followed being that the benign influence
of Government should be exercised as far as can be extended without in any way
increasing the cost of ordinary administration'.[73] Other frontier officials in the
region backed such thinking by invoking long-distance comparisons and
employing moralising rhetoric. One contended that 'the same grounds which
would warrant our interference under certain circumstances in the Congo Free-
State would justify our stopping the existing atrocities that occur in sight of our
out-posts' at the eastern fringes of the Naga Hills Districts.[74] Almost all invoked
the notion that 'barbarism' beyond the border might 'have a disturbing effect' on
people in the Naga Hills District owing to the mobility of populations in the
region, while the Assam Government characterised pushing beyond the acknowledged border as merely facing up to 'the responsibilities of sovereignty'.[75]
These arguments had the desired effect: the Government of India acquiesced to
a series of boundary adjustments that cumulatively meant the Naga Hills
District's dimensions morphed at the behest of men stationed at the frontier.

---

[70] NAI Foreign External A, January 1889, No. 76: Assam Chief Commissioner to Government of
India, Foreign Department, 14/11/1888, ff. 2–3.
[71] NAI Foreign External A, January 1889, Nos. 76–88, Keep-With No. 1: W. J. Crooke, Note, 24/
11/1888, f. 2.
[72] Robert Reid, *History of the Frontier Areas Bordering on Assam from 1883–1941* (Shillong:
Assam Government Press, 1942), pp. 99–100.
[73] Ibid., pp. 132–33.
[74] NAI Foreign External A, July 1908, enclosure to No. 122: H. W. Cole to J. C. Arbuthnot, 20/06/
1907, f. 11.
[75] NAI Foreign External A, July 1908, No. 122: Eastern Bengal and Assam Government to
Government of India, Foreign Department, 07/12/1907, f. 6.

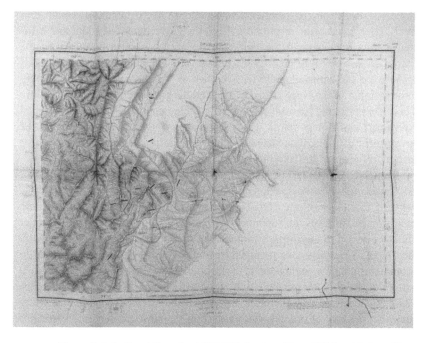

Figure 1.1 Indian Atlas, sheet 130 S.E. (eastern Naga Hills), with three lines
later added showing (from left to right) 'Original', 'Existing', and 'Proposed'
boundaries (1904).[76]

These officials did not aim to create a territory premised on uniform coverage of a defined portion of the earth's surface. State space in this region had the
character of an ever-shifting network of nodes and routes under varying
degrees of control. Rather than implementing increasingly precise boundaries,
colonial administrators instead came to disavow the possibility and desirability
of a fixed border. By way of justification, they claimed that Nagas did not
comprehend the concept of boundaries and engaged in social and economic
relations that confounded efforts to definitively bound homogeneous territories. There is no doubt that they benefitted greatly from the shifting, penetrable
border. For them, just as for the French colonial officials at the Siam-Laos
border during the same era analysed by Andrew Walker, 'the elimination of
[border] ambiguity would have greatly reduced their potential political
influence'.[77] Accordingly, these men successfully advanced the notion that

---

[76] Assam State Archives, Dispur (hereafter 'ASA'), Map Collection, No. 922.
[77] Walker, 'Borders', p. 199.

effective control depended on spatial indeterminacy, meaning that the Naga Hills District remained amorphous and patchy.

1.4 'Breaking the Border Rule': Balochistan's Boundaries, 1866–1892

British officials in the Naga Hills were not alone in seeing fixed boundaries as inimical to their roles as agents of empire. During the quarter-century from 1866 to his death, Robert Sandeman repeatedly broke borders in Balochistan. He started by violating the administrative boundary between Dera Ghazi Khan District in southwest Punjab and the areas nominally under the control of the Khanate of Kalat. After a British military and administrative presence in Balochistan had been established under his charge by the late 1870s, Sandeman spent the remainder of his career (and life) overlooking and undermining boundaries that limited his sphere of action. Much like his contemporaries in the uplands south of the Brahmaputra Valley, Sandeman and his underlings insisted that definitive borders had little meaning in a region of shifting people and complex terrain. They consistently construed upheavals beyond the extant bounds of their jurisdiction as existential threats to colonial interests. As in the Naga Hills, their official subversion brought about substantial results once authorised post facto by the upper echelons of colonial administration: the creation of a new administrative territory, British Baluchistan, and roles – with status and accolades – for themselves.

Sandeman's part in engendering a wholesale shift in frontier policy in the northwest from a defensive 'close border policy' to an active 'forward policy' has been exaggerated both by his contemporaries and in a number of subsequent historical accounts.[78] Previous colonial interactions with the communities beyond the administrative boundary had long been volatile and changeable, rather than wedded to a closed border. Although military actions during the 1840s and the establishment of military posts instantiated British authority in Upper Sind (see Section 4.1), outbreaks of violence among Baloch communities and machinations against the Khan of Kalat among Brahui powerholders

---

[78] Thomas Henry Thornton, *Colonel Sir Robert Sandeman: His Life and Work on Our Indian Frontier* (London: John Murray, 1895), pp. 18–20. Magnus Marsden and Benjamin Hopkins claim that 'Sandeman's actions ultimately proved, in the words of his assistant R. I. Bruce, the "*coup de grace*" to the closed border system': *Fragments*, p. 56; later in the same chapter, Marsden and Hopkins rightly acknowledge the '*ad hoc*' and 'back and forth' nature of frontier policy in the northwest (p. 63). Christian Tripodi divides colonial frontier policy in the northwest into large blocks: 'close border' from 1843 to 1875; 'forward policy' from 1875 to the creation of the North-West Frontier Province in 1901; a modified 'close border' policy from 1901 to the early 1920s; a modified 'forward policy' from the early 1920s. See Tripodi, *Edge*, pp. 16–17; on Sandeman specifically, pp. 50–65.

continued.[79] British ambivalence towards Kalat's rulers and repeated interference in their affairs had been among the drivers of this instability since the First Anglo-Afghan War, when colonial forces attacked the town of Kalat, and replaced the Khan with a man of their choice.[80]

In the 1860s, the community targeted in some of the most severe episodes of violence by British forces during the 1840s, the Bugtis, began to pierce the largely undemarcated boundary with the administered areas in Dera Ghazi Khan District, which lay immediately northeast of Upper Sind. Whereas the manned fortresses of the Upper Sind border presented a formidable deterrent, the boundary further north was sparsely patrolled. Sandeman took up his post as Deputy Commissioner of Dera Ghazi Khan in 1866 against a backdrop of sporadic and generally ineffective measures to prevent border violations and an uncertain British policy towards Kalat Khanate. From the outset of his tenure, Sandeman railed against the existing location of the administrative border, claiming that it divided communities and represented a 'cruel injustice'.[81] He later added that the boundary line the British inherited from the Sikhs 'has proved disastrous to our subjects, and to the frontier clans, and rendered the administration of the frontier tract itself a matter of extreme difficulty'.[82] From shortly after his appointment, Sandeman (as his first biographer T. H. Thornton wrote in 1895) 'broke the border rule repeatedly and successfully'; the latter was certainly true in respect of the growth of his own influence in the region and within the colonial state.[83]

During his first year in Dera Ghazi Khan, Sandeman took his first tour beyond the administrative boundary accompanied by his assistant Richard Bruce, and four Baloch *tumandar*s (chiefs) accompanied by approximately 300 followers. Beyond the border, he met with the Bugti *tumandar* Gholam Mortaza Khan and some of his subordinates who had led infractions into southwest Punjab.[84] In undertaking his own violation of the boundary, Sandeman directly contravened the established chain of command: all dealings with nominal Kalat territory should have gone through the Superintendent of the Upper Sind Frontier or the

---

[79] On fears of a tribal rebellion during the Indian Rebellion of 1857, see NAI Foreign Secret, 25 May 1858, No. 467. On the continuation of forays into Upper Sind after the violence of the mid-1840s, see NAI Foreign Political, 17 May 1853, No. 10. On inter-tribal violence, see NAI Foreign Political, 14 January 1859, No. 21.

[80] Maharashtra State Archives, Mumbai (hereafter 'MSA'), Political, 1838–40, Vol. 21: T. Willshire to Lord Auckland, 14 November 1839, f. 621; MSA, Political, 1841–42, Vol. 74: 'Treaty between Major Outram and Mir Nusseer Khan', 6 October 1841. See also Swidler, 'Kalat', p. 563.

[81] Quoted in Thornton, *Sandeman*, p. 30.

[82] Sandeman, 'Memorandum on the Rectification of the North-West Frontier of India', in Thornton, *Sandeman*, p. 336.

[83] A. L. P. Tucker, *Sir Robert G. Sandeman: Peaceful Conqueror of Baluchistan* (New York: Macmillan, 1921), p. 27.

[84] Richard Isaac Bruce, *The Forward Policy and Its Results, or Thirty-Five Years' Work Amongst the Tribes on Our North-Western Frontier of India* (London: Longmans, Green, and Co., 1900), pp. 26–27

British Resident at the Court of Kalat, who was under the auspices of the Sind and Bombay Governments. As a Punjab official, Sandeman had no official sanction to cross the border. Nonetheless, in the name of the colonial state, Sandeman dictated terms to the Bugtis, including the restoration of stolen property. In return he offered employment in irregular levies and payments to particular chiefs (see Section 5.4).[85] The advent of 'tribal service' as a means of refashioning the frontier was convenient both for the those who benefitted from additional income and for the colonial state, which, as in the case of *posa* in northern Assam, tied 'independent' communities into its political economy. But its primary beneficiary was Sandeman, as it provided an alibi for additional, generally unauthorised, trips beyond the border throughout the rest of the 1860s and into the 1870s. During this period – and again without prior permission – Sandeman also established a summer camp twenty-five miles beyond the acknowledged limits of British territory at which he and Bruce spent a few months each year in contact with the communities of the surrounding hills.[86] Unknown to Sandeman, the contemporary frontier official T. H. Lewin had similarly taken up unauthorised seasonal residence in uplands beyond the administrative border in the region that became the Lushai Hills (see Section 1.6). In both cases, living among upland communities ended up being a precursor to their being brought under formal British administration.

Sandeman's repeated border violations in the late 1860s and early 1870s succeeded in stopping Baloch forays into Dera Ghazi Khan. Rather than ceasing altogether, though, they were merely redirected to Upper Sind – a clear example of administrators provoking instead of salving the 'turbulent frontier'.[87] A protracted battle followed between Sandeman and the Commissioner of Sind, William Merewether, became sufficiently severe that the Punjab and Sind governments convened a 'conference' at the town of Mithankot in February 1871 to broker a resolution.[88] Against previously established protocol, the meeting placed an official stamp on Sandeman's personal authority and involvement with the northern Balochs.[89] As upheavals continued in Kalat, inflamed by the ongoing lack of clarity over which colonial officials had powers to act beyond the administrative border, the Government of India pronounced in 1874 that 'the time has now arrived ... [to] make our own arrangements direct with the frontier tribes and without reference to the Khan'.[90] This marked a significant breakthrough for Sandeman's policy of

[85] Ibid., pp. 28–29. See also Marsden and Hopkins, *Fragments*, p. 57.
[86] Thornton, *Sandeman*, pp. 36–37   [87] Galbraith, "'Turbulent Frontier'".
[88] For example, NAI Foreign A-Political-E, June 1883, Nos. 306–324, Keep-With: Sandeman to C. U. Aitchison, 24 February 1883.
[89] Marsden and Hopkins, *Fragments*, pp. 58–60.
[90] NAI Foreign Political, October 1874, No. 173: Government of India to Sind Commissioner, 9 October 1874, f. 277.

overlooking the administrative border and engaging Baloch chiefs through payments and service. He was chosen to lead two expeditions across the established boundary into Balochistan in 1875 and 1876, which culminated with the establishment of the Baluchistan Agency and the permanent occupation of a British military post at Quetta.[91] The powers assigned to the Agent to the Governor-General in charge of the Baluchistan Agency for intervention in internal Kalat affairs essentially completed the process started during the First Anglo-Afghan War of reducing the Khanate to little more than ceremonial authority.[92] Once again, Sandeman's subversion of his orders was key to these outcomes. The authorised aim of his second mission was to secure the Bolan Pass from tribal depredations. After his return, however, the Government of India pronounced that 'whilst ... we were fully alive to the difficulties and responsibilities of the permanent intervention advocated by Major Sandeman, we could not disguise from ourselves the greater difficulties of renouncing the position in which the success of his mediation had conspicuously placed us'.[93]

Thornton's adulatory rendering of Sandeman's 1876 journey into Balochistan was an 'anti-conquest' narrative in Mary Louise Pratt's terms, masking colonial expansion with a discourse of individual heroism.[94] Thornton wrote of Sandeman's border crossing that 'there were elements of grave anxiety; the hot weather had set in; fifty miles of desert lay before him, then a toilsome journey of sixty miles along the shingly bed of a dry torrent, shut in by stupendous cliffs without a blade of vegetation, before the uplands could be reached; moreover, cholera was in the air'.[95] Thornton also described Sandeman's previous infractions in similarly self-sacrificial terms, claiming they were 'particularly hazardous proceeding[s], because he not only risked his life, but his career'.[96] Sandeman's frontier-redefining tours were acts of a self-promotion, which served to accumulate personal authority within the structures of the colonial state.[97] This strategy was eminently successful: he was knighted and given charge of the Baluchistan Agency.

Sandeman's reconfiguration of the border was in certain respects exceptional at the outskirts of British India in the later nineteenth century, but it also points to certain important elements of frontier making in the nineteenth- and early

---

[91] NAI Foreign Political, November 1875, No. 278: Extract from the Proceedings of the Government of India, Foreign Department, 16 October 1875, f. 6; Bruce, *Forward Policy*, pp. 56–9, 62–6; Thornton, *Sandeman*, pp. 76–95.

[92] The removal of power to levy duties on goods transiting through the Bolan Pass in 1883 might be seen as the conclusion of this process. See NAI Foreign A-Political-E, December 1883, Nos. 74–130.

[93] Quoted in Thornton, *Sandeman*, p. 85.

[94] Mary Louise Pratt, *Imperial Eyes: Travel Writing and Transculturation* (London: Routledge, 1992), p. 7, passim.

[95] Thornton, *Sandeman*, p. 77.   [96] Ibid., pp. 35–36.

[97] T. A. Heathcote, *Balochistan, the British and the Great Game: The Struggle for the Bolan Pass, Gateway to India* (London: Hurst, 2016).

twentieth-century colonial subcontinent. It was indicative of the fact that localised actions and policies shaped frontiers at least as much as grand strategic motivations.[98] There is no doubt that the concern to counter Russian advances in Central Asia over the preceding decade enhanced support for Sandeman's expansionism among senior officials, many of whom sought a hyper-masculine antidote to what they saw as the 'timidity' of supposed recent inactivity.[99] However, although in later writings on Balochistan and Afghanistan addressed to imperial strategists he emphasised the Russian threat,[100] geopolitics were not the primary rationale for advancing into Balochistan in 1877 for Sandeman and his coterie. As one of his assistants put it in 1882, these men believed 'if Persian independence, Khiva, Bokhara, Khokan, and Afghanistan were absorbed by Russia, there would be nothing in this course which we should fear as Englishmen or dread as philanthropists'.[101] Instead, what mattered to them were the issues of tribal control and communication that Sandeman's border-breaking tours both partially engendered and pretended to address.

Violating boundaries and insisting on the temporary nature of existing administrative limits became an essential element of Sandeman's administration of British Baluchistan until his death in 1892. From 1883 on, he undertook a series of tours to the large desert-bound hinterland to the southwest of Quetta, the administrative and military centre of British Baluchistan. During these ventures, he tenuously asserted Kalat's long-standing sovereignty over far-flung communities, thereby drawing them within the ambit of the colonial state and under his own brand of personal administration (see Section 5.4).[102] At the same time, Sandeman worked on undermining boundaries around Zhob, at the mountainous northern fringes of British Baluchistan. This involved two related forms of border disavowal: journeying into and attempting to reclassify territory beyond the colonial state's established administration, and then challenging the dividing line between the remit of the Punjab Government and that of the Baluchistan Agency.

---

[98] Examples of relatively recent claims that high strategy largely dictated frontier policies include Fred Scholz, *Nomadism and Colonialism: A Hundred Years of Baluchistan, 1872–1972*, trans. Hugh van Skyhawk (Oxford: Oxford University Press, 2002 [1974]), p. 93; Tripodi, *Edge*, pp. 17–18.

[99] IOR/L/P&S/7/1: Political letter no. 13 of 1875, Note by Henry Green, 23 October 1874. On Russian expansion in Central Asia, see A. S. Morrison, *Russian Rule in Samarkand 1868–1910: A Comparison with British India* (Oxford: Oxford University Press, 2008).

[100] For example, Sandeman, 'Our Future Policy in Afghanistan (1886)', 'Note on the North-West Frontier and Our Policy in Afghanistan (1887)', and 'On British Relations with the Waziri and Other Frontier Tribes (1890)', in Thornton, *Sandeman*, pp. 342–63.

[101] NAI Foreign A-Political-E, December 1883, No. 91: O. T. Duke to W. G. Waterfield, 17 February 1882.

[102] Thornton, *Sandeman*, pp. 180–2.

Sandeman's rhetorical strategy in relation to Zhob was similar to those in the desert southwest of Quetta. He insisted to his superiors that an outbreak of violence between the Kakar community in Zhob and the Marri community in British Baluchistan constituted a threat to colonial infrastructure, security, and prestige.[103] He also evinced anxiety that the isolated outposts that formed the existing border were 'insufficient', suggesting that the Kakars could corral a force such that 'serious disaster would affect [the] whole policy [of] Government'.[104] He balanced this alarm by suggesting that other men of influence in the region had declared themselves willing to come within the British ambit.[105] After journeying beyond the border to obtain 'justice' and improve access into Zhob – a trip the Government of India judged had failed to meet either of its primary objectives[106] – Sandeman argued that the border would have to be revised to ensure his forces were 'in a position to protect the tribes on the confines of Zhob'.[107] When the Government of India declined to approve this suggestion, further Kakar attacks on British subjects and infrastructure came to Sandeman's rescue, enabling him to make a case for again breaking the border.[108] While there, he worked to entrench colonial involvement in the region such that territorial expansion was a *fait accompli*.[109] There were misgivings within the Government of India over Sandeman's rationales for boundary breaking, with Henry Mortimer Durand, later the architect of the British India-Afghanistan boundary, noting: 'I do not attach much value to Sir Robert Sandeman's predictions of trouble. He is always too much inclined to such predictions in support of his views'.[110] Nonetheless, Sandeman's ability to entangle the colonial state in previously unadministered regions committed his superiors to authorise creeping expansion of a similar sort to that in the Naga Hills at the same time.[111]

Within a few years, Sandeman was again advancing the cause of border adjustments through the usual mixture of pessimistic security assessments, optimistic talk of colonial administration as the driver of 'peaceful development', and assertions of sovereignty that deliberately blurred tribal authority, his own influence, and the colonial state's obligations. He wrote in 1888 that 'until the

---

[103] NAI Foreign A-Political-E, July 1883, No. 30: Sandeman to Foreign Secretary, 30 April 1883, f. 1; no. 31: Sandeman to Foreign Secretary, 21 May 1883, f. 1.

[104] NAI Foreign A-Political-E, July 1883, No. 34: Sandeman to Foreign Secretary, 28 May 1883, f. 2.

[105] NAI Foreign A-Political-E, July 1883, No. 48: Sandeman to Foreign Secretary, 28 June 1883, f. 13; no. 57: Sandeman to Foreign Secretary, 09 July 1883, f. 15.

[106] NAI Foreign A-Political-E, December 1883, Nos. 266–74, Keep-With: Note by J.W.R., 13 November 1883, f. 3.

[107] NAI Foreign A-Political-E, December 1883, No. 271: Sandeman to Government of India, Foreign Department, 16 October 1883, f.7.

[108] NAI Foreign A-Political-E, May 1884, Nos. 210–24.

[109] NAI Foreign External A, May 1885, Nos. 197–300.

[110] NAI Foreign External A, February 1885, Nos. 253–301, Keep-With: Note by H. M. Durand, 3 February 1885.

[111] NAI Foreign External A, July 1886, Nos. 220–30.

whole of the Kakar tribe owning the supremacy of the "Badshah of Zhob" is fully recognised as within my jurisdiction, our frontier railways, frontier road, and position in Baluchistan cannot be considered as safe'.[112] The Government of India acquiesced on the proviso that Kakar territory was not formally annexed but instead brought under British 'protectorate'.[113] Like the 'political control' territory at the eastern fringes of the Naga Hills, this designation served to formalise hazy territory, signalling the colonial government's acceptance of Sandeman's efforts to downplay the meaning of fixed, linear borders.

Amorphous boundaries may have been embraced when it was tribes on the other side of the line, but when the Punjab Government complained that Sandeman was infringing on the boundary between its sphere of influence and that of the Baluchistan Agency, he found persuading his superiors tougher. The clash occurred in 1890, as Sandeman sought to extend the area under his influence northwards from the Zhob Valley, across the Suleiman mountains, into the area to the west of the very District in Punjab where he had started his career, Dera Ghazi Khan. Sandeman once again cited multiple justifications for intervening across this boundary, including attacks on communities under British protection in Balochistan from men in Punjab's sphere of influence, and the notion that 'in these countries there is no such thing as a "no-man's-land"'.[114] This claim of the essentially borderless nature of frontier territory, and therefore the need for officials 'on the spot' to decide the space of administrative intervention, met with resistance from the Chief Commissioner of Punjab and the Government of India. The need to prevent bickering between neighbouring administrations led the latter to set down a newly specific boundary between Punjab and Balochistan's spheres of influence. What form the border should take proved a thorny issue. A division along supposed ethnic lines having been ruled out 'owing to the migratory habits of the tribes', there were extensive discussions on whether watersheds or rivers would best be 'understood by the tribes concerned'.[115] The majority decision in the Government of India – with two dissenters – was that a river would be superior as the watershed would have to be 'mark[ed] out', which might 'have the effect of creating the impression that the two administrations which the boundary would serve to divide were rival and antagonistic'.[116] Having a border convey to nearby semi-subjects such an accurate impression of regional governments as

---

[112] NAI Foreign External A, February 1889, No. 186: Sandeman to Government of India, Foreign Department, 24 February 1888.

[113] NAI Foreign External A, July 1889, No. 468: Government of India, Foreign Department, to Sandeman, 11 July 1889.

[114] NAI Foreign Secret E, November 1890, No. 18: Sandeman, Note on James Lyall's Memo, 1 August 1890.

[115] On watersheds as borders in late-nineteenth-century British India, see Gardner, 'Moving watersheds'.

[116] NAI Foreign Secret E, November 1890, No. 23: Government of India, Foreign Department, to Punjab Government, 7 October 1890. The two dissenters from the majority verdict were Sir

disconcertingly close to warring tribes would never do. This botched resolution to the episode served as an exception that embedded the rule accepted increasingly at all levels of the colonial state: fixed administrative borders should be avoided unless strictly necessary.

As was the case for many officials stationed at the outskirts of Assam, for Sandeman the idea of definitive boundaries was anathema – a block on personal ambition and on the free-ranging interventions he deemed appropriate at the fringes of British India. By the later decades of the nineteenth century, administrators at the upper echelons of the administrative apparatus in British India came to acquiesce in, and even celebrate, such amorphous frontier spaces. After Sandeman's death and before he became Viceroy in 1899, George Curzon wrote of Sandeman as a model frontier official. In doing so, he extolled a combination of hazy and non-limited frontier space and personal authority: 'It is no good to have a "Warden of the Marches" unless you give him a comparatively free hand'.[117] In invoking as a model of the colonial frontier official the men who had controlled the frontier areas between England and Scotland and England and Wales during the late medieval period, Curzon betrayed the extent to which senior officials came to support the subversive tendencies of their subordinates. Some fifty years earlier, Sandeman's role-model John Jacob had defended his own repeated and violent crossings of the boundary between Upper Sind and the Balochs (see Section 4.1) by claiming: 'History gives us an exact counterpart of the frontier as it is and has been (not what it may become) in that of the Marches of Wales and the borders of Scotland ... To keep this Country in safety and quiet there must be in effect, a warden of the Marches, by whatever name called'.[118] By Curzon's time in India, such a sentiment had become orthodoxy. It was widely felt that borders should not act as strict limits on the activities of 'men on the spot'. To a significant extent, official subversion had become the norm. In large part, this can be traced to ubiquitous boundary violations from the mid-1860s by turbulent agents of the colonial state – episodes that shifted the meaning, location, and forms of borders at the fringes of British India.

1.5   'Substantial Pillars': Marking the Boundary in Northern Assam During the 1870s

In Balochistan and Naga Hills, the flurry of frontier making from the mid-1860s consistently worked against the principle of fixed border delineation – that is,

---

Charles Elliott and Sir David Barbour: see NAI Foreign Secret E, November 1890, Nos. 24–25: minutes by Elliott, 29 September 1890, and Barbour, 30 September 1890.

[117] Quoted in Thornton, *Sandeman*, p. 295.

[118] NAI Foreign Secret, 28 April 1848, No. 20: Jacob to Shaw, Commanding in Upper Sind, 24 November 1847, ff. 1238–39.

agreeing boundaries in principle and setting down in written documents and maps. In some other areas during this era, however, borders were not only delineated but also demarcated – marked in material form in the territory itself. But in cases in which material inscription was attempted, erecting and subsequently maintaining boundary markers proved difficult. The limited capacity and will of the British Indian state to impose and uphold materially manifested borders indicate the variability of colonial power in fringe regions.[119] In these areas, officials often perceived that they were losing the struggle to put in place physical objects that would serve as reliably robust devices communicating the colonial state's spatial categories to nearby inhabitants. Officials quickly came to perceive as misguided the hope that squat pillars composed of stones and sand would stand for sovereign power and both instantiate and uphold boundaries of the colonial state's choosing. Border infrastructure at the outskirts of British India frequently remained limited in form and restricted – or even actively problematic – in effect.

In 1873 to 1874, during the cold season when most governmental activity in frontier areas of the northeast took place, the northern boundary of Darrang District in Assam was surveyed and partially demarcated. The process was haphazard and riven with confusion. Officials understood this section of the border in a number of incompatible ways: some thought it was the Inner Line across which colonial subjects could not pass without prior permission; others believed it marked the outer limit of the state's sovereign claims. It was one instance of many in nineteenth-century British India of border directives becoming lost in transmission and creatively adapted at the frontier. The Darrang boundary was also something of an afterthought, set down by a survey party primarily tasked with establishing a border between the sovereign territories of Bhutan and British India.[120] The extension into Darrang did not obtain the approval of the Assam Government: Richard Keatinge, the Chief Commissioner, claimed that 'to survey and define a boundary already laid down by Treaty is one thing, to lay down a new boundary between ourselves and savage tribes who are controlled by no central Government, and with whom Treaties are impossible, is quite another'.[121] Here was another instance of British officials' assumption that borders were first and foremost paper objects coming into conflict with their belief that no such agreements were possible with tribes without written languages or the authority structures necessary to render such agreements durable.[122] Such internal contradictions were significant contributors to the limited realisation of the borders supposed to define colonial frontiers.

---

[119] On the intersection of materiality and state power, see Timothy Mitchell, *Rule of Experts: Egypt, Techno-Politics, Modernity* (Berkeley: University of California Press, 2002).

[120] NAI Foreign Political A, March 1876, No. 505: Keatinge to Government of India, 17 May 1875, ff. 2–3.

[121] Ibid., f. 3.

[122] On similar conflicts in present-day Himalayan India, see Mathur, *Paper Tiger*.

Keatinge's assumption that 'there must ... be a risk that the tribes will look upon the Surveyor and his guard as people who are defining the boundary in their own interests, and who, being few, may safely be opposed' pointed to another common complicating factor in boundary making at British India's outskirts.[123] The assumed proclivity to violence of frontier communities coupled with the notion that they would see material markers of boundaries as unwarranted intrusions generated concerns among many British administrators. The Darrang demarcation party met with no resistance despite the fact that it was simultaneously tasked with enforcing an economic blockade of the Dafla community to the north of the border. But the apprehension of violence alone was sufficient to create problems: one planned boundary pillar was not built on the basis that it was at too great a distance from the Daflas for the party to confidently enforce the blockade.[124] It seems that the Daflas engaged with the logic of making territorial claims through material objects. Unfortunately for the British, this evidence came in the form of a contradictory assertion of where the border should be located. As recorded in a Revenue Survey map published in 1874, inside the dotted line that joined the pillars set down by the British there was 'a post planted by the Dafla Gam [chief] as a boundary mark' (Figure 1.2).

Figures 1.2 and 1.3 Detail of Assam Revenue Survey Map, 'Frontier between District Durrung and the Akha & Dufla Hills' (1874).[125]

---

[123] NAI Foreign Political A, March 1876, No. 505: Keatinge to Government of India, 17 May 1875, f. 3.
[124] NAI Foreign Political A, March 1876, No. 506: Graham to Keatinge, 18 May 1875, f. 4.
[125] ASA, Map, No. 159.

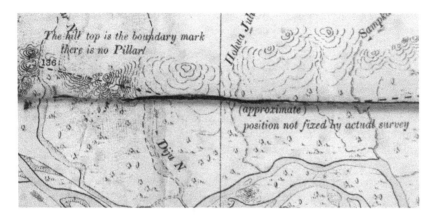

The hill top is the boundary mark there is no Pillar

(approximate) position not fixed by actual survey

Figures 1.2 and 1.3 (cont.)

The issue was not, as some colonial officials supposed, that tribal communities failed to understand the concept of border markers, just that they didn't like where the British had placed theirs.

The demarcation party, 'fearing a collision with the Akas', the community to the west of the Daflas, left another pillar unconstructed, 'although,' the lead officer of the party was careful to emphasise 'he marked the site, carried stones, sand, &c'.[126] Perhaps because of the existence of the alternative Dafla border post and an Aka chief's claims to hold territory south of the colonial boundary,[127] administrators took particular care over the ceremony of placing this particular marker two years later. The official report noted that the 'substantial pillar, measuring 9x7x5 feet' was erected 'in presence of the Akha chief'.[128] Despite this combination of material monumentality and choreographed performance, officials nonetheless doubted the border would become meaningful to the population whose territorial limits it ostensibly defined. Lieutenant-Colonel Graham, the officer in charge of demarcation, opined that

along the Bhootan and Thibet frontiers ... we had tangible and established Governments to deal with, whereas in [Darrang] we had to deal with a population in which almost every third man is a gam or chief, and where one man may repudiate

[126] NAI Foreign Political A, March 1876, No. 506: Graham to Keatinge, 18 March 1875, f. 7.
[127] NAI Foreign Political A, March 1876, No. 503: Keatinge to Government of India, 18 May 1875.
[128] NAI Foreign Political A, March 1876, No. 513: Keatinge to Government of India, 8 December 1875.

to-morrow what another has agreed to to-day ... I cannot look upon it as possessing the degree of stability which a frontier arrangement ought to possess.[129]

Scepticism towards the pillars' communicative potential led the Government of India to agree that demarcation should not be extended any further eastwards along the northern boundary of Assam.

The shortcomings of demarcation generated by officials' apprehensions of human resistance and incomprehension were exacerbated by unruly material elements, especially terrain, in the field. Graham reported that along the portion of the boundary between Assam and Dafla areas, 'no objections were made to our proceedings, the Dufflas merely remarking that "the plain belonged to the sirkar, and the hills to them"'. However, 'an endeavour made by me to get to the hills in this direction failed, owing to the nature of the jungle, which was simply a mass of creepers, thorn-bushes, and broken ground'.[130] The party encountered similar problems along the entire length of Darrang District's northern boundary. 'I had never before seen such a difficult country,' Graham complained. 'The hills ran in any and every direction, their sides were precipitous, and their tops narrow ridges, and when, after hours of climbing and clearing, a view was obtaining, it was found in many cases to be so limited as to prove of no use'. The apparently intractable terrain confounded the original intention 'to place each pillar, if possible at such a height on the first low range as would enable it to be seen from the pillars on either side of it, and give us at the same time a fairly straight boundary line, which would take in all the plain'. Contrary to these orders – and to the presumption that a natural boundary existed between hills and plain – the demarcation party found that

so far from the high hills rising abruptly from the plain, as was the case along the Bhootan frontier, the plains were bounded by a tangled mass of low hills, nearly of the same height, and forming a maze in which days were lost, either in looking for sites for pillars, or in attempting to obtain a glimpse of sites already fixed on.[131]

The material struggles to convey the stones, lime, and sand to hilltops where clearly visible pillars could be located complemented officials' concerns over the communicative hazards of these markers, making the whole enterprise seem relatively futile. The Government of India came to concur with Keatinge's sentiment, expressed in the wake of the Darrang demarcation that 'There is a good deal to be urged in defence of the policy long pursued in Assam of *not* distinctly defining the boundary'.[132]

---

[129] NAI Foreign Political A, March 1876, No. 506: Graham to Keatinge, 18 March 1875, ff. 7–8.
[130] Ibid., f. 6.   [131] Ibid., f. 5.
[132] NAI Foreign Political A, March 1876, No. 505: Keatinge to Government of India, Foreign Department, 17 May 1875, f. 2. Emphasis in original.

1.6   'A Line Shifting': Borders in the Chin-Lushai Hills, 1869–1900

The explosion of official interest in British India's fringes from the later 1860s had a major effect on the upland area sandwiched between eastern Bengal and Burma. Inhabited by Lushais, one of a number of subgroups of the Mizo people from whom the postcolonial Indian state of Mizoram derives its name, this region came within the colonial state's purview as a result of attacks on revenue-paying subjects and the work of hyperactive administrators. In other words, the Lushai Hills emerged from the kind of two-way boundary crossings that were central to frontier making across the colonial subcontinent. After a British military party retreated from the hills in 1869 having largely failed to retaliate against 'the late inroads of the Loosais', administrators still had little idea of the location or meaning of the border. In light of this, the Government of India approved further investigations on the ground by Deputy Commissioner Edgar of the adjacent Cachar District. Edgar's tour of the region and further incursions by Lushais into British-administered areas served primarily to negate any confidence in the possibility of a fixed border. He reported 'constant fluctuations … in the relative power of different [Lushai] Chiefs' and claimed that Lushais intermingled with Kukis, a community largely under colonial administration, to a far greater degree than had been thought. Sometimes the populations of entire villages moved from the jurisdiction of Kuki chiefs in British territory to Lushai chiefs beyond, and vice versa. The Lushais also practiced swidden agriculture, known in the region as *jhuming*, generally clearing different ground for planting crops each year. These migrations made it, Edgar stated, 'almost impossible to deal with them effectually'.[133] His suggested remedy amounted to a repudiation of the idea of spatially fixed borders: 'jurisdiction over them should be made to depend on their race, not their geographical position, at any given time. In other words, I should propose to treat them on somewhat the same principal as that theoretically adopted by the Government of the United States in dealing with the Indian tribes'.[134]

Although Edgar's recommendation was not adopted, frontier officials continued to push for a permeable boundary that could be crossed at their discretion. Following another military expedition against the Lushais in 1871 to 1872 to which he had been attached as a Political Officer, T. H. Lewin wrote a long rationale for such a border. Oblivious of Sandeman's dealings in Balochistan during the same era, Lewin stated:

---

[133] 'Mr Edgar's Notes on the Lushai and other Kookies', in Mackenzie, *History*, pp. 426–36, here p. 428.
[134] Ibid.

The establishment of a line of defence coincident with that of effective jurisdiction, is doubtless a wise and necessary measure on such a frontier as the north-west, where the tribes are pre-eminently warlike and audacious, and where the establishment of a Government officer or soldiers beyond reach of support would be almost equivalent to their destruction; but among the tribes of this frontier such a policy would be out of place. The circumstances, the people, the country, their social habits and character, are all different, and our mode of dealing with them should, I think, be different also ... In all matters connected with these tribes it should be remembered that they are not a nation but a segregation of villages, a collection of small separate republics having no coherence; we are not dealing with the faggot, but the severed bundle of sticks.[135]

Lewin made the case that the lack of social cohesion and effective authority structures among the Lushais rendered the very idea of a fixed and closed boundary ridiculous. Unitary borders were, in his parlance, fit for 'nations', but could not work in the case of 'a collection of small republics', when a zone of indeterminate influence was instead appropriate.[136] Over the following two decades, the boundary between the Lushai Hills and colonial territory developed in a form between the Government of India's vision of a relatively fixed, impenetrable line, and Lewin and the Government of Bengal's preference for a permeable zone. The Deputy Commissioner of Cachar was charged with administering political relations with the Lushai headmen, overseeing trading posts and occasionally visiting the more accessible Lushai villages.[137] Despite quickly falling into disuse among the Lushais, officials elsewhere in Assam during the 1880s heralded these tactics as a means of establishing relations with frontier communities in the aftermath of military violence.[138]

Further south, to the east of Chittagong District in Bengal, Lewin forged his own path. As well as securing Government of India authorisation for a permanent post in the foothills at Demagiri, Lewin of his own volition took to staying in the hills at a place called Sirthay Tlang.[139] His motivations in formulating the idea of permeable borders between administered and 'independent' territory were not limited to the sociological concerns that he focused on in official correspondence, nor were they the product of a strategic impulse to expand Britain's imperial possessions. Having a flexible border mattered to Lewin at a personal level. In his memoirs, he wrote that 'the loneliness and grandeur of [Sirthay Tlang] had a strange attraction for me ... [In the cabin]

---

[135] T. H. Lewin, 'Report of the Political Officer with the Right Column', in Mackenzie (ed.), *History*, pp. 469–70.

[136] For more on Lewin's idea that the Lushais were not a 'nation', see Lewin, *Hill Tracts*, p. 98.

[137] NAI Foreign A-Political-E, September 1883, Keep-With, ff. 1–2.

[138] NAI Foreign Political A, April 1885, No. 163: Cachar Deputy Commissioner to Assam Chief Commissioner, 22 January 1885; NAI Foreign Political A, August 1881, No. 203: McWilliam, Lakhimpur Deputy Commissioner, 'Note on the Abors', f. 9.

[139] Lewin, *Fly*, pp. 436–56.

I sat long, looking eastward, dreaming of fresh explorations, new adventures'.[140] Lewin's longing gaze into an undefined hinterland was indicative of a way of thinking and being that was wholly inimical with the imposition of any fixed boundary.

Despite Lewin's residence in the hills and the more prosaic activities beyond the administrative boundary further north, information about, and activities in, the Lushai country remained scant during the decade-and-a-half following the 1871 to 1872 expedition. The northern boundary set down upon the expedition's conclusion, although marked by three boundary pillars that were found in 1885 to be in 'pretty fair order', was rarely visited and remained shrouded in thick jungle.[141] With the British invasion of Upper Burma in 1885, the area to the east of the Lushai Hills, known as the Chin Hills, nominally came under British sovereignty. As Thant Myint-U has argued, the annexation came at a stage when British technological superiority was such that the colonial state felt able to impose substantially new administrative structures on much of its new territory, rather than incorporating pre-existing elements.[142] By 1889, 'constant and systematic patrols' had broken up the itinerant bands that had operated across much of Upper Burma, while the chiefs of the Shan States in eastern Upper Burma were coerced into submitting to British rule between 1888 and 1890.[143] However, the Chin Hills and Kachin Hills, the latter of which lay to the east of eastern Upper Assam and was inhabited by people with ethnic and cultural ties to the Singphos who fell under nominal Assamese jurisdiction, seemed altogether different propositions. The administrator J. G. Scott characterised the Chins as 'emphatically savages. They lived by raiding and blood feuds between villages made the country impossible for all strangers'.[144] Scott's assessment of the Kachins, meanwhile, echoed Lewin's view of Lushai social structures (or lack thereof): 'In tackling the Kachins we had to deal, not with a nationality, but with groups of small independent savage communities, with no inter-tribal coherence'.[145] The continuation of violent struggles between the Chin and Kachin communities and the colonial state into the 1890s affected the determination of the western and northwestern boundaries of Burma, to which the Government of Burma directed substantial attention after subjugating the Upper Burmese heartland.

Although not as tumultuous as those in Burma, the late 1880s also witnessed key developments on the Indian side of the Lushai Hills. Border infractions into

---

[140] Ibid., pp. 457–9.
[141] NAI Foreign Political A, April 1885, No. 163: Kennedy to Assam Chief Commissioner, 22 January 1885.
[142] Myint-U, *Making*, p. 252.
[143] J. G. Scott, *Burma: From the Earliest Times to the Present Day* (London: T. Fisher Unwin, 1924), pp. 346–9.
[144] Ibid., p. 349.   [145] Ibid., p. 353.

the administered Chittagong Hill Tracts in 1888 provided the rationale for military parties from Bengal, Assam, and Burma to impose administrative posts in the hills. Despite this venture establishing a Political Officer at Aizawl in the northern Lushai Hills and apparently securing commitments from some chiefs, the lack of borders between provincial administrations now became seen as a major problem. Once again, the shifting location of Mizo villages and swidden agriculture worked against colonial spatial logics.[146] The various colonial institutions with interests in the region intensively debated both annual and longer-term movements in the Lushai and Chin Hills region. The Chief Commissioner of Assam proposed that the border between his province's administration and that of Bengal should not be a territorially fixed line but 'a line shifting with Jhums [i.e., shifting cultivated plots] of Lushais'. His reasoning was that 'it would probably be found impossible to maintain an arbitrary line intended to restrict the shifting cultivation of the tribes on either side of it'.[147] For the boundary between the portion of the hills under Assam and that under Burma, he tentatively proposed a more conventional fixed border, the Nankathe or Manipur River, 'which flows from north to south in a fairly straight line so far as our present maps can be depended upon'.[148] But even here, the mutability of the region and its people was of at least as much concern as the potential shortcomings of the extant cartography. He noted that 'the Lushais who in 1871–72 used to inhabit the tract [immediately west of the Manipur River] on the map have all moved westward, and we are ignorant of the people who have taken their place'.[149] To add to these qualms, the Chief Commissioner of Burma protested that he could not accept this border as the largest Chin tribe, the Tashons, who had hitherto been subordinate to British Burma, resided mostly on the west bank of the Manipur River.[150]

As in the late 1860s, these persistent indeterminacies called for further knowledge gathering, but the resulting information still did little to clarify administrative boundaries. British expansion into the central portion of the Chin-Lushai Hills met with widespread resistance. Colonial forces sought to sedantarise communities in the region, but their violence often provoked precisely the opposite effect. Villages were burned and, as in the Naga Hills

[146] NAI Foreign External A, August 1890, No. 255: Assam Chief Commissioner to H. R. Browne, Lushai Hills Political Officer, 22 April 1890.

[147] NAI Foreign External A, August 1890, No. 224: Assam Chief Commissioner to Foreign Secretary of India, 27 March 1890; No. 233: Assam Chief Commissioner to Government of India, Foreign Department, 28 March 1890.

[148] NAI Foreign External A, August 1890, No. 233: Assam Chief Commissioner to Government of India, Foreign Department, 28 March 1890.

[149] Ibid.

[150] NAI Foreign External A, August 1890, No. 262: Burma Chief Commissioner to Foreign Secretary of India, 7 June 1890.

twenty-five years earlier, prohibitions were issued on rebuilding on the same site.[151] Some Lushai chiefs pre-emptively moved their communities beyond the reach of British forces to avoid violence and being coerced into providing labour.[152] Despite these efforts to penetrate the uplands, in 1892 the Foreign Secretary of British India, Henry Mortimer Durand, wrote bluntly about flawed colonial knowledge of the region: 'our information is still too fragmentary to afford a clue to the easiest and most inexpensive method of maintaining peace and order among these hillmen'.[153] The Hills and the people within them remained an unknown, perhaps unknowable, quantity.

The one decision that the British did make in the early 1890s concerned the division of the Lushai Hills into sections administered from Assam and from Bengal. Unable to agree on the proper location of this border, or indeed the principle upon which it might be established, at a conference in Calcutta in 1892 officers from the Assam, Bengal, and Burma governments agreed to abolish the whole idea of a boundary and instead unify the Lushai Hills under the administration of Assam.[154] As with the Mithankot conference of 1871 (Section 1.4), a multi-party meeting was required as clashes between officials attached to various provincial governments generated confusion and friction at frontiers in the later nineteenth century. Like those at Mithankot, the decisions made in Calcutta proved in practice to be indeterminate rather than final. Communications between Aizawl, the administrative post in the northern Lushai Hills, and Lungleh, the post in the southern Hills, were initially inadequate to enable effective unified administration, meaning that the implementation of the non-border was delayed. When the road between the two was completed in 1898, and administration of the southern Hills was handed to Assam, the journey between them still took nearly a month and a separate official remained in charge at each village.[155]

By this stage, the eastern Lushais had tendered their submission to colonial authority following persistent state violence. The Chief Commissioner of Assam pronounced that 'there is not in the Lushai Hills any unexplored "Hinter-land" such as still exists in the Naga Hills to give possible future trouble'.[156] The implication of smooth and even British authority throughout

---

[151] NAI Foreign Secret E, June 1891, No. 88: McCabe to Assam Chief Commissioner, 19 January 1891.

[152] NAI Foreign External A, December 1892, No. 43: McCabe to Assam Chief Commissioner, 23 July 1892; Reid, *History*, pp. 21–4.

[153] NAI Foreign External A, June 1893, Keep-With No. 1: Durand, Note, 18 December 1892.

[154] Anandaroop Sen, 'The Law of Emptiness: Episodes from Lushai and Chin Hills (1890–98)', in Neeladri Bhattacharya and Joy L. K. Pachuau (eds.), *Landscape, Culture, and Belonging: Writing the History of Northeast India* (Cambridge: Cambridge University Press, 2019), pp. 207–36, here p. 207; NAI Foreign External A, September 1892, Nos. 9–62.

[155] NAI Foreign External A, February 1898, No. 60: Assam Chief Commissioner, 'Note on the Transfer of Southern Lushai Hills to Assam', 27 January 1897.

[156] Ward, quoted in Reid, *History*, p. 25.

the Hills was not altogether accurate. The boundary with Burma remained far from complete, with small pockets of space falling between the acknowledged administration of any of the three provincial governments. In 1893, it was found that such an area existed at the southern end of the South Lushai Hills, where it bordered Burma's Arakan Hill Tract. When the Government of Bengal suggested that this portion of the uplands belonged to Burma, the Chief Commissioner of Burma claimed to be unable to locate any record of the survey from the 1850s that had placed the area under his jurisdiction and pointed instead to more recent revenue surveys suggesting that it lay beyond Burma's authority. Contrary to avowed efforts to incorporate the whole of the uplands, the two administrations eventually agreed that this territory could be left as 'no man's land' unless its inhabitants gave any trouble.[157]

Only a year later, the Bengal Government was forced to revise its preparedness to leave the tract unadministered, as quarrels sprang up between inhabitants of the South Lushai Hills and the hinterland beyond. Adopting a similar tone to his counterparts in the eastern Naga Hills, John Shakespear, the Superintendent in charge of the South Lushai Hills, wrote: 'the fact that there are villages within a day's reach of [the administered village of] Sherkor which pay no tribute, are never visited, and are allowed to raid each other just as they like cannot help being bad for our prestige'.[158] Shakespear implemented administrative interventions, including taxation and a labour demand, in this 'anomalous' pocket without any formal revision of the boundary of the South Lushai Hills. Having passed unnoticed until Assam took control of the entire Lushai Hills in 1898, Shakespear's covert expansion suddenly met with the Government of Burma's disapproval. In the ensuing dispute, Shakespear and his superiors in Assam once again deployed the concept of the flexible border. 'The Lushais', the Chief Commissioner of Assam argued, 'are a *jhuming* and nomad folk, and it is difficult therefore to demarcate any permanent boundary which will be respected in practice'.[159] Following the Government of India's ratification, the southern Lushai Hills boundary was left to fluctuate with the cultivation of the area's inhabitants.

Over time, British administration in the Chin-Lushai Hills 'settled' previously mobile communities. In addition, ethnographic stereotyping and Assam and Burma's pursuit of distinct policies made the division between

---

[157] NAI Foreign External A, February 1894, No. 40: Burma Chief Commissioner to Government of India, Foreign Department, 11 September 1893; No. 51: Bengal Government to Government of India, Foreign Department, 24 November 1893.

[158] NAI Foreign External A, October 1894, No. 221: J. Shakespear, 'Report on the Administration of the South Lushai Hills'.

[159] NAI Foreign External A, July 1898, No. 60: Assam Chief Commissioner to Government of India, Foreign Department, 7 June 1898.

inhabitants of the Chin Hills and the Lushai Hills more pronounced. Although border crossings still continued, spatial separation between Chin and Lushai settlements was enforced more vigorously from the later 1890s, beginning with the destruction of a village constructed by Chins in the Lushai Hills after its residents refused to leave. In this instance, the Chief Commissioner of Assam noted, 'the boundary of the Tyao River is one that admits of no dispute ... It is necessary to be very particular in these hills regarding the settlement of outsiders on lands recognized as belonging to the local Chiefs'.[160] Measures to impose spatial fixity developed gradually within the Lushai Hills as well as on the Lushai-Chin boundary. Concerned that with increasingly settled conditions in the Hills, the larger Lushai villages would steadily fragment into smaller hamlets, making tax and labour collection more difficult and weakening chiefly authority, Shakespear instituted 'Land Settlement' around the turn of the twentieth century. Under this system, each chief was assigned a fixed area in which his community could move about.[161] Shakespear summed up the policy and the rationale behind it by stating: 'every chief has his boundaries now and I should not like to subdivide the land further'. The scheme was one of numerous localised borders and continued to operate as the main socio-spatial principle in the Lushai Hills until India's independence.[162]

Placed alongside his simultaneous advocacy of a flexible border at the south of the Lushai Hills, Shakespear's concern with laying down internal boundaries and policing the divide between the Chin Hills and his district was indicative of the wider ambivalence among colonial officials on the efficacy of fixed borders in a shifting area. In the 1870s and again in the 1890s, administrators in Bengal, Assam, and Burma responded to their avowedly limited understanding of the Chin-Lushai Hills and the nomadic tendencies of its inhabitants with a mixture of appeals to institute divisions and suggestions that linear boundaries were not viable or desirable. Making and breaking borders in the Chin-Lushai region, as elsewhere at the frontiers of British India, was never a decisive or unconflicted act but a process of competing interests. It drew on myriad elements beyond purely spatial ones, including sociological understandings of the people who inhabited these regions, and the hopes and fears of administrators themselves. These officials understood that the imposition or violation of a border could constitute their personal authority. The lines between these ambitions and governmental undertakings were as fuzzy as those the British rendered and erased in the frontier hills.

---

[160] NAI Foreign External A, October 1899, No. 40: Assam Chief Commissioner to Government of India, Foreign Department, 13 September 1899.
[161] Reid, *History*, pp. 35–44.   [162] Ibid., p. 44.

1.7   'As If Our Territory': British India's International Boundaries at the Turn of the Twentieth Century

It seems at first glance reasonable to assume that the Durand Line separating Afghanistan and British India was a more authoritative imposition than the earlier borders that defined colonial frontiers. Unlike these boundaries, which had to be negotiated with numerous communities, it was an international border agreed between the Foreign Secretary of British India and the Amir of Afghanistan when the colonial state was by some measures at the peak of its powers. However, it has proved to be deeply problematic: the Afghan and post-colonial Pakistani states have both disavowed its legitimacy.[163] The original resistance to the Durand Line came not only from representatives of Kabul but also from inhabitants of the uplands it bisected; the actions of multiple parties reshaped and undermined the border. And just as in northern Darrang twenty years before, material markers were a key part of the Durand Line's curious border effects, more often prompting subversion than communicating sovereign power.

Despite making some significant departures from the boundary line that had been agreed with other senior members of the Government of India prior to his departure, Henry Mortimer Durand, still Foreign Secretary of British India, returned from Kabul in 1893 satisfied that he and the Amir had agreed 'a well-defined' border.[164] From the perspective of his grand strategic motives, his self-congratulation at the conclusion of the mission seemed justified. The boundary completed the delineation of an Afghan buffer state separating the British and Russian players as they played out what would be the last moves of the 'Great Game'.[165] But the delineation in Kabul had no material reality until Boundary Commission demarcation parties, comprising British and Afghan members, took the field from early 1894. And as Thomas Holdich, the lead surveyor involved in demarcating the border, later acknowledged, 'the process of demarcating a boundary . . . is the crux of all boundary making . . . It is in this process that disputes usually arise, and weak elements in the treaties or agreements are apt to be discovered'.[166] There were persistent disagreements between British and Afghan surveyors over the actual location of the border agreed in Kabul, which were further complicated by numerous inaccuracies in

---

[163] Elisabeth Leake, *The Defiant Border: The Afghan-Pakistan Borderlands in the Era of Decolonization, 1936–1965* (Cambridge: Cambridge University Press, 2017).

[164] MSS Eur D727/4: Durand to Sir Steuart Bayley, 27 November 1893.

[165] On the delineation of Afghanistan's other boundaries during the 1870s and 1880s, see Hopkins, 'Bounds'; Francesca Fuoli, 'Incorporating North-Western Afghanistan into the British Empire: Experiments in Indirect Rule through the Making of an Imperial Frontier, 1884-87', *Afghanistan*, 1, 1 (2018), pp. 4–25.

[166] Thomas H. Holdich, *Political Frontiers and Boundary Making* (London: Macmillan, 1916), p. 208.

the maps that Durand had used in his negotiations with the Amir (see the introductory section to Chapter 2).[167] The result was that, as Holdich himself admitted, 'no part of the boundary defined ... was the actual boundary of the agreement'.[168] A pertinent example of the failures of demarcation at the level of sovereign statehood was the performance of contradictory boundaries that continued to take place every time a caravan passed through the Khyber Pass. British and Afghan guards would accompany the caravans to the different villages through which their respective governments claimed the border ran, so for a distance the two military parties travelled together, locked in a tense impasse.[169]

Although thinly veiled hostility and confusions were rife between British and Afghan boundary commissioners, the opposition to the border of numerous inhabitants of the region between fully administered British India and Afghanistan was more consequential. From the British annexation of Punjab until Durand's agreement with the Amir, many Pashtuns had continued to contest the administrative boundary of Punjab. Like its equivalent in Assam, this border was defined intermittently and hazily, with infrequent material demarcation. Laying down a sovereign boundary between British India and Afghanistan had variable consequences for the administrative boundary. Colonial administrators debated the significance of the Durand Line on the governed limits of Punjab before, during, and after the parties of Boundary Commissioners took to the field. An especially intense and unresolved discussion regarded the region to the west of Dera Ismail Khan District in southern Punjab inhabited by Waziri tribes. Richard Bruce, the Deputy Commissioner of this District and a protégé of Robert Sandeman, saw the imposition of the sovereign border as an opportunity to push for British interventions in Waziri affairs, which he had long advocated.[170] Durand agreed with Bruce that the 'natural consequence' of demarcation in this area was that the colonial government should tax and employ Waziris in militias. 'We should,' he wrote, 'without annexing, bring the whole [Waziri] tribe into order, and insist upon the stoppage of raids and fighting, and gradually make the country free to our political officers'.[171]

Other members of the Punjab Government and the Government of India dissented from these understandings of the border in various ways. The ensuing debates particularly focused on the effect of the 'democratic' structure of

---

[167] IOR/L/PARL/2/284/9: *Agreement Signed by Mr R. Udny and Sipah Salar Ghulam Haidar Khan* (London: Her Majesty's Stationary Office, 1896), pp. 3–4.

[168] Thomas H. Holdich, *The Indian Borderland 1880–1900* (London: Methuen, 1901), p. 242.

[169] MSS Eur F111/315, *Khyber Administration Report, 1899–1900*, f.77; Holdich, *Indian Borderland*, p. 242. See also Robert Warburton, *Eighteen Years in the Khyber: 1879–1898* (London: John Murray, 1900), pp. 142–43.

[170] NAI Foreign Secret E, July 1890, No. 115: Bruce, 'Memorandum', 6 November 1889.

[171] NAI Foreign Secret F, July 1894, Nos. 402–34, Keep-With No. 1.

Waziri communities – that is, their lack of authoritative leaders – on colonial spatial policies.[172] As in the Chin-Lushai Hills around the same time, reworkings of frontier space were bound up with tentative and conflicting notions of internal tribal dynamics. In the face of such difficulties, the Government of India wavered when delivering its verdict on the implications of demarcation ahead of the Waziri Boundary Commission taking the field. It instructed officials 'to interfere as little as [possible] in [the Waziris'] internal affairs'. Contradictorily, it also claimed that the international boundary meant the colonial state had 'assumed a measure of responsibility for the peace of the Afghan border which has not hitherto been ours', demanding more active oversight of the Waziris. The Government of India decided that a military post should be established beyond the existing administrative border and Waziri potentates identified and given financial allowances.[173] However, three members of the Government dissented from this policy, claiming that the post in Waziri country amounted to 'practically assuming . . . administrative control'. Given the loose social constitution of the tribes, these men argued, the outpost was 'eminently calculated to set the whole frontier in a blaze'. This minority instead advocated a continuation of the policy prior to Durand's trip to Kabul, which they described succinctly as 'resting on our present frontiers and influencing the Waziris from without'.[174]

The lack of clarity among officials on the Durand Line's intended impact on nearby inhabitants and tentative talk of extending British authority intersected with heightened suspicions among Waziris. When the Boundary Commission finally assembled in the Waziri uplands in October 1894, it met with the most intensive immediate contestation of the Durand Line. A party of more than 1,200 Waziris assembled and attacked the Commission at the village of Wana, before it had begun to materially inscribe the border by erecting boundary posts or piling up stones.[175] Even Holdich, who suspected the Afghan state's complicity in almost every instance of resistance to colonial projects along the frontier, admitted that 'there was no suspicion of concerted action about this affair at Wana. The Waziris had heard about the boundary that was to be placed between them and their refuge'.[176] Along the Durand Line's entire length, substantial armed brigades accompanied the parties of surveyors, political officers, and civil administrators, purportedly to fight off anticipated resistance

---

[172] The quotations and narrative in this paragraph are drawn from NAI Foreign Secret F, July 1894, Nos. 402–34, Keep-With No. 1.

[173] NAI Foreign Secret F, July 1894, No. 433: Government of India to Secretary of State, 10 July 1894.

[174] NAI Foreign Secret F, July 1894, No. 431: Minute of Dissent signed by Westland, MacDonnell and Pritchard, 6 July 1894.

[175] *Report on the Punjab Frontier Administration, 1894–1895* (Lahore: Punjab Government Press, 1895), pp. 7–8.

[176] Holdich, *Indian Borderland*, p. 238.

but also to display British military might and thereby instantiate the colonial border. Following the attack at Wana, a large military party was sent to attack the groups deemed responsible and thereby clear the way for the return of the demarcation party for a second attempt to inscribe the border materially.[177] Once again, British administrators understood violence to be an essential element of founding a new boundary. The Government of India also deemed it prudent to maintain a permanent garrison of troops at Wana in case of continued border refusals; in fact, this served primarily to further inflame discontent.[178]

Initial British estimates of when the demarcation parties would complete their work were hopelessly inaccurate.[179] Indeed, the idea of finishing the Durand line proved overly optimistic: the demarcation parties left the field – often with fewer men than they had contained at the outset – without setting down material markers along large sections of the proclaimed border. Disagreements with their Afghan counterparts, what Holdich termed 'the geographical impossibility' of laying down some portions of the agreed boundary owing to difficult terrain, and above all resistance from Pashtun and Baloch communities overcame the capacity of the British to transfer the boundary from inadequate map to intractable territory.[180] Furthermore, the cessation of demarcation did not represent an end to the unrest induced by the Durand Line.[181] For many who resided in its vicinity, the border indicated British interference and was therefore a continuing source of irritation. Holdich wrote, sympathetically if simplistically, that from the perspective of upland communities, 'a boundary line indicated by piles of stones had been drawn across their hills to show that theoretically they were shut, and that beyond that line they might appeal no more to people of their own faith and their own language in times of difficulty and disaster'.[182] There may have been widespread awareness of the Durand Line among frontier communities, but this did not translate into practical acknowledgement of the border as a limit that should not be transgressed. As late as 1939, one British official bluntly stated that 'many [Pashtuns] would not admit that the British had any right to control their actions across the Durand Line'.[183] Acts of border subversion continued apace after 1895, ranging from quotidian practices of ignoring the boundary, which concerned the British most

---

[177] *Report on Punjab Frontier Administration, 1894–1895*, p. 7.
[178] H. C. Wylly, *From the Black Mountain to Waziristan* (London: Macmillan, 1912), pp. 459–66; Evelyn Howell, *Mizh: A Monograph on Government's Relations with the Mahsud Tribe* (Karachi: Oxford University Press, 1979 [1931]), pp. 14–7.
[179] Holdich, *Indian Borderland*, pp. 238–39.   [180] Ibid., p. 255.
[181] *Report on the Punjab Frontier Administration, 1895–1896* and *1896–1897* (Lahore: Government of Punjab Press, 1896, 1897).
[182] Holdich, *Indian Borderland*, p. 338.
[183] William Barton, *India's North-West Frontier* (London: John Murray, 1939), pp. 19–20.

when they involved acts such as trading stolen British guns with Afghans, to much grander rejections.[184]

That the border was a difficult-to-control process rather than a stably imposed entity became abruptly apparent to officials in 1897 with numerous outbreaks of unrest, which collectively constituted the largest uprising the British faced in their century of frontier administration in the northwest. As Robert Nichols and David Edwards have shown, the episode was not the 'fanatical' uprising that many stationed at the frontier and more distant commentators claimed.[185] Rather, the border was a vital contributor to a widespread show of resistance directed against heightened colonial intervention. Even the Secretary of State for India acknowledged as much in a letter to the Viceroy, saying that delimiting the Line 'furnished the religious preachers with material for stirring up alarm and jealousy among the tribes, who were thus persuaded to connect the delimitation with the ulterior designs upon their independence'.[186] In 1897, the border also proved problematic to the colonial state in another, somewhat contradictory, sense. Many Pashtuns involved in the uprising crossed the border into Afghanistan to avoid military retaliation, then recrossed – often with kinsmen officially under Kabul's sovereignty – to attack colonial infrastructure and subjects.[187] The border was porous in all the wrong ways from a British perspective – a significant irritant but flimsy deterrent that became detached from its supposed function as a marker of state power and unitary sovereignty.

While the Durand Line provoked intense resistance, the border separating northeastern British India and south-eastern Tibet was ineffective in a distinct way: for decades after its declaration in 1914, it was largely forgotten. As Bérénice Guyot-Rechard shows, the upper echelons of the colonial state engaged in this border-making project reluctantly and subsequently refused to commit the resources needed to instantiate the boundary as a meaningful

---

[184] The trade in stolen arms was a major concern for the British and reached a significant scale towards the end of the nineteenth century: MSS Eur F111/315: 'Report on the Traffic in Arms on the North-Western Frontier by the North-Western Frontier Arms Trade Committee', 18 April 1899, ff. 10–40.

[185] Officials forwarding the 'fanaticism' explanation included, most notably, Robert Warburton and Harold Deane: Warburton, *Eighteen Years*, pp. 290–8; IOR/L/PARL/2/284/13: *Frontier and Overseas Expeditions from India Vol. II*: (London: Her Majesty's Stationary Office, 1898), pp. 59–63. Subsequent histories endorsing this explanation include J. G. Elliott, *The Frontier 1839–1947: The Story of the North-West Frontier of India* (London: Cassell, 1968), pp. 157–58, 165–9. However, some other accounts attributed the rising primarily to the Durand line: for example, Wylly, *Black Mountain*, pp. 311–12. Robert Nichols's historical anthropological account disputed the importance of religious millenarianism in the revolt: Nichols, *Settling*, xxxi. For a critical account of the British discourse of 'fanaticism' in 1897, see David B. Edwards, 'Mad Mullahs and Englishmen: Discourse in the Colonial Encounter', *Comparative Studies in Society and History*, 31, 4 (1989), pp. 649–70.

[186] IOR/L/PARL/2/284/13: Secretary of State for India to Viceroy, 28 January 1898, p. 177.

[187] Peshawar Commissioner to the Amir of Afghanistan, 13 August 1897, p. 75.

object for local populations or British frontier officials.[188] After it had been agreed between Henry McMahon, Foreign Secretary of British India, and the Tibetan Government (and, famously, refuted by the Chinese Government), the boundary was not publicised for fear of antagonising Russia. By this stage, the Chinese expansion into Tibet that had been a prime rationale for the colonial state to set a sovereign boundary had receded.[189] The secrecy of the border and lack of effort to give it shape through material demarcation or performed activities meant that by the mid-1930s, the Assam authorities professed to be entirely unaware of its existence.[190]

Although its effects were very different, this border resembled the Durand Line in more ways than its being colloquially named after the Foreign Secretary of British India who negotiated it. The McMahon Line, like its counterpart on the opposite side of the colonial subcontinent, was not a definitive clarification of British India's sovereign territory. It was thoroughly entangled with extant colonial boundaries to the north of the Brahmaputra Valley, including the *posa* border and the Inner Line, that constituted variegated administrative spaces and enabled frontier officials to operate in the region with limited oversight. Chinese moves into southeast Tibet during what proved to be the final years of the Qing empire was a major imperative for the British to set a sovereign border. The Chinese challenge to the northeast was short-lived relative to the decades-long saga of hypothesised Russian interference in the northwest. But in 1910, it emerged that Chinese administrators were making concrete inroads among communities with direct access to the Assam valley, presenting a more immediate threat to administered colonial India than the Russians ever had.[191] British concerns abounded, typified by the assessment of one diplomat that the Chinese 'spread their influence' among tribal populations 'a little year by year ... [and] are determined to extend their administrative area, until they are met by the outposts of their neighbours'.[192] However, as with the limited role of Russian expansion in dictating British borders in northwest India, imperial rivalry interplayed with colonial officials' desire to modify existing boundary arrangements to the north of Assam.

The short-lived burst of British involvement in the eastern Himalaya that culminated with the delineation of the McMahon Line began two years before Chinese incursions into the uplands at the northeastern fringes of Assam in 1910.[193] Noel Williamson, the Political Officer in charge of overseeing unadministered communities to the north of the Brahmaputra Valley, insisted

---

[188] Guyot-Rechard, *Shadow States*, pp. 31–57.   [189] Ibid., pp. 52–53.   [190] Ibid., p. 59.
[191] NAI Foreign Secret-External, January 1911, Nos. 211–40.
[192] Archibald Rose, 'Chinese Frontiers of India', *The Geographical Journal*, 39, 3 (1912), pp. 193–218, here pp. 203–4.
[193] For initial British reports of Chinese expansion, see NAI Foreign Secret-External, January 1911, Nos. 211–40.

a recent incursion of Adis in pursuit of two escaped 'slaves' revealed major flaws in the region's administrative boundary. Williamson persuaded his immediate superiors that 'there is no doubt that Abors must have known that they were in inside British territory', but as they 'have scarcely been subject to any control and have been permitted to cultivate lands in our territory and even to settle in it without making any payment', they did not respect 'the sanctity of the frontier'.[194] It was these crossings of the administrative border that prompted the provincial government to first raise the spectre of contested sovereignty over upland communities. 'If we show ourselves unable or unprepared to protect our subjects and those of our allies who may enter the hills,' it warned its superiors in the Government of India, 'it is just conceivable that the Government of Tibet may consider there is nothing to prevent them from extending their sphere of influence over these hills'.[195] Here was yet another instance in which colonial administrators based at or near frontiers employed talk of grand strategy to lend urgency to an essentially localised set of concerns.

The following years saw officials in Assam continuing to press for interference in the uplands.[196] After news of the Chinese infractions emerged, the Government of India still generally opposed such moves. The Viceroy, Lord Hardinge, plainly stated in December 1910 that 'any forward movement beyond the administrative frontier was strongly to be deprecated. Chinese aggression would . . . be met, not in the tribal territory bordering Assam, but by attack on the coast of China'.[197] The following year, the border-breaking actions of frontier officials swayed the Government of India's stance in unintended fashion. The same telegram that informed the Government of Eastern Bengal and Assam that Williamson had superseded his authorised remit on a tour in Adi country and crossed the 'Outer Line' denoting the supposed limits of British influence, also contained news that he had been killed.[198] In the wake of Williamson's death, the Government of India began to agree with its subordinate administrators in Assam that existing border arrangements were inadequate. The Adis, British officials claimed, had persistently violated the treaty that underpinned their *posa* relationship with the colonial state.[199] Even Williamson's illicit border crossing was retold as an act of Adi boundary

[194] NAI Foreign External A, September 1908, No. 5: Eastern Bengal and Assam Government to Government of India, Foreign Department, ff. 1–2.
[195] Ibid., f. 2.
[196] NAI Foreign Secret-External, September 1909, No. 299: Eastern Bengal and Assam Government to Government of India, Foreign Department, 29 June 1909, f. 1; NAI Foreign External A, August 1910, Nos. 8–11.
[197] NAI Foreign Secret-External, January 1911, No. 239: Government of India to Secretary of State for India, 22 December 1910, ff. 62–63.
[198] NAI Foreign External A, May 1911, No. 40: Eastern Bengal and Assam Government to Government of India, Foreign Department, 22 April 1911, f. 15.
[199] NAI Foreign External A, August 1911, No. 6: Eastern Bengal and Assam Government to Government of India, Foreign Department, 16 May 1911, f. 3.

breaking: 'It is as much a deliberate attack on us as if the Abors had come into our country, for Mr. Williamson's was a wholly unarmed and peaceful entry solicited by them'.[200] In assenting to military reprisals against the community identified as Williamson's killers, the Government of India for the first time backed 'the determination of a suitable boundary between India and China in this locality'.[201] It was not considerations of great power politics that prompted this shift. Rather, the narrative of Williamson's death spun by officials in Assam prompted new anxieties of the threat that might be posed by upland communities if they were to come under Chinese influence. McMahon averred that the 'tribes . . . are liable to become a serious danger along the length of rich but defenceless British districts', which made it 'more necessary' to communicate to communities along the northern edge of Assam 'that we consider them to belong to us and not to China'.[202] This involved expanding the 'Outer Line', guarding it against Chinese incursions, and taking all inhabitants of the zone between Inner and Outer Lines under 'loose political control'.[203]

In arriving at the notion that a sovereign boundary in this region was necessary, the Government of India and Assam administrators looked to the northwest for justification. The notion of a 'scientific frontier' was notably absent in the northeast due, perhaps, to a combination of its conspicuous vacuity in the northwest and the fact that British knowledge of this boundary region was even sparser than in the northwest. Instead, McMahon suggested that if Chinese influence spread, 'we would then have a series of tribes who would by force of circumstances become as great a local nuisance and danger as the tribes of the North-West Frontier Province'.[204] The Assam administration's comparative perspective was essentially similar: allowing the Chinese to extend their influence up to the existing Outer Line would, it claimed, result in a position 'similar to that on the North-West Frontier if we ceased to control the Khyber and Bolan Passes and retired to the plains, leaving the Afridis and other tribes in possession of all the hill country'.[205] As with many other long-distance comparisons employed to justify frontier activities, invoking the opposite fringe of the subcontinent was a means of replacing local complexities with a simplified tale of events and policies elsewhere. The highly publicised trouble

[200] Ibid., f. 4.
[201] NAI Foreign External A, August 1911, No. 8: Viceroy to Secretary of State for India, 29 June 1911, f. 11.
[202] NAI Foreign External A, August 1911, Nos. 5–17, Keep-With: Note by McMahon, 15 June 1911, ff. 5–6.
[203] NAI Foreign Secret-External, October 1911, No. 60: McMahon to Eastern Bengal and Assam Government, 8 August 1911, ff. 9–10.
[204] NAI Foreign External A, August 1911, Nos. 5–17, Keep-With: Note by McMahon, 15 June 1911, f. 6.
[205] NAI Foreign Secret External, August 1911, No. 439: Eastern Bengal and Assam Government to Government of India, Foreign Department, 25 April 1911, f. 2.

attending the demarcation of the Durand Line might reasonably have been a cause for caution; instead, myths of the northwest's uniquely problematic status became a way of bolstering an already determined course of action.

Regardless of the rhetorical strategies put to work in support of an extended Outer Line, what it entailed in practice remained deeply uncertain in (and long after) 1911. The colonial state had minimal geographical knowledge of the region, and the question of what type of topographic or ethnographic features should properly form the basis for the border's location remained undecided.[206] As plans were set to dispatch three parties into the region with combined punitive, political, and knowledge-gathering functions, disagreements remained even at the very top of the British Government in London as to whether officials on these expeditions should be empowered to determine and demarcate the border. The Secretary of State for India, while recognising potential problems with enabling 'subordinate officers, on their own responsibility' to erect boundary cairns, opined that these men should set the border 'both on account of the difficulty and expense of sending [further] expeditions into these remote and mountainous regions, and in view of the effect likely to be produced on the ignorant tribesmen by repeated incursions of armed parties into their territory'.[207] His counterpart in the Foreign Office disagreed on the basis that a Chinese advance beyond such a border might risk the prestige of the colonial state if it felt unable to respond effectively.[208]

The limited success of all of the expeditionary parties in gathering information on potential border locations complicated this mass of competing concerns further still. Confusion reigned among the officers leading the parties as to the relative priority of surveying the land and securing agreements with tribal potentates.[209] Difficult terrain severely hampered survey and political efforts, with rising rivers, inadequate paths, and struggles communicating with local communities rendering large portions of the uplands inaccessible.[210] Constructing and maintaining a road up the Lohit Valley to the portion of the

[206] NAI Foreign Secret External, October 1911, enclosure to No. 109: 'Memorandum by General Staff Branch' to Survey Parties attached to the Abor Expedition, undated, f.39.

[207] NAI Foreign Secret External, May 1912, No. 202: India Office to Foreign Office, London, 19 October 1911, f. 1.

[208] NAI Foreign Secret External, May 1912, No. 203: Foreign Office to India Office, 26 October 1911, f. 2.

[209] NAI Foreign Secret External, May 1912, enclosure to No. 209: S. G. Burrard, Officiating Surveyor-General of India, to Government of India, Revenue and Agriculture Department, 24 November 1911, f. 6.

[210] NAI Foreign Secret External, May 1912, No. 222: Eastern Bengal and Assam Government to Government of India, Foreign Department, 28 December 1911, f. 14; NAI Foreign Secret-External, May 1912, No. 270: Officer Commanding Abor Expeditionary Force to Chief of General Staff, 10 February 1912; NAI Foreign Secret External, May 1912, Nos. 201–337, Keep-With, Bower, Commanding Abor Expeditionary Force, to Lieutenant-Governor of Eastern Bengal and Assam, 11 December 1911, ff. 9–10.

boundary with Tibet that had been a focus of particular British anxiety since 1910 'proved a matter of much greater difficulty than was anticipated'.[211] The lead officer on this project followed the trend of rendering comparisons with the northwest frontier, but came to very different conclusions to the projection of British authority into the mountains suggested by his superiors a few years previously. Arguing against placing an armed post at the border in the Lohit Valley, he invoked 'a parallel case, when Chitral was occupied in 1895, [and] it was not considered necessary to push forward the post to the actual frontier ... The physical difficulties of this country are much greater than those on the North-West Frontier'.[212] The inaccessibility of portions of the eastern Himalaya coupled with administrators' perceptions that the threat from Chinese expansion had diminished following the Republican revolution in 1911 to 1912 meant that the McMahon Line was realised in only the most partial ways. Material markers were set down in only a few locations, and colonial officials had little will to enact the border as a precisely located, linear object. However, as in Punjab when the Durand Line was set down, making a sovereign boundary with Tibet in the northeast was tied up with the status of the administrative boundary that separated fully governed territory from the irregular zone beyond. A North-Eastern Frontier Tract under the supervision of Political Officers was created, with adjustments to location and significance of the Inner Line boundary and the adoption of a loose legal framework for dealing with the Tract's inhabitants.[213] The burst of border making to the north of the Brahmaputra Valley did not, then, result in the creation of a fixed and singular line. Instead, a permanently exceptional frontier space of patchy, irregular sovereign territory was formally instituted.

1.8   Conclusion: Limits of the Colonial State

The multiple spaces that collectively constituted the frontiers of the colonial state in India were consistently mutating and never definitively settled. Even efforts around the turn of the twentieth century to set absolute outer limits to colonial sovereignty were partially realised, highly contested, and often over-looked. At British India's frontiers, the limitations of the state's ability and will to impose coherent and durable governmental territories were often laid bare. The examples examined in this chapter collectively suggest that from the earliest stages of colonial expansion into Assam, Sind, and Punjab to the end of the nineteenth century, bordering and territory-making were defined by

---

[211] NAI Foreign Secret-External, February 1914, No. 283: Assam Chief Commissioner to Government of India, Foreign Department, 19 June 1913, f. 40.

[212] NAI Foreign Secret-External, February 1914, enclosure 3 to No. 283: E. C. Tylden-Pattenson, 'Proposals for Work in the Lohit Valley, 1913-1914', f. 62.

[213] NAI Foreign External A, April 1915, Nos. 4–10.

multiple slippages rather than being the type of assured projections conventionally assumed to be characteristic of modern state authority. The borders and territories of British India were shifting combinations of practices and ideas, far more complex and less fixed than the areas and lines depicted on maps. They were performed, subverted, and reformulated over time and were subject to interventions by multiple, often conflicting, agents.

Officials variably interpreted most bordering projects, meaning that uncertainties over the location and nature of the boundaries that defined colonial frontiers often existed from the outset. Considering the prevalence of confusions and subversion among agents of the colonial state, it is unsurprising that instantiating borders among populations whose actions they were intended to influence was fraught with difficulties. Such problems were especially apparent in the regions designated by the colonial state as frontiers. These areas were essentially synonymous colonial notions of tribes as generally lacking individuals or institutions with enough authority to enforce binding spatial arrangements. Such stereotypes did not straightforwardly empower the colonial state. Instead, they led many officials to conceive that borders were inevitably doomed to failure, or that repeated bursts of violence were necessary to uphold boundaries. This lent a farcical edge to many colonial frontier-making efforts, as officials sought to implement lines they knew in advance to be impossible.[214]

In frontier India, just as Andrew Walker has shown in the case of the Laos-Siam boundary, the border-making agency of local inhabitants was not only negative.[215] James Scott's famous characterisation of the hill populations of upland South-East Asia as communities seeking above all to escape governmental control fails to capture the variability and complexity of state–tribe relations. Examples from the frontiers of British India suggest that upland and desert- and forest-bound communities (along with the terrain they inhabited) not only opposed the state and its bordering efforts but shaped them in subtler ways.[216] The idea that resistance was a simple act of state refusal was more evident in officials' preconceived apprehensions than in frontier inhabitants' actual responses to bordering projects, which ranged from acceptance to persistent and violent resistance. Even in the case of the Durand Line, which tended towards the latter extreme, the border was not refused outright, but selectively used as a resource – in this instance, for evading colonial violence through crossing to Afghan territory.

Borders were resources for colonial officials every bit as much as for borderland communities. Historians most often approach the spatial

---

[214] On 'impossible lines', see Kar, 'When Was the Postcolonial?'.   [215] Walker, *Legend*, p. 16.
[216] Scott, *Art*, pp. 179–90, passim. On the point of tribes and states constituting each other, see for example Noelle, *State and Tribe*. Scott also argues that tribes and states develop in tandem but exaggerates the role of opposition in this process, arguing that this co-constitution centres on states having a 'tribal problem' and tribes having 'a perennial "state-problem"': *Art*, p. 208.

engagement of the British Indian state during the era of 'high imperialism' in the mid- to late-nineteenth century through strategies, such as irrigation and forest clearance, which sought to render space fixed, productive, and legible.[217] There is no doubt that agents of empire did sometimes seek, in Doreen Massey's words, to 'tam[e] the challenge of the spatial'.[218] But in many cases at India's fringes, such efforts were not only unsuccessful but ambivalent from the outset. Administrators 'on the spot', along with many of their superiors further from frontiers, perceived certain advantages to amorphous boundaries and patchy territories. Unfixed borders were interwoven with notions that the administrative initiatives and interventions of the colonial state should be variable and locally managed, rather than definitively delimited and overseen from distant hubs of empire. This was a trend that fully flourished in the later nineteenth century, when official subversion profoundly shaped frontier spaces in northwest and northeast British India alike. Colonial officials generated conceptions of borders and territory contrary to the clearly delineated and unitary spaces and boundaries generally considered to be integral aspects of the modern state. As soon as we consider the state as a disparate collection of men and materials that had to perform its authority to its subjects and semi-subjects, it becomes apparent that hazy limits and the variegations within territory was a ubiquitous element of colonial spatial engagement, not an exceptional or unusual aberration.

---

[217] See, for example, Imran Ali, *The Punjab under Imperialism, 1885–1947* (Princeton, NJ: Princeton University Press, 1988); Sunil Amrith, *Unruly Waters: How Mountain Rivers and Monsoons Have Shaped South Asia's History* (London: Allen Lane, 2018); Sumit Guha, *Environment and Ethnicity in India: 1200–1991* (Cambridge: Cambridge University Press, 2006), chs. 6–8.

[218] Doreen Massey, *For Space* (London: Sage, 2005), p. 71.

2   Surveys and Maps

During his trip to Amir Abdurrahman's court in Kabul in 1893 to negotiate the boundary that would bear his name in popular parlance, Henry Mortimer Durand spent much of his time worrying about maps. As far as the British were concerned, border delineation required maps, so Durand had in tow a number prepared by the Survey of India. Despite his faith in their accuracy, they proved insufficient for the delineation to be concluded. It turned out that the Amir also held maps in high regard – just not the ones that Durand brought to Kabul. Much to Durand's frustration, Abdurrahman questioned the detail of British maps, insisting on the production of larger copies and demanding a bespoke rendering of the strip a few miles either side of the border that Durand proposed. After four officers in the British delegation rendered these maps, Durand began to feel that progress was being made on agreeing the border.[1] This proved premature, as the Amir began to engage in cartography of his own, 'scoff[ing]', Durand recalled, 'at any maps not drawn by himself'.[2] There followed a prolonged debate over whose maps were more accurate. Durand acknowledged that Abdurrahman's were occasionally 'good', but did some scoffing of his own in claiming that 'when the Amir draws one utterly wrong it is hard work' and describing the Survey of India's image as 'a real map'.[3] Abdurrahman responded by invoking his experience in the field to query British representations: Durand recorded him saying, '"That is no use – it is all wrong. I know – I have been to these places. Your maps are guess work."' He also suggested that colonial map-images were not as impartial as Durand said: '"Whenever you are dealing with one of my alleged encroachments it [is] made very big on the map – When you are dealing with one of your own I notice it is quite a tiny little thing."'[4] Although the Amir's contestations did not shake Durand's fundamental belief in the representations afforded by British surveying and cartographic techniques, they did force him to admit specific imperfections: 'Chageh for instance is quite wrong in our

[1] MSS Eur D727/5: Durand to Lord Lansdowne, 24, 25, and 26 October 1893.
[2] MSS Eur D727/4: Durand to the Marquis of Dufferin, 27 November 1893.
[3] MSS Eur D727/5: Durand to Lord Lansdowne, 3 November 1893.
[4] Abdurrahman, quoted in ibid.

70

survey map. It is more than twice as far from the Helmund [River] as it ought to be'.[5] Following his conversations with Abdurrahman, Durand left Kabul with a sense that British maps of the frontier were imperfect, contestable, and certainly not iron foundations of colonial power.

Abdurrahman and Durand were not the first to call into question colonial frontier maps. Trudging ever deeper into the forested uplands to the east of Bengal in forlorn pursuit of an elusive enemy beyond the control of the British Indian state, members of the 1871 to 1872 Lushai Expeditionary Force pondered how to comprehend and convey their surroundings. In dispatches to the *Indian Express* newspaper of Calcutta, 'Correspondents' with each of the two military parties extolled the contribution to spatial knowledge made by trigonometrical survey detachments accompanying the Expedition. One attested that the surveyors had 'further opened to the ken of Geography and British Indian progress, a not small region deemed an entangled and impenetrable jungle'.[6] Some dispatches drew on the surveyors' work in specifying latitude and longitude at the time of writing to the nearest second. Others supposed that previously published maps would be available to at least some readers, with one advising those 'who [possess] the "Reconnaissance of the Lushai country," Surveyor-General's office, 1870' to locate a topographic feature mentioned in the narrative 'in the letter O in the title of the map, the words LUSHAI COUNTRY'.[7] But as the party travelled further from colonial territory and ennui set in in the face of fleeing communities and unfulfilled objectives, the spatial imaginary described to the readers of the *Indian Express* took on new qualities. Maps were invoked less frequently; the reader was instead called upon to reference a different repertoire of images including 'Gustave Dore's Flood in his illustrations of the Bible', a romanticist rendering intended to evoke the extraordinary climatic conditions and perceptions of existential threat in these frontier environs: '[it] seemed as if we had but the *mauvais quart d'heure* between us and death'.[8] Darkly comic references with more than a hint of self-lampooning also began to jostle with references to longitude and latitude in the effort to make sense of the Expedition's environs for those back in urban Bengal.

It is a melancholy thing when one progresses, as it were, beyond all human ken – out of the sphere of sympathy; a Latitudinarian in fact. Yet so it is; we have arrived at No Man's Land, and Laputa or Brobdingnag may at any time burst upon our view . . . I go to bed, in fact, every night, expecting in the morning to be greeted by the Great Panjandrum with

---

[5] Ibid.
[6] SHL, Lewin Collection, 811-II-29, f. 56: 'The Looshai Campaign, Right Wing', *Indian Observer*, undated.
[7] Ibid., f. 30: 'From Our Correspondent with the Left Column', *Indian Observer*, undated.
[8] Ibid., f. 3: 'From Our Correspondent with the Right Column', 22 December 1871, *Indian Observer*, 6 January 1872.

the button on top, who shall announce our arrival in China. Eastward Ho! is the name of our novel adventure. By the last accurate accounts General Bourchier has marched clean out of the map, a military blunder which the Quarter Master General's Department will find it hard to pardon.[9]

This dense intermingling of allusions to and puns on Christian theology, the novels of Jonathan Swift and Charles Kingsley, Samuel Foote's satire, and colonial military-institutional politics poked fun at the limitations of existing map-images of the region and the fetishisation of accuracy. It conjured up a space defined by unreality, rendered more comprehensible by assimilation into fictional worlds than by global coordinates.

This version of the Lushai Hills was a 'fabulous geography'.[10] It was a product of what Johannes Fabian has described as agents of empire being 'out of their minds', unable and unwilling to purify their accounts of irrational, anarchic qualities.[11] It directly contradicts the notion that high imperial surveyors and their multiple audiences imagined space as an idealised map, there to be dominated, with 'nothing hidden or convoluted, no shadows, no "double entendre"'.[12] As surveying extended further into colonial India's frontiers in the later nineteenth century, British spatial imaginaries became not less but more convoluted, shadowy, and riven with double entendres. Maps, written narratives, and sketches often contained signs of equivocality. The often multiple or indeterminate authors of these representations failed or did not seek to eradicate their particular labours in constituting them. In addition, those involved in the production and reception of cartographic artefacts increasingly called them into question, suggesting they could not truly or comprehensively convey the spaces to which they pertained.

As the nineteenth century progressed, India's frontiers became more intensively mapped. These regions also became increasingly significant as surveyors came to see them not as fragmented and distinct localities, but as part of a unified 'Indian frontier' that provided distinct challenges and opportunities for surveying and mapping. Beneath local specificities, three broad junctures of frontier surveying can be discerned. Sporadic military ventures into the ill-defined fringes of British power during wars and annexations from the 1820s to

---

[9] Ibid., f. 29: 'From Our Correspondent with the Right Column', 16 February 1872, *Indian Observer*, undated.

[10] Sumathi Ramaswamy, *The Lost Land of Lemuria: Fabulous Geographies, Catastrophic Histories* (Berkeley, CA: University of California Press, 2004).

[11] Johannes Fabian, *Out of Our Minds: Reason and Madness in the Exploration of Central Africa* (Berkeley, CA: University of California Press, 2000); the concept of purification in modern knowledge production is discussed in Bruno Latour, *We Have Never Been Modern*, trans. Catherine Porter (Cambridge, MA: Harvard University Press, 1993).

[12] Bruno Latour (referring to paper maps), cited approvingly in Edney, 'Bringing', p. 71. Edney develops this point to contend that maps 'allowed Europeans to conceptualise the world and to think that they could dominate the world itself' (p. 78).

the 1840s involved hasty route surveys – measurements of distance and bearing between places with occasional calculations of location by astronomical sightings. British and Indian agents continued to execute route surveys for various purposes long afterwards; but during the 1850s surveyors began to 'fix' topographical features in frontier regions by trigonometrical observations – the calculation of angles and distances in a series of connected optical observations starting from a physically measured 'baseline'. As colonial state interference increased from the later 1860s, the era of distant sightings gradually gave way to the increasing presence of trigonometrical survey detachments among frontier uplands and deserts. One significant manifestation of this trend was the Survey of India's advent of a 'Superintendent of Frontier Surveys', institutionalising a unified conception of the British Indian frontier stretching from the deserts abutting Persia in the west to the forested highlands of Upper Burma in the east via the high Himalaya.

Surveyors and men of science in colony and metropole widely deemed comprehending the mountains, deserts, and river courses that lay tantalisingly beyond the limits of governed British India to be one of the defining goals of imperial institutions and techniques of knowing space. This chapter shows how these areas were not only considered hinterlands of nearly unparalleled opportunity but also appeared to present challenges that struck at the heart of established means of fixing and rendering space. For many involved in gathering spatial knowledge, it was precisely these difficulties that valorised their efforts. British India's frontiers served a vital role in countering increasingly common insinuations in the later nineteenth century that knowing space involved little more than the application of a standardised set of procedures, and that the era of heroic battles against nature had closed. Explorers and surveyors engaged at frontiers accordingly made sure to foreground their difficulties in a host of official, scientific, and popular accounts. However, the tensions between self-erasure and self-promotion were not always sustainable, nor were the struggles of knowing frontier space merely canny rhetorical ploys.

This chapter engages the recent work of some theorists and historians of cartography on the operative impact of maps and other spatial representations. One of the most fecund aspects of this strand of scholarship is the insistence that we should not assume that particular spatial representations were understood and used in homogeneous, stable ways. As one theoretical intervention puts it, 'maps do not emerge in the same way for all individuals'.[13] Moving away from J. B. Harley's notion of maps as texts, which exaggerated the power of maps to create uniform realities, and towards maps as elements within

[13] Rob Kitchin, Chris Perkins, and Martin Dodge, 'Thinking about Maps', in id (eds.), *Rethinking Maps* (Abingdon: Routledge, 2009), pp. 1–25, here p. 16.

broader assemblages that are performed in various ways leads to a focus on distribution and use.[14] As in equivalent moves in literary theory and intellectual history,[15] this shift involves heightened attention to diversity and scepticism towards the notion that a single representation or representative mode can have a uniform effect. In Michel de Certeau's words, 'a *"polytheism" of scattered practices* survives, dominated but not erased by the triumphal success of one of their number'.[16] This chapter draws out fragmentary evidence of frontier map usage, showing that agents of imperial surveying widely understood maps and narratives of frontier spaces to be fragile communicative devices prone to unstable reception.

It also contends that spatial representations were not only disrupted by processes of collation, production, and reception beyond 'the field' but were equivocal all the way back to initial acts of information gathering. Knowledge of frontier spaces was composed of processes in which 'the actors were trembling'.[17] Moreover, these actors tended to emphasise that they were not only trembling (literally in some cases) but also laughing and being laughed at, stumbling, and dying. Admissions of fallibility were not merely about meeting popular demand for tales of danger. They appeared with surprising consistency across written and visual genres, forming part of private correspondence within the survey establishment as well as mass-market accounts. These crises also had epistemological effects that were not necessarily overcome through the use of 'reason' or in 'centres of calculation'.[18] Surveyors did not assume the existence of an authoritative epistemological domain sealed from a shifting array of challenges to stable knowledge experienced 'in the field'. The persistent presence of particular circumstances in published representations of frontier India suggests that the 'tension between the local view and the broader overview' identified by D. Graham Burnett and others in Britain's American

---

[14] J. B. Harley popularized the notion of 'maps as texts': see especially Harley, 'Texts and Contexts in the Interpretation of Early Maps', in id, *The New Nature of Maps: Essays in the History of Cartography*, ed. Paul Laxton (Baltimore: Johns Hopkins University Press, 2001), pp. 33–49. For critiques of this position, many reflecting the shift to 'maps as performances', see the essays in Reuben Rose-Redwood (ed.), 'Deconstructing the Map: 25 Years on', special issue of *Cartographica*, 50, 1 (2015).

[15] Among the most important works in this vein are: Hans Robert Jauss, *Toward an Aesthetics of Reception*, trans. Timothy Bahti (Minneapolis, MN: University of Minnesota Press, 1982); Roger Chartier, *The Order of Books: Readers, Authors, and Libraries in Europe between the Fourteenth and Eighteenth Centuries*, trans. Lydia G. Cochrane (London: Polity, 1994); Michel de Certeau, *The Practice of Everyday Life*, trans. Steven Rendall (Berkeley, CA: University of California, 1984).

[16] de Certeau, *Practice*, p. 48, emphasis in original.   [17] Bruno Latour, *We Have Never*, p. 126.

[18] On the use of 'reason' in imperial mapping in India, see Edney, *Mapping*, pp. 48–51. On the concept of 'centres of calculation', see Bruno Latour, *Science in Action: How to Follow Scientists and Engineers through Society*, trans. Catherine Porter (Cambridge, MA: Harvard University Press, 1987), Ch. 6.

colonies was a widespread and long-lasting element of spatial knowledge production in the British Empire.[19]

The chapter both develops and departs from Matthew Edney's much-cited assessment of cartography in India during the earlier colonial period.[20] It takes a lead from Edney's concept of 'cartographic anarchy', which brilliantly describes the chaos and heterogeneity of survey work on the ground in British India.[21] However, it dissents from his notion that surveyors and map-makers 'cloaked' these circumstances to a degree that enabled them to believe that 'the cartographic archive and its constituent surveys was indeed a perfect geographical panopticon'.[22] The agents examined in this chapter did not consider maps or any other representative form in such strident terms. They instead diagnosed, bemoaned, and theorised those 'anarchic' processes that Edney claims to have exhumed from a deep grave of colonial erasure and elision. Colonial surveyors were reflexive and anxious about spatial knowledge in multiple ways over the later nineteenth century, engaging just as much as recent scholars in critical assessments of cartography.

These core contentions develop through the five sections that form the rest of this chapter. Broadly chronological, each section also addresses distinct elements and junctures within the broad project of knowing the frontier spaces of colonial India. The first section looks at route surveys at the expanding, shifting fringes of colonial India undertaken up until the 1840s. It argues that while route surveys complemented the logic of British governmental expansion and annexation, they were also diverse and fraught undertakings composed of numerous, often controversial, techniques. Far from being expression of unitary state power, the production and reception of data garnered by these surveys were contingent on a host of local variables. The next section closely examines the activities, actors, and instruments that constituted survey data during the mid-nineteenth-century period when trigonometrical surveyors viewed prominent features of frontiers from a distance. It shows how the challenges of accurate altitude measurement, deemed an essential feature of effective triangulation, led these men not only to undertake a host of much celebrated

---

[19] D. Graham Burnett, *Masters of All They Surveyed: Exploration, Geography, and a British El Dorado* (Chicago and London: University of Chicago Press, 2000), pp. 167–70; Daniel W. Clayton, *Islands of Truth: The Imperial Fashioning of Vancouver Island* (Vancouver: UBC Press, 1999), p. 232.

[20] Edney, *Mapping*; Bernardo Michael also shows the widespread nature of practical difficulties in British surveys in India, but, like Edney, suggests that these challenges were largely occluded in and overcome by the map-image. See Bernardo A. Michael, 'Making Territory Visible: The Revenue Surveys of Colonial South Asia', *Imago Mundi*, 59, 1 (2007), pp. 78–95, here pp. 89–91; Bernardo A. Michael, *Statemaking and Territory in South Asia: Lessons from the Anglo-Gorkha War (1814–1816)* (London: Anthem Press, 2012), Ch. 6.

[21] Edney, *Mapping*, p. 29; Ch. 5.

[22] Ibid., p. 34. See also Edney's claim that '[t]he texts and maps did not present truth, nor do the maps constitute panopticons. The British simply believed that they did' (p. 26).

improvisations but also, contrastingly, to begin to perceive that even perfectly processed survey data could never represent territory with full accuracy. This was a key moment in which doubts about an irreducible limitation in the project of knowing territory started to fester, setting the scene for later shifts in attitudes towards depicting and experiencing space among surveyors at colonial India's frontiers.

Before addressing this later period, the third section focuses on widespread debates among members of the British Indian survey establishment about frontier maps as material objects. Surveyors and users alike were not fixated solely on ideals of accurate data but also sharply aware of the challenges of making and distributing useful images of frontier environs. The advent of surveys of these areas from the 1850s was a key driver of technological shifts in map production and dissemination in colonial India. These were processes entailing multiple concerns as well as apparent triumphs, with flows of geographical information often far from consistent or well directed. The following section takes this story of anxieties about representation back to the field, looking at the period from the 1860s when surveyors ventured into frontier regions rather than gazing at them from distant vantage points. It shows how surveying frontiers came to assume huge significance for colonial agents but was simultaneously beset with multiple difficulties that frequently appeared to constitute insurmountable barriers to gathering effective data. These concerns went beyond those of earlier decades in being seen as unresolvable through the use of reason or by further survey work.

The final section of the chapter demonstrates how trends established over previous decades reached a peculiar resolution during the closing decades of the nineteenth century. Impediments to comprehending frontier spaces combined with cultures of romanticism, mysticism, and anti-empiricism to undergird widely held ideas among surveyors and men of science that these regions were somehow elusive, maintaining a margin of unknowability beyond even the calculations of trigonometrical surveying and the planar projections of map-images. Many agents of empire came to understand frontiers in ways that foregrounded the bodily over the cerebral, the immersed experience over the removed gaze, and the playful over the serious.[23] They operated within and contributed to spatial imaginaries that involved heterogeneous modes of understanding and communicating, and which doubted the value of 'scientific' surveying even as they undertook it. Crucially, unlike conceptions among colonial agents of the earlier nineteenth century of 'jungle' and upland areas

---

[23] Martin Dodge and Chris Perkins note the 'seriousness' with which scholars associated with the New History of Cartography, especially J. B. Harley, treat maps, suggesting an alternative focus on 'the ludic possibilities of mapping'. Dodge and Perkins, 'Reflecting on J.B. Harley's Influence and What He Missed in "Deconstructing the Map"', *Cartographica*, 50, 1 (2015), pp. 37–40; here p. 38.

as regions of disorder but also of potential reform, India's high imperial frontier deserts and mountains came to be understood as permanently resistant to 'improvement'.

Developing this contention of the distinctive nature of late nineteenth-century surveyors and explorers' understandings of frontier space, the chapter concludes by suggesting that knowing frontiers took on forms that incorporated but ultimately exceeded well-developed notions of 'the sublime'. These forms of knowledge, I suggest, can usefully be understood through Martin Heidegger's conception of the 'world-picture'.[24] Recent scholars of imperial representation have employed this theory but have not made use of its core tension. Timothy Mitchell and Derek Gregory, for instance, claim that European empires 'enframed' their colonised territories and communities as 'objects to be viewed', separated absolutely from the viewing subject of the coloniser.[25] They overlook Heidegger's contention that the 'unlimited power for the calculating, planning and moulding of all things' in the 'modern age' produces a sort of surplus – which Heidegger terms 'the gigantic' – which 'becomes ... incalculable'.[26] Many of the late nineteenth-century actors engaged in producing knowledge of India's frontiers construed them in ways akin to Heidegger's 'gigantic': shadowy arenas 'withdrawn from representation' in which to challenge and to lose oneself at a time when technologies of triangulation had apparently fixed the imperial Subcontinent.[27]

2.1 'Getting at the Truth': Route Surveys at Nascent Frontiers

While personnel of the Great Trigonometrical Survey (GTS) laboured over the 'Great Arc' from southern tip of peninsula India to the Himalayan foothills, into the 1840s terrain around and beyond the hazy limits of colonial government continued to be known solely through more rudimentary methods. Extant texts and maps were scoured and local people and travellers were interrogated. When and where it seemed possible and practical – or, sometimes, sufficiently improbable and impractical for someone to be allured by the potential acclaim – British agents of empire undertook route surveys. While they often shared trigonometrical surveys' aspiration to represent terrestrial space in three dimensions, route surveys could dispense with all but a single dimension: that of the line of a path from one place to another. Altitude measurements

---

[24] Martin Heidegger, 'The Age of the World Picture', in *The Question Concerning Technology and Other Essays*, trans. William Lovitt (New York, NY: Harper, 1977), pp. 115–54.

[25] Derek Gregory, *Geographical Imaginations* (Oxford: Blackwell, 1994), pp. 37, 53; Timothy Mitchell, 'The World As Exhibition', *Comparative Studies in Society and History*, 31, 2 (1989), pp. 217–36, here pp. 220, 227.

[26] Heidegger, 'Age', pp. 134–6.   [27] Ibid., p. 136.

and lateral sightings were optional and frequently proved erratic or impossible. In its most sophisticated form, route surveying involved arrays of adapted instruments, fastidious practices of observing features either side of the primary path, and intersecting points and closed circuits that allowed for checks against errors. At its most rudimentary, it merely produced an itinerary – a list of place names, which, as Catherine Delano-Smith shows, was the only means of long-distance wayfinding in most cultures until at least the nineteenth century.[28]

Route surveys around and beyond the limits of governed British India until the mid-nineteenth century were diverse in motive, method, and impact. Various military and civil officials along with travellers with different degrees of connection to colonial administrative bodies garnered arrays of spatial and ethnographic knowledge.[29] There was little by way of central coordination or standardisation before, during, or after these surveys. The earliest forays beyond the colonial state's limits tended not to become fixed reference points for subsequent surveyors and were liable to be denigrated as much as admired.[30] During the brief British military foray into Assam from 1792 to 1794, an officer named Wood collected some geographical information and produced a map. His successors during the colonial invasion of the region in the 1820s did not, however, use his work as a basis for their own. Richard Wilcox, whose surveys of the 1820s will be considered shortly, disparaged the limitation of Wood's survey to the banks of the Brahmaputra River, stating that the spaces beyond remained 'a perfect blank'.[31] George Forster's data on the routes beyond the northwestern limits of the colonial state's territory, gathered during his famed overland 'journey from Bengal to England' in the 1780s, were similarly doubted rather than acclaimed by later surveyors of the region.[32] Mountstuart Elphinstone noted in the influential account of his 'embassy' to the areas around Peshawar in 1808 that, unlike Elphinstone's colleagues, Forster had no instruments and relied on local information for distances. Forster 'could not', Elphinstone pronounced, 'be so good a judge of the length of a stage as a person who had often travelled it, and was besides accustomed to estimate the rate at which camels move'. [33] Unlike Wood's survey data, which did not even

[28] Catherine Delano-Smith, 'Milieus of Mobility: Itineraries, Route Maps, and Road Maps', in James R. Akerman (ed.), *Cartographies of Travel and Navigation* (Chicago, IL: University of Chicago Press, 2006), pp. 16–68.

[29] This was also the case throughout the rest of colonial India: see Edney, *Mapping*, p. 162.

[30] On admiration of earlier travellers and rhetorical strategies among later explorers to position themselves in relation to predecessors, see Burnett, *Masters*, pp. 37–9.

[31] R. Wilcox, 'Memoir of a Survey of Assam and the Neighbouring Countries, Executed in 1825-6-7-8', *Asiatic Researches*, 17 (1832), pp. 314–469; here footnote p. 316. See also Simpson, 'Forgetting'.

[32] G. Forster, *A Journey from Bengal to England* (Calcutta, 1790).

[33] Mountstuart Elphinstone, *An Account of the Kingdom of Caubul, and Its Dependencies, in Persia, Tartary, and India*, 3rd ed. (London: Richard Bentley, 1839), xxxix.

feature in collections of maps assembled for military use during the Anglo-Burmese War during the 1820s,[34] Forster was among the sources for at least one Company-State map of the region beyond its northwestern limits during the First Anglo-Afghan War.[35] This longevity, however, spoke less of confidence in his veracity than the paucity of subsequent information gathering.

The compilation of multiple surveys into regional maps indicates one aspect of the potential for route surveys to transcend the narrow limits of the linear path of a single surveyor. Especially before the advent in the second half of the nineteenth century of widely circulated guides to route surveying such as the Royal Geographical Society's (RGS) *Hints to Travellers*,[36] compilation was fraught with difficulties. It entailed not so much the smooth integration of homogeneous material than the messy melding of diverse ways of seeing and recording.[37] One notable feature of the use of route survey data in later maps of India's nascent frontiers was the tendency not to erase fragments that clearly bore marks of a particular time and place. For instance, a map of 'The North-Eastern Frontier with Burma and part of China' published by the Survey of India in 1862 retained (but mangled) a note lifted from Wilcox's survey narrative: 'On the 24th May 1827 when the Snow was fast melting on the mountains at its source, the Namyen River was here but 80 yards broad and fordable & was fordable [*sic.*]'.[38] Rather than presenting an authoritative, fixed view of regional space in which the moment and location of fieldwork were removed, frontier maps based on route surveys tended to retain signs of these specifics.

The circumstances of route surveying were, above all, highly varied. Many surveys were the work of solo travellers, and many more that relied on supporting retinues were described as if they were lone ventures. These surveys, unlike trigonometrical counterparts, were in word if not in deed 'solitary and nomadic affairs', as D. Graham Burnett puts it in his work on British exploration in South America.[39] While route surveying generally meant an individual human operating in the landscape, in other respects surveyors were required to make clear that they were far from alone. In particular, instruments mattered. During the nineteenth century, barometers and boiling point thermometers (for measuring

---

[34] IOR/H/678.

[35] BL, IOR/X/1620: 'Map of Countries on the North West Frontier of India Compiled from Various Documents. By John Walker Geographer to the Honble. East India Company'.

[36] Felix Driver, *Geography Militant: Cultures of Exploration and Empire* (Oxford: Blackwell, 2001), pp. 49–66. See also James Urry, '"Notes and Queries on Anthropology" and the Development of Field Methods in British Anthropology, 1870–1920', *Proceedings of the Royal Anthropological Institute of Great Britain and Ireland* (1972), pp. 45–57.

[37] For example, Elphinstone, *Account*, 3rd ed. xxxix–xli.

[38] NAI Cartographic, Survey of India, F.98/24–25.   [39] Burnett, *Masters*, p. 10.

altitude), perambulators (for measuring distance), sextants and theodolites (for taking bearings), and notebooks (for recording data) were increasingly taken as markers of credibility.[40] As recent work has amply demonstrated, however, instruments were fragile and unreliable, requiring not only material upkeep and modifications but also 'rhetorical repair' to ensure that they established the authority of the person who wielded them and of the data they supplied.[41]

The 'states of disrepair' of various instruments was a repeated theme in route surveys beyond the established bounds of colonial India and took various forms.[42] Sometimes, instruments were unavailable – a cause not just for concern but also for celebrating the surveyor who sought to overcome this limitation. For instance, Wilcox applauded the work of his colleague Burlton in surveying the eastern portion of Upper Assam in the 1820s 'with a surveying compass only, and unfurnished with any instrument for measuring distances'.[43] The scarcity of instruments and criticisms of their quality was a common refrain. It was evident especially among military officers who, without formal coordination, executed route surveys around and beyond the fringes of Sind during the First Anglo-Afghan War. The Bombay Government received a slew of requests for surveying instruments from its agents in Sind and repeatedly failed to meet this demand. Asked by John Jacob, the Assistant Political Agent in Upper Sind for 'six (6) glass Barometer tubes which will be very useful to me occasionally in measuring the heights of different places', the authorities sent four, 'no more ... being in store'.[44] Nor could they find 'a good surveying compass' that one officer requested to enable him to render 'a rough sketch' of 'parts of the country hitherto unknown'.[45]

---

[40] Lachlan Fleetwood, '"No Former Travellers Having Attained Such a Height on the Earth's Surface": Instruments, Inscriptions, and Bodies in the Himalaya, 1800–1830', *History of Science*, 56, 1 (2018), pp. 3–34; Dane Kennedy, *The Last Blank Spaces: Exploring Africa and Australia* (Cambridge, MA: Harvard University Press, 2013), pp. 25–9; Fraser MacDonald and Charles W. J. Withers (eds.), *Geography, Technology and Instruments of Exploration* (Farnham: Ashgate, 2015); Marie-Noëlle Bourguet, Christian Licoppe and H. Otto Sibum (eds.), *Instruments, Travel and Science: Itineraries of Precision from the Seventeenth to the Twentieth Century* (London: Routledge, 2002). On notebooks, see Marie-Noëlle Bourguet, 'A Portable World: The Notebooks of European Travellers (Eighteenth to Nineteenth Centuries)', *Intellectual History Review*, 20, 3 (2010), pp. 377–400.

[41] Quotation from Eoin Phillips, 'Instrumenting Order: Longitude, Seamen and Astronomers, 1770–1805', in Macdonald and Withers (eds.), *Geography, Technology and Instruments*, pp. 37–56, here p. 45. See also Fleetwood, '"No former travellers"', pp. 17–18.

[42] Schaffer, 'Easily Cracked'.   [43] Wilcox, 'Survey', pp. 316–18.

[44] MSA, Political, 1841–42, Vol. 79: John Jacob, Assistant Political Agent, Upper Sind, to James Outram, Political Agent, Sind, 25 November 1841; J. Dickenson, Chief Engineer, Bombay, to G. M. Anderson, Governor of Bombay, 24 December 1841.

[45] MSA, Political, 1841–42, Vol. 79: C. Benbow to Bombay Government, 11 January 1842.

Even when the beleaguered Bombay Government managed to dispatch the required hardware, instrumental woes continued. Senior officials felt that using instruments was 'likely to alarm and excite [Baloch] prejudices'. The first British surveyor of the portion of Sind adjacent to tribal areas accordingly employed only 'a pocket compass and the occasional use of a sextant'. Furthermore, this surveyor reported that the sextant had 'some imperfection' that meant that he 'cannot depend upon' the latitude measurements it produced.[46] As was later the case in British surveys in the Arabian peninsula during the 1850s and 1860s,[47] in Sind during the 1840s 'distances were determined by the rate of a camel's pace both ambling and walking' rather than by the perambulators that the surveyor had requested.[48] Some complaints about surveying instruments took a more furious tone. One officer vented angrily in the official report on a route to Kalat that:

Unfortunately the surveying instruments with which I was supplied are so extremely bad that my labour has been inconceivably increased & since the hour I left Kilat [*sic.*] the mapping down of my daily outdoor work (rendered extremely intricate by the innumerable observations I have been compelled to take) has so entirely consumed my time and occupied my attention that I have been utterly unable to make enquiries on many points of interest.[49]

Despite his intemperate outburst, within a month this officer found himself in charge of the Sind Survey, after his superior resigned owing to the backlog of work that resulted from the death and ill health of the Indian draftsmen who rendered survey data in map form (e.g., Figure 2.1), and 'the difficulty if not impossibility' of securing adequate replacements.[50] Route surveying at the outskirts of Sind in the 1840s was shot through with problems of instrumentation and expert labour at a time when effective data on and representations of frontier routes was a major priority for colonial forces engaged in Afghanistan and in Sind.

At least surveyors in Sind found one element to be more compliant than they had feared: the landscape. Unlike their successors in the later nineteenth century, who, as discussed later, found the desert terrain and climate wreaked havoc with optical measurements, the first British surveyor into Balochistan reported that 'obstacles . . . were fewer, and of a character less formidable, than we had been led to expect'.[51] The situation that confronted surveyors at the fringes of Assam during and following the war with Burma in the 1820s was

[46] MSA Political, 1840–42: Sinde: G. LeMessurier, Assistant Quarter-Master General, to Outram, 4 March 1840.

[47] Daniel Foliard, *Dislocating the Orient: British Maps and the Making of the Middle East, 1854–1921* (Chicago, IL: University of Chicago Press, 2017), pp. 31–32.

[48] MSA Political, 1840–42: Sinde: LeMessurier to Outram, 4 March 1840, 29 June 1840.

[49] MSA, Political, 1841–42, Vol. 79: Robertson, undated attachment to LeMessurier to Government of India, 29 December 1841.

[50] MSA, Political, 1841–42, Vol. 79: LeMessurier to Bombay Government, 19 January 1842.

[51] MSA Political, 1840–42: Sinde: LeMessurier to Outram, 19 November 1841.

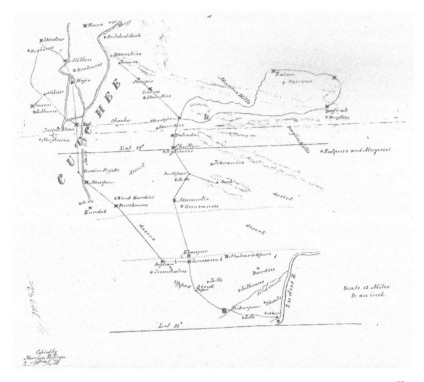

Figure 2.1 Thomas Postans, untitled map of Upper Sind Frontier (1841)[52]

very different in this respect. Once colonial forces invaded Assam in 1824, intensive survey operations were an immediate priority. Surveyors travelled throughout the Brahmaputra Valley and into the hills beyond, including to areas at the northeastern fringes that were not visited again by British personnel until the last decades of the nineteenth century. They accumulated topographical data not only for strategic military purposes, as was the case in the 1840s in Sind. In addition, they aimed to resolve a 'mystery' much debated among leading European men of geography, including the Surveyor-General of India, John Hodgson: whether the Tsangpo river of Tibet became the Brahmaputra River in Assam or the Irrawaddy River in Burma. The data they generated fed into substantial regional maps, most notably one compiled by Wilcox that covered Assam, the uplands north of Burma, eastern Tibet, and part of the Yunnan region of China (Figure 2.2).

[52] MSA Political, 1841–42, Vol. 75: Postans to Outram, 24 May 1841.

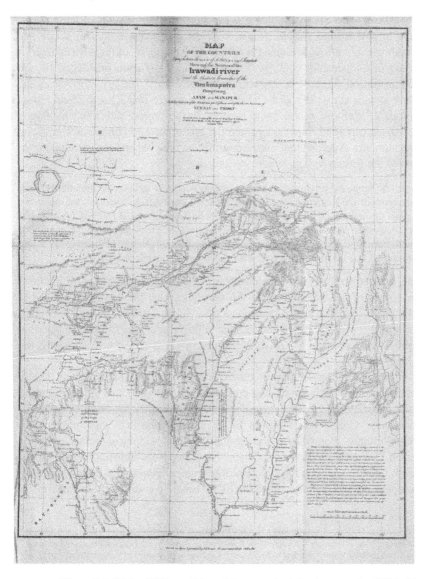

Figure 2.2 Richard Wilcox, 'Map of the countries lying between the 20½ & 30 of N Lat. & 90½ & 99 E. Longitude', in *Asiatic Researches* (1832). Reproduced by kind permission of the Syndics of Cambridge University Library.[53]

[53] Wilcox, 'Memoir', facing p. 314.

Yet route surveys in the densely forested riverine plains and labyrinthine hills in and around Assam proved difficult and were limited in scope and credibility for various reasons. Like the British explorers of the African interior in the mid-nineteenth century,[54] surveyors in this region privileged 'ocular demonstration' – that is, seeing with their own eyes.[55] Yet, just as in Africa and other locales across the globe, there were multiple obstacles to clear vision. Wilcox's 'Memoir' of his route surveys in the region, published in *Asiatic Researches* in 1832, repeatedly cited the landscape and climate as significant impediments. Approaching one summit in the hills beyond the extreme north-east of the Assam Valley, Wilcox recorded:

It may be supposed what interest was excited as each new gain on the mountain's steep face brought me nearer to that height whence I expected to overlook the unknown regions through which the Brahmaputra has its hidden course, but I suffered disappointment. Another mountain rose close to this one on its east, and where the capricious clouds permitted, through their casual openings, a passing glimpse of the rugged country beyond, all I could perceive was fir-clad mountain or a patch of snow.[56]

This was far from an isolated occurrence. Wilcox even assigned some blame to the course of the Brahmaputra – the very thing that his surveys promised to establish – writing that 'its crookedness limited the view and closed it abruptly'.[57] Meanwhile, at the Assam Valley's southern fringes, impassable rapids twice prevented British surveyors in the 1820s from accessing the hills.[58]

These difficulties of terrain made Wilcox and his colleagues unusually dependent on informants among communities in Assam and the surrounding hills, especially those who travelled through the hills for trade or religious purposes.[59] Contrary to Matthew Edney's suggestion that 'local informants' were routinely 'glossed over and submerged' in geographical narratives of this period,[60] Wilcox's 'Memoir' indicated his reliance on, and simultaneous scepticism towards, Asian travellers. His large regional map acknowledged not only European sources but also members of the Singpho community for the hills at

---

[54] Lawrence Dritsas, 'Expeditionary Science: Conflicts of Method in Mid-Mineteenth-Century Geographical Discovery', in Charles W. J. Withers & David N. Livingstone (eds.), *Geographies of Nineteenth-Century Science* (Chicago and London: University of Chicago Press, 2011), pp. 255–78, here p. 268.

[55] Wilcox, 'Memoir', p. 410.   [56] Ibid., p. 380.   [57] Ibid., p. 367.

[58] IOR/X/533/2: 'Map of the Course of the Brahmaputra River', Survey of India (1828).

[59] On tensions concerning 'local knowledge' in European exploration in the nineteenth century, see Kennedy, *Last Blank Spaces*, p. 2; David Lambert, *Mastering the Niger: James MacQueen's African Geography and the Struggle over Atlantic Slavery* (Chicago: University of Chicago Press, 2013), especially pp. 88–118; Innes M. Keighren, Charles W. J. Withers, and Bill Bell, *Travels into Print: Exploration, Writing, and Publishing with John Murray, 1773–1859* (Chicago, IL: University of Chicago Press, 2015), pp. 15–16.

[60] Edney, *Mapping*, pp. 66–8.

the eastern end of the Brahmaputra Valley, Tibetan 'Lamas' cited in the French geographer d'Anville's mid-eighteenth century Atlas, and, for information on Bhutan, 'a Persian sent by Mr. Scott [the Governor-General's Agent in Assam]'.[61] In his written narrative, however, Wilcox repeatedly bemoaned irreconcilable or suspect data, especially on the Tsangpo's route. As 'ocular demonstration' proved beyond him, Wilcox sought out information from 'Lamas' – here meaning Tibetans residing in the uplands northeast of Assam – who 'must know, beyond all doubt, whether their territory is or is not separated from *Thibet* by a large river'.[62] However, an attack on the survey party by members of the Mishmi community that interposed between the Assam Valley and Wilcox's hypothesised 'Lamas' meant that he never reached them.

Other informants on the question of the Brahmaputra's course appeared in Wilcox's 'Memoir' only to be denigrated. The sacred geography within which Assam's Hindu elites located the source of the Brahmaputra particularly vexed Wilcox. 'The *Asamese*', he wrote, 'universally declare [the source] to be utterly inaccessible to man ... At present there appear so many discrepancies between the Hindu legends, and facts, that we are quite at a loss'.[63] Wilcox's irritation towards inhabitants of the area he surveyed was limited neither to lowland communities nor to the provision of topographical information. He also casti-gated the indolence of his guides, reporting that they 'could not conceive that any motive need occasion haste'.[64] In one case, however, he forewent such a racialised attack in order to emphasise his own heroism. Reporting that his 'Woollaston's thermometric barometer' had been 'deranged' by being inverted by 'the man whose business it was to carry it', Wilcox wrote: 'nor can this be wondered at, seeing that all a man's care was employed in preserving his own limbs from injury by a fall from the rugged precipices we occasionally clam-bered over'.[65] Here is one instance of competing rhetorical impulses shaping descriptions in letters and published accounts that were crucial outputs of route surveys.

Obtaining geographical information on the regions at the outskirts of expanding colonial influence during the earlier nineteenth century was a fraught business. The production of data through undertakings both in the field and at the writing desk was diverse and frequently judged inadequate, as admonishing missives from superiors and ongoing controversies among audi-ences indicated.[66] For instance, Wilcox's efforts did not stably resolve the riddle of riverine routes in the uplands around Assam, northern Burma, and Tibet, instead merely strengthening the convictions of those, including

---

[61] Wilcox, 'Memoir', facing p. 314.　　[62] Ibid., p. 410.　　[63] Ibid., p. 354.　　[64] Ibid., p. 383.
[65] Ibid., p. 365.
[66] On efforts to systematise surveys and geographical knowledge gathering, see Kennedy, *Last Blank Spaces*, pp. 46–59; Driver, *Geography Militant*, pp. 49–66.

members of the British Indian survey establishment, who were already convinced that the Tsangpo joined the Brahmaputra rather than Burma's
Irrawaddy.[67] There was no universally agreed measure of the validity of survey
data or of what constituted topographical precision, even between the various
institutions of the colonial state.[68] The Military Department, for example, was
generally content with plans of routes between strategic locales; by contrast,
Presidency Governments and scientific institutions in colony and metropole
alike increasingly sought area coverage.[69]

The heterogeneous ways in which route survey data were produced and
received were both products of, and contributors to, the indeterminacy of
colonial India's morphing fringes during the first half of the nineteenth century.
As D. Graham Burnett and Daniel Foliard have shown in the cases of British
Guiana and Arabia, respectively, 'mobile and exploratory' route surveying
fosters a view of 'expandable' rather than fixed imperial space.[70] As such,
this form of surveying was a significant aspect of an era in which colonial
frontiers in northeast and northwest India were not bounded by even a pretense
of precision linear boundaries. As will be discussed later in this chapter,
trigonometrical surveying did not straightforwardly supersede route surveying
at and beyond British India's frontiers. In some cases, atmospheric circumstances rendered long-distance trigonometrical sightings impossible, reducing
surveyors' fields of vision to narrow routes. And deliberate route surveys
continued to be vital but precarious and disputable elements of spatial knowledge in the later nineteenth century, especially useful in the fractured terrain
and politically fractious environs beyond the fully governed colonial state
territory. As in the famous 'transfrontier' explorations into Central Asia undertaken by colonial-trained local personnel known as 'pandits', such surveys
remained bound up with expansive definitions of colonial interests beyond
sovereign state space.[71] While they were a key element in the projection of
colonial activity beyond already established territorial limits, this section has
shown that route surveys and the maps that (sometimes) resulted were not

---

[67] Simpson, 'Forgetting'.
[68] On the historicity and heterogeneity of 'accuracy', see M. Norton Wise (ed.), *The Values of Precision* (Princeton, NJ: Princeton University Press, 1995); Simon Schaffer, 'Late Victorian Metrology and Its Instrumentation: A Manufactory of Ohms', in Mario Biagioli (ed.), *The Science Studies Reader* (London: Routledge, 1999), pp. 457–78.
[69] See, for example, debates over maps of the Sind frontier in the early 1840s: MSA Political, 1840, Vol. 95: Government of India to Bombay Government, 22 June 1840, f. 432; MSA Political, 1844, Vol. 95: Quarter-Master General to Government of India, Political Department, 7 September 1844.
[70] Quotation from Burnett, *Masters*, p. 10; Foliard, *Dislocating*, pp. 31–41.
[71] Derek Waller, *The Pundits: British Exploration of Tibet and Central Asia* (Lexington, KY: The University Press of Kentucky, 1990); Kapil Raj, *Relocating Modern Science: Circulation and the Construction of Knowledge in South Asia and Europe, 1650–1900* (Basingstoke: Palgrave Macmillan, 2007), pp. 181–222.

expressions of a stable and unitary project of colonial power/knowledge. Beset with difficulties in the field, which were only occasionally overcome through forms of 'rhetorical repair', route surveys at the limits of British political control were a diverse set of undertakings, and the circulation of resulting maps was limited. As the remainder of the chapter shows, trigonometrical surveying at India's frontiers held out new promise for generating authoritative data for the colonial state but continued to be afflicted by a range of problems, old and new.

2.2 'Impossible to Level': Frontiers and the Problem of Altitude in the 1850s

According to those who planned and executed it, the run of triangles extended during the 1850s from a coastal base-line at Karachi to the Attock River at the northern limits of recently annexed Punjab fully deserved the appellation 'Great', which was applied to only a select few trigonometrical series. From the outset, however, the Great Indus Series was riddled with difficulties that had palpable effects on its final form. In his initial instructions to the lead surveyor, Surveyor-General Andrew Waugh classified the undertaking as 'essentially a frontier series', and accordingly told him to route the survey 'as near the boundary as political circumstances will admit or physical circumstances render desirable'. Waugh's reiteration of this point – 'keep as near the western frontier as practicable' – amounted to little in the field. Broken terrain and lurid imaginings of tribal violence pushed the line of survey further east, well into colonial territory. In the first season he took the field, the lead surveyor of the southern portion of the Series had a host of complaints: the difficulty of ascending hills, lack of water, severe storms and torrential rain, freezing temperatures, dilapidation to previously built observation towers, and inadequate *puckals* (water carriers). An attack by local inhabitants on a trigonometrical station, which destroyed one heliotrope and damaged another, capped this succession of problems, prompting the lead surveyor to state plainly that 'the series should never have approached so near the frontier'. He abandoned the originally agreed route along the hills that formed the designated boundary of colonial sovereignty in Sind, shifting the series further east – and thereby further from its original designation as a frontier series.[72]

Relocating the Great Indus Series from the hills to the plains may have mitigated the anxieties related to 'political circumstances', but the terrain generated a new array of concerns. Substantially adapted instruments and surveying methods were put to work to surmount these challenges, with varied

---

[72] Details and quotations from R. H. Phillimore, *Historical Records of the Survey of India. Volume V. 1844 to 1861: Andrew Waugh* (Dehra Dun: Survey of India, 1968), pp. 44–45.

perceived success. Their shortcomings were not limited to the realm of temporary aberrations but were understood by leading surveyors to have profound epistemological implications for the possibility of accurate spatial knowledge. Along with the difficulties of limited resources, competing calls on survey parties' time and personnel, and damaged equipment that were part and parcel of what Edney terms the 'cartographic anarchy' of trigonometrical surveying throughout colonial India,[73] the length of the Great Indus Series and the environs through which it was routed generated specific concerns. The components of 'cartographic anarchy' could in theory be overcome: instruments repaired, resources allocated, terrain covered at a later stage. But as GTS parties made their way across the plains of western Punjab and narrated their difficulties, senior survey officials came to perceive an apparently irreducible void between the territory and their representation of it. This was a moment of realisation for those at the apex of the colonial surveying establishment that the map – and even the raw observational data that undergirded map-images – was not, nor could ever aspire to be, the territory.

What precipitated this realisation, and why did it happen during the Great Indus Series rather than in another place, at another time? The surveyors engaged in the field during the mid- to late 1850s wrote mostly of quotidian problems and of overcoming them. They repeatedly discussed their apprehension towards using the 'great theodolite' (a 34-inch theodolite manufactured by Troughton & Simms that reached India in 1830[74]), deemed 'too valuable to risk' in case of attack by frontier communities, especially when armed guards were unavailable during the Indian Rebellion of 1857 to 1858. The difficulty of obtaining labour to construct towers from which to make observations in flatter terrain was another recurring theme in their reports. But these were surmountable difficulties, causing postponements and in some instances requiring re-surveys with the larger theodolite, rather than terminally compromising the accuracy of the work.[75] A knottier issue emerged in the correspondence between John Walker, a lead surveyor on the Series and later Surveyor-General, and Andrew Waugh. The problem concerned 'levelling', the measurement of vertical angles in trigonometrical observations necessary to calculate altitude. Levelling came to Walker's notice as he worked in the flat plains at the western outskirts of Punjab, where the proximity to the ground of the visual 'rays' (lines of sight) that constituted single observations made them prone to distortion in the vertical axis. This phenomenon, generally termed 'refraction', was widely discussed among nineteenth-century surveyors.[76] In

---

[73] Edney, *Mapping*, Ch. 5.   [74] Phillimore, *Historical Records*, Vol. 5, pp. 150–51.
[75] Ibid., pp. 46–9.
[76] Kathryn Yusoff, 'Climates of Sight: Mistaken Visibilities, Mirages and "Seeing Beyond" in Antarctica', in Denis Cosgrove and Veronica della Dora (eds.), *High Places: Cultural Geographies of Mountains, Ice and Science* (London: I.B. Tauris, 2009), pp. 48–63.

this instance, however, Walker claimed that it presented difficulties that con-founded the levelling technique employed on triangulated surveys throughout India of taking vertical angles by theodolite. For Waugh, meanwhile, the Great Indus Series was prominent among an array of considerations that seemed to necessitate new levelling techniques. The error figure in the altitude calculated by connected trigonometrical series that ran from sea level at Hooghly in Bengal to sea level at Karachi was, Waugh complained, 'not sufficiently in keeping with the wonderful precision attainable in all the other results of the survey'.[77] The ongoing extension of the Great Indus Series deep into the continental interior sharpened Waugh's concern. It was, he said, 'a matter of great interest to bring up an accurate datum from the sea to the Himalayas, in connexion with the deter-mination of the heights of those stupendous pinnacles of the earth'.[78] Frontier peaks loomed large in the Surveyor-General's imagination as the ultimate challenge for the determination of altitude by his men and instruments, acting as a key impulse to the development of new ways of levelling.

The adapted technique, using spirit levels in place of problematic theodolite observations, emerged through the interplay of a vast array of elements. Waugh's numerous instructions and his ongoing analysis of the results of Walker's team while they remained in the field constituted attempts at direction from the GTS's headquarters in distant Dehra Dun. But the experimentations of Walker and his retinue in the shadow of frontier uplands at the outskirts of Punjab diluted and sometimes directly contradicted these centralising efforts. Walker assembled a levelling party that included newly recruiting Indian surveyors and assistants. He employed one of these surveyors, Ramchand, on the basis of previous experience with the German explorer Adolf Schlagintweit in Central Asia,[79] seemingly overlooking the low regard in which many Survey officials held the ventures of Schlagintweit and his two brothers.[80] Instruments came from various sources, including three Troughton and Simms spirit levels cadged from the Punjab Canal Department. 'Precision' measuring devices were lost en route and those that remained required a great deal of tinkering in the field to make them work tolerably.[81] Some underwent substantial redesigns, such as the addition of glass cases to levels to protect them from 'currents of air'.[82] Working practices also fluctuated, with surveyors and sets of instruments

[77] IOR/X/39/2: A. S. Waugh, *Report on the Survey of India for the Three Years Ending 1858–59* (London: Her Majesty's Stationery Office, 1863), p. 6.
[78] Ibid. [79] Phillimore, *Historical Records*, Vol. 5, pp. 76–7.
[80] Ibid., pp. 146–7. On the Schlagintweits, see Moritz von Brescius, *German Science in the Age of Empire: Enterprise, Opportunity and the Schlagintweit Brothers* (Cambridge: Cambridge University Press, 2018).
[81] For more on this aspect of instrumental practice in the nineteenth century, see Richard Dunn, 'North by Northwest? Experimental Instruments and Instruments of Experiment', in MacDonald and Withers (eds.), *Geography*, pp. 57–76; Schaffer, 'Easily Cracked'.
[82] Waugh, *Report 1858–59*, p. 7.

deployed in varying combinations in an attempt to mitigate against, in Waugh's words, errors whose 'constant character gave reason for anxiety in regard to their accumulating tendency in a long line of 960 miles'.[83] The Great Indus Series' length was not the only distance that mattered to the surveyors and their superiors in Dehra Dun. Waugh and Walker extolled the production of new levels based on Walker's drawings, a process of communication and manufacture which successfully bridged the 1,500 miles between western Punjab and the GTS's Mathematical Instrument Department in Calcutta tasked with executing modifications.[84] Walker also boasted that 'in the whole distance from the sea to Attock' each levelling observation was exactly equidistant, insinuating that the 'long line' of the Great Indus Series that caused Waugh so much anxiety could be mastered by rigorous sub-division.[85]

The stories that Walker and Waugh told sought to valorise the sprawling assemblage of people, correspondence, and instruments that constituted the ever-shifting levelling operation on the Great Indus Series, acclaiming its ability (under their direction) to overcome the tyranny of distance. In both his 'Short Account of the Levelling Operations of the Great Trigonometrical Survey' submitted to his Survey of India superiors in 1860 and in his paper to the Royal Astronomical Society in London four years later, Walker presented the complex conjunctions of men and instruments he put to work as a pioneering triumph.[86] To his London audience, he compared his undertakings favourably to the levelling executed between Bristol and the English Channel in 1837 for the British Association for the Advancement of Science under the direction of William Whewell, thereby not-so-humbly insinuating that he and the GTS had bettered a leading man of science and institution in the metropole.[87] This element of Walker's renderings of his operations had a long-term impact. In his *Records of the Survey of India* published fifty years after Walker's 'Short Account' (and shortly before his own appointment as Surveyor-General of India), Sidney Burrard stated that 'in 1858 Indian levelling was started upon correct and scientific lines'.[88] Burrard's acclamation of Walker's undertaking echoed Waugh's assessment that 'the work was most ably and scientifically executed'.[89]

In this supposedly monumental feat of 'planning and calculating and adjusting and making secure', it is tempting to detect Heidegger's 'World Picture' in

[83] Ibid.   [84] Ibid.
[85] Waugh, *Report 1858–59*, appendix: J. T. Walker, 'Short Account of the Levelling Operations of the Great Trigonometrical Survey of India', 25 September 1860, p. 27.
[86] Walker, 'Short Account'; J. T. Walker, 'On the Methods of Determining Heights in the Trigonometrical Survey of India', *Memoirs of the Royal Astronomical Society*, 33 (1863–4), pp. 103–14.
[87] Walker, 'Determining Heights', pp. 107–8.
[88] Burrard, quoted in Phillimore, *Historical Records*, Vol. 5, p. 80.
[89] Waugh, *Report 1858–59*, p. 8.

the making.[90] Yet Waugh's report and Walker's narratives indicated something quite different as well. Both detailed their immense frustration at an
insurmountable gap between the survey data and the territory. The newly
developed levelling practices meant that 'differences between observers were
much reduced', but only 'in some cases' did Waugh judge them to have been
'counteracted'. Despite increasingly intricate systems for noting errors and
computing corrections, Waugh opined that 'it is, humanly speaking, impossible to level an instrument practically without some residual error'.[91]
Walker, meanwhile, lingered in his paper to the Royal Astronomical
Society on the 'good deal of uncertainty that exists in reading the [standard]
level', owing to optical distortion of the air bubble within the liquid by which
readings were taken, 'which some observers might guard against more than
others'. Despite the promises of spirit-levelling to have 'no place for personal
errors' on the part of individual surveyors, the experience of the operation in
the Great Indus Series 'lead[s] to the eventual conclusion that these [errors]
may be the largest and most serious of all'.[92] Moreover, Walker avowed, these
'discordances' between individual observers appeared to have been 'continuous' in stable conditions 'of bright sunshine and calm, such as is of frequent
occurrence in tropical countries'.[93] His admission acted contrary to his earlier
effort to raise the colony above the metropole, suggesting instead that, in this
respect, climate terminally disadvantaged the Subcontinent relative to the
British Isles.

Waugh and Walker's accounts exhibit profound ambivalence to the capacities of surveying. While aggrandising the amalgamations of men, missives, and
machines that constituted the GTS as it extended to the mountain fringes of the
Subcontinent (and taking extra care to foreground their own roles in these
processes), they also pondered the seepage of subjective perceptions into
survey data despite their intricate efforts to stem the flow. They acknowledged
that this practical shortcoming had effects well beyond the field. It could not be
elided through sleights-of-hand in centres of calculation and compilation but
instead impacted trigonometrical surveying's epistemological status. However
intricate the instruments, however efficient the passage of materials in networks spanning key offices across the colonial Subcontinent, however well
suited to specific terrains of plains or hills the working methods, however
'scientific' the structure of checks and balances applied to the calculation of
altitude, the experience of the Great Indus Series led leading surveyors of
British India to perceive that human fallibility would always intrude, constituting an unbridgeable void at the most fundamental level between map and
territory.

---

[90] Heidegger, 'Age', p. 135.   [91] Waugh, *Report 1858–59*, p. 7.
[92] Walker, 'Determining Heights', p. 110.   [93] Ibid., p. 114.

2.3   'Rough Accurate Maps': Frontier Representations as Material Objects

Just as the advance of trigonometrical surveying to the edges of colonial India's frontiers from the 1850s had a major impact on the perceived epistemological limits of survey data, so too did it have substantial effects on maps as material objects. It coincided with significant shifts in the production and dissemination of spatial representations of the colonial Subcontinent. This was much more than mere temporal concurrence: effectively representing frontier spaces was among the elements driving the Survey of India to turn to new methods of image reproduction. The Survey's earliest attempts at the unusually laborious, materially intensive, and delicate process of colour lithography were motivated by the desire to depict the extreme topography captured in recent surveys of the Himalaya and portions of the Punjab frontier by allowing for visually striking altitude shading.[94] These attempts were variously successful. The sheets of the Himalaya surveys were widely celebrated, winning a prize medal at the Great Exhibition of England in 1862. On the other hand, an attempt at reproducing a map of the Derajat region to the west of Punjab was a thorough failure, with ill-aligned printing stones and warped paper proving inadequate to the task in hand.[95] The introduction from 1865 of photographic reproduction techniques at the Survey's printing office, following instruction from the Ordnance Survey in Southampton, seemed to have particular merits for frontier maps.[96] Far quicker than lithographic reproduction, which required the preparation of stone imprints for each image, photozincography was heralded for fulfilling what the head of the India Office's Geographical Department Clements Markham termed 'the great demand in India ... not for highly finished, but for rough accurate maps'.[97] Senior surveyors also assumed it would have the benefit of reducing reliance on the 'often uneducated ... Natives' who were an integral part of lithographic reproduction.[98] Photozincography was put to use during frontier military expeditions and the Second Anglo-Afghan War (1878–80), when it allowed for the swift dissemination of such 'rough' maps of relevant regions to army officers.[99]

---

[94] Phillimore, *Historical Records*, Vol. 5, pp. 330–31.   [95] Ibid., p. 330.

[96] Ibid., p. 331; Clements R. Markham, *A Memoir on the Indian Surveys*, 2nd ed. (London: W.H. Allen and Co., 1878), p. 176.

[97] Markham, *Memoir*, p. 177. On photozincography, see Michael Twyman, 'The Illustration Revolution', in David McKitterick (ed.), *The Cambridge History of the Book in Britain. Volume VI: 1830–1914* (Cambridge: Cambridge University Press, 2009), pp. 117–43, here p. 131.

[98] IOR/X/39/6: J. T. Walker, *General Report on the Great Trigonometrical Survey of India and the Topographical Surveys of the Bengal Presidency for 1864–65* (Dehra Dun: GTS, 1866), pp. 40–41.

[99] An example of such a map for use at the northeast frontier, on the 1874 Dafla Expedition, is Cambridge University Library, Maps.B.364.87.1.

This was not, however, a case of the unmitigated triumph of imperial technologies for representing space. The Surveyor-General acknowledged that printing these map-images on calico rather than paper to make them sufficiently hard-wearing to take into the field slightly reduced printing precision and rendered them 'not so well suited for the insertion of correction and additional matter'.[100] By the early twentieth century, the leading frontier surveyor turned London-based man of science Thomas Holdich critiqued photozincography for producing 'crude unfinished-looking sheets which might well lead to an impression of absolute inaccuracy'.[101] These comments remind us that high imperial surveyors and map-users understood maps as working documents designed for specific purposes, which had particular flaws and limitations, rather than perfected and authoritative representations. The demands of depicting frontiers and using maps in them pushed the Survey of India to explore new methods of production that were tolerably fit for purpose. And while leading survey officials extolled the supposed successes, they also fretted over drawbacks and limitations, understanding maps as imperfect material artefacts rather than idealised assertions of spatial mastery.

In some important respects, maps and map-series covering frontier and 'trans-frontier' spaces were consolidated and rationalised through processes that began in earnest from the 1870s. Up to this point, the most widely circulated maps of the northwest and northeast frontiers were relatively small-scale images manufactured on an individual basis. Many of these images drew upon (and acknowledged) numerous sources, combining disparate information and representational conventions with some difficulty, and often recycling idiosyncratic details from the originals. Map-images of particularly sensitive frontier areas were also produced on an ad hoc basis.[102] Commercial presses such as J. B. Tassin's Calcutta-based operation produced frontier maps for public consumption.[103] In part this gap in the market existed because the Survey's own printing capacity was very limited at this time, which also meant that frontier maps such as the 1856 'Map of the Trans-Indus Frontier' had to be sent to London to be lithographed – work that apparently proceeded at a leisurely pace.[104]

From the mid-1860s, the number of maps of frontier regions in circulation increased with the expansion of the Survey of India's printing department. In

---

[100] IOR/V/24/3978: J. T. Walker, *General Report on the Operations of the Survey of India ... during 1879–80* (Calcutta: Government Press, 1881), pp. 40–41.

[101] T. H. H[oldich], 'Report of the Indian Survey Committee, 1904–1905', *The Geographical Journal*, 27, 4 (1906), pp. 392–5, here p. 394.

[102] See, for example, maps of Hazara during the 1850s: NAI Cartographic, Survey of India, F.11/11 (1851 image); NAI Cartographic, Survey of India, F.5/17 (1856 update).

[103] IOR/X/1562/1–4: J. B. Tassin's Map of North-Western Frontier (1848); Phillimore, *Historical Records*, Vol. 5, p. 325.

[104] Phillimore, *Historical Records*, Vol. 5, p. 317.

1864 to 1865 more than 3,000 lithographed copies of the six-sheet 'Map of the North-Eastern Frontier of Bengal, Bhootan and Assam' were produced. A series of trans-frontier maps to represent both trigonometrical surveying and the route surveys of British and Indian explorers was initiated in 1871 to 1872, with the intention of '[proving] useful in studying questions connected with any part of our extensive frontier or with any of the foreign territories lying beyond it'. Accompanying written route plans were printed 'for the use of travellers who are constantly applying to [the Survey] for such information'.[105] A 'North-Eastern Frontier' series was produced from 1884, with multiple editions of most sheets produced to accommodate new survey data. The Intelligence Branch, founded in 1878, took centre stage in compiling and representing spatial information concerning frontiers in map-images and route books, including for military parties sent to enact violence beyond administered British India.[106] In addition, frontier areas were finally included within the published sheets of the 'Atlas of India' project, which had been initiated in the 1820s and was to remain incomplete when superseded in 1905.[107]

A number of factors belied the impression of order given by the incorporation of frontier spaces into new and existing map series. Many sheets within these series continued to draw on multiple data sources, combining various surveying techniques and levels of details. They often contained large blank areas and codified uncertainty in forms such as question marks after toponyms and dashed lines to convey conjectural river courses. A typical example was a note in a 1911 map of uplands to the north of the Brahmaputra Valley: 'Broken lines on this map indicate conjectural features. The position of many villages is doubtful'.[108] Such omissions were not necessarily prompts to expansion or even further surveying, contrary to J. B. Harley's reading of *terra incognita* on European imperial maps in the North American context.[109] For instance, the incumbent Surveyor-General opined in 1861 (wrongly, as it turned out) that the patchy data gathered on the northwest frontier during the 1850s were 'the best and only information we are ever likely to possess' for the sheets of the 'Atlas of India' covering the region.[110] There were also perceived problems with the circulation of even those series

---

[105] IOR/X/39/13: T. G. Montgomerie, *General Report on the Operations of the Great Trigonometrical Survey of India, during 1871–72* (Dehra Dun: GTS, 1872), p. 17.

[106] James Hevia, *The Imperial Security State: British Colonial Knowledge and Empire-Building in Asia* (Cambridge: Cambridge University Press, 2012). An example of an Intelligence Department map is ASA, Maps, No.195: 'Map to Accompany the Preliminary Report on the Chin-Lushai Country Dated December 1892'.

[107] Phillimore, *Historical Records*, Vol. 5, p. 311; British Library, Maps Collection, Survey of India (S.I.) 13.

[108] ASA, Maps, No. 246.   [109] Harley, *New Nature*, pp. 190–91.

[110] H. L. Thuillier, quoted in Phillimore, *Historical Records*, Vol. 5, p. 311.

with large print runs. Holdich claimed in 1906 that there was 'little or no outflow' of maps 'into the thirsty regions of the frontier', meaning that 'officers commanding frontier stations were often lamentably ignorant of their own immediate geographical surroundings'.[111] Many maps, even those in series that aspired to even and universal coverage of portions of the colonial Subcontinent, contained unmistakable marks of fallibility and did not necessarily contribute to projects of frontier administration.

These images were also only an element within a far broader array of frontier spatial renderings produced in the later decades of the nineteenth century. Despite the ostensible strategic sensitivity of the regions to which it pertained, new information on frontiers seeped well beyond the colonial state's departments and personnel. There were significant exchanges of information pertaining to India's frontier regions with French, German, and Russian geographers during this period.[112] These communications resulted in quirks such as the first map of one journey into Central Asia by 'native explorers' being produced not in India or Britain but in Germany by the founding editor of the prominent geographical journal *Petermanns Mittheilungen* (who apologised for the image failing to do 'full justice' to the survey information).[113] The cultural cache of India's frontiers often strained or overrode imperatives to secrecy.[114] As in the case of the Lushai Expedition's 'Correspondents' for the *Indian Express*, agents of empire disseminated spatial knowledge in a range of guises blurring the boundaries of the official and the public. Survey officials were central to the increasing prominence of depictions and descriptions of frontier and trans-frontier spaces in books, periodicals, newspapers, and the meetings and journals of learned societies, especially the RGS.[115] These processes and publications constituted an explosion of fascination among agents of empire and various publics in colony, metropole, and beyond, which was both effect and cause of the bursts of colonial expansion from the late 1860s. The term 'explosion' alludes not only to the quantity of representations but also their frequent mutual incompatibility. Their impact was diverse and dynamic; India's frontiers were not subsumed within unitary and rigid modes of cartographic depiction.

---

[111] T. H. H., 'Report', p. 393.

[112] Waller, *Pundits*, Ch. 9; Royal Geographical Society archives, London (hereafter 'RGS'), JWA/3.

[113] RGS, JWA/3: August Petermann to J. T. Walker, 27 March 1869.

[114] On J. T. Walker's uneasy relationship with the Government of India on issues of secrecy concerning explorations in Central Asia, see Waller, *Pundits*, Ch. 9.

[115] The leading surveyors and publications involved are detailed in the remainder of the chapter. Among the earliest books to foreground frontier surveying was R. G. Woodthorpe, *The Lushai Expedition* (London: Hurst and Blackett, 1873). T. G. Montgomerie began reporting the work of Indian surveyors to the Royal Geographical Society from the late 1860s.

2.4   Sites for 'Sore-Eyes': Surveying in Frontier Regions from the Late 1860s

Let us return from offices, printing presses, and learned societies to 'the field'. The complex and sometimes contradictory nature of colonial knowledge of frontiers during the explosion of the later nineteenth century was not only a product of multiple representations and audiences. Surveyors and 'explorers' were often at the crest of the imperial wave as it broke over portions of India's fringes. From the outset, however, they relied on a host of others: military escorts, locally embedded administrators, and, not least, informants and labourers drawn from frontier populations. The aims, actions, and spatial imaginaries of the heterogeneous actors involved in networks of surveying were frequently far from coordinated, which could have substantial effects on survey data and representations.[116] Perhaps surprisingly, professional surveyors in particular interpreted their roles and the spaces in which they operated in multiple ways. It is to some leading instances of this variation that I now turn, taking forward the story of the Great Indus Series and focusing on moments of crisis during the subsequent decades in which established surveying practices, instruments, and representational techniques seemed inadequate to comprehend India's frontiers.

During the 1850s and 1860s, frontier surveying generally took place from distant vantage points, consisting primarily of theodolite sightings of topographical features beyond the colonial state's administrative limits. Surveyors were primarily concerned with issues of accuracy, seeking to discipline refractory instruments, generate robust working practices, and find means by which the vast distances involved in cartographic data production and transmission could be overcome. Despite their feverish (and not infrequently fever-ridden[117]) activity and efforts to foreground successes in their narratives, they acknowledged their frequent failures to innovate and maintain methods that worked tolerably well. To an even greater extent than the Great Indus Series, trigonometrical surveying in Assam proceeded fitfully and relied on compromises and ad hoc experimentation in working practices to counteract the 'truly lamentable' progress.[118] The glacial pace of progress up the Brahmaputra Valley led to the abandonment of a core principle of the Survey of India that triangulation preceded revenue surveying, forming 'the colossal skeleton' from which the 'sinews and flesh' of the latter could hang.[119]

---

[116] On the complexities of such reliance in the exploration of Central Africa, see Fabian, *Out of Our Minds*, Ch. 2.

[117] Phillimore, *Historical Records*, Vol. 5, p. 467.

[118] NAI Cartography, Dehra Dun Vol. 431: Walker to W. G. Beverley, i/c Assam Valley Triangulation, 28 August 1873.

[119] 'Calcutta Review', undated, quoted in Markham, *Memoir*, p. 118. See also IOR/X/39/14: J. T. Walker, *General Report on the Operations of the Great Trigonometrical Survey of India, during 1872–73* (Dehra Dun: GTS, 1873), pp. 7–8.

Obtaining good sightings with theodolites was a recurrent concern. In contrast to variable refraction in the northwest, visual occlusion in Assam occurred because of profuse vegetation and smoky haze generated by agriculturalists' fires to clear ground for crops.[120] Later surveyors heavily criticised the fixing of frontier peaks during these surveys, suggesting that haste and visual obstructions had caused prominent mountains to be mistaken for each other.[121]

Two central aspects of frontier trigonometrical surveying in the mid-nineteenth century – observing frontiers from a distance and the problematic of 'accuracy' – altered during the following decades. Trigonometrical and topographical survey parties began to enter frontier regions and lone route surveyors, including 'native explorers' or 'pandits', went beyond into Tibet and Central Asia.[122] While concerns over limitations to the accuracy and coverage of survey data persisted as mapping parties took to the frontier hills and deserts, a new anxiety arose among surveyors and others engaged in the construction and assessment of spatial knowledge. Many frontier surveyors and other interested agents began to express what might be termed ontological doubts about whether the numerical data of trigonometrical surveying and the maps that followed could constitute true or complete spatial knowledge. Even as technologically advanced trigonometrical surveying spread to the very outskirts of colonial influence in southern Asia, alternative means of understanding and representing frontier spaces seemed increasingly valid and necessary.

A key aspect of British scepticism towards spatial knowledge of frontier India concerned the roles of Asian people. Non-Europeans were involved in frontier surveying in many forms, ranging from porters, to informants and guides, to assistant surveyors. Only in rare instances was their involvement perceived to achieve the kind of 'circulation' between British and Indian actors that Kapil Raj has identified in the case of Thomas Montgomery 'transforming' his Indian assistant Abdul Hamid into 'an intelligent instrument of measure' able to conduct route surveys in frontier regions.[123] There were fierce debates in India and in metropolitan institutions, especially the RGS, over the reliability of data generated by Indian route surveyors. The 'pandits' had many steadfast supporters, especially among British frontier surveyors such as Thomas

---

[120] X/39/10: J. T. Walker, *General Report on the Operations of the Great Trigonometrical Survey of India, during 1868–69* (Dehra Dun: GTS, 1869), pp. 6–7; NAI, Cartography, Dehra Dun Vol. 431: Walker to W. C. Rossenrode, i/c Eastern Frontier Party, GTS, 13 July 1870; NAI Cartography, Dehra Dun Vol. 431: Walker to Beverley, i/c Assam Triangulation, undated; Walker to H. J. Harman, i/c Assam Triangulation, 14 September 1874.

[121] IOR/V/24/3986: 'Notes by Colonel H. B. Tanner, on Reconnaissances and Explorations in Nepal, Sikkim, Bhutan and Assam', xlviii.

[122] Waller, *Pundits*; Raj, *Relocating*, Ch. 6.

[123] Raj, *Relocating*, pp. 181–3. On circulation, see also Kapil Raj, 'Beyond Postcolonialism ... and Postpositivism: Circulation and the Global History of Science', *Isis*, 104, 2 (2013), pp. 337–47.

Holdich, but other men of geography opined that their data required exceptional validation to make it dependable.[124] For instance, the retired Indian Army officer and orientalist scholar Henry Rawlinson argued that the 'value' of one 'native explorer's' narrative was 'very much enhanced by the fact that his notes had been put together by the Head of the Survey Department, General Walker, whose name was a sufficient guarantee of minute accuracy of detail combined with sound general views of the physical geography of Central Asia'.[125] Racialised notions of variable expertise meant that data produced by non-European personnel were prone to doubt and contestation. In many other cases in frontier locales, knowledge did not circulate between surveyors and local informants, instead meeting immovable obstacles.

British surveyors in the Lushai Hills during the 1880s complained at length of difficulties in fixing villages on their maps as the inhabitants of the hills employed various naming practices and many of the villages moved with annually shifting cultivation.[126] The Surveyor-General noted that in maps of much of the Lushai Hills, he and other surveyors 'considered [it] useless to show the village sites or enter the names of the chiefs, as the information would soon be obsolete'.[127] This region of swidden agriculture seemed fundamentally inimical to the type of fixed information represented on the Survey of India's maps. A distinct difficulty with ascertaining place-names in frontier locales showed on the opposite side of the colonial Subcontinent during a survey operation in 1898 in Malakand. In his public-facing account of this venture, the young journalist Winston Churchill reported a farcical solution to the impossibility of obtaining reliable information when racialised assumptions dominated geographical knowledge production.

Our guide . . . squatted on the ground and pronounced the names of all the villages, as each one was pointed at. To make sure there was no mistake, the series of questions was repeated. This time he gave to each an entirely different name with an appearance of great confidence and pride. However, one unpronounceable name is as good as another, and the villages of the valley will go down to official history, christened at the caprice of a peasant.[128]

---

[124] Waller, *Pundits*, pp. 125–7; Felix Driver, 'Hidden Histories Made Visible? Reflection on a Geographical Exhibition', *Transactions of the Institute of British Geographers*, 38 (2013), pp. 420–35, here p. 427; J. T. Walker, 'Four Years' Journeyings Through Great Tibet, by One of the Trans-Himalayan Explorers of the Survey of India', *Proceedings of the Royal Geographical Society and Monthly Record of Geography*, 7, 2 (1885), pp. 65–92.

[125] Rawlinson, quoted in Walker, 'Four Years', p. 87.

[126] IOR/V/24/3988: 'Report on the Survey Operations with the Chittagong Column, Chin-Lushai Expeditionary Force, by Lieutenant W. J. Bythall', in H. R. Thullier, (ed.), *General Report on the Operations of the Survey of India during 1889–90* (Calcutta: Government Press, 1891).

[127] IOR/V/24/3996: C. Strahan, *General Report on the Operations of the Survey of India during 1897–98* (Calcutta: Government Press, 1899), pp. 24–25.

[128] Winston Spencer Churchill, *The Story of the Malakand Field Force: An Episode of Frontier War* (London: Longmans, Green, and Co., 1899), p. 159.

In this case, toponymic data gathering was portrayed as a comic venture, facilitating the creation of maps that fulfilled the formal expectation of representing named places but lacked any pretension to accuracy. Churchill's anecdote gestures towards moments of incomprehension in the encounters that constituted spatial knowledge even in the era of trigonometrical surveying, which surveyors understood to destabilise the authority of colonial maps.

Another perceived barrier to obtaining spatial knowledge of frontiers was the reliance of large trigonometrical survey parties on a significant number of labourers to carry unwieldy equipment such as theodolites, plane tables, and food supplies. In forested uplands of the northeast, recruits from nearby hill regions were also made to clear ground to enable observations. Obtaining labour was frequently fraught with violence, and in many cases colonial officials found effective communication with porters impossible. The lead surveyor of a triangulated series stretching to the Burmese boundary reported in 1882 that 'I turned the telescope to search for the first of my new stations, and found that the hill had not been touched, but that, through laziness probably, my cutters must have taken to a low hill at half the distance, on which I saw a signal put up'.[129] What colonial personnel derided as indolence was often a result of porters being overburdened and poorly equipped to deal with harsh conditions. One expedition into the Mishmi Hills to the northeast of the Brahmaputra Valley left half of the thirty-strong porterage party frostbitten, with some requiring partial amputations of their feet.[130] The violent and practically problematic use of local labour by survey parties generated difficulties that impacted the quantity and quality of the data collected and showed up as sparsely detailed areas in resulting maps.

When they entered regions beyond the full administration of the colonial state, survey parties often induced fierce resistance, as the march of military retinues coupled with demands for food and supplies constituted an intolerable intrusion. A British surveyor understood Lushais to perceive thirty-foot-high survey marks for theodolite sightings as 'effigies of [Queen Victoria], placed on their hill tops as evidence of her greatness and the power of her army to penetrate where it would'. This perhaps provides a distorted glimpse into how threatening survey materials and practices appeared to some unadministered communities.[131] On other occasions, it seems that frontier inhabitants objected specifically to colonial surveying and maps. One surveyor reported that a community to the north of Assam agreed to allow him into their hills only

---

[129] IOR/V/24/3980: 'Report by Major W. F. Badgley on the Survey of Part of the Burma-Manipur Boundary, Dated February 1882', in J. T. Walker, (ed.), *General Report on the Operations of the Survey of India during 1881–82* (Calcutta: Government Press, 1883), p. 35.

[130] IOR/V/24/3998: 'Narrative Report of Capt. C. L. Robertson on Survey Operations with the Mishmi Expedition', in St. G. C. Gore, (ed.), *General Report on the Operations of the Survey of India during 1899–1900* (Calcutta: Government Press, 1901), appendix pp. 18–19.

[131] Woodthorpe, *Lushai Expedition*, pp. 193–94.

on the conditions that he journey without his military retinue and 'provided I made no map for the Queen to see'.[132]

Violent resistance could impinge on the material ensembles crucial to colonial cartographic knowledge. Accompanying an army column through the Kurram Valley during the Second Anglo-Afghan War in 1878, the surveyor Robert Woodthorpe was shot at. Although his body was merely grazed, 'a piece of his clothes [was driven] into his sketch book, which was considerably damaged'.[133] The bullet had a material impact on the knowledge generated from an opportunistic foray into an otherwise inaccessible region, highlighting the fragility of even the least sophisticated elements within the instrumental repertoires of surveying.[134] Woodthorpe also avowed that on the same expedition, 'the circumstances of hasty marches and hostile people' who deliberately destroyed target marks for theodolite observations rendered the resulting data less accurate than they should have been.[135] The limitations of the survey showed on the map that followed, which contained details only in the valleys and left the uplands largely blank.[136] Here as in many other instances, 'silences' in maps were not only the product of wilful colonial elision as Harley posits[137] but also of all manner of 'states of disrepair' in the complex and delicate assemblages of humans, instruments, and communicative technologies that constituted cartography in high imperial frontiers.[138]

Surveyors' perceptions of resistance to their activities in frontier regions often refused any strict division between human and non-human elements. Nature appeared purposive and threatening. In his diary of a military-survey expedition north of Brahmaputra Valley in 1884, Woodthorpe noted: 'we were attacked but not by Abors: the river had risen rapidly & suddenly a great wave coming down [*sic.*] like a wall'.[139] When attempting to comprehend and convey their more troubled attempts to know frontier spaces, agents of empire often anthropomorphised features of the landscape. One administrator in the Naga Hills claimed to his superior that the Lanier river, flowing through the hills, 'has finally laughed us to scorn by disappearing through the great

---

[132] IOR/X/39/17: J. B. N. Hennessey, *General Report on the Operations of the Great Trigonometrical Survey of India, during 1875–76* (Dehra Dun: GTS, 1877), p. 7.

[133] Walker, *General Report 1878–79*, pp. 49–50.

[134] On the importance of notebooks as instruments of exploration and survey, see Eugene Rae, Catherine Souch and Charles W. J. Withers, '"Instruments in the Hands of Others": The Life and Liveliness of Instruments of British Geographical Exploration, c.1860–c.1930', in Macdonald and Withers (eds.), *Geography, Technology and Instruments of Exploration*, pp. 139–60.

[135] V/24/3978: 'Extract from a Report by Major R. G. Woodthorpe, R. E., Season 1879–80', in J. T. Walker, (ed.), *General Report on the Operations of the Survey of India during 1879–80* (Calcutta: Government Press, 1881), p. 23.

[136] NAI Cartographic, Survey of India, F.113/10.   [137] Harley, *New Nature*, pp. 83–107.

[138] Schaffer, 'Easily Cracked'.

[139] Pitt Rivers Museum archives, Oxford (hereafter 'PRM'), Woodthorpe papers: 'Aka Diary, 1884', 11 March 1884.

Saramethi range instead of continuing on in its northerly course ... the very reverse of that we had all anticipated'.[140] Colonisers' sensations of becoming objects of derision tended to be powerful: we might think of George Orwell's comment some decades later that 'every white man's life in the East ... was one long struggle not to be laughed at'.[141] To those concerned with knowing space rather than just governing people, topography could be every bit as mocking as humans. The explorer Francis Younghusband, meanwhile, conceived of the landscape in Gilgit as actively restrictive when writing of 'precipitous moun-tains which forbade [his travel companion] following any route than that which led down the valley of the river he was in'.[142] Surveyors' and explorers' attributions of agency to particular features of frontier landscapes were numer-ous and significant. Collectively, they indicate that agents at the fringes of the colonial subcontinent often perceived themselves surrounded by all too lively natural forces, under threat of being mastered by all they sought to survey.

During the later nineteenth century, surveyors increasingly felt that climate and terrain in frontier India presented major impediments to generating satis-factory data. Although when viewed from a distance or summited with favour-able conditions, mountains were integral to the production of spatial knowledge of India's frontiers, being among the peaks and ridges often under-mined trigonometrical and topographical surveying. In written accounts, many frontier surveyors oscillated between admitting the cartographic shortcomings induced by extreme topography and celebrating these elements in the course of aggrandising their own labour. This was particularly apparent in surveys north of Assam from the mid-1870s on, which tended to accompany military exped-itions, giving them limited time and few opportunities to rectify shortcomings. Woodthorpe and his retinue were unable to progress far into the Miri and Mishmi Hills in 1877 and 1878 as although 'the few inhabitants of the country were friendly, ... the physical difficulties were great and the weather most unfavourable, rain poured in torrents, rendering the jungle paths almost impass-able, and greatly impeding the movements of the party'.[143] Operating in broken terrain with few major paths, the surveyors were forced to travel by unusual means. A keen artist (see Section 3.4), Woodthorpe delighted in sketching his travails and pronounced himself satisfied with the 'very fairly reproduced' lithographed version of one image for the GTS's annual report (Figure 2.3).[144] Clearly, the labour of surveying mattered to Woodthorpe and his

[140] NAI Foreign Political A, April 1874, No.177: John Butler, Naga Hills Deputy Commissioner, to Assam Chief Commissioner, 25 February 1874, f. 3.

[141] George Orwell, *Shooting an Elephant and Other Essays* (London: Penguin, 2003), p. 38; see also Fabian, *Out of Our Minds*, pp. 95–8.

[142] RGS, Younghusband papers, CB7/102: Younghusband to Douglas Freshfield, 13 June 1893.

[143] IOR/V/24/3976: J. T. Walker, *General Report on the Operations of the Survey of India during 1877–78* (Calcutta: Surveyor General's Office, 1879), p. 16.

[144] RGS, JWA/2: Woodthorpe to Walker, 27 June 1878.

Figure 2.3 Robert Woodthorpe, sketches to illustrate 'a curious kind of bridge'
across the Dibong River (1878). © The British Library Board.[145]

institutional superiors, the act of crossing the Dibong River by a 'curious kind
of bridge' being presented as an exotic curiosity and a heroic undertaking.[146]
But the sketch also indicated Woodthorpe's inability to progress far through the
frontier hills. This shortcoming showed on maps that relied on this survey,
including the 1882 Indian Atlas sheet covering the region, which contained
blank patches and one sizeable tract without topographical detail labelled
'uninhabited jungle'.[147]

---

[145] Walker, *General Report 1877–78*, facing p. 125.

[146] On masculine heroism as a key component of British field sciences in the Victorian era, see
Bruce Hevly, 'The Heroic Science of Glacier Motion', *Osiris*, 11 (1996), pp. 66–86. On
representations of bridges across rivers as a colonial visual trope, see Mueggler, *Paper
Road*, pp. 39–41.

[147] ASA, Maps No.1079: Indian Atlas, sheet 138 N.W.

Occasionally, reaching a frontier summit afforded surveyors viewpoints from which to take in far greater expanses than was possible in lower areas. But often lines of sight remained limited and underwhelming: in the northeast especially, fog and smoke from fires used by both *jhuming* and sedentary agriculturalists rendered the sightings necessary for trigonometrical and topographical surveying 'an absolute impossibility'.[148] During his trigonometrical work in the Naga Hills during the 1870s, Woodthorpe reported that mist limited the visual field to 'the country immediately bordering our march'. The resulting observations were akin to those on a route survey rather than the comprehensive triangulation intended.[149] Reporting to his superiors on his work in similar atmospheric conditions on the opposite side of the Brahmaputra Valley eight years later, Woodthorpe repeated a phrase he had employed in his private diary in the Naga Hills, admitting that he identified some topographical features through '"guesses at truth"'.[150]

Topographical surveying could be even more difficult than triangulation in labyrinthine hills. As the Surveyor-General described in 1865, 'to execute work of this style, the ground must be open to view, and not hid by forests and jungle, as is very frequently the case; it is often impossible to see the same point from two places'. To hack down forests in order to unveil every topographical detail, he opined, 'would be too laborious and expensive, and would cause much havoc and injury'.[151] For this reason, surveys in the Khasi and Garo Hills during the 1860s were conducted at half the standard topographical scale.[152] Surveyors engaged in the region also estimated distances to particular points from a single view, meaning that the accuracy of data seemed to the Survey of India to depend to an even greater extent than usual 'on the skill and integrity of the Surveyor'.[153] All manners of problems could compromise these very qualities, not least the extreme prevalence of illness including one case that struck at the visual foundations of topographical surveying, self-diagnosed as

---

[148] The quotation relates to surveying in the Lushai Hills in 1898–99. IOR/V/24/3997: St. G. C. Gore, *General Report on the Operations of the Survey of India during 1898–99* (Calcutta: Government Press, 1900), p. 27.

[149] IOR/L/P&S/7/11, ff. 115–20, pp. 5–6.

[150] IOR/V/24/3983: 'Extract from the Narrative Report of Lieutenant-Colonel R.G. Woodthorpe, in charge No. 6 Party, North-East Frontier Topographical Survey', in G. C. De Prée, (ed.), *General Report on the Operations of the Survey of India during 1883–84* (Calcutta: Government Press, 1885), ix; Pitt Rivers Museum archives, Oxford (hereafter 'PRM'), Woodthorpe Papers: 'Naga Hills Diary, 1876', f. 15.

[151] IOR/X/39/6: J. T. Walker, *General Report on the Great Trigonometrical Survey of India and the Topographical Surveys of the Bengal presidency for 1864–65* (Dehra Dun: GTS, 1866), p. 5.

[152] IOR/X/39/7: J. T. Walker, *General Report on the Great Trigonometrical Survey of India and the Topographical Surveys of the Bengal Presidency for 1865–66* (Dehra Dun: GTS, 1866).

[153] Walker, *General Report 1864–65*, pp. 4–5.

'sore-eyes'.[154] The lack of internal checks and balances in topographical surveying (unlike trigonometrical surveying) further exacerbated these problems, the only method of verifying data being to re-survey. When such work was undertaken in the Khasi and Garo Hills, it was discovered that the surveys of the 1860s contained such 'very glaring discrepancies' that the 'offending Surveyors' were fined and dismissed.[155] 'Defective' data continued to be unearthed over a decade later, requiring laborious revisions to maps of the area.[156]

The expansive deserts of the Sind frontier and Balochistan came with their own problems of vision during the simultaneous extension of triangulation, topographical surveying, and reconnaissance work from the late 1870s. The region's drifting sands prompted questions over the appropriateness of representing it through conventional data and maps. G. P. Tate, who was deputed to the northwestern reaches of Balochistan with the Baloch-Afghan boundary commission in 1895, noted that maps of the area based on reconnaissance work undertaken less than a decade previously were wholly unreliable. The majority of the region, he reported, 'is covered with a sea of sand-hills'. These were inexplicable by extant western terms, Tate opined, instead requiring Baloch categories of 'drift sand and those sand-hills which are fairly stable; the former they call *bud*, and the latter *reg* or *rek*'.[157] The extreme temperatures in Balochistan led survey parties to race through as quickly as possible, abandoning efforts at ascertaining altitude by levelling and instead using boiling point observations, which senior survey officials widely disparaged.[158] Sandstorms and mirages frequently obscured or distorted vision, making it 'most difficult to take observations during the greater portion of the day'.[159] Adjustments to raw data or the use of different instruments could not overcome these problems. It was not only the sand that moved: the degree of refraction fluctuated wildly and, as one surveyor admitted, 'delude[d] even the most experienced. Objects invisible at one moment would at the next be seen far above the eye of the spectator'.[160]

Among the high mountains north of Punjab and Kashmir, visual occlusion took another form. In his account of surveying the towering landscape near Chitral in the mid-1880s, Woodthorpe recounted the distinctly limited field of sight. 'From the low elevation of his route', he wrote,

[154] Thuillier, *General Report 1888–89*, p. 70.   [155] Ibid., p. 5.
[156] Walker, *General Report 1877–78*, pp. 22–23.
[157] IOR/V/24/3994: C. Strahan, *General Report on the Operations of the Survey of India during 1895–96* (Calcutta: Government Press, 1897), ii.
[158] Ibid., iii.
[159] Quotation from Walker, *General Report 1878–79*, p. 7. See also G. P. Tate, *The Frontiers of Baluchistan: Travels on the Borders of Persia and Afghanistan* (London: Witherby and Co., 1909), p. 35.
[160] De Prée, *General Report 1883–84*, x.

BRIDGE AND PATH, CHITRÁL.

Figure 2.4   G. M. J. Giles, 'Bridge and Path, Chitral' (1885) © The British Library Board.[161]

it is seldom that the traveller sees the higher peaks and ranges on either side. His view is bounded by the bare precipices and fantastic pinnacles of the lower ranges, and as he crosses, with discomfort, the shingle slopes every [*sic*] ready to move down under his weight, he gazes upwards with wonder at their vast height and at the frowning rocks above.[162]

A photograph on the following page, labelled 'Bridge and Path, Chitral', reinforced the integral features of this space as described in the text. The image is significantly underexposed, and its right quarter wholly occupied by a dark, looming cliff (Figure 2.4). A small, silhouetted figure stands on the narrow path bounding the cliff face – the same path from which the photograph was taken – with a river lurking below.

In stark contrast to Romanticist landscape images depicting an individual occupying the 'summit position' above the surrounding environs,[163] neither the

---

[161] Ibid., facing p. 15.
[162] W. S. A. Lockhart and R. G. Woodthorpe, *The Gilgit Mission 1885–86* (London: Eyre and Spottiswoode, 1889), p. 14.
[163] I have adopted the term 'summit position' from Peter H. Hansen's account of modernity and mountaineering, *The Summits of Modern Man: Mountaineering after the Enlightenment* (Cambridge, MA: Harvard University Press, 2013). For more on Romanticist images of individuals within landscapes, see Hugh Honour, *Romanticism* (New York, NY: Westview, 1979), pp. 78–79.

photographer nor the figure in shot has a privileged vantage point. They are trapped within the maze of mountains, with no immediate prospect of attaining the surrounding heights. The photograph portrays the overwhelming scale of the surrounding terrain while supporting a narrative of the intrepidness of those men who laboured through it. Surveyors' tales of being overcome by the scale and knottiness of frontier spaces were, then, simultaneously expressions of anxiety and self-attributions of heroism. The tension maintained in these accounts and images represented instances in which the surveyors' vision was not so much that of Apollo, gazing down serenely, as that of fallen Icarus, or of Dionysus, befuddled and intoxicated by the surrounding grandeur.[164]

2.5   'A Higher Land': Theorising the Unknowable Frontier

When vision failed or seemed unreliable, surveyors and explorers often admitted a sense of being lost in frontier space. The sense of being engulfed by the vastness and complexity of frontier landscapes is especially apparent in the soldier-mountaineer Charles Bruce's claim that a party of troops marching through the high peaks of Chilas 'had to all intents and purposes disappeared into space'.[165] In contrast to the immovable labyrinths of uplands, the danger of deserts to the British lay in their lack of features and mutability. A report written by a newspaper correspondent who travelled with the surveyors and political agents of the Baloch-Afghan boundary commission told of how a number of guides became separated from the main party in 'a perfect hurricane' and 'were only accidentally found, nearly dead'. The correspondent continued, 'One can imagine no more horrible death than that from being lost in this desert country'.[166] The overriding sensation that many surveyors and explorers conveyed not only to the adventure-hungry public but also in ostensibly authoritative reports to institutional superiors was that of being overwhelmed by frontier spaces. In such instances, we can discern a 'sentimental' protagonist akin to the figure that Mary Louise Pratt identifies in many British travel accounts around the turn of the nineteenth century.[167] The appearance of the narrator in accounts of frontier spaces as a man 'composed of a whole body rather than

---

[164] On Icarian knowledge, see de Certeau, *Practice*, pp. 91–110; Burnett, *Masters*, pp. 175–76. On the opposition of Apollo and Dionysus, see Friedrich Nietzsche, *The Birth of Tragedy and Other Writings*, ed. Raymond Geuss and Ronald Speirs, trans. Ronald Speirs (Cambridge: Cambridge University Press, 1999).

[165] C. G. Bruce, *Twenty Years in the Himalaya* (London: Edward Arnold, 1910), p. 197.

[166] F. P. Maynard (ed.), *Letters on the Baluch-Afghan Boundary Commission of 1896* (Calcutta: Baptist Missionary Press, 1896), pp. 61–3.

[167] Pratt, *Imperial Eyes*, Ch. 4.

a disembodied eye' to whom 'things happen ... and he endures and survives' suggests that the travelling, corporeal self was not always minimised or erased in knowledge-producing ventures in the later nineteenth century.[168] Instead, this subject was not only revivified but enhanced by a distinct formulation of the spaces in which he operated. Unlike British representations of India's jungles and uplands in the earlier nineteenth century as dangerous but also amenable to improvement,[169] the mountains and deserts of the high imperial frontier were generally constructed as unreformable.

The significance of this shift is apparent if we consider the man whose writings most vividly expressed the benefits of maintaining frontiers as fundamentally elusive spaces in which to lose oneself: Francis Younghusband, the explorer, Indian Army officer, and later President of the RGS. In both official and popular accounts of his explorations in the late 1880s and 1890s of the high mountains between northern British India and Central Asia, Younghusband first expressed the spiritualist leanings that were to become an integral feature of his perceptions of geography and empire. 'Separated from the haunts of civilisation by chain after chain of inhospitable mountains', he wrote in his official report of an 1889 mission to gather knowledge of routes between Kashmir and Central Asia, 'I seemed, indeed, to be intruding on the abode of some great invisible but all-pervading Deity – the Emblem of Eternal Rest – and to have risen from the world beneath to a higher land'.[170] Notwithstanding his fastidious perusal of *Hints to Travellers* to learn the basics of surveying, and his rendering of numerous map-images,[171] Younghusband later conveyed that his experiences north of Kashmir led him to doubt the efficacy of disenchanted vision alone. 'Clearly it is not the eye, but the soul that sees ... The whole panorama may be vibrating with beauties that we ordinary men cannot appreciate'.[172] Younghusband's conception of the mountainous frontier as an essentially spiritual space, the seminal features of which could not be fixed by a mechanical gaze nor represented by maps, were widely communicated and deemed sufficiently credible for him to reach the institutional pinnacle of imperial geography. He was also far from alone in describing portions of British India's frontier as exceeding conventionally knowable space. George

---

[168] The quotation is from ibid., p. 78. See also David Arnold, *The Tropics and the Traveling Gaze: India, Landscape, and Science 1800–1856* (Delhi: Permanent Black, 2005), pp. 228–29; Lorraine Daston and Peter Galison, *Objectivity* (New York, NY: Zone Books, 2007).

[169] Arnold, *Tropics*, chs. 3–4; K. Sivaramakrishnan, 'British Imperium and Forested Zones of Anomaly in Bengal, 1767–1833', *The Indian Economic and Social History Review*, 33, 3 (1996), pp. 243–82.

[170] F. E. Younghusband, *Report of a Mission to the Northern Frontier of Kashmir in 1889* (Calcutta: Government of India Press, 1890), p. 41.

[171] See RGS, GFY/1/4: Younghusband's copy of *Hints to Travellers* used on his 1887 overland journey from Peking to India.

[172] Francis Younghusband, *Kashmir* (London: Adam and Charles Black, 1909), pp. 15–16.

Robertson, a doctor in the Indian Army, wrote of his travels to the same region a year before Younghusband: 'the fantastic thought arose in my mind that behind that transparency, that translucent cloud-film, a veritable faery country had been revealed to me, stretching far into the nothingness beyond'.[173] Feeling lost, not being able to trust sensory data, and experiencing a connection between self and surroundings that eluded description or depiction: these were exactly the sensations that many high imperial explorers and surveyors sought, and claimed to find, at India's frontiers.

These men also perceived that topographical features or spatial knowledge could become 'lost' at frontiers. In a heavily illustrated paper to the RGS on the uplands north of Punjab and Kashmir, Younghusband labelled a moodily stylised rendering of a jagged mountain, from a drawing by the senior surveyor Henry Tanner (of whom more shortly), 'a lost snowpeak, Hindu Kush' (Figure 2.5). Notions of being adrift also occurred in some attempts to extend trigonometrical series into the frontier hills. These undertakings had to depart from previously 'fixed' stations, requiring that the surveyors first rediscovered such a station. Moments of belated connection with existing series were celebrated as near-providential events.[174] But at other times no such connection was made. One such instance was the survey of the Mishmi Hills at the turn of the twentieth century, undertaken to rectify the omissions of Woodthorpe's party with its crossing of the 'curious kind of bridge' two decades earlier. The lead surveyor found that the many of the stations established twenty years earlier in the Assam Triangulation Series

had been entirely carried away by the different large rivers, and the forest had everywhere grown up to such an extent which not only made it very difficult to find such stations as were still extant, but which, when they were found, rendered it impossible to see anything from them without an expenditure of time and labour in jungle-clearing which, in the present instance, it was not possible to undertake.[175]

These circumstances meant that trigonometrical calculations in the frontier hills could not be integrated into the GTS's grid that spread across colonial India: the entire survey itself was lost, unmoored from the rest of the triangulated subcontinent.

Into the last decades of the nineteenth century, there remained a strong concern among imperial agents with obtaining the types of appropriately noted theodolite sightings and topographical details that were taken to constitute accurate survey data. There was also a keen awareness of the potential

---

[173] George Scott Robertson, *The Kafirs of the Hindu-Kush* (London: Lawrence & Bullen, 1896), vii–viii.

[174] For example, Thomas Holdich's description of the Pamirs triangulation in 'The Use of Practical Geography Illustrated by Recent Frontier Operations', *The Geographical Journal*, 13, 5 (1899), pp. 465–77; here pp. 474–75.

[175] Gore, *General Report 1899–1900*, appendix p. 18.

Figure 2.5 Henry Tanner, 'A lost snowpeak, Hindu Kush' (1895). Reproduced by kind permission of the Syndics of Cambridge University Library.[176]

limitations to obtaining such information, along with plentiful discussion of what constituted appropriate cartographic representation. However, frontier surveyors and officials during this period increasingly called into question whether survey data and maps could ever convey the truth of frontier spaces. Some suggested that the extreme topography and sublime vistas that formed the essence of frontiers demanded direct experience and could not be reduced to textual or visual representations, especially not a top-down, flattened map perspective. Frontier maps were prone to sceptical receptions, especially from those with first-hand experience of the regions represented. Take, for example, a Punjab frontier official's claim in his 1890 memoir that 'to look at a frontier map, even one of those famous India Office "large maps," ... does not convey much idea of that country'.[177]

Surveyors' accounts of frontiers increasingly diverged from Edney's observation that colonial geographical narratives were 'textual equivalent[s] of the purely mechanistic vision that creates an unassailable distance between the observer and observed'. Instead of 'reject[ing] self-reference' such that 'geographical observation was turned outward from, not in toward, the British self', surveyors in the late nineteenth century described themselves as thoroughly

---

[176] F. E. Younghusband, 'Chitral, Hunza, and the Hindu Kush', *The Geographical Journal*, 5 (1895), pp. 409–26, here p. 410.

[177] Edward E. Oliver, *Across the Border or Pathan and Biloch* (London: Chapman and Hall, 1890), p. 274.

entangled with the surrounding environs.[178] Many accounts placed the surveyor's vulnerable body centre stage. In his memoirs, Thomas Holdich described himself at the high mountain summit of the Takht-i-Suliman in 1883, 'chained ... to the theodolite in spite of chattering teeth and numbed fingers'.[179] Holdich and most other frontier surveyors also wrote extensively in both published accounts and official correspondence of the journeys they undertook to reach the sites at which they collected their data. In contrast to Tim Ingold's claim that agents of modern western knowledge presented processes of data collection as a uniform series of immediate and static observations,[180] frontier surveyors' accounts freely attested to involuntary corporeal movements and celebrated improvised instrumental practices. Admitting the potential failings of knowledge production seemed a price worth paying for the opportunity to emphasise heroic labour.

As part of this tendency to place themselves within the landscape, surveyors frequently invoked sublime aesthetics. One instance was G. P. Tate's popular account of surveying the Neza-i-Sultan, a steep-sided shaft of rock near the meeting point of the Persian, Afghan, and Balochistan borders. 'It was a brilliant moonlit night', Tate wrote, 'and the shaft of the great mass of agglomerates standing out against the dark blue sky oppressed our minds by its towering heights and vast dimensions. The description we had read of this stupendous column in Sir Charles Macgregor's book[181] entirely failed to convey the impression we derived from our visit to the Neza'.[182] His description implied that certain features of the frontier could not be accessed from removed representations, the immersive experience being accessible only from a grounded, embodied vantage point. The critique of Macgregor's recent written description indicated that imperial spatial knowledge was far from cumulative or uniform. And Tate's view of the scene was a disconcerting experience, not an exercise in assured mastery and stable understanding.

One of the most significant attempts to formulate alternative modes of representing frontier spaces appeared in the writings of one of Tate's contemporaries, Henry Tanner. Tanner was part of a generation of surveyors whose work centred on the fringes of the colonial subcontinent, ranging from Balochistan to the high mountains north of Punjab and the Himalaya around Darjeeling and north of Assam. His concerns returned to the problems of understanding altitude that had been in play since the extension of triangulation

---

[178] Edney, *Mapping*, pp. 66–8.   [179] Holdich, *Indian Borderland*, p. 88.
[180] Tim Ingold, *Lines: A Brief History* (London: Routledge, 2007), pp. 88–89.
[181] The reference is to Charles Metcalfe Macgregor's *Wanderings in Balochistan* (London: W.H. Allen & Co., 1882), which has a sketch of the Neza facing p. 191 and describes it (p. 170) as a 'really wonderful peak' that 'looked as if it was the ruin of one of the towers which are seen in various parts of Persia. Yet of course it could not be one of these, as it was of too enormous dimensions to be the work of man'.
[182] Tate, *Frontiers*, p. 44.

to the mountainous fringes of British India under Andrew Waugh. After leading a trigonometric survey party to Gilgit in 1879 to 1880, which claimed to have 'fixed' 145 peaks beyond the bounds of administered British India, Tanner became acutely aware of the shortcomings of data collected when working among frontier mountains and valleys. 'I do not wish it to be understood that the points have the accuracy of those hitherto accepted by the Great Trigonometrical Survey', he stated, since he was able to take observations from only a few viewing points owing to the difficulty of moving among the valleys and passes of Gilgit. Individual observations were also liable to inaccuracies, Tanner warned, as 'on some of the peaks it was necessary to place the instrument [theodolite] at the very edge of giddy precipices, and then, sometimes, one only of the verniers of the horizontal limb could be read, and that with considerable risk and difficulty'.[183] Here once again we see agents of imperial cartography 'trembling', but, *contra* Latour, choosing not to 'purify' these experiences through narrative elision and instead admitting the epistemic consequences of their fallibility even in official correspondence.

Under these circumstances of dubious instrumental practices, Tanner turned to alternative registers to convey the landscape. Even his official report to the Survey of India overlooked data, instead focusing impressionistically on the 'fantastic shapes', the 'vast wilderness of isolated mountains', and 'the faint, cloud-like group round [the high peak] Tirich Mir' that he had discerned as he stood at Gurunjur, then the most northerly station connected to the grid of GTS triangulation. In the same narrative, he characterised the view of the northern slopes of the huge peak of Nanga Parbat as 'the most magnificent snow view on the globe', beyond description by his 'feeble pen'.[184] In a retelling of his vision of Nanga Parbat to the RGS in 1891, Tanner delighted in the absolute removal of this frontier scene from British India, saying: 'Facing you stretch the slopes of pure snow, untainted with the dust of the plains'.[185] Having taken charge of the Darjeeling and Nepal boundary surveys, which afforded opportunities to observe the highest Himalayan peaks further to the east, Tanner returned to question of what constituted knowledge of mountain spaces at the fringes of the subcontinent. Far from being rectified, his faith in the possibility of precisely calculating the heights of these peaks continued to wane. 'From an extensive experience in Himalayan surveying', he wrote to the Surveyor-General in 1884,

I can safely state that even when carrying on our work with the aid of the best maps, instruments, and requisite knowledge of surveying, we are liable, until we compute the

---

[183] Walker, *General Report 1879–80*, p. 42.   [184] Ibid., p. 43.

[185] H. C. B. Tanner, 'Our Present Knowledge of the Himalayas', *Proceedings of the Royal Geographical Society and Monthly Record of Geography*, 13, 7 (1891), pp. 403–23, here p. 407.

positions of our points, to mistake one mountain for another, even though we may have learnt their appearance by heart from other stations ... Two of my assistants last year mistook other mountains for Everest, and I myself recorded "Everest" against a mountain 5,000 feet lower than it.[186]

In this same report, Tanner admitted that he assumed different distances to Himalayan mountains even after numerous theodolite observations, giving a range of possible altitudes and 'never pretending to fix the peaks absolutely'.[187]

As well as freely admitting the difficulties of ascertaining altitude and the tendency for the Himalaya to remain elusive even after extended experience of them, Tanner suggested the limitations of defining high peaks by altitude above sea level. In his 1884 report and again in the paper he gave to the RGS in 1891, he provided a table comparing various mountains in the Greater Himalaya along with Mont Blanc.[188] The table relegated the importance of altitude – the metric that Waugh had couched as the pride of GTS operations, but which Tanner merely termed their 'accepted' rank – and instead advanced the heights of the faces of these mountains relative to the surrounding topographical features as the true measure of their significance. By this measure, he crowned Nanga Parbat, which was widely celebrated and depicted in non-map forms by his contemporaries in the survey cadre (Figure 2.6), as 'king of mountains'. His rationale for this alternative measure was aesthetic. Notwithstanding his claim that Nanga Parbat 'baffles description', Tanner described his experience as a grounded observer taking in the north face of the mountain in 1880:

It is a scene that is not grasped or taken in at once, but after a while the stupendous grandeur of the view is appreciated. It is quite overwhelming in its magnitude; it is in fact one of the grandest spectacles that nature offers to the gaze of man. Great height, vast breadth, and appalling depth are combined, and like the panorama of the Tibet snow, as described to me by Captain Harman, it is "immense." There is nothing small or mean about it; it is on a scale which is gigantic.[189]

In rendering Nanga Parbat, Tanner evoked the sense of gargantuan scale and hints of terror that were central constituents of the sublime. His conclusion that Nanga Parbat's unique importance lay in its 'immense' and 'gigantic' appearance also provides an opening for understanding the distinctive character of late nineteenth-century frontier surveying from what went before and elsewhere: through reading it alongside Martin Heidegger's notion of 'the gigantic'. Heidegger posited that 'the gigantic' – for example, huge numbers in the sciences and the annihilation of distances through technologies – advances as modern man 'brings into play his unlimited power for the calculating, planning

---

[186] De Prée, *General Report 1883–84*, xxxii.   [187] Ibid., xxxiii.
[188] Ibid., xxxiii–xxxv; Tanner, 'Present Knowledge', p. 408.
[189] De Prée, *General Report 1883–84*, xxxiii–xxxiv.

Figure 2.6 Thomas Holdich, 'Nanga Parbat from the Bunji Valley of the Indus' (*c*.1895) © Royal Geographical Society (with IBG).[190]

and moulding of things'.[191] This conception broadly accords with familiar renderings of high imperial mapping that foreground its fantastically huge calculations and supposed power to generate univocal renderings of space. But in exploring what was at stake in conceiving frontier spaces in late nineteenth-century British India, we should work with Heidegger's subsequent claim that

as soon as the gigantic ... becomes a special quality, then what is gigantic, and what can seemingly always be calculated completely becomes, precisely through this, incalculable. This becoming incalculable remains the invisible shadow that is cast around all things everywhere when man has been transformed into *subiectum* and the world into a picture. By means of this shadow the modern world extends itself out into a space withdrawn from representation.[192]

Tanner's admission of the limitations of trigonometrical surveying in the face of the 'gigantic' scales at play in frontier topography points towards the ambivalence that Heidegger conjures here. The seeming triumph of immense technological assemblages centring on a masterful subject – in this case the extension of theodolites, men, and instrumental paraphernalia to some of the

[190] RGS, X610/023579.   [191] Heidegger, 'Age', pp. 134–35.   [192] Ibid., pp. 135–36.

most intractable places on earth – seemed simultaneously to reveal a margin that remained elusive and unknowable through such means. This margin developed from the realisation among leading surveyors engaged in the Great Indus Series during the 1850s that there was an irreducible gap between raw survey data and territory, and thereby a limit to cartographic improvement. By the 1880s and 1890s, the concept of 'a space withdrawn from representation' took on an enhanced, distinctive form among frontier surveyors and explorers. Often construed as both integral constituent and ultimate product of the construction of the world-as-picture in 'the modern age',[193] as the nineteenth century drew to a close maps seemed to many surveyors whose fieldwork undergirded them to be unable to represent frontier spaces in full. These regions instead seemed to demand embodied, spiritualised experience. Having developed the means to calculate them completely enough for almost any practical purpose, surveyors insisted that frontier environs had become incalculable.

2.6   Conclusion: 'Clean Out of the Map'

Surveyors and explorers of Tanner's era began to call into question the value and meaning of survey data in regions that seemed to call for embodied, sublime experience. Frontiers went from being the ultimate challenge for calculation and representation, to instead become spaces that called in question the ability of such practices to constitute true and complete spatial knowledge. Immersed in the vertical and horizontal expanses of the high imperial frontier, surveyors imagined themselves to be 'clean out the map' not only in having ventured beyond extant cartographic knowledge but by virtue of being in locales that seemed to reveal the limitations of such knowledge.

This chapter has shown how the rigours of trigonometrical sightings of frontier regions in the mid-nineteenth century caused leading surveyors in colonial India to perceive an irreducible margin between survey data and territory. It has suggested that agents involved in frontier surveying were intensely aware not only of the potential shortcomings of producing data but also of representing it, extensively pondering the labour-intensive processes of producing and circulating maps. It has traced the appearance of seemingly intractable barriers to the successful prosecution of surveys when trigonometrical parties began to enter frontier regions in the later decades of the nineteenth century. Finally, it has suggested that one key development of this era was the advent of a widely shared notion of frontiers as spaces that eluded map representation, demanding alternative modes of engagement. In sum, the

---

[193] For example, Martin Jay and Sumathi Ramaswamy, 'Section I: The Imperial Optic', in id (eds.), *Empires of Vision: A Reader* (Durham, NC: Duke University Press, 2014), pp. 23–43, here p. 33.

chapter presents surveying and spatial knowledge in the era of high empire as an altogether more fraught and uncertain endeavour than has been generally understood. Far from considering themselves masters of the surrounding terrain, surveyors and explorers were sharply conscious of limitations to survey data and maps that could not always be elided or fixed at a later stage. Unlike their predecessors in the jungles and uplands of the subcontinent, they did not maintain faith in the possibility of adapting and improving the landscapes in which they were entangled, instead maintaining that these regions posed challenges of an insurmountable nature. They were altogether more reflective and reflexive – and their numerical, written, and visual representations were far less assured and monolithic – than many recent accounts of modern imperial cartography have allowed for. A shadow accompanied their attempts to proclaim their own heroism and celebrate the gigantic technological assemblages that they put to work: the idea that frontier spaces could overwhelm both the surveyor's self and the knowledge he produced.

This oscillation between celebrating and fearing the notion that India's frontiers exceeded representation was among the earliest and most influential doubts among British agents of empire over the value of spatial knowledge. Concerns first expressed in the 1860s that opportunities for 'discovery' were becoming ever sparser drove a pervasive sense of crisis in British imperial exploration and geography around the turn of the twentieth century.[194] And as Priya Satia has elucidated, a conjuncture of cultural or 'metaphysical' uncertainties, preferences for a pure, minimalist aesthetic, and epistemological doubts generated among imperial agents of the early twentieth century the notion that Arabia was a 'land of mirage, myth, and imprecise borders'.[195] To Satia's list of factors we can add the prevalence of officials who had cut their teeth at India's frontiers among the British cadre in the Middle East.[196] As this chapter has evidenced, a similar set of concerns encompassing knowledge, self, and spirituality were entangled with understandings of high imperial India's mountain and desert outskirts. Going 'clean out of the map' may have expressed limits to spatial knowledge but also provided a new playground for men bored by unprecedented imperial domination.

---

[194] Charles W. J. Withers, *Geography and Science in Britain, 1831–1939: A Study of the British Association for the Advancement of Science* (Manchester: Manchester University Press, 2010), p. 85.

[195] Priya Satia, *Spies in Arabia: The Great War and the Cultural Foundations of Britain's Covert Empire* (Oxford: Oxford University Press, 2008), quotation on pp. 13–14.

[196] Toby Dodge, *Inventing Iraq: The Failure of Nation Building and a History Denied* (London: Hurst, 2003), pp. 120–21.

3   Ethnography

On an unseasonably warm February evening in 1897, members of the Anthropological Institute of Great Britain and Ireland gathered in London for a paper on inhabitants of 'the wild hill tracts' between Upper Burma and Assam.[1] It was not the first time that the Institute hosted a talk on the Nagas of northeast India, nor would it be the last.[2] A potent mixture of limited but gradually increasing data, competing conjectures over origins and migrations, and notions of 'exoticism' rendered the Nagas important subjects in the emerging discipline of anthropology. The 1897 paper was written by one of the Institute's recently inducted female members, Gertrude Godden.[3] Unlike her more famous contemporary Mary Kingsley who journeyed to West Africa to undertake fieldwork, Godden was a so-called armchair anthropologist.[4] She synthesised information on the Nagas from scholarly articles and administrative reports, and acknowledged that the transmission of data from northeastern India to London was both essential and problematic. 'In some cases', she

---

[1] The manuscript of the spoken version of the paper is in the Royal Anthropological Institute's Archives (hereafter 'RAI'), MS 156. An extended version was published in two parts in the Institute's Journal: Gertrude M. Godden, 'Naga and Other Frontier Tribes of North-East India', *The Journal of the Anthropological Institute of Great Britain and Ireland*, 26 (1897), pp. 161–201; Gertrude M. Godden, 'Naga and Other Frontier Tribes of North-East India (continued)', *The Journal of the Anthropological Institute of Great Britain and Ireland*, 27 (1898), pp. 2–51.

[2] Earlier papers include: S. E. Peale, 'The Nagas and Neighbouring Tribes', *The Journal of the Anthropological Institute of Great Britain and Ireland*, 3 (1874), pp. 476–81; R. G. Woodthorpe, 'Notes on the Wild Tribes Inhabiting the So-Called Naga Hills, on Our North-East Frontier of India. Part I', *The Journal of the Anthropological Institute of Great Britain and Ireland*, 11 (1882), pp. 56–73; R. G. Woodthorpe, 'Notes on the Wild Tribes Inhabiting the So-Called Naga Hills, on Our North-East Frontier of India. Part II', *The Journal of the Anthropological Institute of Great Britain and Ireland*, 11 (1882), pp. 196–214. Among many later papers are: J. P. Mills, 'Certain Aspects of Naga Culture', *The Journal of the Royal Anthropological Institute of Great Britain and Ireland*, 56 (1926), pp. 27–35; J. H. Hutton, 'The Significance of Head-Hunting in Assam', *The Journal of the Royal Anthropological Institute of Great Britain and Ireland*, 58 (1928), pp. 399–408.

[3] On Godden and the growing membership of the Anthropological Institute, see George W. Stocking Jr., *After Tylor: British Social Anthropology, 1888–1951* (London: Athlone, 1996), p. 373.

[4] On Mary Kingsley, see Kennedy, *Last Blank Spaces*, p. 265.

warned, 'information may have been given as Naga in the following pages which should include, or be referred to, other inhabitants of this frontier; these pages are published as open to correction on this point, especially as regards possible error in the use of Dalton's "Ethnology of Bengal"'.[5] Godden was far from alone in doubting the reliability of Edward Tuite Dalton's heavily illustrated 1872 work on the people of northeastern India, as will be discussed later.

Other men with direct experience of the Nagas played a less contested part in her paper. Godden did not present her research at the Institute's meeting; Robert Woodthorpe, a former British Indian frontier surveyor who had retired a year earlier, read her typescript. While stationed in northeast India, Woodthorpe had developed a second specialism in ethnography, producing an unparalleled array of pen-and-ink and watercolour sketches (discussed in Section 3.5). Woodthorpe took the liberty of illustrating Godden's paper with projectable versions of more than a dozen of his images alongside some Naga weapons and clothes from his own collection and that of Guybon Damant, the late Deputy Commissioner of the Naga Hills District.[6] The talk thus became a composite of heterogeneous elements well beyond the authorship of a single person. It was a bricolage of materials that were conveniently to hand and deemed sufficiently trustworthy by the relatively small, but by no means univocal, cadre involved in studies of frontier India. Fortunately, given that she seems not to have been consulted in advance, Godden pronounced herself impressed with the 'beautiful lantern slides'.[7] Whether the written form of Godden's paper, published in the Anthropological Institute's *Journal*, impressed Woodthorpe is rather less certain: Godden either overlooked or omitted two papers on the Nagas that he had delivered to the Institute only fifteen years earlier.[8] This was an instance of how prosaic processes such as oversight or exclusion were key elements of ethnographic knowledge in transit.

Godden's paper also casts light on broader features of ethnography in the era of high empire. The transcript for the spoken version of the paper concluded by 'point[ing] out how vividly the Naga tribes of the Indian frontier illustrate the mutual tie that should exist between the scientific aim of this Institute and the administrative work of Empire'.[9] But Godden's suggestion that 'surely the value of a scientific equipment in frontier work should be obvious' was, like most statements containing an appeal to their own self-evidence, an attempted intervention rather than a description of the existing state of affairs.[10] Just as the high priests of British social anthropology would discover in the interwar period, advocates of state backing for ethnography in nineteenth-century

---

[5] Godden, 'Naga (continued)', footnote p. 2.
[6] 'Front Matter', The Journal of the Anthropological Institute of Great Britain and Ireland, 27 (1898), p. 1.
[7] RAI, MS 156, f. 1.   [8] Woodthorpe, 'Wild Tribes, Part I'; Woodthorpe, 'Wild Tribes, Part II'.
[9] RAI, MS 156, f. 37.   [10] Ibid., ff. 37–38.

India found fostering formal links between colonial administrative institutions and anthropological ventures very difficult.[11] Shortly after her paper at the Anthropological Institute, Godden attempted to circulate 'an organised series of Anthropological questions . . . to the members of the Indian Civil Service, & officers administering the NE Frontier of India, in order that their collaboration might if possible be obtained in carrying on Anthropological work'.[12] Nothing, it seems, came of this proposal: it was one of the many failed rapprochements between colonial states and anthropologists.[13]

The audience discussion that followed Godden's paper was indicative of the tendency for ethnographic data to be harnessed to a range of competing and even mutually incompatible theories. Godden placed information from the Naga Hills into a framework informed primarily by James Frazer's compendious work of evolutionary ethnology, *The Golden Bough*.[14] Some audience members pursued radically different agendas. The former Chief Commissioner of Assam, Steuart Bayley, directly contradicted Godden's Frazerian evolutionary analysis of myth and ritual, pronouncing that he expected that the analysis of the Nagas should rest on anthropometry, 'the work so well begun by Mr. Risley, a comparison of the measurements of the facial angle and other physical characteristics'.[15] (As discussed in Section 3.6, during the following decade or so Herbert Risley had a great deal to say about frontier inhabitants.) Bayley also questioned whether, in light of linguistic and physical differences, the Nagas were a single 'race' as Godden suggested, thereby continuing a debate over the origins and

---

[11] On the linkages between social anthropology and colonial states, see Henrika Kuklick, *The Savage Within: The Social History of British Anthropology, 1885–1945* (Cambridge: Cambridge University Press, 1991), pp. 182–241. On this subject and on the flimsiness of connections between anthropology and colonialism in the late nineteenth century, see Stocking, *After Tylor*, pp. 367–426.

[12] RAI, Council minutes, 30 March 1897, Council Minutes 1882–1900 Volume, f. 316; see also Stocking, *After Tylor*, p. 373.

[13] On other schemes in a similar vein from the 1870s to 1930s, see Kuklick, *Savage Within*, pp. 196–204.

[14] On *The Golden Bough* and its place in British anthropology, see Stocking, *After Tylor*, pp. 124–78. Godden most notably forwarded a Frazerian reading of headhunting as symptomatic of 'a belief in the special potency or efficacy attached to the head or brain': Godden, 'Naga (continued)', p. 15.

[15] Godden, 'Naga (continued)', p. 48. Risley's primary publication during until his appointment as Indian Census Commissioner in 1899 was the four-volume *The Tribes and Castes of Bengal* (Calcutta: Bengal Secretariat Press, 1891). On anthropometry in colonial India, see Crispin Bates, 'Race, Caste, and Tribe in Central India: The Early Origins of Indian Anthropometry', in Peter Robb (ed.), *The Concept of Race in South Asia* (Delhi: Oxford University Press, 1995), pp. 219–59; Elizabeth Edwards, 'Science Visualized: E. H. Man in the Andaman Islands', in id (ed.), *Anthropology and Photography 1860–1920* (New Haven and London: Yale University Press, 1992), pp. 108–21; Elizabeth Edwards, *Raw Histories: Photographs, Anthropology and Museums* (Oxford and New York: Berg, 2001), pp. 131–56; Sen, 'Savage Bodies'.

unity of the Nagas that was co-extensive with sustained British contact with these communities.[16] Other commentators on Godden's paper repurposed the textual and visual material she (and Woodthorpe) had presented to fit their own conjectures. Gottlieb Leitner and William Crooke, both well-established ethnographers in India, mooted geographically expansive connections between Nagas and other upland communities across the subcontinent based on material culture and customs rather than physical data advocated by Risley and Bayley.[17] Even on the evening of the paper, then, Godden and Woodthorpe's spoken and visual material gave rise to a host of wide-ranging speculations and interpretative clashes. This was highly unstable knowledge, prone to persistent reconfigurations rather than definitive closures.

Frontier ethnography was less a linear path, and more a series of false starts and doublings back. It was, appropriately, akin to the tight hairpins and slippery paths winding through the steep-sided valleys of the Naga Hills rather than the plumb-line straight boulevards of Edwin Lutyens' New Delhi that were completed towards the end of the period considered in this chapter.[18] Nonetheless, India's frontiers were areas of extraordinary human interest for agents of empire and metropolitan commentators throughout the nineteenth century. As the previous chapter showed, surveys and maps provided definitions – albeit always fluctuating and contested ones – of where and what frontier regions were. Characterisations and representations of people were also vital elements of colonial notions of the frontier. Frontier ethnography and cartography shared notable overlaps and intersections: assessments of populations and spaces often appeared in the same letters, articles, and books. In addition, as in Woodthorpe's case, surveyors were among the leading producers of ethnographic knowledge.

There were also significant distinctions between the two fields. Although spatial knowledge claims were not limited to state-trained and -authorised surveyors, ethnography lacked any central, coordinating institution equivalent to the Great Trigonometrical Survey and Survey of India. It remained a more diffused, contested, and methodologically and theoretically variegated venture than cartography, not just in frontier India but across the colonial Subcontinent, in metropolitan Britain, and throughout the wider world. Until well into the twentieth century, it was something that colonial personnel tended to engage in alongside their primary functions, whether

---

[16] Godden, 'Naga (continued)', p. 48. William Robinson's account of the Nagas published in 1841 showed uncertainty over their origins and unity: William Robinson, *A Descriptive Account of Asam* (Calcutta: Ostell and Lepage, 1841), pp. 380–2.

[17] Godden, 'Naga (continued)', pp. 48–9.

[18] On the conception and execution of imperial modernity in New Delhi, see Stephen Legg, *Spaces of Colonialism: Delhi's Urban Governmentalities* (Oxford: Blackwell, 2007).

military, administration, trade, or survey. Despite these characteristics, ethno-graphic knowledge mattered. It was produced in tandem with British engage-ments with the populations at the fringes of state control, and it inflected subsequent interactions. In many cases, it was also among the most widely travelled information on India's frontiers, influencing popular and official understandings of the essential characteristics of these areas in geographic-ally and temporally far-reaching ways.

In this chapter, I explore four main areas: how colonial understandings of the people who lived and moved at the outskirts of state space were formed; the frameworks that structured these understandings; the representational forms of ethnographic knowledge; and how, and with what effects, ethnographic data and theories moved. The previous chapter showed how the extraordinary qualities of frontier space generated both problems and opportunities for colonial surveyors and led to these areas being widely valued in the age of high empire for their productive challenges. Frontier people were cast in a similar role: their apparent differences from 'settled' agrarian communities that comprised the bulk of fully governed India provided an ongoing source of intrigue for ethnographers. Even prior to the annexation of adjacent lowland areas, ethnographers saw upland and desert-bound communities at what became the fringes of the colonial subcontin-ent as unusually significant. The imagination of India's frontier communities as key subjects of ethnography continued as the discipline of anthropology became more formalised during the later nineteenth and early twentieth centuries, as discussed later in the chapter, and beyond.

This widespread recognition among British personnel in colonial India and metropolitan Britain alike that frontier people were important did not, how-ever, emanate from or lead to unanimity on the questions of why they were important and how they should be understood. Quite the opposite was true. Doubts over the validity of particular informants and modes of representa-tion, disputes over competing theoretical frameworks, and controversies over the nature of frontier communities were at the heart of colonial ethnography. Like spatial knowledge, ethnographic understandings did not simply accu-mulate as British interference in frontier regions tended to increase through the nineteenth century. In some ways, fragmentation and contestation increased rather than diminished as greater quantities of data were produced. Among the most pervasive indeterminacies concerned frontier communities' supposed tendencies towards violence and the possibility of colonial inter-vention in these tendencies. Even individual agents of empire and specific texts could evince contradictory perspectives on 'tribal violence', and the persistent nature of this uncertainty was a major driver of continued ethno-graphic investigation and representation.

The interest in violence was foremost among the themes and problematics that drew together ethnographic investigations in the northwest and northeast of British India. But in contrast to the development of a notion of 'frontier surveying' that drew together regions at opposite edges of the colonial subcontinent, in other important respects ethnography during the last third of the nineteenth century took on distinct characteristics in the northwest and northeast. From the late 1860s, zones of extended encounters between colonial personnel and previously ungoverned communities emerged as Balochistan and the Naga Hills came under irregular forms of British administration. The predilections of key individuals and distinct modes of encounter meant that very different forms of ethnography emerged in the two regions. The Naga Hills became a site of innovative field-based knowledge that mixed written and visual material with effects lasting into the twentieth century, while in Balochistan ethnography focused on already established concerns with identifying powerholders and authority structures. Even publications that incorporated ethnographic depictions and descriptions of groups from across the subcontinent, such as the monumental multi-volume *The People of India* published from 1868 to 1875, bore strong traces of variations between different frontier regions. However, the spread of the decennial colonial census to frontiers along with other projects of ethnographic survey around the turn of the twentieth century drew together populations of the northwest and northeast in hypotheses on the nature and deep history of the subcontinent's tribes (Section 3.6).

This chapter's analysis of the motives, means, and effects of frontier ethnographies draws on and intervenes in the historiography of anthropology and theories of the relationship between anthropology and imperial power. It develops two trends in this scholarship: the contention that anthropology was not straightforwardly a prop of (colonial) state power and a focus on knowledge-gathering practices 'in the field' and theorists in the colony rather than prominent anthropologists in the metropole.[19] Interactions between colonial administration and ethnographic knowledge were diverse, as were the effects on ethnographers of studying frontier

---

[19] The classic statement that anthropology was the handmaiden of colonial power is Talal Asad, 'Introduction', in id (ed.), *Anthropology and the Colonial Encounter* (Atlantic Highlands, NJ: Humanities Press, 1973), pp. 9–19. The leading works linking theories of human diversity to agendas of British power in India are Dirks, *Castes*, and Cohn, *Colonialism*. Pioneering historians of anthropology in the 1980s and 1990s such as Henrika Kuklick and George Stocking tended to focus on elites and their theories. Kuklick, *Savage Within*; George W. Stocking Jr., *Victorian Anthropology* (New York, NY: Maxwell Macmillan, 1987); Stocking, *After Tylor*. Kuklick is among those who pushed back against the equation of anthropology and colonial power: Kuklick, *Savage Within*, p. 26. Recent works in this vein include Peter Mandler, *Return from the Natives: How Margaret Mead won the Second World War and lost the Cold War* (New Haven, CT: Yale University Press, 2013). On the importance of varied knowledge-gathering practices in the field, see Sera-Shriar, *Making*; and James Poskett, *Materials of the Mind: Phrenology, Race, and the Global History of Science, 1815–1920* (Chicago, IL: University of Chicago Press, 2019).

populations. Anthropologists were, as Simon Schaffer has commented, '*subjects* in every sense: topics of disciplined enquiry, subordinates of regimes of power, and bearers of consciousness'.[20] Ethnographers in frontier India did not simply apply pre-formed agendas and observe as instructed by the proliferating range of guidebooks and questionnaires that emerged from the mid-nineteenth century.[21] As Zak Leonard argues in relation to India's northwest frontier, differences between individual ethnographers and 'the micro-politics of knowledge' mattered.[22] Frontier ethnography not only pertained to spaces at the colonial margins, it was absolutely of those marginal spaces, retaining distinctive features when incorporated into broader studies of human variation.

This chapter presents a broadly chronological analysis of frontier ethnographies and their influence on ethnological and anthropological theories. The first section examines the core assumptions of the agents of empire who produced assessments of communities at the upland and desert fringes of the subcontinent prior to British annexations of adjacent lowland regions. It then traces the emergence of British ideas of the 'mountain tribes' at the fringes of Assam during the two decades immediately following annexation, before turning to the Sind and Punjab frontiers as British interference grew during and in the wake of the Anglo-Afghan War (1839–42). The fourth section returns to the northeast and looks at the results of more intensive, field-based encounters, showing how visual representations and ethnological theories alike were controversial and fragmented. It then zooms in on photography, showing that this was a disputed and limited technology for depicting frontier communities during the later nineteenth century, but one that embedded the notion of frontier tribes as inherently violent. Finally, the sixth section considers the vital importance of frontier communities in British Indian anthropology around the turn of the twentieth century. I suggest that, despite significant shifts in theories of human diversity and in data collection and representation, India's frontiers remained spaces of ethnological mystery and contestation at this juncture in ways comparable to a century earlier.

---

[20] Simon Schaffer, *From Physics to Anthropology—and Back Again* (Cambridge: Prickly Pear, 1994), p. 28.

[21] Ibid., pp. 32–33. On guidebooks and questionnaires, see Urry, '"Notes"'; George W. Stocking, 'The Ethnographer's Magic: Fieldwork in British Anthropology from Tylor to Malinowski', in id (ed.), *Observers Observed: Essays on Ethnographic Fieldwork* (Madison, WI: University of Wisconsin Press, 1983), pp. 70–120; Efram Sera-Shriar, *The Making of British Anthropology, 1813–1871* (London: Pickering & Chatto, 2013), pp. 53–79.

[22] Zak Leonard, 'Colonial Ethnography on India's North-West Frontier, 1850-1910', *The Historical Journal*, 59, 1 (2016), pp. 175–96, here p. 176. See also Martin Bayly's notion of the 'epistemic insurgency' of local circumstances and encounters: Bayly, *Taming*, pp. 34–35.

3.1 'Entirely Distinct from the Ordinary Population': Ethnographic Encounters During the 1810s

The first British forays into the uplands and deserts that became colonial India's frontier regions took place against a backdrop of intense European interest in the origins, migrations, and divisions of mankind. The linguistic ethnology of the judge and polymath William Jones in the epistemic 'contact zone' of Calcutta during the 1780s established India as a vital site within globe-spanning theories of human diversity.[23] Epistolary networks and expanding print cultures enabled Jones's methodological focus on grammatical structure as the best guide to human variation to retain influence deep into the nineteenth century. His core conjecture that Persia, India, and Egypt formed the cradle of civilisation in the wake of the biblical deluge was more immediately controversial but also widely discussed long after Jones's death in 1794.[24] Of particular interest to administrator-scholars working in Madras and Bombay Presidencies was the possibility that an aboriginal population (or populations) predated Sanskrit-speaking incomers to the subcontinent. These theories encouraged increased attention to supposedly isolated communities, which were conjectured to hold the key to resolving the mystery of linguistic and physical diversity of colonial India and its peripheries.[25] As will be discussed shortly, this way of thinking meant that leading ethnologists in Europe made extensive use of information about communities beyond the agrarian plains of fully governed British India.

It would be a mistake, however, to suggest that Jones and his successors firmly dictated the ways in which frontier administrator- and traveller-ethnographers understood and represented the people they encountered. Those operating at the outer edges of imperial influence at northwest and northeast India during the first half of the nineteenth century tended not to be concerned with speaking to Jones's world-spanning conjectures. Nor did they exclusively privilege linguistic data in their ethnographic assessments. In addition, while many were undoubtedly interested in the deeper history of frontier communities and adopted broad racial categories shaped by Jones

---

[23] Thomas Simpson, 'Historicizing Humans in Colonial India', in Efram Sera-Shriar (ed.), *Historicizing Humans: Deep Time, Evolution and Race in Nineteenth-Century British Sciences* (Pittsburgh, PA: University of Pittsburgh Press, 2018), pp. 113–37, here pp. 116–20. On Calcutta as epistemic 'contact zone', see Kapil Raj, 'Mapping Knowledge Go-Betweens in Calcutta, 1770–1820', in Simon Schaffer, Lissa Roberts, Kapil Raj, and James Delbourgo (eds.), *The Brokered World: Go-Betweens and Global Intelligence, 1770–1820* (Sagamore Beach, FL: Watson, 2009), pp. 105–50. On William Jones, see Garland Cannon, *The Life and Mind of Oriental Jones: Sir William Jones, the Father of Modern Linguistics* (Cambridge: Cambridge University Press, 1990); Thomas R. Trautmann, *Aryans and British India* (Berkeley, CA: University of California Press, 1997), pp. 28–61; Ballantyne, *Orientalism*, pp. 18–55.

[24] Simpson, 'Historicizing', p. 118; Ballantyne, *Orientalism*, pp. 30–55.

[25] Simpson, 'Historicizing', pp. 120–5; Trautmann, *Aryans*, pp. 131–64.

and his successors, much of their knowledge was relatively ahistorical in terms of positing essential characteristics and being geared towards contemporary administrative imperatives. Frontier officials and travellers instead drew on a host of models beyond those at the cutting edge of European ethnology. Biblical and ancient historical reference points were especially influential in theorising populations at the northwestern fringes of the subcontinent. Perhaps most significant of all were the profound effects that interactions with populations in different regions had on the ethnographic work that followed. Frontier peoples and Asian travellers with experience of these regions were not only subjects of colonial knowledge but active participants in shaping it.[26]

The British collected information on the inhabitants of the regions beyond Sind and Punjab prior to colonial annexations of the adjacent areas. The first of what Martin Bayly terms 'periodic bouts of engagement and retrenchment' with Afghanistan during the nineteenth century began with the dispatch of a diplomatic mission led by the Scottish administrator Mountstuart Elphinstone to the Afghan Amir, Shah Shuja, in 1808.[27] Two years later, another expedition motivated by fears of Napoleon's designs on India was launched further south, with two British soldiers, Charles Christie and Henry Pottinger, journeying to Persia via Balochistan. The publications that eventually emerged from these undertakings, Elphinstone's *An Account of the Kingdom of Caubul* (1815) and Pottinger's *Travels in Beloochistan and Sinde* (1816), provided the first substantial accounts of the populations that would later be considered 'frontier tribes'.[28] Elphinstone's volume proved immensely influential in subsequent decades, while Pottinger's was also the primary source of information on the region it covered until the late 1830s.

There was no direct equivalent to these accounts and their ethnographic details for the uplands surrounding the Brahmaputra Valley. The one notable British foray into Assam prior to war with the Burmese in the mid-1820s was a military expedition to help the Ahom kingdom suppress an uprising from 1792 to 1794. The only major written output of this venture was a report by the lead officer, Captain Welsh, which provided answers to thirteen questions put by the Government of Bengal and made no mention of communities beyond the valley's fringes.[29] British administrators did, however, have relatively

---

[26] On 'go-betweens' in the history of science, see Simon Schaffer, Lissa Roberts, Kapil Raj & James Delbourgo (eds.), *The Brokered World: Go-Betweens and Global Intelligence, 1770–1820* (Sagamore Beach: Watson, 2009).

[27] Bayly, *Taming*, p. 1.

[28] Mountstuart Elphinstone, *An Account of the Kingdom of Caubul, and its dependencies, in Persia, Tartary, and India* (London: Longman, Hurst, Rees, Orme, and Brown, 1815); Henry Pottinger, *Travels in Beloochistan and Sinde* (London: Longman, Hurst, Rees, Orme, and Brown, 1816).

[29] Captain Welsh to Bengal Government, 6 February 1794, in Mackenzie, *History*, pp. 377–94.

extensive contact prior to annexing Assam with two adjacent groups that were counted among the northeast's 'frontier tribes' throughout the nineteenth century. These were the Garos and Khasis, inhabitants of the uplands that lay to the northeast of British Bengal. Although ostensibly beyond colonial sovereignty, these communities were subject to repeated bouts of British interference from the late eighteenth century owing to merchants' interest in limestone located in the hills and violent skirmishes between uplanders and lowland subjects of the Company-State.[30] In 1815, the administrator who would do much to shape British involvement in the northeast for the remaining sixteen years of his life, David Scott, became the Magistrate of Rangpur District at the foot of the hills. Colonial engagements with the Garos and Khasis intensified from this point, entailing written assessments that, although embedded in official correspondence and more fragmentary than Elphinstone and Pottinger's near-contemporaneous accounts, constituted the region's first colonial ethnographies.

Difference of genre was not the only distinction between descriptions of inhabitants of the northeastern hills by Scott and his colleagues, and those in the upland and desert-bound northwest during the 1810s. In addition, despite sharing the same London publisher, the ethnographic portions of Elphinstone and Pottinger's books were far from standardised. These discrepancies went all the way back to the beginning of the ethnographic enterprise: the circumstances under which Elphinstone, Pottinger, and Scott obtained information varied substantially. Elphinstone only travelled as far northwest as Peshawar, which although beyond the River Indus and thus across 'the boundary of India' as he understood it,[31] meant that he did not venture into any portion of what would become the frontier beyond colonial Punjab. He instead assembled a substantial information-gathering network to garner knowledge of populations under Kabul's sway.[32] As he acknowledged in his *Account*, though, this network was patchy and based partly on chance encounters, especially when it came to providing information on upland communities. The first that Elphinstone heard on the large Waziri community, for instance, came from Sikh merchants at the ferry on the Indus near Dera Ismail Khan. He reported them as 'describ[ing] the Afghaun tribes as generally kind to travellers, and honest in their dealings; but one tribe (the Vizeerees), they said were savages, and eat human flesh'.[33] While apparently doubting the claims of cannibalism,

[30] Simpson, 'Forgetting'; Cederlöf, *Founding*, pp. 51–52; David Ludden, 'Investing in Nature around Sylhet: An Excursion into Geographical History', *Economic and Political Weekly*, 29 November 2003, pp. 5080–8; David Ludden, 'The First Boundary of Bangladesh on Sylhet's Northern Frontiers', *Journal of the Asiatic Society of Bangladesh* (2003).

[31] Mountstuart Elphinstone, *An Account of the Kingdom of Caubul, and Its Dependencies, in Persia, Tartary, and India*, 3rd ed. (London: Richard Bentley, 1839), Vol. 1, p. 34.

[32] Bayly, *Taming*, pp. 58, 63–64.   [33] Elphinstone, *Account*, 3rd ed., Vol. 1, pp. 37–38.

Elphinstone confessed that his final account of the Waziris 'is derived from travellers: it is superficial, and may be incorrect'.[34] Information from other travellers and from violent forays into the uplands by members of his party tended to confirm Elphinstone's assumptions of the hill communities' 'predatory character'.[35] While he clearly attempted to highlight the specificities of different tribes, his efforts to obtain granular information were hampered by the linguistic limitations of his British underlings, who generally lacked knowledge of Pashtu.[36] The peculiarities and limitations of Elphinstone's informants were clearly apparent in his ethnographies.

Pottinger and Christie, by contrast, travelled in person through much of Balochistan. In what became a common trope of British adventure beyond governmental limits in India and beyond, Pottinger emphasised that he and Christie 'completely metamorphosed ourselves, by having our heads shaved, and adopting the entire native costume'.[37] As he admitted elsewhere in his narrative, however, these disguises achieved relatively little. He and Christie instead depended for translation, wayfinding, and guarantees of safe-passage on 'two Hindoostanee men' who accompanied them from the outset, and an array of travelling merchants and local potentates they encountered.[38] Although not as reliant as Elphinstone on these intermediaries for ethnographic data – and inclined to a dim view of the observational capacities of 'all the natives of those parts of Asia which I have traversed' – these informants undoubtedly shaped Pottinger's knowledge.[39] Some of his most egregious criticisms of portions of Baloch society, such as the claim that hill communities 'out of the immediate precincts of the Khan [of Kalat's] authority ... infested the roads and committed the most atrocious robberies', bore clear marks of originating in the Khan's court.[40] Pottinger struggled to obtain what he considered important information, complaining that the 'romantic fiction and tales of wonder' in Baloch genealogical narratives made them difficult to render in 'credible form'.[41] He also found that information on the contemporary structures and appellations of Baloch society was elusive; even the principal tribal divisions were a 'perplexing subject'.[42] His knowledge of communities to the northeast of Kalat, the very groups that were to be of primary interest to colonial administrators on the Upper Sind frontier during the 1840s, was especially sparse as he and Christie did not travel there in person and lacked informants with extensive direct contact.[43]

---

[34] Elphinstone, *Account*, 3rd ed., Vol. 2, pp. 96–97.

[35] He used this term to describe inhabitants of the Khyber Pass: Elphinstone, *Account*, 3rd ed., Vol. 1, p. 55.

[36] Ibid., pp. 40–3.   [37] Pottinger, *Travels*, p. 10.   [38] Ibid., quotation p. 5.

[39] Ibid., quotation p. 45; see also p. 36.   [40] Ibid., p. 60.   [41] Ibid., pp. 53–54.

[42] Ibid., p. 55.

[43] In his list of Baloch tribal subdivisions, the 'Bugothees' and 'Murees' (Bugtis and Marris) are among the few without estimated population or the name of the chief listed. Ibid., pp. 55–8.

That David Scott and his colleagues were administrators rather than diplomats or travellers meant that their methods of ethnographic data collection differed again from those of Elphinstone and Pottinger. Initially, Scott and his co-Magistrate in Rangpur district, Thomas Sisson, had no direct contact with the upland communities, and instead relied on men of influence in the landowning communities at the foot of the hills for all information. When violence between Garos and the landowners broke out in 1815, however, Sisson became convinced that the landowners were preventing the British from obtaining key information so as to misrepresent the two-sided nature of the conflagration.[44] He instead began to seek reports directly from Garos, eventually establishing contact with an individual who, unusually and 'from a long intercourse with the lowlanders', spoke some Bengali.[45] As with Pottinger and Elphinstone, Sisson's account clearly bore the traces of specific limitations of knowledge gathering. 'I have spared no pains or trouble', Sisson avowed, 'to acquire some knowledge of the nature of the connexion which subsists between the commonality and their Chief, but the accounts I have heard have in this particular proved so contradictory that I am unwilling to trouble government with the actual detail of their inconsistencies'.[46] The circumstances encountered 'in the field' were, then, drivers of major variations in ethnographies in the 1810s and, as we shall see, remained so even as colonial engagements with frontier communities became more intensive.

Another significant distinction between accounts in this era lay in the analytical frameworks into which the administrator- and soldier-ethnographers placed their information. Sisson's account, as with much of the writing on the Garos and Khasis by Scott's generation, was concerned primarily with immediate administrative necessities. The main focus was, accordingly, on comprehending recent social and political dynamics along with structures of authority, as Sisson's frustration towards inconsistent information on the role of chiefs suggests. It was also knowledge that undergirded colonial expansion into the uplands. Regulation X of 1822, drafted by Scott and forming the legal basis for British administrative interference in Garo villages, was founded upon the contention established by earlier ethnographic writings that the Garos were among those 'races of people entirely distinct from the ordinary population' who required special consideration to avoid being 'at the mercy of [Bengali] Zemindars [sic.]'.[47] By contrast, neither Pottinger nor Elphinstone were concerned with immediate imperatives to govern the populations they encountered. While both

[44] IOR F/4/533: Thomas Sisson to Judicial Department, 15 February 1815, ff. 137–40.
[45] Ibid., f. 145.   [46] Ibid., f. 149.   [47] Mackenzie, *History*, pp. 250–51.

took an interest in tribal authority (or lack thereof),[48] they also sought to explain relations between different communities across a wider area. Elphinstone's account was structured in encyclopaedic fashion, providing details of the upland communities proceeding from north to south – a format subsequently repeated in numerous ethnographies of the Punjab frontier.[49] Both he and Pottinger were concerned with wider questions of tribal origins and migrations, rooting their analyses less in philology than in speculative ancient chronologies. Elphinstone picked up on the cartographer James Rennell's hypothesis that the inhabitants of Kafiristan descended from Alexander the Great, while Pottinger suggested that marriage and dowry rituals gave some credence to the notion that the Balochs' antecedents were Israelites.[50] Such an interest in the deep histories of upland communities in the northeast only emerged in the wake of the British invasion of Assam.

Elphinstone's and Pottinger's writings also differed from those of Scott and his colleagues in being read and used by leading ethnological theorists of the first half of the nineteenth century. Elphinstone's *Account* in particular proved to be popular and widely influential. Its updated third edition was produced in London by a renowned publishing house as British forces invaded Afghanistan in 1839, and copies were distributed to officers going to war.[51] The work was also closely studied by James Cowles Prichard for the third edition of his own prominent book, *Researches Into the Physical History of Mankind*, published in five volumes between 1836 and 1847.[52] From the publication in 1813 of the first edition of this work until his death in 1848, Prichard was the leading figure in British ethnology.[53] Deeply influenced by William Jones's philological methodology, he became ever more convinced of India's significance to understanding human diversity at a global scale, especially because the lack of mixing between castes and the seclusion of certain 'tribes' seemed to assure the continuity of divisions fixed in the distant past.[54] As such, he greatly expanded the space given over to analysing the

---

[48] For example, Pottinger commented on the 'more despotic authority' among Brahuis relative to Balochs (*Travels*, pp. 71–72), and Elphinstone repeatedly commented on limited authority among upland populations, including the claim that "none of [the Yusufzai] chiefs have authority equal to that of a constable in England' (*Account*, 3rd ed., Vol. 2, pp. 21–22).

[49] Bayly, *Taming*, pp. 59–63.   [50] Bayly, *Taming*, p. 55; Pottinger, *Travels*, pp. 64–9.

[51] Elphinstone, *Account*, 3rd ed. On London publishing of imperial travel narratives, see Keighren, Withers, and Bell, *Travels*. On the distribution of copies to the officers of the Army of the Indus, see Bayly, *Taming*, p. 73.

[52] James Cowles Prichard, *Researches into the Physical History of Mankind*, 3rd ed. in five vols. (London: Sherwood, Gilbert, and Piper, 1836–47).

[53] Stocking, *Victorian Anthropology*, pp. 48–53. The first edition of Prichard's work is: James Cowles Prichard, *Researches into the Physical History of Man* (London: John and Arthur Arch, 1813).

[54] Prichard, *Researches*, Vol. 4, 3rd ed., p. 150.

subcontinent in the third edition of his magnum opus, paying special attention to supposedly remote tribes.[55]

Drawing on Elphinstone and, as discussed below, the traveller Alexander Burnes,[56] Prichard asserted that 'no ethnological discovery of recent times is calculated to excite greater interest than that of the aboriginal race ... termed Kafirs by the Mohammedan neighbours' (now known as the Kalash).[57] Prichard named and praised Elphinstone's local informants on Kafiristan while explicitly disregarding Elphinstone's hypothesis of descent from Alexander the Great.[58] Instead, Prichard highlighted Elphinstone's discovery that the inhabitants' 'language is nearly allied to the Sanskrit', which, he stated, firmly placed them among 'the Indo-European or Arian race'.[59] This philological evidence, coupled with their having 'the sanguine or xanthous complexion of the northern Europeans', made the 'Kafirs' one of the major pieces of evidence in Prichard's core argument against increasingly influential arguments that racial groups were physically fixed.[60] Elphinstone's ethnography of communities at the upland margins of India, gathered through a network of diverse informants, became, then, a vital element within leading metropolitan debates on human diversity.

3.2 'Raising, Not Solving, Doubts': The Advent of Assam's 'Mountain Tribes', 1820s–1840s

Prichard also incorporated upland communities at the fringes of Assam into the third edition of his *Researches*,[61] drawing extensively on a slew of accounts on these regions and their inhabitants published during the two decades following British invasion in the mid-1820s. As the seal broke on the information vacuum that existed prior to annexation, colonial administrators, soldiers, and scientific travellers undertook intensive geographic and ethnographic research. By the late 1830s, there was an established chain of transmission from officials at the outskirts of the Brahmaputra Valley to the Asiatic Society in Calcutta. Francis Jenkins, the lead colonial administrator in the northeast from 1834 to 1861, was a key intermediary, passing many letters and reports on to the Political Department of the Government of India in Calcutta, which, in turn, sent some on to the Asiatic Society.[62] The Asiatic Society's periodicals, *Asiatic Researches* and the *Journal of the Asiatic Society of Bengal*, were widely read

---

[55] James Cowles Prichard, *Researches*, Vol. 4, 3rd ed., pp. 91–248.

[56] Alexander Burnes, 'On the Siah-posh Kaffirs with Specimens of Their Language and Costume', *Journal of the Asiatic Society of Bengal*, 7 (1838), pp. 325–33.

[57] Prichard, *Researches*, 3rd ed., Vol. 4, p. 213.

[58] Elphinstone, *Account*, 3rd ed., Vol. 2, pp. 373–87.

[59] Prichard, *Researches*, 3rd ed., Vol. 4, p. 214.   [60] Ibid., p. 218.   [61] Ibid., pp. 219–28.

[62] See, for example, E. R. Grange, 'Extracts from the Journal of an Expedition into the Naga Hills on the Assam Frontier', *Journal of the Asiatic Society*, 106 (1840), pp. 947–66, here p. 947.

within and beyond the colonial Subcontinent, and were a key source for Prichard. The late 1830s and early 1840s also saw the publication in Calcutta of influential travel accounts and works of synthesis that included comparative and connected accounts of the various upland peoples surrounding Assam.[63] Before turning to these books, let us examine how ethnographic knowledge was produced during the earliest years of the British occupation of Assam.

Ethnography marched in lockstep with administrative imperatives as the British mission to expel Burmese forces from Assam turned into annexation. In the later 1820s, two regions at the fringes of Assam became especially signifi- cant. The extreme eastern end of the Brahmaputra Valley was deemed stra- tegically vital for its proximity to Burma and China, and the hills inhabited by the Khasi community (now eastern Meghalaya) were seen as prime territory for *dak* and transport links between Bengal and Assam.[64] In understanding the Khasis, David Scott, the lead administrator in Assam following the British invasion, and his underlings did not draw explicitly on local precedents such as Regulation X of 1822 or the experiences of earlier limestone mining prospect- ors among the Khasis. Instead, they employed primitivist models drawn from across the world. Adam White, one of Scott's assistants, attested in his account of Scott's administration that the '[Khasi] Parliament . . . brought vividly to my recollection, the eloquent description of the North American Indians by Robertson, Chateaubriand, and Cooper; and, for once, I found my boyish dreams realized'.[65] Such admiration for the Khasis' political institutions did not preclude colonial coercion, nor a scheme for two Bhutias to teach the Khasis methods for cultivating upland regions – an undertaking that met with incomprehension.[66]

Growing Khasi irritation at colonial interference came to a head in April 1829 when two of Scott's junior officers in charge of building a road through the hills were killed. White used this episode and the violent colonial response as the basis for assessing the Khasis' fighting resolve, with classically informed expectations as the yardstick.

The resistance made by the Cassyas did not evince that heroic spirit which the martial appearance of their warriors had led us to expect, and which, they said, was displayed in the encounters of their tribes with each other. In these contests, we were told, that the hostile bands, like Ossian's heroes, rushed from their opposite hills against each other "like the dark storms of autumn and dire was the result when their conflicting shields

---

[63] Notable works in this vein were: Pemberton, *Report*; John M'Cosh, *Topography of Assam* (Calcutta: Bengal Military Orphan Press, 1837); Robinson, *Descriptive Account*.

[64] The following analysis of British understandings of the Khasis during the late 1820s and early 1830s is a shortened version of the account in Simpson, 'Forgetting'.

[65] Adam White, Memoir of the Late David Scott, Esq. Agent to the Governor-General, on the North-East Frontier of Bengal (Calcutta: Baptist Mission, 1832), pp. 35–36.

[66] Ibid., footnote p. 40.

dashed against each other in the vale below." Here no such display of manhood took place.[67]

In the wake of this violence, a combination of admiration and disgust for the Khasis persisted among Scott and his colleagues.[68] The Court of Directors in London later commented upon the peculiarity of their ambivalence, opining that 'Mr. Scott and all the Officers under him, must have been completely misinformed as to the state of feeling among the Cossyahs'.[69] This was, in fact, an extremely productive shortcoming, rooted in modes of understanding defined by forgetting and circularity rather than progressive accumulation. Sparse communication networks and ambivalent ethnographic assessments allowed for the repeated re-engagement of the colonial state in areas in which previous attempts to gain traction had failed conspicuously. Comparisons with textual ideals, especially tales of heroic daring such as Ossian's and James Fenimore Cooper's, were rather easier than engaging close-at-hand complexities. So were reductively optimistic parallels with models across the British imperial world, such as Scott's suggestion almost immediately after the Khasi uprising that Europeans should settle in the hills just as they had colonised New South Wales in Australia.[70] Capacious and ambiguous representations of the Khasis afforded British officials the freedom to propose and pursue diverse, even contradictory, schemes.

Knowledge of the communities at the eastern end of the Brahmaputra Valley had very different features: there substantial and significant variations in how ethnographic data were collected and represented even between men within David Scott's small cabal of underlings. Whereas Adam White sought to comprehend the Khasis by reference to textual models and classical ideals, soldier-ethnographers further east principally attempted to untangle the complex relations between and within communities by engaging with local informants. The most detailed account of the people of this region was an article by John Neufville, an army officer and Political Agent, published by the Asiatic Society of Bengal in 1828.[71] The accessibility of informants and the administrative concern to gather knowledge of the region's most troublesome communities dictated the depth of Neufville's analysis of various communities. At the intersection of both elements were the Singphos, located at the fringes of the hills at the extreme eastern edge of the valley. In 'endeavoring to trace their manners, customs, and traditions', Neufville placed particular emphasis on the

---

[67] Ibid., pp. 43–46.   [68] Ibid., pp. 49–50.
[69] IOR/E/4/742: Court to Government of India, 3 December 1834, f. 322.
[70] Ibid., ff. 322–7; Nirode K. Barooah, *David Scott in North-East India, 1802–1831: A Study in British Paternalism* (New Delhi: Munshram Manoharlal, 1970), pp. 220–9.
[71] John Bryan Neufville, 'On the Geography and Population of Assam', *Asiatic Researches*, 16 (1828), pp. 331–52. Wilcox's 'Memoir', also published in *Asiatic Researches* (in 1832), contains ethnographic material but is more directly concerned with geography.

Singphos' accounts of their creation and dispersal. His rendering of these theories stated that the original Singphos were created atop a mountain located in present-day northern Myanmar and thereafter washed downstream toward the Irrawaddy River. For a period they halted and 'were immortal, and held celestial intercourse with the planets and all heavenly intelligences, following the pure worship of the one supreme being', but upon descending to the plains, twenty-one generations prior to Neufville's day, 'they fell in with the common lot of humanity, and . . . soon adopted the idolatries and superstitions of the nations around them'.[72] At the point of the Singphos' supposed descent into the valley lowlands, British administrative interests began more clearly to guide Neufville's narrative. A history of labour systems and authority structures took centre stage, focusing on claims of slaveholding among the Singphos and the identification of powerholders within the community.[73]

The preceding narrative of Singpho origins and migrations, however, contained a tension that ran through much colonial ethnographic discourse. Neufville was never quite sure how much credence to give to his informants' stories. He quoted at length a testimony largely derived from a Singpho potentate, the Bisa Gam, which conferred upon it a degree of authority. He claimed to have chosen the account from a number given by various Singpho sources as 'it appears to be the most consistent' and the informant was 'the most intelligent of them'.[74] The political alliance that Neufville was in the process of constructing with the Bisa Gam – eventually positioning him as leader of all Singphos – was almost certainly another factor.[75] Here, as in many other instances, reliability as an ethnographic informant was entangled with considerations of frontier politics. The Bisa Gam was both a supplier of information and the beneficiary of Neufville's firm division of the Singphos into 'twelve *Gaums*, or clans' and characterisation of the Bisa Gam as one of the four 'most influential' clan chiefs.[76] These were claims that, after recapitulation in subsequent texts, became a core facet of colonial understandings of the Singphos and guided policy for more than a decade after Neufville's death in 1830.[77]

Despite these dynamics, Neufville was not wholly convinced by the Bisa Gam's tale. He cross-referenced elements with other Singpho narratives and excised what he termed its 'fabulous portions', confining the unabridged version to an appendix.[78] He also omitted the universal

---

[72] Neufville, 'Geography', pp. 339–40.
[73] On the colonial focus on slavery, see Sadan, *Kachin*, pp. 50–70.
[74] Neufville, 'Geography', p. 339.   [75] Sadan, *Kachin*, pp. 65–7.
[76] Neufville, 'Geography', p. 338.
[77] The twelve clans hypothesis appears in, among others, M'Cosh, *Topography*, p. 149, and Robinson, *Descriptive Account*, p. 376. On Neufville's death, see NAI Foreign Political, 3 September 1830, No. 39: David Scott to Secretary to Government, 6 August 1830, ff. 1–2.
[78] Neufville, 'Geography', pp. 339–40.

categories – 'mankind' and 'the race of man' – that appeared in the Bisa Gam's account (in Neufville's translation, of course), instead saying merely 'the *Sinh-phos* were originally created' and thereby localising the theory's explanatory power.[79] He did not, however, remove the narrative's particularities through placing the Singphos within a biblical framework with global pretensions, nor did he invoke the authority of philological or physical analyses. Instead, by authoring a distinct version of the Singpho creation story, Neufville simultaneously positioned himself as the proper arbiter of a reasonable theory and suggested that Singpho narratives provided credible information on how the community came to occupy its current geographical and social position.

Neufville and White's works were among those incorporated into the first accounts that drew the communities at the outskirts of Assam into a single analysis. Although he did not write ethnographic overviews, Francis Jenkins again played a significant role here, collecting and distributing the manuscript sources for the overviews.[80] An 1836 article in the *Journal of the Asiatic Society of Bengal* and 1837 book *The Topography of Assam* by the Assistant Surgeon John McCosh established what became a conventional format for listing Assam's frontier communities, proceeding west from Bhutan across the mountains north of the Brahmaputra, then turning south along the eastern edge of the valley before going from east to west along the southern edge.[81] More fundamentally, works such as McCosh's and William Robinson's *A Descriptive Account of Asam* (1841) configured upland northeast India as a space of primitive and remote tribes with suspiciously 'democratic' organisational structures,[82] exotic appearance and customs, and violent predilections. The colonial frontier became defined ethnographically as well as geographically.

While seeking to define essential characteristics of 'the tribe' in the northeast, McCosh and Robinson's writings also bore witness to how British activities in Assam impinged on the social and political structures of communities at Assam's fringes. Colonial upheavals affected which groups were seen as primary subjects of ethnography and which areas were understood as frontier space. Most important in this respect was tea. Tea cultivation quickly overtook immediate concerns of attacks from Burma as the defining feature of the British

---

[79] Ibid., pp. 339–40, 348–50.

[80] J. McCosh, 'Account of the Mountain Tribes on the Extreme N.E. Frontier of Bengal', *Journal of the Asiatic Society of Bengal*, No. 52 (1836), pp. 193–208, here p. 193; Robinson, *Descriptive Account*, vii.

[81] McCosh, 'Account'; M'Cosh, *Topography*, pp. 131–66. This format was repeated in Robinson's *Descriptive Account*, pp. 333–421 and Alexander Mackenzie's influential 1884 *History*.

[82] For instance, Robinson wrote of the Abors that 'each clan or village forms a democratic republic by itself', noting 'the very singular coincidence between the political institutions of these people, and those of the inhabitants of the Alps in the country of Grison [in Switzerland]': *Descriptive Account*, p. 359.

presence in Upper Assam in the 1830s. This had a direct impact on ethnographic knowledge production. William Griffith, a botanist deputed to the region in 1836 to investigate the presence and prospects of tea plants, also wrote accounts of people, especially the Mishmi community in the hills beyond the northeastern corner of the Brahmaputra Valley.[83] The spread of tea 'gardens' led to the displacement of Singphos and members of adjacent groups, Hkamtis and Mataks, forcing them to move and adapt to new labour regimes.[84] A profound shift in ethnographic assessments of these communities followed. In 1837, McCosh had judged Singphos to be 'by far the most powerful and the most formidable of these hill tribes [surrounding Assam]'.[85] Four years later, Robinson opened his section on the Singphos by echoing some of this sentiment: 'the Singphos are by far the most powerful tribe bordering on the valley'.[86] While much of his account was taken directly from McCosh, the differences mattered. Robinson cut the reference to the Singphos being 'formidable' and went on to heavily qualify the statement by detailing recent developments which had, he wrote, led to 'altered habits [in] this rude but energetic race'. 'Latterly ... feeling the necessity of submitting to a power which has so nearly approached them, and whose strength they now perceive they cannot resist, they have shewn an inclination to abandon their old habits of lawlessness and rapine, and to turn their attention to agriculture, now become necessary for their subsistence'.[87] The perception that acculturation was taking place among the Singphos called into question their status as a 'mountain' or 'frontier' tribe. A year after the publication of Robinson's book, control of Singpho and Hkamti areas was transferred from the Political Department to the Revenue and Judicial Department of the Government of India, suggesting a shift in status from frontier to settled community.[88]

An uprising by a large portion of the Singphos in 1843 shook sanguine British assessments of the spread of tea gardens.[89] Nevertheless, in the years that followed, the focus of frontier ethnography in Assam continued to shift from the eastern end to the southern edge of the valley inhabited by communities lumped together by the British as 'Nagas'.[90] Contact between colonial officers and Nagas began in 1825, when Robert Boileau Pemberton

---

[83] William Griffith, 'Journal of a Visit to the Mishmee Hills in Assam', *Journal of the Asiatic Society of Bengal*, 65 (1837), pp. 325–41. Reprinted in William Griffith, *Journal of Travels in Assam, Burma, Bootan, Affghanistan and the Neighbouring Countries* (Calcutta: Bishop's College Press, 1847), pp. 54–9.

[84] Sadan, *Kachin*, pp. 72–73; Jayeeta Sharma, 'Making Garden, Erasing Jungle: The Tea Enterprise in Colonial Assam', in Deepak Kumar, Vinita Damodaran and Rohan D'Souza (eds.), *The British Empire and the Natural World: Environmental Encounters in South Asia* (Oxford: Oxford University Press, 2010), pp. 119–41, here pp. 125–26.

[85] M'Cosh, *Topography*, p. 149.   [86] Robinson, *Descriptive Account*, p. 375.   [87] Ibid., p. 376.

[88] Sadan, *Kachin*, pp. 78–79.   [89] Ibid., pp. 79–91.

[90] On the advent of 'Naga' as an ethnographic category, see Alban von Stockhausen, 'Naga: Lineages of a Term', in Neeladri Bhattacharya and Joy L. K. Pachuau (eds.), *Landscape,*

accompanied the Raja of Manipur, Gambhir Singh, on a mission to displace the Burmese force occupying Manipur. In an article in the Calcutta *Government Gazette*, Pemberton described Naga dwellings, marriage rituals, and physical appearance (noting 'some degree of resemblance to the Chinese' and their 'muscular strength').[91] Little of the information contained in this report appeared in McCosh's overviews of the 'mountain tribes' in 1836 and 1837, nor did the journey of Francis Jenkins and Pemberton to Manipur in 1832 yield substantial ethnographic assessments of the Nagas.[92]

A glut of information on particular sections of the Nagas emerged during the years that followed McCosh's accounts, deriving from two distinct engagements in different locations. Starting in 1839, British forces undertook a series of incursions into western portions of the Naga uplands (see Section 4.2).[93] The narrative accounts by the officers commanding these military parties passed, through Jenkins and the Political Department of the Government of India, into the pages of the *Journal of the Asiatic Society*.[94] The expeditions partially resolved some basic confusions, such as the location of the Angami tribe held responsible for the attacks on Cachar as well as the more fundamental fact that 'Angami' was the name of a community, not a place.[95] Further east, as tea plantations expanded at the fringes of Upper Assam to the south of Dibrugarh and Sibsagar, American Baptist missionaries had by the late 1830s established extensive contact with a Naga community bordering the valley known as Namsangias. Although the colonial authorities rebutted their requests for assistance, the missionaries published a series of vocabularies and phrasebooks in 1839, the first sources on a language understood to be a Naga dialect.[96] These

Culture, and Belonging: Writing the History of Northeast India (Cambridge: Cambridge University Press, 2019), pp. 131–50, here p. 133.

[91] H. H. Wilson, *Documents Illustrative of the Burmese War* (Calcutta: Government Gazette Press, 1827), appendix 13, from the *Government Gazette*, 29 December 1825, xvii-xix.

[92] On contact with Nagas during Jenkins and Pemberton's journey, see NAI Foreign Political, 1832, No. 69–71; NAI Foreign Political, 23 July 1832, Nos. 64–9.

[93] IOR/F/4/1832.

[94] E. R. Grange, 'Extracts from the Narrative of an Expedition into the Naga Territory of Assam', *Journal of the Asiatic Society*, 90 (1839), pp. 445–70; Grange, 'Extracts' (1840), pp. 947–66; 'Despatch from Lieut. H. Bigge, Assistant Agent, Detached to the Naga Hills, to Capt. Jenkins, Agent Governor General, N. E. Frontier, Communicated from the Political Secretariat of India to the Secretary to the Asiatic Society', *Journal of the Asiatic Society of Bengal*, 110 (1841), pp. 129–36; Mr. Browne Wood, 'Extracts from a Report of a Journey into the Naga Hills in 1844', *Journal of the Asiatic Society of Bengal*, 154 (1844), pp.771–85; Capt. Brodie, 'Narrative of a Tour over That Part of the Naga Hills Lying between the Diko and Dyang River', *Journal of the Asiatic Society of Bengal*, 168 (1845) pp. 828–44.

[95] These confusions had been evident in correspondence from the British Superintendent in Cachar, J. G. Burnes, during the preceding years: NAI Foreign Political 20 February 1837: Burnes to J. Lewis, Commissioner of Revenue, Dacca, 23 December 1836, f. 242; IOR/F/4/1832: Burnes to Bengal Government, Political Department, 7 November 1838, f. 13.

[96] 'Report of the Board: Mission to Asam', *The Baptist Missionary Magazine*, 22 (1841), p. 192. On colonial authorities' rebuttal of requests for assistance, see Mackenzie, *History*, p. 92. On

missionaries and the British officers in the western Naga region were key informants for William Robinson's *Descriptive Account*, in which he devoted a fifth of the section on 'hill tribes' to the Nagas (whereas McCosh had enough information for only a single page).[97] Robinson quoted a missionary account of Naga funeral rites at length, and his commitment to a philological methodology, which he termed 'the most important aid . . . in tracing the origin of these tribes', led him to depend especially on the Baptists and their linguistic expertise.[98] Robinson continued throughout the 1840s to obtain information from the missionaries. His long article of 1849 in the *Journal of the Asiatic Society of Bengal* on the languages of Assam and 'its mountain confines' drew still more extensively on their data. The analysis of Naga languages in this article was based entirely on the Namsangia dialect in which the Americans worked, and the sample sentences – such as 'There is one God . . . He made me and you and all men . . . He sees in all places' – clearly bore the imprint of missionary priorities.[99]

The Baptists' influence among ethnologists stretched beyond Robinson to a more widely renowned individual who also followed William Jones in conducting ethnology through linguistic analysis, Brian Houghton Hodgson.[100] Hodgson was a polymath with a particular interest in unearthing the 'aboriginal' communities that he hypothesised predated the Aryan 'invasion' of India.[101] In the late 1840s, as he extended this project to account for upland inhabitants in the northeast, Hodgson entered into correspondence with Nathan Brown, one of American missionaries based in Upper Assam. Hodgson was initially sceptical of the value of Brown's comparative vocabulary of 'the mountaineers round Assam' as a source for philological ethnology, claiming that the 'very limited number of words' served to 'raise, not to solve, doubts'.[102] However, he praised Brown as an 'able and zealous enquirer' and later quoted him at length in the

---

Baptist missions among the Nagas more generally, see Arkotong Longkumer, '"Along Kingdom's Highway": The Proliferation of Christianity, Education, and Print amongst the Nagas in Northeast India', *Contemporary South Asia*, 27 (2019), pp. 160–78.

[97] Robinson, *Descriptive Account*, pp. 380–98; M'Cosh, *Topography*, pp. 356–57.

[98] Robinson, *Descriptive Account*, quotation on p. 337; see also the language tables based on information from the missionary Nathan Brown, p. 340. On Naga funeral rites, he quoted Miles Bronson (while misspelling his name), pp. 396–8.

[99] William Robinson, 'Notes on the Languages Spoken by the Various Tribes Inhabiting the Valley of Asam and Its Mountain Confines', *Journal of the Asiatic Society of Bengal*, 27 (1849), pp. 183–237, 310–49, here pp. 324–30.

[100] For more on Hodgson's ethnography, see Martin Gaenszle, 'Brian Hodgson as Ethnographer and Ethnologist', in David M. Waterhouse (ed.), *The Origins of Himalayan Studies: Brian Houghton Hodgson in Nepal and Darjeeling 1820–1858* (Abingdon: Routledge, 2004), pp. 206–26; Simpson, 'Historicizing', pp. 122–23.

[101] Trautmann, *Aryans*, pp. 158–60; Gaenszle, 'Brian Hodgson', pp. 208–20.

[102] B. H. Hodgson, *On the Aborigines of India. Essay the First; on the Kooch, Bodo and Dhimal tribes* (Calcutta: Baptist Mission Press, 1847), iv–v

Asiatic Society's *Journal* on Naga languages. [103] Hodgson also attached special significance to the Nagas, conjecturing that they were at the boundary of a major ethnological division, marking the western limit of 'the monosyllabic-tongued' people that he supposed to be of Chinese origin (in distinction to the 'aboriginal' Indians found in uplands across the rest of the subcontinent). [104]

Although Hodgson's hypothesis was disputed, other scholars of the 1840s also believed that the Nagas were of particular ethnological importance. What Robinson termed the Nagas' 'apparent diversity', especially in languages, led him to infer that 'many of the tribes have not sprung from one common origin'. Robinson's hypothesis – like Hodgson's, explicitly provisional – was that some Nagas had 'emigrated from the north-west borders of China, probably during ... the thirteenth and fourteenth centuries', while others 'have been driven into the fastnesses of these hills from Asam and Bengal, and brought with them languages very different from each other'. [105] While often discussed as one 'hill' or 'mountain tribe' amongst many, it was the Nagas' variety as revealed by the disparate ventures of colonial officers to the west and American missionaries to the east that made them simultaneously intriguing to ethnologists and problematic to officials. They seemed to pose not only an open-ended administrative challenge to the expansion of colonial state and capital (as discussed in chapters one and four) but also a deep ethnographic mystery. It was, then, a combination of their political importance at the fringes of growing commercial interests and their internal socio-cultural diversity that rendered the Nagas such important ethnographic subjects during the 1840s. As will be discussed later, the idea that distinctions between Naga communities indicated unusually convoluted patterns of migration and social change kept them at the forefront of frontier ethnography through into the twentieth century.

3.3 'Aboriginal Remnants': Ethnography in the Time of War and Annexation at the Sind and Punjab Frontiers, 1830s–1850s

Following the short-lived Napoleonic threat to India that prompted Elphinstone's embassy and Christie and Pottinger's journey, there was a lull in British engagements in the uplands beyond Punjab and in Balochistan. [106] This ended in the 1830s, with a proposal for commercial schemes on the Indus and increasing interference in regional politics. Especially important were the

---

[103] Quotation from Hodgson, *Aborigines*, iv. Hodgson quoted Brown in: B. H. Hodgson, 'On the Aborigines of the Eastern Frontier', *Journal of the Asiatic Society of Bengal*, 18 (1849), pp. 967–75; and B. H. Hodgson, 'Aborigines of the North East Frontier', *Journal of the Asiatic Society of Bengal*, 19 (1850), pp. 309–16.

[104] Hodgson, *Aborigines*, x, p. 141.   [105] Robinson, *Descriptive Account*, pp. 381–82.

[106] There was also a lull in interest in Afghanistan and Persia: see Bayly, *Taming*, pp. 52–53.

travels and subsequent writings of Alexander Burnes and Charles Masson.[107] These men were indebted to Elphinstone's work and patronage within what Martin Bayly terms the British 'knowledge community' of the regions beyond the limits of northwest colonial India.[108] Despite journeying through sizeable portions of the uplands in person, Burnes's immensely popular 1834 book *Travels into Bokhara* largely retained Elphinstone's fixations on outlining tribal structures of authority and violent tendencies.[109] Burnes also followed Elphinstone's fascination with the Kalash, making special efforts to obtain information that would, in Burnes's words, 'gratify . . . the extreme interest' in this community.[110] Like Elphinstone, Burnes believed that their exceptional physical appearance and cultural and linguistic distinctions from adjacent groups denoted unusual ethnological significance. He wanted to travel to Kafiristan in person but lacked opportunities and instead remained dependent on informants he encountered in Kabul.[111] In an article in the *Journal of the Asiatic Society of Bengal* published four years after *Travels into Bokhara*, Burnes provided extensively details of these informants. He quoted one, 'a young Kaffir, about eighteen years of age' named as 'Deenbur', at length on Kalash customs, without any significant interjections of his own.[112] He also assigned credibility to a Muslim informant who had visited four Kalash villages and reported the inhabitants as closely 'resembling Europeans in their intelligence, habits and appearance as well as in their hilarious tone and familiarity, over their wine'.[113] Burnes evidently preferred this information, in keeping with the suggestion that the Kalash were pristine remnants of a population from much further west in Eurasia over the conjecture of most Afghans that they emanated from Arabia.[114]

Along with these fragmentary hints as to the Kalash's deep history, Burnes' compilation of a short vocabulary in the article meant that it became a key source for James Cowles Prichard's assertion of the Kalash's importance in the third edition of *Researches into the Physical History of Mankind*. To Prichard, the language specimen was 'of the greatest importance'. He used it to underpin the claim (following the German geographer Carl Ritter) that the 'Kafirs of the Hindu-Khuh [*sic.*] belong to the Indian race, and that the Sanskrit, which has long been a learned and dead language in Hindustan, is

---

[107] Charles Masson was the pseudonym of James Lewis, who deserted his role as East India Company soldier.

[108] Bayly, *Taming*, pp. 71, 92–116.

[109] Alexander Burnes, *Travels into Bokhara; Being an Account of a Journey from India to Cabool, Tartary, and Persia*, Vol. 1 (London: John Murray, 1834), pp. 113–14, 178–79.

[110] Burnes, 'Siah-posh' p. 325. Largely similar material on the Kafirs later appeared in Alexander Burnes, *Cabool: A Personal Narrative of a Journey to, and Residence in that City in the Years 1836, 7, and 8* (London: Carey and Hart, 1843), pp. 73–82.

[111] Burnes, 'Siah-posh', footnote pp. 325–26.   [112] Ibid., pp. 326–8.   [113] Ibid., p. 329.

[114] Ibid., p. 326.

still preserved in a peculiar dialect among the mountaineers of the Indian Caucasus'.[115] In short, one of the most significant components of the leading British ethnological thesis of the first half of the nineteenth century came directly from Burnes's information gathering, which, in turn, relied on a few contacts with whom he came into contact in Kabul. This process of transmission involved selective readings and interventions at each stage. Burnes preferred the informants who enabled him to hint at a link between Europeans and the Kalash; Prichard largely overlooked Burnes's account of customs, especially the suggestion that there was no similarity between Kalash religious practices and Hindu beliefs.[116] Ethnographic knowledge travelled from the outskirts of empire to ethnological schema that reached large European audiences through the omission as well as recapitulation of information.

Burnes's account of the Kalash, like much frontier ethnography, was not only tenuous and mutable but also contentious knowledge. Writing in 1859, H. G. Raverty, a soldier turned administrator in the Peshawar district immediately following British annexation of Punjab, launched a concerted attack on Burnes's information gathering.[117] Burnes, he charged, had been remiss during his years in Kabul in not either travelling in person to Kafiristan, 'a journey of only four or five days', or sending a British officer there.[118] Raverty extolled his own informant network, which included 'a native of Kandahar' who stayed for two years at his behest, and a Maulvi of the Peshawar District who had previously lived 'close to the Kafir ... frontiers' in Dir.[119] As Zak Leonard shows, most of Raverty's writings from his time in Peshawar focused on written language rather than the contemporary life-worlds of frontier populations.[120] However, his article on Kafiristan instead dealt at length with present-day tribal divisions and 'customs and ceremonies', with an eye constantly on what these suggested about the Kalash's origins.[121] This focus on extant Kalash culture allowed Raverty to critique Burnes. For instance, he discerned a link between Kalash and Hindu belief through a shared deity, going against Burnes's disavowal of any such overlap.[122] While echoing Burnes's comments on the European appearance of the Kalash, Raverty confidently posited that they 'appear ... unquestionably to be the remnant of the Aboriginal inhabitants

[115] Prichard, *Physical History of Mankind*, Vol. 4, 3rd ed., pp. 215–16.
[116] Burnes, 'Siah-posh', p. 327.
[117] H. G. Raverty, 'Notes on Kafiristan', *Journal of the Asiatic Society of Bengal*, 28 (1859), pp. 317–68.
[118] Ibid., pp. 317–18. On Raverty's career, see Leonard, 'Colonial Ethnography', pp. 179–82.
[119] Raverty, 'Notes', pp. 319–20.
[120] Leonard, 'Colonial Ethnography', p. 180. Raverty was especially renowned for his book *A Grammar of the Pukhto, Pushto, or Language of the Afghans* (Calcutta: Baptist Mission Press, 1855).
[121] Raverty, 'Notes', pp. 338–68, quotation on p. 362.   [122] Ibid., p. 363.

of ... central Afghanistan as at present constituted' and were displaced to their current location during the spread of Islam.[123] These conclusions, as well as Raverty's attacks on other scholars' works on the Kafirs, were themselves hotly disputed in the decades that followed.[124] Like the Nagas in the colonial northeast, the Kalash became enduring objects of peculiar ethnographic speculation through the combination of two elements. On the one hand, information on both of these groups remained limited and unstable, liable to challenge and contestation. On the other, there was widespread agreement among interested Europeans that Nagas and Kalash were exceptional communities, likely to reveal important truths about human diversity at the regional and global scales.

Further south, the tumultuous British involvement in Balochistan during the years leading up to, during, and following the Anglo-Afghan War generated enhanced ethnographic interest. As with the Nagas and the Kalash, the widespread notion that Balochs were ethnological outliers distinct from surrounding groups fuelled speculations about their origins and historical migrations. These hypotheses mingled with military and administrative imperatives that gave rise to investigations into the recent political history of the Khanate of Kalat and accounts of the inhabitants of the hills to the northeast of Kalat territory. The upland Balochs, who had been beyond the reach of Henry Pottinger's informant network in 1810, were of special interest as they posed persistent challenges to colonial soldiers and administrators (see Section 4.1). Much British writing on these groups consisted of assertions that they were inherently violent, with the collisions during and after the war configured as windows onto their essential nature.[125] Thomas Postans, the Assistant Political Agent in Sind and Balochistan during the Afghan war, wrote that 'in person, these [upland] tribes differed much from those seen in Sindh, being larger in bulk and stature, and much more ferocious in aspect'.[126] This analysis of Baloch violence presented a claim of distinct appearance that represented the frontier as a space set apart by its inhabitants' fearsome physical character-istics, a tendency also found in numerous writings on the Assam and Punjab frontiers.

As with ethnographies of the Punjab-Afghan frontier and the uplands around Assam, accounts of Balochistan generally warned of the limitations of material pertaining to past movements and events, bemoaning the lack of written

[123] Ibid., p. 365.

[124] See especially G. W. Leitner, 'Siah Posh Kafirs', *The Journal of the Anthropological Institute of Great Britain and Ireland*, 3 (1874), pp. 341–69, here p. 351.

[125] For example, Charles Masson, Narrative of a Journey to Kalat, Including an Account of the Insurrection at That Place in 1840; and a Memoir on Eastern Balochistan (London: Richard Bentley, 1843), p. 348.

[126] T. Postans, 'On the Biluchi Tribes Inhabiting Sindh in the Lower Valley of the Indus and Cutchi', *Journal of the Ethnological Society of London*, 1 (1848), pp. 103–26, here pp. 117–18.

records.[127] These shortcomings were highly productive, however, prompting a slew of competing conjectures as to the deep history of the Balochs and the racial composition of the present inhabitants of the region. On even basic points regarding the Balochs, explorer- and administrator-ethnographers disagreed. In his 1843 *Narrative of a Journey to Kalat*, Charles Masson pronounced that 'physiological distinctions' were sufficient for him to deduce that Balochs 'are comprised [of] many tribes of very different descent'.[128] In a paper delivered the following year, Postans acknowledged Masson's work but went on to contradict it completely. 'I am not aware that there are any physical peculiarities distinguishing tribes generally', he stated, surmising that all Balochs were likely 'of an Arabian stock'.[129] Like a number of British ethnographers of the Kalash, Postans also kept open the possibility that India's frontiers might contain remnants of the 'lost tribes' of Israel. He whetted the appetites of the metropolitan audience by highlighting 'the conformation of feature' between Jews and Balochs along with cultural similarities, before coyly suggesting that until 'deeper and more learned antiquarian research' had been conducted on the subject, it 'had better be left alone'.[130]

Postans's humility in this instance notwithstanding, it is notable that he and most other soldiers, administrators, and explorers who dabbled in ethnography at India's frontiers during this period did not merely collect data. They advanced theories. Their claims tended to be methodologically haphazard, melding fragments of physical, linguistic, and cultural data rather than asserting the primacy of particular types of evidence. Nonetheless, many frontier ethnologists actively engaged with leading European scholarship. Masson, for instance, disputed the renowned German historian Arnold Heeren's claim that language indicated that the Brahuis of Balochistan were connected to Afghans.[131] And, as we have already seen, frontier ethnographers' work was widely distributed in influential circles beyond colonial India. One salient example relating to the burst of interest in Balochistan during the 1840s was publication of Postans's research by the Ethnological Society of London, the first major British institution in the field, in the inaugural volume of its *Journal*.[132] Postans's work thus brought into contact two concurrent trends of the late 1830s and early 1840s: intense interest in Balochs as the British colonial state expanded to its northwest and institutional developments in British ethnology.

---

[127] For example, Robert Leech, 'Brief History of Kalat, Brought Down to the Deposition and Death of Mehrab Khan, Braho-ee', *Journal of the Asiatic Society of Bengal*, 12 (1843), pp. 473–512, here p. 473; Postans, 'Biluchi Tribes', p. 106; Masson, *Narrative*, p. 336.

[128] Masson, *Narrative*, p. 337.   [129] Postans, 'Biluchi Tribes', pp. 104, 107–8.

[130] Ibid., pp. 105–6.   [131] Masson, *Narrative*, p. 338.

[132] Postans, 'Biluchi Tribes'. On the Ethnological Society, see Stocking, *Victorian Anthropology*, pp. 244–7.

Postans was also notable for being among the earliest to engage prolifically in visual representation of frontier populations, which became more prominent during the mid- to late nineteenth century. This was partly a case of the particular habits of an individual agent of empire. Although during the early nineteenth century an increasing number of British army officers were trained in drawing, Postans chose to execute a series of pen-and-ink and watercolour sketches of people and places and to compile these into an album while most of his predecessors and contemporaries did not.[133] But his images were also bound up in broader dynamics and processes. His particular vantage point onto the Balochs – a product of the turbulent frontier politics of Upper Sind – was one crucial element. Pottinger and some of Postans's contemporaries, such as Masson, encountered Balochs primarily in their journeys inland from the coast to Kalat, spending no time in the Kachhi region further to the northeast. By contrast, Postans was stationed for a prolonged period in Shikarpur, imme-diately adjacent to Kachhi and the Bolan Pass and home to those Baloch communities that particularly irritated and interested colonial officials. Extended contact with the groups in Kachhi that the colonial state managed to settle in Upper Sind through force and with Balochs already residing in Sind led to the encounters at which Postans produced his sketches.

Three of the images in his album depicted different Kachhi communities. In these images and those of Balochs in Sind, weapons featured heavily.[134] One of the most ornately finished sketches purports to represent the Dombkis, a group from Kachhi that Postans elsewhere wrote had been 'peaceably settled as cultivators' and 'enlisted for police duties' by the British (Figure 3.1).[135] In the image and the written narrative, Postans concealed the violence of the colonial intervention that was the key prerequisite of his having contact with Dombkis (see Section 4.1). Instead, the sketch suggests the Balochs' violent tendencies by positioning two figures in stylised fashion to show a range of rifles, swords, and shields. Postans had no such opportunities to depict com-munities that remained an active threat to colonial territory and subjects in Upper Sind. The Marris, located near the Bolan Pass beyond Kachhi, figured in the album only as a visual absence in an image labelled 'The attack on the Muris', which showed distant colonial troops firing at people concealed in rugged uplands (Figure 3.2).[136]

---

[133] Postans's album is at the British Library, IOR/WD485. On the rise of training in drawing for army officers, see Twyman, 'Illustration Revolution', p. 119.

[134] IOR/W485, 13b, 58b, 59a, 67a, 108.

[135] T. Postans, 'Report on Upper Sindh and the Eastern Portion of Cutchee, with a Memorandum on the Beloochee and Other Tribes of Upper Sinde and Cutchee, and a Map of Part of the Country Referred to', *Journal of the Asiatic Society of Bengal*, 12 (1843), pp. 23–44, here p. 40.

[136] In 1843, Postans wrote that the Maris were 'the most numerous and powerful of any below the Bolan Pass . . . [and] are essentially predatory and warlike': 'Report', pp. 38–39.

Figure 3.1 Thomas Postans, 'Dumki Biluchi' or 'Biluchi armed & accoutred'
(*c*.1840) © The British Library Board.[137]

Postans's sketches were also tied up with changing print technology during
the first half of the nineteenth century. From the 1820s, steel engraving and
lithography began to replace woodblock and copperplate printing in European
publishing houses. As a recent study has outlined, this 'made the production of
illustration cheaper and more versatile ... allowing for the continued use of the
plates and maps from edition to edition and the easier integration of text and
image on the same page'.[138] Sketches rendered in Upper Sind appeared in
Postans's London-published 1843 book *Personal Observations on Sindh* thanks
to this technological shift. Whereas the lavishly produced quarto first edition of
Elphinstone's *Account* (1815) featured expensive aquatint illustrations of particular individuals and ethnographic 'types' on heavyweight paper inserted into
the typescript when it was bound, monochrome renderings of some of Postans's
depictions were embedded within the text in his more humbly produced, octavo

---

[137] IOR/W485, 13b.   [138] Keighren, Withers, and Bell, *Travels*, pp. 156–57.

Figure 3.2 Thomas Postans, 'The attack on the Muris at the Surtaf Pass 1840' (*c*.1840) © The British Library Board.[139]

format book.[140] The publishers also commissioned a colour-tinted lithograph of 'A Biluchi soldier and Hindu trader of Sindh' for the frontispiece (Figure 3.3).[141] Like many published ethnographic sketches, the frontispiece image was a composite of individuals originally rendered separately. The body, clothing, and accoutrements of the 'Biluchi soldier' were taken, with minor adjustments, from a drawing Postans executed in 1839, which another London company had already lithographed separately (Figure 3.4). The change of caption from the earlier lithograph's 'Jemidar of Beloochees Kurachee' is notable: a specific rank and location gave way to a much wider category, suggesting that this heavily armed figure typified Balochs in general. As we

[139] IOR/W485, 68b.

[140] On details of the format of the first edition of Elphinstone's *Account* and on the significance of different formats (including the prestige of quarto relative to octavo), see Keighren, Withers, and Bell, *Travels*, pp. 228, 236. On British depictions of Indian 'types' in the earlier and later nineteenth century respectively, see C. A. Bayly, 'From Company to Crown. Nineteenth-Century India and Its Visual Representation', in id (ed.), *The Raj: India and the British 1600–1947* (London: National Portrait Gallery, 1990), pp. 130–40, here p. 134; Christopher Pinney, 'Colonial Anthropology in the "Laboratory of Mankind"', in Bayly (ed.), *The Raj*, pp. 252–63, here p. 256.

[141] Thomas Postans, *Personal Observations on Sindh* (London: Longman, Brown, Green, and Longmans, 1843), frontispiece, pp. 44, 323.

Figure 3.3 Thomas Postans, 'A Biluchi soldier and Hindu trader of Sindh', lithograph by W. Walton (1843). Reproduced by kind permission of the Syndics of Cambridge University Library.[142]

shall see in the next section, efforts to broaden the representative scope of images remained commonplace as ethnographic images became more widespread.[143] But, as was the case with Postans in Upper Sind, particular encounters and local dynamics mattered in the colonial production of knowledge of India's frontier communities. Traces of specificity and contestation often remained embedded within images, making them potent but volatile means by which to represent the people who formed the limits of British India.

[142] Postans, *Personal Observations*, frontispiece.
[143] On the adaptation of images for mass-audience publications, see Keighren, Withers, and Bell, *Travels*, p. 157.

Figure 3.4 Thomas Postans, 'Jemidar of Beloochees Kurachee', lithograph by Day and Haghe (*c*.1839) © The British Library Board.[144]

3.4   'Patient, Painstaking Care': Fragmented Ethnography in Northeast India during the 1870s

Scholars recently have called into question the idea that a monolithic 'ethnographic state' developed in British India in the wake of the Rebellion of 1857 to 1858.[145] The 1860s and 1870s undoubtedly saw an explosion of ethnography at the northeast frontier, some of which came under the auspices of major projects

---

[144] IOR/WD485, 67a.

[145] Nicholas Dirks is the foremost advocate of the 'ethnographic state' theory: Dirks, *Castes*, pp. 16–17; Nicholas B. Dirks, 'Annals of the Archives: Ethnographic Notes on the Sources of History', in Brian Axel (ed.), *From the Margins: Historical Anthropology and Its Futures* (Durham, NC: Duke University Press, 2002), pp. 47–65. Critiques of this idea include: Leonard, 'Colonial Ethnography', pp. 188–89, 195; Anastasia Piliavsky, 'The "Criminal Tribe" in India before the British', *Comparative Studies in Society and History*, 57, 2 (2015), pp. 323–54.

with state patronage. New impulses to centralise and standardise ethnographic data also emerged from the metropole. Fierce debates over methodologies for understanding the significance and basis of race were not resolved but were brought within a single organisation, the Anthropological Institute of Great Britain and Ireland, in 1871.[146] The Institute produced a guide to ethnographic work, *Notes and Queries in Anthropology*, in 1874, which went beyond previous efforts to discipline fieldwork practices and records.[147] As will be outlined in this section, these developments did impact some of the ways in which frontier inhabitants were understood, and how knowledge of them was transmitted. However, ethnography remained fragmented in terms of representative techniques, core contentions, and the transit of knowledge. Such fragmentation was, in a sense, built into the way in which key individuals practised ethnography in the northeast. They emphasised the particularity of the encounters they had with upland populations, employed varied representative techniques, and often foregrounded rather than effaced their own activities and those of their colonial colleagues in the region. In short, the intensification of ethnography in the northeast and the advent of enhanced state and institutional involvement did not result in uniformity but generated diversity and dissensus.

This was the case even in projects directly backed by the upper echelon of the colonial state. Two prominent publications touched extensively on frontier communities: J. Forbes Watson and John Kaye's eight-volume *The People of India* (1868–75) and the retired administrator Edward Tuite Dalton's *Descriptive Ethnology of Bengal* (1872).[148] They shared a similar format, offering encyclopaedic overviews of 'racial types' through photographs and potted written descriptions. Their authors admitted the contingency and uncertainties involved in their compilation and production.[149] Watson and Kaye famously professed that 'the photographs were produced without any definite plan, according to local and personal circumstances, by different officers' and that the written descriptions 'varied greatly in amplitude and value'.[150] Dalton

---

[146] Stocking, *Victorian Anthropology*, pp. 248–56; Sadiah Qureshi, *Peoples on Parade: Exhibitions, Empire, and Anthropology in Nineteenth-Century Britain* (Chicago, IL: University of Chicago Press, 2011), pp. 212–5.

[147] Urry, '"Notes"', pp. 47–48; Stocking, *Victorian Anthropology*, pp. 258–61. On earlier questionnaires, see Sera-Shriar, *Making*, pp. 53–79.

[148] J. Forbes Watson and John William Kaye (eds.), *The People of India. A series of photographic illustrations, with descriptive letterpress, on the races and tribes of Hindustan*, 8 vols. (London: India Museum, 1868–1875); Edward Tuite Dalton, *Descriptive Ethnology of Bengal* (Calcutta: Office of the Superintendent of Government Printing, 1872).

[149] On the production of *The People of India*, see John Falconer, '"A pure labor of love": A publishing history of *The People of India*', in Eleanor M. Hight and Gary D. Sampson (eds.), *Colonialist Photography: Imag(in)ing race and place* (London: Routledge, 2002), pp. 51–83.

[150] Watson and Kaye, *The People of India*, Vol. 1, ii; James R. Ryan, *Picturing Empire: Photography and the Visualization of the British Empire* (London: Reaktion Books, 1997), pp. 155–56; Falconer, 'Passion', p. 81.

confessed that the *Descriptive Ethnology* emerged from the failure to hold an 'Ethnographic Congress in Calcutta' as an adjunct to the Asiatic Society of Bengal's general industrial exhibition in 1869 and 1870.[151] The event had not materialised because the Commissioner of Assam claimed that bringing 'typical specimens' of frontier communities to Calcutta might result in 'casualties that the greatest enthusiast for anthropological research would shrink from encountering ... [and] might lead to inconvenient political complications'.[152] Such caution over possible resistance to attempts at human display may have been prudent.[153] An attempt in 1883 to pay Akas to the north of the Brahmaputra Valley to take part in an exhibition in Calcutta resulted in the colonial agent concerned being killed. In a deposition to the local British official following the death, Aka chiefs stated: 'This fact is well known that we may sell and may give our goods, but we can never sell a human being. To send a [man] to buy a raja and rani was not a good thing to do on the part of the Government'.[154]

Dalton's theoretical and methodological framework mixed older and newer components. Echoes of Brian Houghton Hodgson and other work focused on tracing remnants of the 'aboriginal' pre-Aryan peoples of India can be discerned in his claim that the population of 'the North-Eastern Frontier' constituted 'the most archaic form we possess of the materials out of which the ancient population was formed'.[155] But Dalton disavowed the priority that these ethnologists gave to language as the key to human diversity. Instead, he followed the growing trend towards physical anthropology during the middle decades of the nineteenth century in colonial India and metropolitan Britain, and sought cranial and facial measurements.[156] However, huge variations in the techniques of different photographers and the information captured in their images stymied Dalton's search for standardised data. The surgeon Dr. Benjamin Simpson, who he commissioned to add photographs for the *Descriptive Ethnology* to the prize-winning ones Simpson showed at the London Exhibition of 1862, received Dalton's praise for 'add[ing] much to [the images'] value by contributing also the measurement of the individuals photographed'.[157] He judged some other contributions more harshly. In the textual commentary on one particular photograph, Dalton professed to 'know nothing of this miserable looking creature [who] does not at all correspond with the [written] description'.[158] That the image still found its way into the

---

[151] Dalton, *Descriptive Ethnology*, i-ii.   [152] Ibid., i.
[153] On the impact on anthropology of displayed people in Britain, see Qureshi, *Peoples*.
[154] NAI Foreign External A, October 1884, No. 58: Medhi Raja and fourteen other Rajas to Deputy Commissioner, Darrang District, 26 November 1883.
[155] Dalton, *Descriptive Ethnology*, p. 1.
[156] On the short-lived bastion of physical anthropology, the Anthropological Society of London (operative from 1863 to 1871), see Stocking, *Victorian Anthropology*, pp. 247–56.
[157] Dalton, *Descriptive Ethnology*, iii.   [158] Ibid., plate 26.

Descriptive Ethnology was a clear sign of the unevenness of his information-gathering network.

Dalton's own doubts over the veracity and utility of his images paled alongside the criticism he faced from some officials posted to Assam's frontier regions. Scepticism towards the *Descriptive Ethnology* began long before Gertrude Godden queried his reliability in 1898.[159] Dalton obtained information from published works including Robinson's *Descriptive Account* and the *Journal of the Asiatic Society of Bengal*, and from his own journals written while 'employed in various expeditions amongst the hill tribes', despite the fact that some of the latter had been lost during the Rebellion of 1857 to 1858.[160] John Butler, the Deputy Commissioner of the Naga Hills District when Dalton's book was published, recorded in his diary:

Amused myself by reading some of Dalton's work on the Ethnology of Bengal and was much surprised to find that the letter press at all events as far as the Naga Tribes are concerned is not in my humble opinion worth very much and yet this is the very portion of the book for the accuracy of which he states in his preface that he himself is alone responsible. It seems strange that he should not apparently ever have considered it worth his while to refer to any of the Frontier Officers in Assam.[161]

Butler's objection was not merely that of a jilted would-be contributor. It pointed to a deeper schism within ethnography in the northeast over how to comprehend frontier inhabitants. It is notable that Butler was particularly critical of the photography in Dalton's *Descriptive Ethnology*, claiming that it did not accurately illustrate particular communities. Butler and his colleagues at the Assam frontier in the 1870s shared with Dalton an emphasis on the physical appearance and material culture of tribes, and relative disinterest in questions of language. But unlike Dalton's compilation that listed communities and represented them as 'types', they practised forms of ethnographic representation and theorising that relied on prolonged contact with inhabitants of a smaller area. During the decades of creeping expansion that followed its inauguration as a colonial District in 1866 (see Section 1.3), the Naga Hills became the primary arena for a more immersive type of ethnography in the colonial northeast. Butler and his contemporaries in the region were at pains to foreground rather than diminish their own presence among the Nagas, positioning their labours as the guarantee of accurate information. In the single article he authored before his premature death in 1876, Butler described his passage to Naga villages 'often up through tortuous, narrow, covered ways, or

---

[159] Godden, 'Nagas (continued)', footnote p. 2.
[160] Dalton, *Descriptive Ethnology*, iii, passim.
[161] Centre of South Asian Studies archives, University of Cambridge (hereafter 'CSAS'), Stewart papers, Box 2: John Butler, *Volume III: Tour Diary of the Deputy Commissioner for 1873* (Shillong: Assam Government Press, 1942), p. 3.

lanes, with high banks on either side, lined with a overhanging tangled mass of prickly creepers and brushwood, sometimes through a steep ravine and along a bed of an old torrent'.[162] As we have already seen, the location and credentials of observers tended to feature prominently in frontier ethnographies: these were not accounts that sought to construct objectivity by occluding the observer.[163] The works of Butler and his colleagues strengthened these established features, as they sought to tie ethnographic expertise to the extended contact made possible by administering a frontier region.

Synchronous developments at the northwest frontier had notable similarities. There too, sustained contact with Pashtun and Baloch communities from the 1870s allowed administrator-ethnographers such as S. S. Thorburn and Mansel Longworth Dames to develop new forms of frontier ethnography focused on what Zak Leonard terms 'socio-cultural analysis of present life worlds on the frontier'.[164] However, while investigations in the northwest focused significantly on folklore and oral traditions, enhanced contact in the Naga Hills tended to underpin studies of material culture and social structure. Of particular importance in the latter respect was Butler's realisation that the Angami Nagas were divided less between villages, as previously assumed, than between clans.[165] The dynamics between these groups – a number of which inhabited each village – were of interest to Butler and his immediate successors for political reasons, as they sought to intervene in conflicts among people under their growing jurisdiction. It seems that in grappling with this feature of Angami society, Butler initiated a particular mode of comparison between frontier communities in northwest and northeast by applying the Pashtun term 'khel' to Naga clans. Certainly, his previous experience of the Punjab frontier was on his mind: he wrote of his '3 years [sic.] sojourn in Peshawar' two days after first alluding to 'khel' in his tour diary in 1870.[166] We might speculate that Butler deemed the term appropriate because it imbued Angamis with the same combination of social fragmentation and violent tendencies that British administrators of his era assigned to the inhabitants of the uplands west of Peshawar. At any rate, the borrowing caught on and from the 1890s transitioned from being a category of primarily administrative interest to a key object

---

[162] John Butler, 'Rough Notes on the Angami Nagas', *Journal of the Asiatic Society of Bengal*, 44 (1875), pp. 307–46, here pp. 317–18.

[163] On the development of this model of objectivity during the nineteenth century, see Daston and Galison, *Objectivity*.

[164] Leonard, 'Colonial Ethnography', quotation on p. 176. S. S. Thorburn, *Bannu; or Our Afghan Frontier* (London: Trübner & Co., 1876); M. Longworth Dames, *A Text Book of the Balochi Language, Consisting of Miscellaneous Stories, Legends, Poems, and Balochi-English Vocabulary* (Lahore: Government Press, 1891).

[165] Butler, 'Rough Notes', p. 315.

[166] John Butler, *Volume I: Tour Diary of the Deputy Commissioner, Naga Hills. 1870* (Shillong: Assam Government Press, 1942), pp. 4–5.

of anthropological study once the 'khel' came to be identified as the exogamous unit of Naga society (see Section 3.6).[167]

Butler may have adopted terminology from the northwest, but his ethnography differed from contemporary administrator-ethnographers in that region – and shared a common feature with Dalton's work – in making extensive use of visual representations. Images became a core component of frontier ethnographies in the northeast from the 1870s on. Lithographed sketches of some frontier 'types' by Butler's father (also called John Butler) had appeared in the London-published 1847 book *A Sketch of Assam*.[168] The decades that followed saw the uptake of cameras and photographic reproduction techniques in India, enabling substantial and rapid changes in ethnographic representation.[169] The seven plates that accompanied the younger Butler's article of 1875 were reproduced by means of photozincography at the Surveyor General's Office in Calcutta, a method introduced to India less than a decade before for the primary purpose of copying maps (see Section 2.3). However, as is the case for the late 1830s and 1840s, technological changes are necessary but not sufficient to explain the growing importance of images in frontier ethnography. Individuals mattered too: none more so, in the case of visual representations of Nagas, than the man who rendered what Butler termed the 'admirable illustrations' for his article and who later read Gertrude Godden's paper to the Anthropological Institute in London, Robert Woodthorpe.[170]

In his obituary, his fellow surveyor Thomas Holdich suggested that Woodthorpe's passion for sketching derived from encounters in the upland northeast with 'people so exceptional in their physical characteristics, and so entirely aboriginal in their manners and customs'.[171] In fact, Woodthorpe was a prolific sketch artist prior to his arrival in India, creating a heavily illustrated 'Journal' of his first voyage from Southampton to Calcutta in 1869.[172] He generated a visual corpus that went well beyond any previous or contemporary frontier ethnographer. Woodthorpe was an army officer in the Royal Engineers, employed by the Survey of India from 1871. Following early assignments to the Khasi and Lushai uplands, he gained a reputation as a frontier specialist. Along with stints in the Naga Hills, Woodthorpe undertook survey work during

---

[167] Especially important was its use in A. W. Davis's report on Nagas in E. A. Gait, *Census of India, 1891. Assam. Vol. I—Report* (Shillong: Assam Secretariat Printing Office, 1892), pp. 237–51, here p. 238.

[168] An Officer [John Butler], *A Sketch of Assam with Some Account of the Hill Tribes* (London: Smith, Elder and Co., 1847).

[169] On photography in India during this period, see Christopher Pinney, *Camera Indica: The Social Life of Indian Photographs* (London: Reaktion Books, 1997); Christopher Pinney, *The Coming of Photography in India* (London: British Library, 2008).

[170] Butler, 'Rough Notes', quotation on p. 327, plates following p. 328.

[171] T. H. Holdich, 'Obituary: Major-General R.G. Woodthorpe, C.B., R.E.', *The Geographical Journal*, 12, 2 (1898), pp. 195–201, here p. 195.

[172] PRM, Woodthorpe Papers: 'Journal of an "overland" voyage from Southampton to Calcutta'.

the 1870s and 1880s to the north of Assam and in northern Burma. He also accompanied British military parties into the northwest frontier during the Second Anglo-Afghan War and during an expedition north of Kashmir in the mid-1880s. He gained influence in leading metropolitan institutions, giving talks at the Royal Geographical Society and the Anthropological Institute.[173] Although Woodthorpe's ethnographic sketching was an adjunct to his survey duties, Butler was not alone among his colleagues in extolling the images. Holdich pronounced that they 'must be considered unique in value, not only for the extent of them, but for their minute accuracy, and the patient, painstaking care with which comparatively small ethnographical traits and details are preserved in them'.[174]

There is no doubt that Woodthorpe's sketches had a significant impact on frontier ethnography from the 1870s through into the twentieth century. They continued to be used by administrator-anthropologists J. H. Hutton and J. P. Mills in the 1920s.[175] However, neither the images nor their influence were uniform or straightforward. The outstanding feature of Woodthorpe's visual corpus, which included photographs that he collected alongside his own drawings, is its huge variety of perspectives and of circulation. He continually sought new ways of viewing the territories and inhabitants of frontier regions, and the material he produced and collected bears marks of adaptations in the face of practical constraints and limitations. Woodthorpe's images are, then, key examples not only of the growing reputation of the northeast – and the Naga Hills in particular – as an ethnographic hotspot but also of the contingency and diversity that marked the production and use of representations of frontier communities.

Woodthorpe rendered a number of set-piece scenes that depict inhabitants of the northeastern uplands alongside British officials and members of their retinues. These were some of his most reproduced and widely viewed images; as such, they illuminate some of the possibilities (and potential perils) associated with the circulation of visual representations. One of these sketches was reproduced in monochrome and published in the London-based weekly *The Graphic* in 1873. It presents a highly selective rendering of British benevolence in dealing with uplanders, centring on Captain Williamson, the lead colonial

---

[173] Woodthorpe, 'Naga Hills Part I'; Woodthorpe, 'Naga Hills Part II'; R. G. Woodthorpe, 'Explorations on the Chindwin River, Upper Burma', *Proceedings of the Royal Geographical Society and Monthly Record of Geography*, 11, 1 (1889), pp. 197–216; R. G. Woodthorpe, 'The Country of the Shans', *The Geographical Journal*, 7, 6 (1896), pp. 577–600; R. G. Woodthorpe, 'Some Account of the Shans and Hill Tribes on the State of the Mekong', *Journal of the Anthropological Institute of Great Britain and Ireland*, 26 (1897), pp. 13–28.

[174] Holdich, 'Obituary', p. 195.

[175] Thomas Simpson, 'A Fragmented Gaze: Depictions of Frontier Tribes and the Beginnings of Colonial Anthropology', in Marcus Banks and Annamaria Motrescu-Mayes (eds.), *Visual Histories of South Asia* (New Delhi: Primus, 2018), pp. 73–92.

official, as a paternalistic figure receiving the 'submission' of 'lately independent Garo chiefs'.[176] This image fed growing metropolitan demand for news of colonial engagements in frontier locales, a process that depended crucially on photographic reproduction technologies. However, these techniques could be flawed. As Woodthorpe wrote underneath his personal copy of the version that appeared in *The Graphic*, the photographic reduction of the original sketch to enable it to fit in the periodical was 'not very accurately done' (Figure 3.5). Even in the age of mechanical reproduction, transmitting ethnographic representations was an imperfect enterprise that often produced less-than-satisfactory results.

Following this disappointment, Woodthorpe went to significant lengths to ensure adequate reproductions of another of his ethnographic tableaux. Drawn

Figure 3.5 Robert Woodthorpe, 'Indian sketches – the lately independent Garo chiefs tendering their submission to Captain Williamson', in *The Graphic* (1873). © Pitt Rivers Museum, University of Oxford.[177]

---

[176] *The Graphic*, 196 (30 August 1873), p. 196.   [177] PRM, 1914.5.2, 1.

Figure 3.6 Robert Woodthorpe, 'Captn. J. Butler receiving submissions of Naga chiefs' (1874). © Pitt Rivers Museum, University of Oxford.[178]

in 1874 during Woodthorpe's first survey expedition to the Naga Hills, the image represents at its centre John Butler, surrounded by a range of Nagas and colonial personnel. Woodthorpe deliberately prepared the original sketch for reproduction, tinting in white some features such as a turban and a spear-point to aid the photographic process (Figure 3.6). He personally hand-coloured one of the large-format copies (Figure 3.7), and at least one more coloured image was produced in this format.[179] A host of monochrome copies of various sizes were also printed onto cheaper paper. One recent interpretation of the sketch suggests that it 'combines the realism of the figures with a representation of a desired set of relations in the colonial system: exoticism tempered by the order and harmony of the Raj'.[180] By this reading, the image was essentially similar to Woodthorpe's earlier depiction of the Garos and Williamson: a sanitised rendering of colonial control over ostensibly undeveloped and picturesque frontier peoples. In fact, the specificities embedded across the multiple copies of this sketch suggest that ethnographic representation was a more fragmented venture. Unlike the Garos in the Williamson image, the Nagas are not arrayed around Butler in a manner suggesting paternalistic oversight. The idea that they are

[178] PRM, 1910.45.19.
[179] Another image sold at auction in 2008 for £10,000. Alban von Stockhausen, *Imag(in)ing the Nagas: The Pictorial Ethnography of Hans-Eberhard Kauffmann and Christoph von Furer-Haimendorf* (Stuttgart: Arnoldische Art Publishers, 2014), p. 54.
[180] Jacobs et al, *The Nagas*, p. 17.

Figure 3.7 Robert Woodthorpe, 'Naga Hills, Assam' (1874). © Pitt Rivers Museum, University of Oxford.[181]

tendering 'submission' to Butler appears in the title only of the original pencil sketch and does not appear in the caption of any other copy.

The image is also highly unusual among Woodthorpe's sketched oeuvre and colonial visual representations more generally in depicting acts of ethnographic representation. The right-hand portion of the image portrays Dr. Brown, the Political Agent at Manipur, and Woodthorpe himself.[182] Brown was a keen photographer who contributed to Dalton's *Descriptive Ethnology* and is shown grasping a leg of a photographic tripod whilst a Manipuri assistant stands by, holding a photographic plate to be loaded into the camera.[183] Woodthorpe, meanwhile, appears in profile in the act of sketching one of the three Lhota Nagas who stand posed, partly obscured by Brown and Brown's camera apparatus and attendant. This is the visual equivalent of Butler's emphasis on his own bodily labour as an administrator-ethnographer in the Naga Hills. Woodthorpe's depiction of himself at work – a peculiarly pallid, ghost-like form in the reproduction that he coloured – is especially indicative of the reductive nature of the conventional set-up for ethnographic sketches. The rigidly staged men lined up to come under the scrutiny of Woodthorpe's pencil

---

[181] PRM, 1910.45.18.
[182] Brown is mislabelled on some later reproductions as 'Dr. O'Brien': PRM 1910.45.18; PRM 1998.219.2.2.
[183] Dalton, *Descriptive Ethnology*, iii; plate 19.

and Brown's camera lens stand in stark contrast to the more varied figures arrayed in the foreground and those that can be distantly glimpsed in the background of the sketch. These features suggest the need to go beyond some influential recent theories of how modern states, especially colonial ones, assemble knowledge. In contrast, for instance, to James C. Scott's notion that such states 'see' with 'resolute singularity', Woodthorpe's 'Butler' sketch gives an insight into the multiplicity of British ethnographic representations of Nagas during the 1870s.[184] It is an image that should be understood with reference to anthropologist Erik Mueggler's caution against assuming that 'imperial gazes could, in reality as well as in ideology, be modelled on the kind of vision commonly attributed to the camera'. The sketch instead provides an opening onto the reality that, in Mueggler's words again, 'acts of vision are . . . always embedded in social fields of vision, composed of intersections of multiple pairs of eyes'. As they depicted people at the edges of empire, ethnographers such as Woodthorpe were exposed to 'the gazes of others'.[185]

Variable annotations on different versions of the sketch indicate the multiple ways in which it was seen, prompting us to consider how Woodthorpe's visual ethnographic corpus took on diverse meanings and uses, even for Woodthorpe himself.[186] On the reverse of one of the smaller format photographic reproductions of the 'Butler' sketch, Woodthorpe dated and located the scene: 'Lakmuti – Rengma Naga village – Season 73-74'. He also noted parenthetically that 'all portraits [were] taken from actual sitters' (omitting to add that not all these individuals were ever at Lakmuti).[187] These details seem to have been added for the benefit of other viewers. After all, particulars did matter to imperial men of science of Woodthorpe's generation, as shown by Holdich's comment that Woodthorpe's drawings were valuable because of 'their minute accuracy' and 'small ethnographical traits and details'.[188] There are, therefore, reasonable grounds to speculate that Woodthorpe assumed such specifics would add credibility and utility to the image as an ethnographic source for members of the Anthropological Institute in London, where the image is now held. He also recorded particular dates, places, and names on some of the preliminary sketches of the individual 'actual sitters' that he executed at various junctures and places during his journey through the hills in 1873 and 1874 (Figures 3.8 and 3.9).[189] These details set the images apart from the 'types' that dominated previous and contemporary representations of frontier inhabitants. They were diverse in terms

---

[184] Scott, *Seeing*, p. 347.   [185] Mueggler, *Paper Road*, p. 60.

[186] On the importance of text to colonial images in the mid-nineteenth century, see Clare Anderson, 'Oscar Mallitte's Andaman Photographs, 1857-8', *History Workshop Journal*, 67 (2009), pp. 152–72, here p. 155.

[187] RAI, MS 442/1.   [188] Holdich, 'Obituary', p. 195.

[189] The preliminary sketches held in the Pitt Rivers Museum archives aside from the two reproduced below are PRM 1914.5.2, 14 and 37.

Figure 3.8 Robert Woodthorpe, 'Sézelé, an Angami of Cepama, Naga Hills' (1874). © Pitt Rivers Museum, University of Oxford.[190]

of poses and material accoutrements, and clearly bore marks of intensive encounters with particular individuals in specific locations.[191]

Woodthorpe's images did not derive ethnographic significance through specificities alone. Adapted annotations and subtle visual amendments to subsequent versions of the preliminary studies partially transformed them into broader 'types'. Equally important, though, was that these 'types' were sometimes contradictory and did not resolve into a single authoritative categorisation. As Clare Anderson has written of ethnographic images of Andaman Islanders, reproduction and alteration entailed 'the possibility of visual and textual disruption of various kinds'.[192] When photozincographed in monochrome to illustrate John Butler's 1875 article, one of studies also incorporated

<hr />

[190] PRM, 1993.17.1.
[191] On the significance of named individuals in British colonial ethnographic images around this time, see Ryan, *Picturing Empire*, p. 142. Joy Pachuau and Willem van Schendel point out that ethnographic sketches of Mizo people during the 1870s and 1880s 'allow us to see individuals': Joy L. K. Pachuau and Willem van Schendel, *The Camera as Witness: A Social History of Mizoram, Northeast India* (Delhi: Cambridge University Press, 2015), p. 34.
[192] Anderson, 'Oscar Mallitte', p. 162.

Figure 3.9 Robert Woodthorpe, 'Dotsoll – Chedema. Angami Naga' (1874).
© Pitt Rivers Museum, University of Oxford.[193]

into Woodthorpe's 'Butler' sketch underwent notable alterations. It was re-captioned without the sitter's name and given additional exoticised features: a head-dress with three feathers (akin to those that Woodthorpe depicted on Nagas of a different tribe in the 'Butler' tableau) and an animal-hide pattern on the shield (Figure 3.10). Butler's written description of the image claimed that this individual had his 'loins girt up, and carrying two spears, [was] ready for action'.[194] This set the man in substantially different terms to his appearance in Woodthorpe's tableau, in which the removal of the second spear enhanced the scene's impression of relative tranquillity. The amended version in Butler's

[193] PRM, 1914.5.2, 83.   [194] Butler, 'Rough Notes', p. 328.

Figure 3.10 Robert Woodthorpe, 'Angami Naga of Chedema',
photozincographed print (1875). Reproduced by kind permission of the
Syndics of Cambridge University Library.[195]

article also went on to influence future accounts of the Nagas, appearing
alongside a pair of mugshot photographs to typify Angamis in a 1900 article
by the surgeon-anthropometrist Laurence Waddell.[196]

When transferring this individual from the preliminary study to the tableau,
Woodthorpe also undertook additional interventions. He substantially nar-
rowed the man's eyes, altering a physical feature that he and contemporary
British anthropologists afforded significance as a marker of tribal distinction

[195] Butler, 'Rough Notes', plate 19.
[196] L. A. Waddell, 'The Tribes of the Brahmaputra Valley:—A Contribution on Their Physical
Types and Affinities', *Journal of the Asiatic Society of Bengal*, 69, 3 (1900), pp. 1–127, plate 8.

among the Nagas.[197] Like the other individuals incorporated into this image, Woodthorpe removed the name and village of this man. In this way, Woodthorpe's sketches contributed to administrator-ethnographers' intensified, but still uneven, efforts to classify Naga tribal groupings during the later nineteenth century.[198] By highlighting the particularities of Angamis in the visual field of the 'Butler' tableau and the captions he appended to some copies, Woodthorpe also promoted his preferred theory that the Angamis were a wholly distinct group that had immigrated to the hills more recently than all other Nagas.[199] It is clear, then, that the presence of specific markers in ethnographic images was useful in some ways, but that the erasure of such markers and subsuming of individuals into 'types' were equally useful in others. Woodthorpe's sketches were especially effective when they were adaptable. As Nick Hopwood suggests of a very different type of scientific image, 'copying, the epitome of the unoriginal, [was] creative, contested, and consequential'.[200] Across various versions and copies, drawings of Nagas were spliced, re-captioned, and harnessed to contrary anthropological contentions.

There is some cause for thinking that the significance of the 'Butler' tableau changed for its creator and many viewers a little over a year after Woodthorpe rendered the original. Butler died in January 1876 following a skirmish between a colonial survey party and Nagas, an event noted in captions on a number of copies of the image. One of the monochrome reproductions is labelled 'Major Butler Political Agent Killed by Nagas 1875', and rather than being identified by tribe, the annotation 'Nagas' covers all depicted except the agents of empire.[201] This description might imply that the ethnographic order of the assembled Nagas in the 1874 original gave way to a sense of a generally threatening mass. Butler's death and those of other British officials clearly impacted Woodthorpe's affective engagement with the region. He created a watercolour landscape entitled 'Pangti – village and camp where Butler died', and later annotated one copy of another landscape with: 'where Lt. Holcombe [another surveyor] was cut up 1874'.[202] Prior to Butler's death, Woodthorpe's tableau with him central stage may have been seen as a representation of harmonious relations under beneficent colonial guidance; after this well-publicised event, its significance clearly changed for Woodthorpe and would have been very different for many of its likely audience.

---

[197] On eyes as a marker of distinction, see the discussion following Woodthorpe's 1882 paper to the Anthropological Institute in London: Woodthorpe, 'Wild Tribes Part I', p. 73. See also Woodthorpe, 'Wild Tribes Part II', p. 197.

[198] Jacobs et al, *The Nagas*, pp. 17–20.   [199] Woodthorpe, 'Wild Tribes Part I', pp. 58–59.

[200] Nick Hopwood, *Haeckel's Embryos: Images, Evolution, and Fraud* (Chicago, IL: University of Chicago Press, 2015), p. 4.

[201] PRM, 1916.47.1, 18.   [202] PRM, 1982.2.2; RAI, MS442/6.

The violence that pervaded survey expeditions into the Naga Hills affected not only understandings of extant images but also Woodthorpe's subsequent sketches. One image from 1875 shatters any assumption that ethnographic representations uniformly sought to present British engagements as peaceful.[203] Labelled by tribe and village – 'Lhota Naga of Wokha' – this image does not position its subject in a standard pose designed to facilitate comparison and categorisation but instead depicts a victim of colonial violence presumably as he died, slumped face-down (Figure 3.11). Although unique among the sketches now held in his main archival collections, there is evidence that Woodthorpe produced another image of a Naga killed by colonial troops.[204] Victims of the violence that attended British intrusions further east into the uplands appear, then, to have formed a small but distinct 'type' in Woodthorpe's ethnographic sketches. We might tentatively bracket these images with visual (normally photographic) corpuses that represented victims of other late-nineteenth-century moments of 'catastrophic colonial violence'. Unlike these collections of images, which, in Branwyn Poleykett's words, 'appeared to be designed and circulated with virtuous intent',[205] the level of sympathy with which Woodthorpe depicted these subjects is ambiguous. There is no evidence that either of the images of dead Nagas were reproduced, and their impact – affective or ethnographic – seems to have been limited. The only record of their reception was the claim in a 1924 letter from the administrator-anthropologist J. H. Hutton to the Curator of the Pitt Rivers Museum Henry Balfour that one of the images 'isn't to my mind an attractive sketch, though very clear'.[206] But as Erik Mueggler has commented on Westerners' photographs of indigenous suffering at another imperial borderland, such images hold the potential to demand unusual empathetic engagement from viewers, 'slicing through the "chronotopic certainties" that put subject and viewer each in his own place'.[207] At the very least, these sketches show that Woodthorpe's ethnography was sufficiently capacious to represent very different forms of encounter between Nagas and colonial personnel. His images did not generate a single vision of empire, nor did they reduce their subjects to a distinct order or framework. They instead afforded glimpses of the fragmented – even chaotic – nature of British attempts to control and to know frontier people in the later nineteenth century.

---

[203] On the suppression of the violence of encounters in another key arena of ethnography in British India, the Andaman Islands, see Anderson, 'Oscar Mallitte', pp. 158–59.

[204] J. H. Hutton described a Woodthorpe sketch of a 'dead Rengma' in a letter to Henry Balfour of 10 October 1924: PRM, Mills Box.

[205] Branwyn Poleykett, 'Pasteurian Tropical Medicine and Colonial Scientific Vision', *Subjectivity*, 10, 2 (2017), pp. 190–203, here p. 194.

[206] PRM, Mills Box, Hutton to Balfour, 10 October 1924.   [207] Mueggler, *Paper Road*, p. 209.

Figure 3.11 Robert Woodthorpe, 'Lhota Naga of Wokha' (1875). © Pitt
Rivers Museum, University of Oxford.[208]

3.5   'Insufficient Intimacy and Confidence': Photographing 'Frontier Tribes' in the Later Nineteenth Century

Woodthorpe's renderings of frontier inhabitants by hand were uniquely prolific
and influential. Visual ethnography expanded enormously during his era primarily because of the rise of photography rather than sketches. Recent scholarship has suggested the limitations of theories that either rigidly link
photographs to projects of state power or argue that by the later nineteenth
century western elites widely saw photography as producing necessarily truth-
ful representations.[209] Christopher Pinney's influential work proposes that,
with the spread of photographic technologies to Indians, photography became

---

[208] PRM, 1914.5.2, 28.

[209] The most influential work linking photography and state power is John Tagg, *The Burden of
Representation: Essays on Photographies and Histories* (Basingstoke: Macmillan Education,
1988). On shifts beyond these paradigms, see Daston and Galison, *Objectivity*;
Elizabeth Edwards, 'Tracing Photography', in Marcus Banks & Jay Ruby (eds.), *Made to Be
Seen: Perspectives on the History of Visual Anthropology* (Chicago, IL: University of Chicago
Press, 2011), pp. 159–89, here pp. 171–4; Jay and Ramaswamy, 'Imperial Optic', in id (eds.),
p. 36; Elizabeth Edwards, 'Anthropology and photography: A long history of knowledge and
affect', *Photographies*, 8, 3 (2015), pp. 235–52, here p. 239–40.

a *pharmakon* – both cure and poison – to the colonial state.[210] We can extend this argument to cover British uses of photography in India, especially when faced with the unusual challenges of frontier conditions. Ethnographic photographs were produced under diverse circumstances and with different intentions. They often bore marks of dispersed agency between photographer, subject, and technology. In contrast to sketches and texts, the indexicality of photographs – their capture of the array of light during a brief moment – preserves moments of contingency and contestation.[211] The relative reproducibility of photographs did not necessarily give rise to widely agreed ethnographic truths.[212] As Ariella Azoulay puts it, when 'the photograph is out there, an object in the world, ... anyone, always (at least in principle), can pull at one of its threads and trace it in such a way as to reopen the image and renegotiate what it shows'.[213] This means, in Branwyn Poleykett's words, that photographs' 'evidentiary efficacy requires careful arrangement and labour' – features often lacking in relation to frontier ethnographic images.[214]

Until the advent of more portable cameras in the very last years of the nineteenth century, photography was an expensive and laborious enterprise practised by relatively few.[215] The difficulties of transport and political sensitivities in frontier areas further added to this exclusivity: a small number of men in very particular circumstances produced images of the inhabitants of these regions. As Erik Mueggler puts it, 'in the ambiguously colonized peripheries of empire', photography was 'a cumbersome machiner[y], laborious to master and difficult to apply to daily experience'.[216] Photographs constituted a substantial portion of Woodthorpe's collections; he was one of the many frontier administrators and soldiers to compile albums depicting the regions in which they operated.[217] Woodthorpe interspersed photographic prints among his own sketches in some of the albums he assembled, suggesting that he considered them to be a significant to his vision of frontiers. Some of the images that Woodthorpe amassed were studio images of 'tribal types' on cheap, glossy paper, complete with captions designating the community embedded prior to reproduction.[218] Most were almost certainly produced by

---

[210] Pinney, *Coming*, pp. 47–9.   [211] Edwards, 'Tracing Photography', pp. 167–8.

[212] On the importance of reception in studies of colonial ethnographic photography, see Poskett, *Materials*, ch.6.

[213] Ariella Azoulay, *The Civil Contract of Photography* (New York, NY: Zone Books, 2008), p. 13.

[214] Poleykett, 'Pasteurian', p. 193.

[215] On the material processes involved in photography in India during this era, see Poskett, *Materials*, ch.6.

[216] Mueggler, *Paper Road*, p. 54.

[217] On the increasing popularity of photo-albums among the British in India from the 1860s onwards, see Gary D. Sampson, 'The Success of Samuel Bourne in India', *History of Photography*, 16, 4 (1992), pp. 336–47, here p. 338.

[218] For example, PRM, 1914.5.2, 80.

members of Woodthorpe's parties into the upland northeast, although Woodthorpe himself may not have taken many of these shots.[219] Unlike the studio images, the photographs produced on the survey expeditions seem not to have been widely reproduced.

These photographs bear clear signs of the contingent circumstances of their production, varying substantially in terms of visual modalities and quality of execution. Woodthorpe's contemporaries had to improvise their attempts to create effective images. One conspicuous issue was creating a plain backdrop. In the sketch portraits that Woodthorpe drew, simply leaving the background blank clearly defined the human or material subject of the image.[220] In photographs, achieving the same effect was more difficult. Sometimes, especially in shots of larger groups, Woodthorpe did not attempt any such backdrop or used an available setting, such as a hut wall (see Figure 3.13 for examples of both). More deliberately constructed backdrops included a line of large leaves and a sheet, which in some cases only covered a portion of the photographic field (Figure 3.12).[221] Some images also failed to contain a large number of human subjects from spilling beyond their edges. In others, people moved while the shutter was open, blurring their features.[222] These diverse and often haphazard representations remind us that a single participant never exclusively determines any photograph.[223] Elizabeth Edwards's caution against the sometimes 'quasi-romantic' move to attribute agency to people depicted in ethnographic images is certainly applicable to these photographs' unnamed and fleetingly captured subjects, about whose deliberate actions we can only speculate. But we can say, with Edwards, that humans (and materials) are active 'presences' in images taken during British forays into frontier regions.[224]

One aspect over which the photographer ostensibly had a fair degree of control, especially when backed by threat of violence, was the arrangement and poses of subjects. Pinney has argued that during the second half of the nineteenth century, two primary colonial ethnographic modalities developed: the 'mugshot', in which the head and shoulders of the subject was photographed; and the depiction of human subjects alongside supposedly 'typical' elements of their material culture.[225] None of the images in Woodthorpe's albums were mugshots, and although many might be grouped into the latter category, these varied substantially in other respects. The unstable intermingling of physical

---

[219]   In his account of his time in the Lushai Hills in 1871–2, Woodthorpe noted that another officer, Captain Cookesley, used a camera and made no mention of taking any photographs himself: Woodthorpe, *Lushai Expedition*, p. 250.

[220]   On the removal of backdrops as a strategy to render an individual 'a specimen', see Anderson, 'Oscar Mallitte', pp. 163–9.

[221]   PRM, 1916.47.1, 47 and 56.   [222]   For example, PRM, 1914.5.3, 12.

[223]   Azoulay, *Civil Contract*, pp. 11–12   [224]   Edwards, 'Anthropology', p. 242.

[225]   Pinney, 'Colonial Anthropology', p. 256.

Figure 3.12 Unknown photographer, R. G. Woodthorpe collection, 'Miri' (c.1877). © Pitt Rivers Museum, University of Oxford.[226]

and cultural traits in photographs of frontier inhabitants is typified in two images on a single page of one of Woodthorpe's albums (Figure 3.13). The upper photograph is of a group of five men, two crouching and three standing. One of the standing men is in profile – a pose found in many portraits in publications such as *The People of India* – while the remainder more or less face the camera. This profile pose is unique among Woodthorpe's collections at the Pitt Rivers Museum and the Royal Anthropological Institute. It appears to have been a brief, experimental foray into a particular photographic modality to which most photographers of Nagas in the 1870s did not return. This image is captioned '? Nagas. ?'; the uncertain categorisation points towards its strictly limited circulation and usefulness as a carrier of ethnographic information, despite conforming to an established visual form. It indicates that the colonial ethnographic gaze was hardly an unwavering one, and that without captions photographs could be, if not mute, then extremely quiet.[227] It also points

[226] PRM, 1916.47.1.64.
[227] On the muteness of photographs without captions, see James L. Hevia, 'The Photography Complex: Exposing Boxer-Era China (1900–1901), Making Civilisation', in Rosalind C. Morris (ed.), *Photographies East: The Camera and Its Histories in East and Southeast Asia* (Durham, NC: Duke University Press, 2009), pp. 79–119, here pp. 94–6.

Figure 3.13 Unknown photographer, R. G. Woodthorpe collection, '? Nagas.
?' and 'Angami' (c.1875). © Pitt Rivers Museum, University of Oxford.[228]

towards the broader truth in colonial locales that, in Ann Laura Stoler's words,
'producing rules of classification was an unruly and piecemeal venture at
best'.[229]

The second photograph is also a group shot but taps into a very different
modality. It features seven men posed in front of a hut with full battle regalia, as
if preparing to attack. This set-up was one that Woodthorpe's contemporaries

[228] PRM, 1914.5.3, 14–15.   [229] Stoler, *Archival Grain*, p. 1.

used often, and it continued to be popular among photographers through into the twentieth century.[230] Such representations in the late nineteenth century interwove the two paradigms that Pinney suggests structured photography of tribes in colonial India: the 'salvage' paradigm, which sought to preserve something of tribal life as it supposedly fractured under external encroachment; and the 'detective' paradigm, which presumed the continued vitality of sections of 'ancient' Indian society in the face of 'modern' colonial interference.[231] Images of tribal weaponry and warmongering in the northeast (and, as discussed shortly, the northwest too) were sufficiently numerous to constitute the visual equivalent of the ability that Mary Louise Pratt assigned to colonial texts, 'to constitute the everyday with ... numbing repetition'.[232] These representations collectively served simultaneously as cautious assertions of colonial control – implied by the ability to corral subjects to pose – and as key means by which frontier communities were assigned the character of innate violence.

Relative to the northeast, visual representations of peoples of the northwest frontier remained relatively scarce. There is little evidence that most officials who had extensive interactions with inhabitants of this region took photographs or rendered sketches. Those who partially bucked this trend, such as the surveyor Thomas Holdich, did not produce conventional ethnographic images. Instead, Holdich's images documented no more than hints of habitation within the landscape (Figure 3.14), redolent of the lack of sustained encounters of the type that Woodthorpe experienced in the Naga Hills. In the case of the Punjab section of frontier, this distinction may be partly ascribed to less sustained administrative intervention, but the same contention does not hold for Balochistan, which saw increased British interference concurrent with that in the Naga Hills (Sections 5.3 and 5.4). This reiterates that individuals mattered in colonial ethnography. The northwest had no direct equivalent to Woodthorpe, although Woodthorpe himself conducted two surveys in the northwest during which he executed some ethnographic and landscape sketches.[233] Photographs of peoples of the northwest frontier did, however, feature prominently in *The People of India* and among the catalogues of leading professional photographers in colonial India. Like those of the northeast, these images were clearly shaped by contingencies of technology and of colonial power. Another shared feature was the circumscribed capacity of photographs to differentiate and specify frontier communities. Instead, they often merely reiterated the impression that the key characteristic of 'frontier tribes' was violence.

---

[230] For a later depiction of Naga violence, see CSAS, Macgregor Collection, Album 1, Image 46.

[231] Pinney, *Camera Indica*, pp. 45–6. On salvage photography, see also Edwards, *Raw Histories*, pp. 157–80.

[232] Pratt, *Imperial Eyes*, p. 2.   [233] PRM, 1929.87 series, and 1957.10.3.

Figure 3.14 Thomas Holdich, photograph labelled: 'This section shows the scattered nature of the Tirah villages' (c.1879) © Royal Geographical Society (with IBG).[234]

The images of inhabitants of the Sind and Punjab frontiers in *The People of India* typified these features. The Sind photographs were originally commissioned for the 1862 International Exhibition in London.[235] The two soldier-photographers, W. R. Houghton and Henry Tanner, who later became Superintendent of Himalayan Surveying, mostly depicted Balochs residing in fully governed colonial territory.[236] Watson and Kaye admitted that this generated uncertainties over the photographed subjects' connections and similitude with their unadministered 'clansmen', who were implied to be purer types.[237] Regarding the Punjab frontier population, the comprehensiveness of the whole project was doubtful. Watson and Kaye professed that

illustrations of the border Afghan tribes have been supplied as far as the Photographic representations extended; but they are far short of including the whole of the tribes or their branches ... It can only be inferred that as yet sufficient intimacy and confidence

[234] RGS, PR/090896.

[235] Janet Dewan, 'Delineating Antiquities and Remarkable Tribes: Photography for the Bombay and Madras Governments 1855–70', *History of Photography*, 16, 4 (1992), pp. 302–17, here p. 307. On the commission of photographs for the International Exhibition, see Falconer, '"Pure labor"', p. 61.

[236] Tanner's personal album, including some images taken for *The People of India*, is housed at the British Library: IOR Photo 143.

[237] Watson and Kaye, *People*, Vol. 6, photograph 289.

does not exist between our officers on the frontier and these tribes; that their mountains and their varied peoples cannot as yet be explored or thoroughly understood.[238]

Lacking locally collected information on these communities, the editors focused little on distinguishing cultural features and only occasionally suggested relevant physical distinctions.[239] Instead, the written descriptions reinscribed the neuroses and limitations of the few texts that Watson and Kaye relied upon for source material, including W. W. Hunter's anxiety-saturated *Our Indian Musalmans* (1871) and R. H. Temple's 1856 Punjab Government publication on frontier communities (see Section 4.3).[240] Nearly all of the illustrative photographs did little to consolidate or extend the editors' written ethnographic analysis beyond providing vague allusions to violence through posing subjects with weaponry. *The People of India* ostensibly separated distinct 'tribes' and 'branches' along the Punjab frontier. However, the lack of clear-cut differences between the photographs and the slippages between communities in the text instead contributed to an impression of an indistinguishable mass, interrupted only by the occasional named potentate about whom more was known.[241] In addition, the volumes that dealt with northwest frontier communities, published in 1872, circulated less extensively among colonial institutions than the earlier volumes as interest in the project waned.[242] Their impact among ethnologists was, it seems, very limited.

Commercial photographers produced images of the northwest frontier's inhabitants that featured heavily in officials' albums of the region and contributed to processes of ethnographic 'typing'.[243] Prominent studios such as Burke & Baker and Bourne & Shepherd, both of which originated in the early 1860s, were at the forefront.[244] In 1863, William Baker received permission to accompany a colonial military venture into the Punjab frontier hills; his business partner John Burke accompanied many more 'expeditions' until the late 1890s.[245] Photography and imperial militarism bolstered each other through the British Empire during the second half of the nineteenth

---

[238] Watson and Kaye, *People*, Vol. 5, after photograph 258.   [239] Ibid., photograph 244.

[240] Ibid., Vol. 5, photograph 244; after photograph 258; W. W. Hunter, *Our Indian Musalmans: Are They Bound in Conscience to Rebel Against the Queen?* (London: Trübner & Company, 1871); R. H. Temple, *Report Showing the Relations of the British Government with the Tribes on the North-West Frontier of the Punjab, from Annexation in 1849 to the Close of 1855* (Lahore: Punjab Government Press, 1856).

[241] Watson and Kaye, *People*, Vol. 5, photographs 249 and 251.

[242] Falconer, '"Pure Labor"', p. 77.

[243] For example, D. C. Macnabb's and H. W. Bellew's albums: IOR, Photo 752/12; IOR, Photo 50/1.

[244] John Falconer, 'Photography in Nineteenth-Century India', in Bayly (ed.), *The Raj*, pp. 264–77, here p. 266. On Bourne & Shepherd, see Sampson, 'Success'.

[245] Omar Khan, From Kashmir to Kabul: The Photographs of John Burke and William Baker, 1860–1900 (Munich: Prestel, 2002), pp. 10–6.

century.[246] However, journeys with colonial parties into the northwest frontier rarely afforded numerous opportunities for ethnographic portraits, as the violent purpose of these missions made close encounters with potential subjects relatively scarce. Even Burke's most famous and varied series, comprising 100 images shot as he accompanied the Peshawar Valley Field Force during the Second Anglo-Afghan War, was threadbare in terms of ethnographic depictions, primarily out of aesthetic choice. Many of the images include frontier inhabitants, but with a very few exceptions these figures are dwarfed by the primary subject: the surrounding mountain landscape. In the handful of photographs in which men other than the newly installed Amir of Afghanistan, Yakub Khan, were placed centre-stage, they were depicted in groups in named British camps.[247]

This paucity meant that a great deal was made of the images in which frontier inhabitants did appear. Among the most widely circulated of Burke's photographs was one from this series featuring a heavily armed band of men against a craggy, vertiginous backdrop (Figure 3.15). Nestled inconspicuously among

Figure 3.15 John Burke, 'The Khan of Lalpura & followers, with Political Officer' (*c.*1879) © The British Library Board.[248]

[246] Ryan, *Picturing Empire*, pp. 73–98.   [247] IOR Photo 487/58; IOR Photo 487/86.
[248] IOR Photo 487(55). See also National Army Museum archives, 1955–04–39–55.

the group, almost all of whom look directly at the camera while cradling their rifles, is one without a gun who gazes to the side of the shot. Look more closely and it becomes obvious that, headwear aside, this man's clothing is also different from that of the others. The odd-one-out is Robert Warburton, the Political Officer of the Khyber Pass region, where the photograph was taken. The band of men are followers of the Khan of Lalpura, a leading Mohmand potentate who sits by Warburton's left knee and fought with the British forces during their second invasion of Afghanistan in the late 1870s. Although Burke's own title for this image explained the identity of its subjects, many viewers overlooked Warburton's presence and the allegiance of the armed men to British forces during the conflict. The photograph was instead presented as a marker of the supposed violent proclivities of the Punjab frontier's Pashtuns in general.[249] This process was essentially the reverse of the pursuit of 'mechanical objectivity' that Lorraine Daston and Peter Galison describe as the key impulse behind much scientific illustration in the later nineteenth century. Rather than being valuable for their assumed ability to faithfully depict individual specificities instead of generalising according to the subjective predilections of the artist, frontier ethnographic photographs tended away from the specific and towards the general.[250] On this point, we might revisit Holdich's comment on the 'comparatively small ethnographical traits and details' preserved in Woodthorpe's sketches: high-quality hand-drawn images were often thought to be better than photographs at capturing the minute and the particular.

Visual semantic slippages, most of which removed specificities and contributed to the increasingly pronounced stereotype of 'fanatical' frontier violence, were common features of commercial images and their various reproductions.[251] For instance, the *London Illustrated News* captioned a woodcut version of a photographic image: 'the people of the Khyber Pass ... are a bold and active race of highlanders, fond of predatory warfare. It will be remembered that they inflicted terrible losses upon the British army in its hurried retreat from Cabool, nearly thirty years ago'.[252] In other cases, images were substantially altered prior to reproduction to foreground tribal violence. During the Second Anglo-Afghan War, the French illustrator Emile Bayard adapted a Charles Shepherd photograph (Figure 3.16) to represent a dynamic battle scene, complete with a firing matchlock gun, in place of the more static if still closely staged original.[253] The fixation in commercial images

---

[249] Khan, *Kashmir*, pp. 130–31.   [250] Daston and Galison, *Objectivity*, pp. 115–90.

[251] On colonial tropes of frontier 'fanaticism', see Hevia, *Imperial Security*, pp. 191–237; Condos, '"Fanaticism"'; Charles Lindholm, *Frontier Perspectives: Essays in Comparative Anthropology* (Karachi: Oxford University Press), pp. 3–16.

[252] *Illustrated London News*, 18 June 1870; Khan, *Kashmir*, pp. 36–37.

[253] Columbia University, 'Afghans' images, www.columbia.edu/itc/mealac/pritchett/00routes data/1800_1899/northwest/afghans/afghans.html (accessed 23 September 2018).

Figure 3.16 Charles Shepherd, 'Afreedees from Khyber Pass' (*c*.1878)
© The British Library Board.[254]

on tribal violence continued in series such as Bourne & Shepherd's 'The Tribes on Our Frontier', produced during the 1890s.[255] These photographs were again diverse in terms of the number of subjects and their carefully managed poses, but a clear allusion to violence was a common thread connecting them all. Ethnographic photographs in the northeast and northwest alike tended to be less intimate than many of Woodthorpe's sketches. A more distanced gaze did not mean a singular one, though. It was instead epistemically shallow, flirting with the twin limitations of 'collapsing into the illustrative' rather than demonstrating general truths,[256] and of merely reaffirming, time after time, the already embedded trope of tribal violence.

3.6   'Purely Tribal': Frontiers and Anthropology at the Turn of the Twentieth Century

Contemporaries stationed at the Assam frontier may have scorned Dalton's *A Descriptive Ethnology of Bengal*, but a leading figure in the next generation

---

[254] BL, MSS Eur G91(153).   [255] IOR, Photo 576/65–67; Photo 867/2/1–3.
[256] Edwards, *Raw Histories*, p. 150.

of colonial anthropologists managed to make use of it. Herbert Risley, Commissioner of the 1901 Census of India, Director of the Ethnographic Survey of India, and leading exponent of anthropometry, illustrated his magnum opus *The People of India* (1908) with twenty-four lithographed renderings of photographs that originally appeared in Dalton's work.[257] These were the only images aside from a frontispiece photograph to feature in the first edition of Risley's book. Yet Risley seemed somewhat uncertain about their place in his work. Although he described them as 'fine pictures', he acknowledged that they 'represent only two out of the seven main types' that he identified as distinct races in India.[258] This lack of uniform coverage in a work with firmly stated comprehensive aspirations was not the only flaw. In the introduction to *The People of India*, Risley asked the sole surviving photographer, Benjamin Simpson, to 'pardon the shortcomings of the process employed' in reusing the images.[259] In addition, the photographs were far removed from the methods that Risley extolled and employed throughout the text, with no pretensions to facilitate cranial or nasal measurements. It does not seem that Risley found the images valuable as anthropometric documents, as Dalton had intended them.[260]

Why, then, did they appear in Risley's book? He suggested that he sought to rescue from obscurity Dalton's 'rare' work, 'the entire stock' of which 'was destroyed by an unfortunate accident some years ago'. Here was a twist on the notion of salvage anthropology as the preservation of communities under threat of acculturation or extermination. Risley professed 'a pious duty, to preserve from oblivion' not colonised peoples but a British ethnologist and his cohort of European photographer-informants.[261] A further motive can be inferred from Risley's private correspondence. Despite advances in print technology, publishing images remained an expensive business.[262] When a second edition of *The People of India* was discussed in 1909, John Murray, the London publishing house whose stock-in-trade was popular travel accounts, raised concerns about its public appeal and suggested that its heavy factual content meant that 'the book is not one which seems ... to lend itself very much to artistic illustration'.[263] And Thacker, Spink & Co., the Calcutta publisher of the first edition (and the eventual second edition, four years after Risley's death), seems

---

[257] Herbert Risley, *The People of India* (Calcutta and Simla: Thacker, Spink & Co.; London: W. Thacker & Co., 1908).

[258] Ibid., vi.   [259] Ibid., vi.   [260] Dalton, *Descriptive Ethnology*, ii–iii.

[261] On salvage anthropology, see Pinney, *Camera Indica*, pp. 45–46. Quotation from Risley, *People*, vi.

[262] Risley discussed the cost of publishing images at length with Assam administrators in relation to a projected but unfinished book on the people of Assam's plains regions: Risley Papers, British Library, MSS Eur E295/21: B. C. Allen, Secretary to Eastern Bengal and Assam Government, to Risley, 17 January 1910; P. R. Gurdon to Allen, 21 December 1909, ff. 8–11.

[263] MSS Eur E295/21: John Murray to Edward Ommanney, 15 August 1909, 18 August 1909, 21 September 1909, ff. 18–23, quotation from 18 August 1909, f. 22.

to have advocated using images from Dalton's book in order to minimise expense. Risley vaguely mentioned in his introduction the role of 'my publishers' in choosing images, and it was only when the first edition was 'selling steadily' that Thacker, Spink & Co. wrote positively to Risley about more innovative visual strategies.[264] The publishing house's mention of the possibility of stereoscopic illustrations for a future edition (a prospect that did not transpire) was one of a number of indications that the images in the original were considered inadequate.

Reproduction did not mean that the photographs were considered of unquestionable ethnographic value. In fact, it subjected them to a second round of criticisms.[265] With an eye to the mooted second edition, a retired soldier-administrator friendly with Risley pointedly offered sixteen hand-sketched 'good portraits of very excellent types' covering the full array of Risley's seven racial groups.[266] And William Crooke, the administrator-anthropologist who edited the second edition of The People of India, published in 1915 after Risley's death, removed two photographs and added thirteen new ones. Crooke justified this amendment in blunt terms: 'to render the book more interesting and useful to Anthropologists'.[267] The story of why and with what effects images from Dalton's 1872 book ended up being reproduced thirty-six years later in Risley's work typifies key quirks of ethnographic transmission. Photographic images were not 'immutable mobiles' that could be relied upon to travel well across time and space. Their presence was an outcome of contingent factors and fraught negotiations, and was as liable to produce confusion and controversy as to be a conduit of settled knowledge.

The unrepresentative nature in Risley's work of Dalton's images of upland communities from around Assam and Bengal was one of many ways in which frontiers remained unusually prominent in late-nineteenth-century colonial anthropology. Continuities mattered, not least the sustained notion that India's frontier communities were archaic fragments that gave clues to the ancient migration patterns by which India was populated. Locales that had been subject to intense ethnological theorising since the earlier nineteenth century, especially the Naga Hills, Balochistan, and Kafiristan, remained productive zones of uncertainty and speculation for anthropologists around the turn of the twentieth.[268] But this was a period of substantial change in studies of human diversity in the subcontinent and beyond. New paradigms and modes of data

---

[264] Risley, People, vi; MSS Eur E295/21: Thacker, Spink & Co. to Risley, 15 May 1908, ff. 45–46.

[265] On the reproduction of scientific images as a key constituent of new controversies, see Hopwood, Haeckel's Embryos, p. 301.

[266] MSS Eur E295/21: Edward Ommanney to Risley, 7 February 1909, ff. 2–4.

[267] William Crooke, 'Preface to the New Edition', in Herbert Risley, The People of India, 2nd ed., W. Crooke (ed.) (Calcutta and Simla: Thacker, Spink & Co.; London: W. Thacker & Co., 1915), ix.

[268] Works on Kafiristan included: Leitner, 'Kafirs'; Robertson, Kafirs.

collection came to the fore. The most notable of these were the expansion of India-wide censuses, new schemes of anthropometric and linguistic data gathering, increased (although still intermittent) backing for ethnographic projects from the colonial state and leading scientific institutions in the metropole, and intensified discussions on the foundations of social organisation, especially caste and tribe.[269] All of these elements combined in Risley's *The People of India* and the works of administrator-anthropologists opposed to him on key issues. Among these new data and theories, frontiers retained a prominent place.

The advent of the decennial census in British-administered frontier regions was a piecemeal venture. The first all-India census in 1881 enumerated populations in a few portions of the upland northeast and spread to encompass the whole Naga Hills District in 1891.[270] Balochistan lagged behind, as Robert Sandeman declared his opposition to the census on the grounds of potential resistance and lack of state resources.[271] Accordingly, the data collected in 1891 was sparse, and no detailed report was produced. The 1901 India-wide census, under Risley's superintendence, saw greatly expanded operations in Balochistan. But substantial areas were still entirely excluded and fewer data were collected on particular communities owing to 'political considerations'.[272] As instruments for the accurate enumeration of populations in British-governed frontier districts and provinces, censuses were, then, avowedly limited. However, many of the regional census reports written by senior officials became influential documents, mined for information by distant anthropologists. The reports rehearsed established stereotypes of frontier communities, especially ambivalent claims of barbaric violence and romantic simplicity.[273] In addition, though, they played a vital role in stimulating debates on social, cultural, and physical distinctions across the subcontinent, contributing especially to a topic of increasing interest among anthropologists and administrators: the basis and significance of tribal communities.

---

[269] On the census, see: Bernard S. Cohn, *An Anthropologist among the Historians and Other Essays* (Delhi: Oxford University Press, 1987), pp. 224–54; Arjun Appadurai, 'Number in the Colonial Imagination', in Carol A. Breckenridge and Peter van der Veer (eds.), *Orientalism and the Postcolonial Predicament* (Philadelphia, PA: University of Pennsylvania Press, 1993), pp. 314–40. On contested notions of caste and tribe, see Susan Bayly, *Caste, Society and Politics in India from the Eighteenth Century to the Modern Age* (Cambridge: Cambridge University Press, 1999), pp. 97–143; Bates, 'Race'.

[270] Gait, *1891 Assam Census Report*, p. 1.

[271] R. Hughes-Buller, *Census of India—1901. Volume V. Baluchistan. Part I—Report* (Bombay: Times of India Press, 1902), p. 24.

[272] Hughes-Buller, *Census 1901*, i–ii.

[273] For instance, Denzil Ibbetson, *Panjab Castes* (Lahore: Government Press, 1916), pp. 42, 58–59 (this book was a posthumous reprint of Ibbetson's chapter on ' The Races, Castes, and Tribes of the Panjab' in the *Report on the Census of the Panjab in 1881* (Lahore: Government Press, 1883); A. W. Davis, 'The Naga Tribes', in Gait, *1891 Assam Report*, pp. 237–51.

A great deal of scholarship focuses on the role of colonial censuses in India in shaping and reflecting debates on caste, especially whether it was essentially racial as Risley argued, or based on occupation as Denzil Ibbetson and William Crooke (among others) proposed.[274] The closely related discussion of tribes – broadly construed as communities based on the idea of common descent – has received notably less historiographical attention.[275] However, leading figures from both sides of this debate commented extensively on the concept of the tribe, and in fact shared much common ground on this subject.[276] Not least, they widely assumed that frontier populations were among the least compromised examples of tribal community, relatively isolated from the influence of caste.[277] The nearby presence of the 'purely tribal … Pathan or Biloch of the frontier hills' influenced and evidenced Ibbetson's core argument in his report on the Punjab census of 1881 that tribe rather than caste was the essential basis of social organisation throughout the region.[278]

Conceptions of the tribe set down in census reports on frontier populations also fed into anthropological studies with a Subcontinent-spanning scope. Despite their direct opposition over the basis and stability of caste groupings, Risley's *The People of India* and Crooke's *Natives of Northern India* shared Ibbetson's contention that tribe temporally preceded caste in India.[279] Risley and Crooke also gave identically worded definitions of 'the tribe', which included the notion that 'in some parts of the country the tribesmen are held together by the obligation to assist their brethren in blood feuds, rather than by the tradition of common ancestry'.[280] We might speculate that the ingrained stereotype of the 'fanatical' northwest frontiersman underpinned this definition, which positioned violence as the foundation of the tribal community. It is more probable still that Crooke's and Risley's shared characterisation was informed by the commentary on communities along the northwest frontier in Ralph Hughes-Buller's 1901 census report on Balochistan, an analysis both

---

[274] Bayly, *Caste*, p. 127.

[275] Susan Bayly and Crispin Bates mention tribes in their analyses of nineteenth-century colonial debates on race but focus primarily on caste: Bates, 'Race'; Bayly, *Caste*. Others focus exclusively on caste, for example, Pant, 'Cognitive Status'; Dirks, *Castes*.

[276] For instance, the different approaches on caste of Risley on the one hand and Ibbetson and J. C. Nesfield on the other that were clearly apparent at the 'conference on ethnography' the three men held in Lahore in 1885 were absent from their discussions on tribe. See H. H. Risley, *The Tribes and Castes of Bengal. Ethnographic Glossary, Vol. II* (Calcutta: Bengal Secretariat Press, 1891), appendix II, pp. 143–73.

[277] Risley, *People*, 2nd ed., p. 123.   [278] Ibbetson, *Panjab Castes*, quotation on p. 22.

[279] W. Crooke, *Natives of Northern India* (London: Archibald Constable, 1907), pp. 36–37; Risley, *People*, p. 61. For Crooke's arguments against Risley, see W. Crooke, 'The Stability of Caste and Tribal Groups in India', *The Journal of the Royal Anthropological Institute of Great Britain and Ireland*, 44 (1914), pp. 270–80; W. Crooke, 'Preface to the New Edition' and 'Introduction', in Risley, *The People of India*, 2nd ed., ix–xxi.

[280] Crooke, *Natives*, p. 36; Risley, *People*, p. 61.

men admired.[281] Among its key claims was that Pashtun and Baloch tribes were formed 'by inverse processes' – one version of the broader tendency among colonial administrators to oppose Pashtun and Baloch social organisation.[282] Hughes-Buller argued that although they shared the 'underlying principle' of being united 'by common good and common ill', Pashtun tribes maintained the 'fiction of common blood', while Baloch and Brahui tribes did not.[283] Hughes-Buller's analysis underpinned the Crooke and Risley's mutually agreed basic concept of the tribe – a concept that both anthropologists took to reveal a fundamental structure of Indian social organisation antecedent to caste.

Crooke and Risley also concurred on the basic features and the ethnological significance of frontier communities in the northeast. Both referred to a 'Mongoloid' type of tribe typified by the Nagas. And, drawing on A. W. Davis's tract on Nagas in the 1891 Assam Census Report, Crooke and Risley alike highlighted the division of the tribe into 'khels' as a central feature of Naga social organisation. Working with Scottish ethnologist J. F. McLennan's categories of exogamy and endogamy,[284] which became increasingly influential among British ethnographers in India from the 1880s, Davis had gone beyond Butler (see Section 3.4) in identifying khels as 'exogamous sub-divisions' of 'Naga society'.[285] By the early 1890s, the search for exogamous clans had become a guiding principle for administrator-ethnographers in the northeast. The fixation of this principle is evident in Davis's comment on the 'Kuki-Lushai' inhabitants of the Lushai Hills: 'I have not been able to trace any division into exogamous clans . . . It is possible, however, that the village names are also the names of clans, or that the eight tribal subdivisions . . . are really clans, and not sub-tribes'.[286] Even the Khasis, whose distinctive language and matrilineal society had long provoked British interest and confusion,[287] seemed to follow the supposed 'Mongoloid' basis of 'exogamous clans or septs', even if in this case these were defined by descent from female rather than male ancestors.[288] Crooke and Risley followed Davis and E. A. Gait, the Commissioner of the 1891 Census in Assam and later Census Commissioner of India, in highlighting the exogamous clan as the feature that distinguished the 'Mongoloid tribe' of the northeast from the tribes

---

[281] For their admiration for Hughes-Buller's work, see Risley, *People*, p. 63; Crooke, *Natives*, p. 58.

[282] On oppositions of Baloch and Pashtun social organisation, see Paul Titus, 'Honor the Baloch, Buy the Pushtun: Stereotypes, Social Organization and History in Western Pakistan', *Modern Asian Studies*, 32, 3 (1998), pp. 657–87.

[283] Hughes-Buller, *Census 1901*, pp. 116–28.

[284] John F. McLennan, Primitive Marriage: An Inquiry into the Origin of the Form of Capture in Marriage Ceremonies (Edinburgh: Adam and Charles Black, 1865).

[285] Davis also pointed out that Angamis referred to 'khels' as 'tepfu' or 'tino': Davis, in Gait, *1891 Assam Census Report*, p. 238.

[286] Davis, in Gait, *1891 Assam Census Report*, p. 251.

[287] Gait, *1891 Assam Census Report*, p. 187.   [288] Ibid., p. 258.

of the northwest.[289] Quoting Hughes-Buller, Risley indicated that the 'khel' of the northwest was very different to that of the northeast.[290] The 'Turko-Iranian tribe' – encompassing Pashtuns, Brahuis, and Balochs – was, he argued, notably endogamous, 'result[ing] from the practice of marrying a woman of the same group, a near kinswoman, or, if possible, a first cousin'.[291] Risley's distinction was all the more striking for playing on the common term of the 'khel', shared between British descriptions of Nagas and Pashtuns because it had been transported across the Subcontinent to do work within a very different set of ethnographic theories almost four decades earlier.

For all of their shared features, India's frontiers also figured as key points of contestation between Crooke and Risley. Crooke argued that Risley's anthropometric methodology came under particular strain at frontiers and interior upland regions. Risley went to significant lengths to incorporate anthropometric data of frontier communities into *The People of India*, overseeing measurements in the northwest himself.[292] But he could only access people that he grouped under the 'Turko-Iranian type' in administered regions of British Baluchistan and western Punjab. This limitation meant that the number of subjects in each sub-group varied greatly, from 271 'Marri, Bugti and Rind, etc., from the country around Sibi' that Risley took to represent the 'Baloch', to a mere six 'Kafirs'.[293] Similar inconsistencies marked the data on northeast frontier communities, with measurements of inhabitants of the uplands north of the Brahmaputra Valley taken from small groups that had journeyed to or settled in the administered lowlands.[294] Crooke latched onto such shortcomings, claiming that branches of 'border tribes' that had been 'exposed to foreign influence' by residing in the plains tended to undergo physical change. He configured frontiers as regions of anthropometric information famine, stating that 'we are not at present in possession of a complete series of skull measurements of the people of India, still less of its borderlands'.[295]

The contested rise of anthropometry was interwoven with an equally fraught set of debates over language in colonial India, in which frontier tribes also had a central role. Disavowals of any connection between language and race had become commonplace among ethnologists by the last decades of the nineteenth century. But this had the perverse effect of opening a distinct space for philological studies, which proliferated through the Census and the loosely

---

[289] Crooke, *Natives*, pp. 39–40. Risley, *People*, p. 64. See also H. H. Risley and E. A. Gait, *Census of India, 1901. Volume I. India. Part I—Report* (Calcutta: Government Press, 1903), p. 515.
[290] Risley, *People*, p. 66.   [291] Ibid., p. 67.
[292] Herbert Risley, 'Presidential Address. The Methods of Ethnography', *The Journal of the Royal Anthropological of Great Britain and Ireland*, 41 (1911), pp. 8–19, here pp. 16–17.
[293] Risley, *People*, 2nd ed., p. 395.
[294] Ibid., p. 402. Risley drew some of the data for inhabitants of uplands around Assam, including seven 'Abors', from Laurence Waddell: see Waddell, 'Tribes', p. 13.
[295] Crooke, *Natives*, pp. 18–19, 23–24.

related Linguistic Survey of India, established in 1894. So too did conjectures as to what insights linguistic data could offer into the origins and movements of communities, and connections between them.[296] A salient episode within these broader discussions was Crooke and Risley's opposing interpretations of an anomaly in Balochistan first established in 1880.[297] Both men agreed that the Brahui language was Dravidian, and thus an erratic among the surrounding Persianate languages. Risley cited this as 'perhaps the most notable illustration of the weakness of the argument from affinity of language to affinity of race'.[298] Crooke, while also disclaiming language as 'a test of race', argued that it 'may explain tribal migrations'. He accordingly insisted that the linguistic status of Brahui lent weight to the hypothesis that Dravidians had once inhabited the subcontinent as far northwest as Kalat.[299] A variant on Crooke's theory, supported by Thomas Holdich among others, was that the Brahui language indicated that Dravidians had entered India from the northwest rather than the south, as Crooke preferred.[300] This was one instance of many in which an influx of linguistic data from India's frontiers in the late nineteenth century seemed to provide a significant clue to ethnological questions but generated dissensus rather than closure.

Languages of the upland northeast seemed to pose intense challenges and hold great promise for linguists and ethnologists. 'The thorny path of Assam Hill philology', warned the Commissioner of the 1891 Census of India, 'requires as cautious treading as those of the country itself, where stockades, pitfalls, and bamboo caltrops beset the unwary at every turn'.[301] Increasingly intensive colonial engagements with communities around the fringes of Brahmaputra Valley produced a glut of information on tribal lexicons and grammars. Placing this information within theoretical structures remained a convoluted and contested business. The lack of written scripts for most of these languages not only posed problems of data collection but was also assumed to render the languages unusually mutable. In 1891, E. A. Gait complained that 'these nomad forms of speech are so constantly changing that it is

---

[296] Javed Majeed, *Colonialism and Knowledge in Grierson's* Linguistic Survey of India (Abingdon: Routledge, 2019), pp. 78–81. See also Gait, *1891 Assam Census Report*, pp. 158–59.

[297] George Grierson, superintendent of the Linguistic Survey of India, discussed this anomaly at length in his chapter on 'Language', in Risley and Gait, *1901 Census Report*, pp. 247–348, here pp. 279–89. E. A. Gait, the Census Commissioner in 1911, contested Grierson's hypotheses on this point: E. A. Gait, *Census of India, 1911. Volume I. India. Part I—Report* (Calcutta: Government Press, 1913), pp. 325–8.

[298] Risley, *People*, p. 12   [299] Crooke, *Natives*, pp. 25–26, 32–33.

[300] T. H. Holdich, 'The Arab Tribes of Our Indian Frontier', *The Journal of the Anthropological Institute of Great Britain and Ireland*, 29, 1/2 (1899), pp. 10–20, here p. 12.

[301] J. A. Baines, *General Report on the Census of India, 1891* (London: Eyre and Spottiswoode, 1893), p. 149.

often difficult to trace linguistic kinship'.[302] Gait's contemporaries also related linguistic fragmentation to tribal violence: 'it is hardly necessary to point out that with so many tribes close together, each under hereditary obligations to lay by a store of the skulls of its neighbour, the diversity of language is ... great'.[303] The profusion of languages and patchy data rendered the classification of tribal languages in the northeast in 1891 'purely tentative'.[304]

A particularly productive problem for administrator-ethnologists in this region was the Khasi language, which Gait noted was 'in every way dissimilar' to those of other frontier communities.[305] Over the following two decades, Khasi was the subject of multiple conjectures from scholars in India and Europe.[306] In 1901, the Census Reports for Assam and for India relayed the German philologist Ernst Kuhn's theory that the Khasi language formed a 'Mon-Khmer' group with dialects used by tribes inhabiting the upper Mekong region.[307] British commentators generally assumed that this philological theory had ethnological ramifications. George Grierson, superintendent of the Linguistic Survey of India, hypothesised in 1903 that the Khasi people were a surviving remnant of the first group of 'Indo-Chinese' migrants, 'who must once have occupied a large area, if not the whole, of what is now Assam and Indo-China'.[308] The broad principle of multiple waves of migration from the north and east gained widespread acceptance among interested British parties, even if administrators based in Assam staked out their expertise by suggesting revised categories based on first-hand experience of the tribes concerned.[309] The period of settled knowledge on this issue proved short-lived. Within a decade, the Austrian linguist Wilhelm Schmidt convinced Grierson and other key authorities that 'Mon-Khmer' languages were a small part of a 'great family' of Austric languages, which extended across Australasia and the South Pacific.[310] But what this meant for the origins and historic migrations of the Khasis remained, according to the administrator-scholar

---

[302] Gait, *1891 Assam Census Report*, p. 158. Gait's successor as Census Commissioner of Assam in 1901, B. C. Allen, made a similar point, as did George Grierson: B. C. Allen, *Census of India, 1901. Volume IV. Assam. Part I. Report* (Shillong: Assam Secretariat, 1902), p. 89; Grierson, in Risley and Gait, *1901 Census Report*, p. 266.

[303] Baines, *1891 Census Report*, p. 150.   [304] Gait, *1891 Assam Census Report*, p. 158.

[305] Ibid., p. 187.

[306] For a near-contemporary account of these developments, see P. R. T. Gurdon, *The Khasis*, 2nd ed. (London: Macmillan & Co., 1914), xviii-xix, pp. 200–1.

[307] Allen, *1901 Assam Census Report*, p. 91; Grierson, in Risley and Gait, *1901 Census Report*, p. 257.

[308] Grierson, in Risley and Gait, *1901 Census Report*, p. 252.

[309] Allen, *1901 Assam Census Report*, p. 120.

[310] George van Driem, 'Hodgson's Tibeto-Burman and Tibeto-Burman Today', in David M. Waterhouse (ed.), *The Origins of Himalayan Studies: Brian Houghton Hodgson in Nepal and Darjeeling 1820–1858* (London: RoutledgeCurzon, 2004), pp. 227–48, here p. 235; Javed Majeed, *Nation and Region in Grierson's Linguistic Survey of India* (London: Routledge, 2019), pp. 60–61; Gait, *1911 India Census Report*, p. 324.

who authored the first monograph on the Khasis in 1907, 'a vexed question' that could not be resolved by reference to linguistic data alone.[311] Like the seemingly disconnected Burushaski language spoken by inhabitants of Hunza-Nagar in the northern portion of the Punjab-Kashmir frontier,[312] Khasi was the kind of anomaly upon which fixed categories floundered but colonial ethnologists and linguists thrived.

3.7   Conclusion: Productive Problems

Henry Pottinger had noted the mystery of the Brahui language during his travels in Balochistan nearly a century before Risley and Crooke published their competing analyses.[313] That this persisted as an unresolved and extremely productive ethnographic problem for so long provides a microcosm of some of the main continuities in frontier ethnography across the nineteenth century. Through a combination of limited and contestable data and their apparently stark differences from people elsewhere in the subcontinent, frontier communities continued to be subjects of intense speculations and conflicting theories. British official-ethnologists celebrated tribes in the northwest and northeast on the basis of their being 'free' from the influence of caste structures.[314] These groups were widely seen to have extreme significance for questions of historic migrations, the durability of various physical and cultural markers, and social structures. Yet they consistently eluded conclusive answers. In the early decades of the twentieth century every bit as much as in the early decades of the nineteenth, an array of British administrators and scholars saw frontier inhabitants as vexing but vital ethnological mysteries.

In this chapter, I have suggested that frontier ethnographies went through a series of distinctive but overlapping phases from the early nineteenth to the early twentieth centuries. Much changed across this period. The intensity of British engagements with India's frontiers generally increased, although major differences remained between particular localities. Coupled with imperatives for the production of new types of data emanating from methodological shifts, and innovations in representation through advances in print and photographic technologies, shifting encounters led to very different forms and amounts of ethnographic information. There was undoubtedly a move towards the visual in frontier ethnography during the mid-nineteenth century. This was also a period when studies of human diversity gradually crystallised into the discipline of anthropology. Although significant, these changes did not, however, add up to standardised ways of knowing frontier peoples, nor did they give rise to a field

---

[311] Gurdon, *Khasis*, pp. 10–8.
[312] See Grierson in Risley and Gait, *1901 Census Report*, p. 340.   [313] Pottinger, *Travels*, p. 54.
[314] Gait, *1911 Census Report*, p. 370. See also Risley and Gait, *1901 Census Report*, pp. 554–55.

that marched in lockstep with a particular form of colonial power. Networks of informants generally grew denser across the century considered in this chapter, but the components they comprised and the materials they generated continued to be fragile and to bear traces of local specificity that could only be removed partially or with difficulty. Ethnographic data, anthropological theories, and representative modalities remained partial and controversial, all the more so when the things that carried this information – images, books, objects – were copied and travelled. The transit of materials across time and space was fundamental to the production of knowledge, but almost always involved selective appropriations and dissensus. In fact, shortcomings and contests were essential features of frontier ethnography and anthropology. Colonial knowledge of people thrived on the persistence of productive problems, and such problems clustered around particular communities at the subcontinent's fringes.

4   Violence

David Scott, Agent to the Governor-General for the North-East Frontier after the position was created during the Anglo-Burmese War in 1824, began his frontier career ten years earlier at the hazy fringes of British authority in northeastern Bengal. Within months of taking up his post, he received alarming news. Garos had 'committed excesses of the most atrocious nature', attacking lowland cultivators before 'return[ing] into the Jungle'.[1] Scott's missive contained tropes that were already well rehearsed in colonial administrators' writings on upland communities: the unprovoked and excessive nature of their violence, their defenceless victims, and their escape to impenetrable terrain. He recommended that a military force be sent against the entire Garo community, giving two justifications for this course of action. First, it was in keeping with the tactics of precolonial rulers of the region. Second, although the Garos were not subjects of the colonial state, 'they enjoy the advantages of that State, [and] cannot complain if they are also subjected to the inconveniences that unavoidably attend it, amongst which is to be reckoned the probability of the innocent suffering with the guilty'.[2]

Further investigations, however, rendered Scott's call to punish a collective tribal subject somewhat shaky. It appeared that the landowners of the estates at the foot of the hills were not innocent targets but had pushed into the hills upon the advent of British rule in the region and perpetrated 'oppression and cruelty' against the Garos.[3] When a colonial military force deputed to protect cultivators against depredations from the hills attacked a party of Garos who came down not to commit violence but to trade cotton, the sense that the uplanders might not be the only aggressors was enhanced further still.[4] In light of these developments, Scott's co-Magistrate Thomas Sisson advanced a very different conception of the tribal subject. Instead of focusing on inherent aggression and apparent invulnerability as Scott's initial report had, Sisson suggested that the

---

[1] IOR/F/4/533 (12847): Scott to Judicial Department, Bengal Government, 16 January 1815, ff. 1–2.
[2] Ibid., f. 4; IOR/F/4/533 (12847): Scott to Judicial Department, 17 January 1815, ff. 9–10.
[3] IOR/F/4/533 (12847): Sisson to Judicial Department, 15 February 1815, ff. 67–76, 96–105.
[4] IOR/F/4/533 (12847): Scott to Bengal Government, 14 February 1815, ff. 31–5.

landowners' violence 'overawed the timid Mountaineer'. This characterisation evidently surprised someone higher in the imperial chain of command: in the copy of Sisson's letter sent to the Court of Directors in London the term 'timid' is underlined, with the marginal note, 'a very unusual epithet for a mountaineer'.[5] Scott remained uncertain, caught between differing notions of the Garos' character and, therefore, hesitant about the legitimacy of state violence directed against the community as a whole. He acknowledged that the Garos were victims of zamindars' violence, but also believed, a colleague later recalled, that 'a Garrow never would listen to reason, until he had been beaten: then he kissed the rod, and acknowledged the person who wielded it as his superior'.[6]

Scott was far from alone among British administrators dealing with India's frontiers in vacillating between the protective and the punitive, and between individual and collective tribal subjects. As outlined in the previous chapter, British characterisations of frontier populations repeatedly foregrounded proclivities towards violence. Such representations did not remain at the level of epistemic violence; they were crucial alibis for large-scale acts of physical violence perpetrated by the colonial state.[7] Recent work focusing on the Punjab frontier from the 1860s onwards shows how claims of innate tribal violence undergirded legal interventions and categories that facilitated violent state responses, especially the Murderous Outrages Act, the Frontier Crimes Regulation, and the concept of 'fanaticism'.[8] In this chapter, I focus on a related but distinct form of violence targetting frontier communities: military ventures that the British widely called 'expeditions'. This epithet was part of a lexical distinction that sought to establish the justice of the colonial state's violence as it rendered illegitimate the 'raids', 'robbing', and 'murders' of frontier populations.[9] These pejorative terms lumped together such diverse enterprises as horseback forays for food by Balochs, headhunting by Nagas, and blood-feuds among Pashtuns, along with widespread resistance to increasing colonial interference and infrastructure.

This chapter shows how the motivations, tactics, and frequency of violence varied substantially between different communities, as did the environmental features that shaped clashes at frontiers. In addition, changing British understandings of frontier spaces and social dynamics went hand-in-hand with

---

[5] IOR/F/4/533 (12847): Sisson to Judicial Department, 15 February 1815, f. 65.

[6] White, *Memoir*, p. 30.

[7] On the importance of focusing on physical as well as epistemic violence, see Elizabeth Kolsky, *Colonial Justice in British India* (Cambridge: Cambridge University Press, 2010), p. 8.

[8] Kolsky, 'Colonial Rule of Law'; Hopkins, 'Frontier Crimes Regulation'; Condos, 'Licence to Kill'; Condos, '"Fanaticism"'.

[9] On the importance of linguistic distinctions to the perpetuation of British Indian state violence covered with a veneer of legality, see Simon Layton, 'Discourses of Piracy in an Age of Revolutions', *Itinerario*, 35, 2 (2011), pp. 81–97.

shifting targets and agents of colonial violence. Nonetheless, the reductive distinction between expedition and raid was a core element of a basic model for justifying state violence at India's frontiers, repeated by administrators throughout the nineteenth century. The first widely shared element of this model was that state violence was reactive – a response to prior violence. The second was that violence was educational – it was a 'language' that violent tribals understood, precipitating changes in their behaviour to their own benefit and that of nearby subjects of British India.[10] The analysis in this chapter will show that both elements of this narrative (which continues to underpin 'counter-insurgency' operations at the frontiers of postcolonial South Asia[11]) are deeply problematic. Colonial violence frequently preceded any violence by frontier populations and was often sufficiently disproportionate as to render ridiculous the claim that it was reactive. In addition, the repeated instances of frontier communities responding violently to state violence undermined the claim that it was educational.

The chapter also shows that critiques of state violence are not merely the preserve of postcolonial historians but were already in circulation among agents of empire in the nineteenth century. Frontier violence was riven with tensions and disputes. Even as it was deployed in myriad locales, many administrators questioned it and some viewed it as scandalous, in the sense of threatening or outright contradicting the moral basis of imperial rule. Unlike 'scandals' of empire in India and beyond, such as the impeachment of Warren Hastings and the Indian and Jamaican Rebellions,[12] the use of violence in frontier regions was primarily problematic to administrators in the colony. Metropolitan commentators such as J. A. Hobson, who in 1902 wrote that the 'well nigh incessant' violence along Indian frontiers and in Africa rendered 'the *pax Britannica* . . . a grotesque monster of hypocrisy', were relatively belated in their critiques.[13] Frontier violence during the nineteenth century had no London-based figure calling the colonial state to account as Edmund Burke

---

[10] On violence as a 'language' supposedly understood by frontier inhabitants, see Kolsky, 'Colonial', p. 1223.

[11] Sanjib Baruah, *Durable Disorder: Understanding the Politics of Northeast India* (New Delhi: Oxford University Press, 2005).

[12] On Hastings's impeachment, see Nicholas Dirks, *The Scandal of Empire: India and the Creation of Imperial Britain* (Cambridge, MA: Harvard University Press, 2006). On the Indian Rebellion, see Rudrangshu Mukherjee, *Awadh in Revolt 1857–1858: A Study of Popular Resistance* (Delhi: Oxford University Press, 1984); Stokes, *The Peasant*; Ranajit Guha, *Elementary Aspects of Peasant Insurgency in Colonial India* (Durham, NC: Duke University Press, 1999); On the Jamaican Rebellion, see Gad Heuman, *'The Killing Time': The Morant Bay Rebellion in Jamaica* (London: Macmillan, 1994); R. W. Kostal, *A Jurisprudence of Power: Victorian Empire and the Rule of Law* (Oxford: Oxford University Press, 2005).

[13] J. A. Hobson, *Imperialism: A Study* (Ann Arbor, MI: University of Michigan Press, 1965), p. 126.

had in the 1780s. Even after Hobson's intervention, frontier violence never became a full-blown scandal at the imperial level. But there was a constant susurrus of competing discourses in India, where some British officials believed violence was both ineffective and morally corrosive. This chapter shows how the 'scandal' of frontier violence was a protracted and often inconclusive affair that played out in subtly differing ways across varied regions.

The cyclical discussions and episodes of colonial violence examined in this chapter had a quality that, following Ricardo Roque's study of Portuguese imperialism in Timor, can be termed 'atavism'.[14] Colonial power in frontier India, like that in Portuguese Timor, tended to be fragile and reliant on frequent violence. Administrators' attempts to differentiate their violent practices from those of frontier populations and local polities such as Kalat, Agror, and Manipur were fraught with slippages. Even as some agents of the colonial state insisted on the distinctiveness of its violence, others either revelled in or abhorred the use of the same methods – and sometimes the same personnel – of violence practised by its rivals and subsidiary allies in frontier locales. Bruno Latour has outlined how practitioners of modern science try, and fail, to suppress the non-modern elements of the networks they seek to master even as they actively engage these elements.[15] The struggle for the colonial state to instantiate its ostensibly modern authority through practices that were almost indistinguishable from those its personnel admonished as backward necessitated similar, and similarly insecure, processes of 'purification'. It was in the repeated slippages of these processes, and the consequent need for frequent and unconvincing restatements of the civilising potential of state violence, that colonial atavism showed up at spatially dispersed frontier regions throughout the nineteenth century.

In this chapter, I substantiate these contentions in relation to three key – and in many respects very different – zones of frontier violence. The first section looks at a period from the late 1830s to the late 1840s of intense colonial violence against Balochs in the desert and arid hills to the northwest of Upper Sind. These actions culminated in the large-scale slaughter of members of the Bugti tribe, which proved controversial even among British administrators in the region. The eruption and suppression of this short-lived scandal was indicative of the way in which violence was bound up in disputes and indeterminacies rather than being stable projections of state power. The next section examines repeated bouts of violence against Nagas, especially Angamis, in the wet, steep-sided uplands south of the Brahmaputra Valley. It focuses on shifting rationales and means of violence from the late 1830s to the end of the nineteenth century. Throughout this period, debates raged between British

---

[14] Roque, *Headhunting*.   [15] Latour, *We Have Never*.

administrators for decades over the character of Naga violence, who and what colonial violence should target, and who was competent to enact violence on the state's behalf. Although these arguments were fraught and inconclusive, violence remained a key plank of colonial interference in this region even after the establishment of the Naga Hills District in 1866. The final section turns to expeditions in the Punjab frontier. Focusing first on shifting justifications and methods of state violence in the fifteen years following the annexation of Punjab in 1849, it then looks at a series of four expeditions in the Black Mountain region towards the north of frontier from the 1850s to the 1890s. In this area, administrators became ever less sure of the efficacy and ethics of large-scale military operations as a means of founding the colonial state's authority, even as they continued to resort to this method.

Frontier violence caused huge destruction across these three regions in human and environmental terms. Large numbers of people were killed, and colonial strategies of destroying food stores, crops, and buildings left entire communities exposed and lacking essential goods. This occurred despite the fact that in all of these areas, some administrators who initiated and oversaw violence saw it as liable to fail on both moral and practical levels. These spectacular but sporadic episodes worked in tandem with the colonial state's confused knowledge structures and antagonistic rationales at India's frontiers. As Ann Laura Stoler proposes in relation to Dutch colonial Java, it was precisely the 'allusive, muddy register' of colonial discourse, replete with 'inconsistencies', 'that set the terms for new repressions, subsequent violences, and renewed commitment to retaliating against what were perceived as counterinsurgent acts'.[16] Although – and because – it rarely lived up to British expectations as a means of instantiating colonial power among communities beyond administrative borders, military force continued to devastate people in northwest and northeast alike as the twentieth century dawned.

4.1   'Terrible to Behold': Violence on the Upper Sind Frontier, 1839–1848

During the Anglo-Afghan War of 1839 to 1842, the British Indian Army faced the challenge of maintaining supply and communication routes through the Kachhi desert and hills to the northwest of Sind that led to the Gomal Pass into southern Afghanistan. In part, this was a problem of information. John Jacob, an officer who went on to have a renowned career on the Upper Sind frontier, recalled that as the British invasion began, 'the country, its people, and all belonging to it, were ... completely unknown to the officers and men of the

---

[16] Stoler, *Archival*, p. 187.

Indian army'.[17] It was also an issue of establishing relations with the Baloch tribes of Kachhi. Lieutenant Eastwick, the Political Agent in the region, opined in March 1839 that 'the state of this part of the country is at present most lamentable, robberies & murders are of daily occurrence, & were it not for the exertions of the native cavalry the communications would be entirely cut off'.[18] This account was unsurprisingly partial: colonial forces travelling to and from Afghanistan had overestimated the supplies available in the region and compensated by taking grain from the Balochs' stores.[19] In response, Baloch horsemen harried colonial troops and took food and goods from convoys. Regional potentates including the Amirs of Sind and Khan of Kalat, Eastwick claimed, were unable to prevent or punish these occurrences. The British instead relied on irregular cavalry manned and commanded by South Asians to maintain supplies to the regular units in Afghanistan. Eastwick persuaded the Government of India to adopt two measures. First, a militia drawn from the very communities that harassed the supply route through the Gomal Pass would both co-opt and police the Balochs. The use of military service as an attempted means of simultaneously defusing and punishing opposition was repeated at frontiers in northwest and northeast throughout the nineteenth century. Second, Eastwick informed tribal potentates that he held them responsible for their underlings' behaviour. Like his contemporaries in the Naga Hills (discussed in Section 4.2), the Political Agent in Upper Sind supposed that each major community had a chief who could compel obedience.[20] Although more true in Baloch communities than among Nagas, in both regions this proved a dubious assumption leading to results that frustrated British administrators.

Eastwick believed that 'force & violence are the worst instruments of Gov[ernmen]t ... by a great & enlightened nation'.[21] Nonetheless, the Government of India invested him with discretionary authority in the event of 'any formidable body of depredations'.[22] Fearing that continued skirmishes with Balochs might cut off British forces in Afghanistan, and disenchanted by the refusal of many tribal chiefs to supply men for the proposed militia, this provision was put to use before the end of 1839. Eastwick's successor Ross Bell

---

[17] Lewis Pelly (ed.), *The Views and Opinions of Brigadier-General John Jacob, C. B.*, 2nd ed. (London: Smith, Elder & Co., 1858), pp. 298–99.

[18] NAI Foreign Secret, 3 July 1839, No. 48: Eastwick to Government of India, 18 March 1839, ff. 6481–82.

[19] H. T. Lambrick, *John Jacob of Jacobabad* (London: Cassell, 1960), p. 33.

[20] NAI Foreign Secret, 3 July 1839, No. 48: Eastwick to Government of India, 18 March 1839, f. 6482; No. 50: Eastwick to Government of India, 7 March 1839, ff. 6491–3.

[21] NAI Foreign Secret, 3 July 1839, No. 50: Eastwick to Government of India, 7 March 1839, f. 6493.

[22] NAI Foreign Secret, 1 May 1839, No. 11: Government of India to Eastwick, 8 April 1839, f. 2840;

authorised an attack on the Dombki community after a chief, Bijar Khan, refused to relinquish goods taken from British convoys. Bell intended this attack to communicate the colonial state's authority to other communities in the region. It was 'necessary that Beeja Khan's band should be destroyed', he claimed, both to '[free] us of the most formidable body of plunderers which infests these parts' and '[check] the disposition to plunder so general amongst the other Belooch tribes'.[23] The military action was based on a fundamental misreading of tribal dynamics in the region. Bijar Khan had in fact turned against his kinsman and erstwhile chief and established a group opposed to the main body of the Dombkis. What the British read as predations involving multiple communities was in fact the work – at least initially – of this single faction.[24] The assumption that Baloch tribes were static entities in thrall to single chiefs, rather than dynamic groups with shifting allegiances, led the British to undertake violence that alienated rather subjugated people of the Kachhi region. The military action also failed in a more immediate sense, as the party of around 400 colonial troops lost its way having 'wandered into the jungle', and eleven died from exposure to heat.[25]

Despite this episode, extreme violence became commonplace in British dealings with Balochs around Kachhi.[26] Although the Dombkis and a number of other major tribes entered into agreements with the colonial state during 1840, outbreaks of fighting persisted.[27] Bell and his successor as Political Agent, James Outram, acknowledged that these were largely induced by ill-advised colonial interference in the tribal hills and the tendency of the British to break agreements.[28] But their underlings situated beyond administered Sind tended to argue that innate characteristics of the Balochs drove the violence. They also consistently assumed that 'an organized assemblage of hill tribes' lay behind attacks on British soldiers and infrastructure.[29] Thomas Postans, whose ethnographic work later became influential, proclaimed early in his tenure as Assistant Political Agent at the Upper Sind frontier: 'averse as every British officer must be, to indiscriminate cruelty or a blood thirsty spirit of revenge, these Belooch tribes generally . . . can only [be dealt] with by force of arms; & by treating them as open enemies'.[30] Throughout the Anglo-Afghan War, then, British soldiers and administrators widely believed that the

---

[23] NAI Foreign Secret, 21 August 1839, No. 105: Bell to Government of India, undated, ff. 3–4.
[24] Lambrick, *John Jacob*, pp. 34–35.
[25] NAI Foreign Secret, 21 August 1839, No. 105: Bell to Government of India, undated, ff .4–5.
[26] NAI Foreign Secret, 26 December 1839, Nos. 94–6.
[27] NAI Foreign Secret, 29 June 1840, Nos. 55–7.
[28] NAI Foreign Secret, 29 June 1840, No. 55: Bell to Government of India, 1 June 1840; MSA Political, 1842, Vol. 70: Outram to Government of India, 23 December 1841, ff. 201–3.
[29] NAI Foreign Secret, 29 June 1840, No. 56: Postans to Bell, 21 May 1840, f. 5.
[30] Ibid., ff. 6–7.

large-scale extirpation of groups beyond the boundary of Upper Sind was both permissible and effective.

In 1840, following a British-led coup against the Khan of Kalat Mihrab Khan, with whom the colonial state had previously been allied, a revolt arose in which the British Agent at Kalat was killed.[31] Colonial administrators' attention turned to the Brahui tribes in Kalat, who relied on trade with Sind to obtain food and other necessities. Following the revolt, Bell advised that 'no advance should be made against [Kalat] until famine shall have convinced the Brahoee Tribes that no effectual opposition can be offered by them so long as the provinces from which their supplies must necessarily be drawn are commanded by us'. Although he disavowed that the British were 'wag[ing] an exterminatory war against the Brahoees',[32] the tendency towards extreme violence against nebulously and capaciously defined communities was again clear. British correspondence does, however, contain traces of an alternative narrative of violence during the revolt. Without any pre-established authority to do so, the colonial state put the men accused of 'murdering' the Agent on trial. One of the accused, named 'Kaissoo' in colonial documents, was asked: 'What had the Sahib [British Agent] done to you that you should kill him?' He replied that 'the guns had been firing on our people and killed many so in the excitement of moment I slew the Sahib'. Kaissoo's claim that his act followed rather than preceded colonial violence did not significantly alter British administrators' conviction during the Anglo-Afghan War that military actions against Balochs and Brahuis were necessary and justified.

After the annexation of Sind in 1843, violence became a more contested issue among agents of empire. The newly minted Sind administration led by the bombastic army officer Charles Napier came into prolonged contact with Balochs of Kachhi, who abutted the ill-defined administrative boundary proclaimed in Upper Sind. A year after annexation, Napier configured the problem as one in which topography and the Baloch mode of warfare – bands of horsemen conducting swift operations and carrying off goods – conspired against colonial forces now tasked with defending revenue-paying cultivators rather than a military supply line. 'The Desert, which divides our frontier from these tribes . . . is no protection to us', Napier wrote in one of his many rambling and melodramatic missives, 'but enables them to assemble without our knowledge . . . About 15 villages have abandoned their land and fled . . . This is a pressing danger'.[33] Lacking a force on the scale that had been present in the

---

[31] *Frontier and Overseas Expeditions from India. Vol. III: Baluchistan and the First Afghan War* (Calcutta: Government Printing, 1910), p. 44.

[32] NAI Foreign Secret, 23 November 1840, No. 84: Bell to Captain Bean, Political Agent, Quetta, 25 October 1840, f. 4.

[33] NAI Foreign Secret, 13 July 1844, No. 15: Napier to Ellenborough, 24 April 1844, f. 2 (emphases in original).

region during the War, Napier instead persuaded two ostensibly independent Baloch communities to attack the Dombkis, who he considered among the leading 'marauders'. He claimed to be partially reassured by one chief, who said that 'he will destroy the Doomkies; and promises me not to hurt women or children'. But, Napier admitted, 'how far his promises are to trusted I do not pretend to say – time will show'.[34] The Governor-General supported subcontracting state violence to tribal agents as a practical expedient: 'however much we may dislike the mode of warfare pursued by these Tribes against each other, and regret having any connection with it, it is impossible not to feel that it is better that they should be divided against each other than united against the innocent and peaceful cultivators of our Frontier lands'.[35] Atavism was, then, deemed a risk worth running to instantiate colonial authority in Upper Sind.

Officials increasingly referred to Kachhi Balochs by animalistic metaphors such as 'a flight of locusts', part of their efforts to normalise the use of severe violence throughout the 1840s against people nominally subject to the Khan of Kalat rather than British India.[36] The claim that these communities were in 'open rebellion' against a helpless Khan was also used to justify the blurring of boundaries through military interventions.[37] John Jacob, in charge of the Sind Horse and Camel Corps, innovated the strategy of pursuing Baloch parties through the desert and into the hills. A number of subsequent accounts extolled his heroism, popularising Jacob's actions and rendering them a reference point for later frontier officials.[38] Jacob and his colleagues proudly took to announcing the death toll of their missions, eliciting acclaim from their superiors.[39] Their increasingly bloody efforts to repress people beyond the Upper Sind boundary culminated in the wholesale slaughter in October 1847 of a substantial portion of the Bugti tribe, who resided in the hills to the north of Kachhi. For the preceding three years, colonial officials had considered the Bugtis to be especially problematic. In January 1845, Napier described them as 'the Pindarees of the Indus'.[40] By referring to the group with whom the British had a long and vicious struggle in western India between 1816 and 1818, Napier invoked the kind of violence unconstrained by legality commonly associated with colonial actions prior to paramountcy rather than in the 1840s.[41] The fight against the Bugtis took on the same character as the

---

[34] Ibid, ff. 3–4.
[35] NAI Foreign Secret, 13 July 1844, No. 16: Ellenborough to Napier, 11 June 1844, f. 1.
[36] NAI Foreign Secret, 25 April 1846, No. 15: Postans to Bombay Government, 24 December 1845, f. 18.
[37] Napier, 'Manifesto', 13 January 1845, quoted in Pelly (ed.), *Views*, pp. 330–31.
[38] For example, Thornton, *Sandeman*, p. 15.
[39] For example, NAI Foreign Secret, 25 September 1847, No. 60–2.
[40] Napier, 'Manifesto', 13 January 1845, quoted in Pelly (ed.), *Views*, p. 334.
[41] On the Pindaris, see Radhika Singha, *A Despotism of Law: Crime and Justice in Early Colonial India* (Delhi: Oxford University Press, 1998), pp. 176–77.

Pindari campaign, which had been described by one military officer as aiming at 'their extirpation ... and not their defeat as enemy entitled to the rights of war'.[42]

Intermittent skirmishes between a colonial force led by Napier and the Bugtis had already taken place from 1845.[43] Upon assuming command of the Upper Sind frontier for a second time in January 1847, Jacob enforced an aggressive policy of constant patrols in the Kachhi desert. This included maintaining a military presence in the desert during the hot season, which Napier had previously seen as an immutable environmental barrier that would cause 'great loss of life' among colonial troops.[44] Frequent acts of violence against Balochs culminated with the attack on the Bugtis by a section of the Sind Irregular Horse, which involved violence on a scale previously unparalleled on this frontier. In his report on the fighting, the commanding officer Lieutenant William Merewether emphasised that the Bugtis had 'attempted to plunder' villages before his force responded, and that they 'obstinately continued to fight until the destruction was so great that their numbers were reduced to about 120' of an initial 700.[45] These were important rhetorical strategies in justifying his actions, the extremity of which moved Merewether to inform Jacob that 'the destructive effect of our little carbines ... were [sic.] quite terrible to behold'.[46] Jacob's assessment was still more triumphalist. He couched the victims as men without a right to life, not on the basis on their being at war with the colonial state but because of their supposedly inveterate criminality. It was, he reported, 'the most perfectly successful affair of the kind I have ever witnessed or heard of ... The loss of life on this occasion has been terrific, but it is satisfactory to know that the men slain were robbers and murderers who were the terror of all the peaceable persons within their reach'.[47]

Other officials did not wholeheartedly endorse these rationales for violence against the Bugtis. Richard Pringle, who had just succeeded Napier as the Commissioner of Sind when the administration passed from military to civilian authority, initially described the violence to the Governor-General as 'a sanguinary engagement ... in which one of the hill tribes has been almost annihilated ... a very complete affair'. He also proclaimed that Merewether's action 'must at this moment have an important moral influence in impressing the other tribes with a sense of our power and securing the peace of the Frontier'.[48] Violence, by this assessment, was educative, serving to instantiate

[42] Fitzclarence, quoted in ibid., p. 177.
[43] MSA Political, 1848, Vol. 147, Napier to Governor-General, 9 March 1845, ff. 13–7.
[44] NAI Foreign Secret, 13 July 1844, No. 15: Napier to Governor-General, 24 May 1844, ff. 1–2.
[45] MSA Political, 1847, Vol. 107: Merewether to Jacob, 2 October 1847, ff. 34–6.
[46] Ibid., f. 37.
[47] NAI Foreign Secret, 27 November 1847, No. 18: Jacob to M. M. Shaw, 2 October 1847, ff. 17–18.
[48] NAI Foreign Secret, 27 November 1847, No. 15: Pringle to Governor-General, 8 October 1847, ff. 1–2.

the boundary by displaying the colonial state's power to the 'independent' communities beyond. Writing to the Governor of Bombay that same day, however, Pringle appeared less confident. While reiterating that the Bugtis' aggression and 'obstinate resistance' justified Merewether's actions, he suggested that the Bugtis' infractions of the British border were due to their having been 'latterly distressed by scarcity of food'.[49] Bugti actions, Pringle insinuated, were not merely brazen but a desperate response to the colonial state's interference in Balochs' partially pastoralist modes of subsistence, which involved obtaining food from cultivated Upper Sind.

As part of the transition from military to civilian government in Sind, Pringle placed Jacob under the control of the civilian Collector and Magistrate of Shikarpur District, which abutted the Kachhi frontier. He also queried Jacob's methods. Jacob claimed that violence beyond the administrative boundary was 'founded on reason, on common sense, and mercy to our own people' and a necessary response to the 'system of private warfare ... constantly carried on' at the frontier when he arrived in the region.[50] He admitted, however, that the Bugtis' food supply had been cut off to a point where, immediately before Merewether's action, some 'were literally dying of starvation'.[51] The foundational principle of Jacob's policy of violence was to treat all Bugtis as enemies. Their disavowal of Kalat's authority meant, he insisted, that 'the ordinary rules of international law do not ... apply. All experience shows that some special remedy is necessary'.[52] In short, Jacob sought to establish that circumstances justified – indeed, made unavoidable – the suspension of principles of ordinary law and the criminalisation of an entire community that were ostensibly subjects of another state. He went further still in insisting that the security of the frontier 'should be in one man's hands', garlanded with the title 'Warden of the Marches', establishing the term that Robert Sandeman and George Curzon would later use to describe their model frontier official (see Section 1.4). Even after the annihilation of the Bugtis, any reduction of the powers invested in that individual would be a great mistake, Jacob said, as all Baloch communities 'continually pine after the stormy and lawless freedom they have lost, and are always on the watch for a renewal of the joys of a robber life'.[53] Jacob presented cross-border Baloch pastoralism and inter-tribal conflicts as inherently criminal and in need of violent correction.

---

[49] MSA Political, 1847, Vol. 107: Pringle to G. Russell, 8 October 1847, ff. 14–6.
[50] NAI Foreign Secret 28 April 1848: Jacob to Sind Government, 11 November 1847, ff. 1201–5; Jacob to Shaw, 24 November 1847, ff. 1234–5.
[51] NAI Foreign Secret, 28 April 1848: Jacob to Government of Sind, 11 November 1847, f. 1206.
[52] NAI Foreign Secret, 28 April 1848: Jacob to Shaw, 24 November 1847, f. 1238 (emphasis in original).
[53] NAI Foreign Secret, 28 April 1848: Jacob to Government of Sind, 11 November 1847, f. 1206; Jacob to Shaw, 24 November 1847, f. 1239.

Pringle's assessment of Jacob's methods was very different. Deploying military force against people attempting to obtain means of subsistence 'may be justifiable against an Enemy with whom we are at open war', he wrote, but no such state of war existed with the Bugtis.[54] (It is notable that a member of the Government of India censured Sandeman's tribal engagements of the 1880s in similar terms: 'we are engaged in no war ... consequently a heroic policy is not required'.[55]) Citing a lack of corroborating documentary evidence, Pringle also denied that Jacob had ever been invested with the authority to employ violence against the Bugtis, and that this violence served merely to 'perpetuate ... hostilities'. By detaining individuals 'against many of whom no other charge can be brought then that they have the misfortune to belong to a tribe which has incurred our displeasure', Jacob also assumed a collective tribal subject contrary to 'any principles of justice or sound policy'.[56] For Pringle, Jacob's actions in the name of the colonial state against the Balochs constituted 'an indefinite & uncompromising warfare', wholly against legal and ethical precepts.[57]

The debates between Pringle's newly empowered civil establishment in Sind and military men over the violence against the Bugtis crystallised some key concerns about colonial frontier violence, which were replicated at other frontiers and other times throughout the nineteenth century. They showed that fixed legal norms did not precede deployments of British military force; colonial violence proceeded on the assumption of a legal vacuum. It was a peculiar version of martial law, defined, as Nasser Hussain outlines, by being 'punishment ... not caused by questions of innocence or guilt or a specific transgression of the law'.[58] Ascriptions of terms such as 'raiders', 'robbers', 'marauders', and 'wild tribes' generated a collective tribal subject, punishable with indiscriminate violence. Under these conditions, members of frontier communities became what Giorgio Agamben terms 'bare life', meaning they could be killed with impunity.[59] But Pringle's contributions to the debates constituted a counter-narrative of violence. This logic characterised as scandalous the excesses of violence and the entwined conception of the tribal subject as bare life and the frontier as a space of legal exception. This was a particular version of the phenomenon that Taylor Sherman identifies in state violence across British India: 'the state's penchant for ruling collectives

---

[54] NAI Foreign Secret, 28 April 1848: Sind Government to Goldney, 23 October 1847, ff. 1105–7.

[55] J. W. Ridgway, in NAI Foreign A-Political-E, June 1883, Nos. 306–24, Keep-With.

[56] NAI Foreign Secret, 28 April 1848: Sind Government to Dundas, Commanding in Sind, 16 November 1847, f. 1211.

[57] NAI Foreign Secret, 28 April 1848: Pringle to Governor of Bombay, 14 December 1847.

[58] Nasser Hussain, *The Jurisprudence of Emergency: Colonialism and the Rule of Law* (Ann Arbor, MI: University of Michigan Press, 2003), p. 124.

[59] Giorgio Agamben, *Homo Sacer: Sovereign Power and Bare Life*, trans. Daniel Heller-Roazen (Stanford, CA: Stanford University Press, 1998).

[running] up against the self-imposed liberal desire to govern individuals'.[60] Pringle preempted later critiques of colonial violence, such as J. A. Hobson's, in suggesting that violence threatened the state's claims to 'pacify' and 'improve'. This challenge forced those who enacted frontier violence, such as Jacob, to develop rhetorical strategies and theoretical rationales that did not simply revel in the excess of their actions, but invoked principles such as reason and justice. Significant, and often retrospective, labour was required to proclaim the guilt of the punished subject and its educating effect on other would-be transgressors.

Pringle's assessment of violence at the Upper Sind frontier in 1847 generated a scandal only within a small circle of administrators. His superiors in the Bombay Government sought from the outset to dismiss his concerns. Responding to Pringle's suggestion that 'every endeavor [should] now be made to alleviate the suffering of the [remaining Bugtis]', the Governor of Bombay George Clerk commented, 'the less we make known of sympathy in the regrets ... the better perhaps'.[61] Clerk claimed that Pringle's critique of Jacob's methods was made 'in the absence of ... knowledge' of the environmental and social conditions of the Kachhi region.[62] He also reinstated Jacob on the basis that with 'his great experience of and influence over the various tribes on the frontier, it must be obvious that Major Jacob on the spot, can more efficiently adopt measures for the protection of the frontier, than Captain Goldney [the Collector and Magistrate] at Shikarpoor'. Far from the sympathetic subjects that Pringle had proclaimed, Clerk characterised the Balochs of Kachhi as 'the plundering tribes that infest [the frontier]', thereby sharing in Jacob and Merewether's dehumanised and collective tribal subject.[63] Finally, Clerk and the Bombay Government retrospectively validated the use of colonial force back as far as Napier's time on the basis that 'the Khan of Kelat was unable to control the plundering tribes who made inroads into our territory, [so Napier] was at liberty to coerce them'.[64] By this reckoning, the void of state authority in Kachhi gave British officers the right to execute violence without the prior authorisation of the colonial state's upper echelons.

Dealing with a tract over which conventional state sovereignty of British India or Kalat did not apply, and faced with the combined threats of heat, hills, and horsemen, the Bombay Government instituted Jacob as sovereign. His discretionary power might with good reason be termed 'frontier sovereignty', since it had clear similarities with arrangements for violence instigated to the south of the Assam Valley during the 1840s (discussed in the next section).

---

[60] Taylor C. Sherman, *State Violence and Punishment in India* (London: Routledge, 2010), p. 6.
[61] NAI Foreign Secret, 28 April 1848, No. 4: Clerk, 'Minute', 20 October 1847, f. 1075.
[62] NAI Foreign Secret, 28 April 1848, No. 8: Clerk, 'Minute', 29 November 1847, f. 1163.
[63] NAI Foreign Secret, 28 April 1848, No. 27: Clerk, 'Minute', 5 February 1848, f. 1275.
[64] Ibid., f. 1278.

Authority to decide to perpetrate violence was vested in an individual with minimal oversight; it extended over a hazily delimited area defined primarily by the movement of semi-nomadic tribes; and it was rooted in spectacular displays of killing carried out by irregular forces manned primarily by frontier inhabitants. Regarding this last aspect, upon being reinstated Jacob removed all Indian Army troops from the border posts and replaced them with a new band of Baloch recruits. He thereby constituted a militia connected to the colonial state only through him. He also proclaimed himself 'certain that I shall be able successfully to maintain profound peace and tranquillity within our own territory, although the Cutchee side might be a scene of violence and disorder'.[65] Kachhi was, then, the zone of violent excess that supposedly allowed the recently conquered territory of Sind to be governed 'normally'. There was appropriate symbolism in the fact that Pringle was forced to accept this state of affairs while he cruised along the Indus in a ship named *Napier*: his civil government had formal control of its northern frontier, but affairs there rested on the basis set by his military predecessor.[66] As discussed in Section 5.1, colonial violence also continued to shape the lives of the Balochs of Kachhi long after Jacob's troops had slaughtered the party of Bugtis.

4.2   'Often Repeated Outrage': State Violence and the Nagas, 1838–1900

The frontier of southern Assam was unlike Upper Sind in many respects. The two regions were ecologically distinct: heavy rainfall instead of scorching sun; swirling mists instead of shimmering mirages; dense forests instead of sand and baked earth. The inhabitants of these areas were also thoroughly different in crucial respects: blade-wielding Nagas who moved exclusively on foot rather than rifle-carrying Baloch horsemen; rice cultivation in terraced plots among the Angamis rather than pastoralism with limited agriculture among the Balochs; forays into colonial territory motivated by trade and obtaining labour and skulls rather than by the need for food. Yet there were similarities in how British administrators understood and responded to the movements of populations who were able to return to upland environs resistant to conventional colonial military force. As in Kachhi, among the Nagas the British partially adopted the fighting tactics of their targets. Cavalry troops raised from the local population harassed the Balochs, while parties of men from upland regions navigated the steep paths between Naga villages on foot before ambushing their targets. The violence deployed by the British was also similar in terms of

---

[65] NAI Foreign Secret, 28 April 1848, No. 32: Jacob to Sind Government, 23 February 1848, ff. 1310–11.

[66] NAI Foreign Secret, 28 April 1848, No. 31: Pringle to Clerk, 17 February 1848, f. 1287.

targetting food supplies and directing violence against loosely defined communities. In both regions, violence also provoked and emanated from prolonged debates between administrators over its effectiveness and legitimacy. As British administration in the Naga Hills expanded from 1866, infrastructure including roads and a permanent 'police force' developed, and knowledge grew of the myriad variations within Naga society. Yet broad features of how violence was performed and discussed were persistent, remaining central to colonial engagements with unadministered Nagas until the end of the century.

In 1869, the Bengal Government official Alexander Mackenzie wrote a memorandum reviewing British policy on 'the North-East Frontier'. It included a lengthy justification of colonial violence against Angamis over the preceding three decades. 'The majority of the so-called military expeditions into the Angami Hills were designed', Mackenzie claimed, 'not mainly or primarily to burn, destroy, and slay, but to bring our Officers with safety into and out of a position in which they could personally negociate [*sic.*] with the Naga Chiefs'.[67] Not only was violence supposedly a means to an honourable end, but the alternative was wholly ineffective. 'Moderation was of course misunderstood. It was too thoroughly English to be appreciated by ignorant Nagas'.[68] Mackenzie's notion that British violence was the only form of communication that Nagas understood had an extensive lineage among British officials at the Assam frontier. After their pioneering 1832 journey through the Naga uplands to Manipur, Francis Jenkins and Robert Pemberton called for a permanent military post on the boundary between Naga country and northern Cachar and predicted that the British would have to 'detach a military force to subdue them ... should they prove refractory'.[69] The colonial state's previous dealings with other marginal populations, such as the Bhils and littoral communities in western India, influenced these views.[70] More proximate comparisons emerged from violent interactions with communities such as the Singphos and Mishmis at the eastern fringes of Upper Assam and the Khasis and Garos (discussed previously) to the southwest of Lower Assam.[71]

Some administrators in Assam also suggested that the colonial state's supposedly effective and moderate violence distinguished it from its regional competitors, allies, and predecessors. In 1839, six years after it installed him as the Raja of the tributary state of Upper Assam, the Company-State removed

---

[67] Mackenzie, *History*, p. 369.   [68] Ibid.

[69] NAI Foreign Political, 5 May 1832, No. 70: Jenkins to Agent to Governor-General, Northeast Frontier, 6 February 1832, ff. 5–6; NAI Foreign Political, 23 July 1832, No. 67: Pemberton to Government of India, 12 July 1832.

[70] On the Bhils, see Ajay Skaria, *Hybrid Histories: Forests, Frontiers and Wildness in Western India* (Delhi: Oxford University Press, 1999). On the application of the label of 'pirates' to littoral communities in Western India, see Layton, 'Discourses'. On the process of criminalising communities in colonial India, see Singha, *Despotism*, pp. 169–224.

[71] On colonial state violence against the Singphos, see Sadan, *Kachin*, pp. 41–85.

Purunder Singh from office. This change of policy was justified on the grounds that, in the region where tea had been discovered and was soon to become a major colonial concern,[72] 'the incursions of the Mountain Tribes adjacent have been repressed in a more feeble manner than the Military strength at his disposal, and command of his resources would have warranted'.[73] Jenkins, by then the Governor-General's Agent to the North-East Frontier, ascribed Purunder's inadequate violence to his 'being a Bengali by education and habits', drawing on the established colonial trope of effete Bengali men.[74] He expressed confidence that actions directed by British officers would ensure 'the tranquillity of all our frontiers but if [the tribes] be left to the Rajah we shall never be free from anxiety'.[75]

Officials did not, however, unanimously agree that violence against communities of the upland northeast was either justified or qualitatively distinct from that of the Assamese, Burmese, and Manipuris. During the late 1830s there was significant uncertainty over how to respond to incursions by Nagas into Assam and North Cachar in pursuit of prized items such as cowrie shells, skulls, and captives for labour.[76] The administrator overseeing North Cachar, E. M. Gordon, opined that there were 'insuperable objections' to attempting 'one of those hostile expeditions'.[77] Gordon expressed concern at the improbability of securing the responsible parties given the 'scanty' information on, and 'inaccessible nature' of, the country in which a military party would have to operate.[78] The only extant sketch map of the relevant portion of Cachar derived, its renderer admitted, 'from the information of the captured Nagas ... obtained through the medium of an indifferent Interpreter'.[79] Alongside this dearth of information, Gordon critiqued 'the expeditions resorted to by native states' in the region, which he characterised as 'one indiscriminate plow of murder, arson and rapine'.[80] Nevertheless, he advised

[72] Sharma, 'Making Garden', pp. 122–6.
[73] NAI Foreign Political, 18 April 1838, No. 56: White to Jenkins, 10 March 1838, f. 45.
[74] NAI Foreign Political, 16 May 1838, No. 55: Jenkins to Government of India, 4 April 1838, f. 176. On colonial constructions of Bengali 'effeminacy', see Mrinalini Sinha, *Colonial Masculinity: The Manly Englishman and the Effeminate Bengali* (Manchester: Manchester University Press, 1995).
[75] NAI Foreign Political 16 May 1838, No. 53: Jenkins to Government of India, 3 April 1838, f. 124.
[76] On the role of labour shortages as a motive for incursions, see Jangkhomang Guite, 'Civilisation and Its Malcontents: The Politics of Kuki Raid in Nineteenth Century Northeast India', *The Indian Economic and Social History Review*, 48, 3 (2011), pp. 339–76, here p. 374.
[77] NAI Foreign Political, 20 February 1837, No. 1A: E. M. Gordon to Bengal Government, 5 January 1837, f. 237.
[78] Ibid., f. 238.
[79] NAI Foreign Political, 20 February 1837, No. 1A: Burnes to Lowis, 23 December 1836, ff. 241–42.
[80] NAI Foreign Political, 20 February 1837, No. 1A: E. M. Gordon to Bengal Government, 5 January 1837, f. 238.

that if violent action was to be taken against the Nagas, the British should contract one of these states – Manipur – to conduct it, 'not only because the system of warfare, hitherto practised against the Hill Tribes (and indeed the only one that is practicable) could be discreditable to the Company's troops, but because the climate would prove fatal to our officers and men'.[81] Here was an instance of colonial atavism. Gordon understood that deploying violence against Nagas threatened to call into question the colonial state's distinctness from ostensibly less civilised subordinate polities. Yet he advocated using precisely these tactics and personnel, claiming that the upland environment and fighting style of the Nagas demanded them.

Gordon also doubted the capacity of violence to educate. 'Expeditions', he wrote, 'not only do not effectually stop, but seem to increase the plundering habits of their unfortunate victims'.[82] Some of his contemporaries in the sparse administrative cadre in the northeast disagreed with him on this point, insisting on the potential of military violence to communicate state power to frontier inhabitants. George Gordon, the Political Agent in Manipur, claimed that a joint military undertaking involving colonial and Manipuri troops against Naga transgressors would 'strike such terror as may prevent a recurrence of the aggressions'.[83] The two Gordons did not remain on different sides of the argument for long. In 1838, less than two years after his critique of expeditions, E. M. Gordon called for a military response to a case of Naga headhunting in Cachar, a custom that British administrators in this era knew little about but had already categorised as unacceptable barbarism.[84] This was one of many instances of inconsistent positions on violence being espoused not only by different colonial personnel but also by an individual official.

In the cold season of 1838 to 1839, a military force was sent to attack the Nagas held responsible for the violence in Cachar. Frontier officials believed that operations earlier in the year were 'impracticable from the number of Rivers ... intersecting the Country, and which during the season of Rain are never fordable'.[85] As in Upper Sind (at least until Jacob), colonial military power was a seasonal affair in this region. At both frontiers, it was also dependent on employing locals. The Superintendent of Cachar, J. A. Burnes, suggested that an irregular party of hill-dwelling Cacharis – 'a robust manly race acclimated to the Hills' – accompany the regular colonial infantry.[86] Along with perceiving them as an antidote to the peculiar conditions of the uplands,

---

[81] Ibid.   [82] Ibid.

[83] NAI Foreign Political, 20 February 1837, No. 2A: G. Gordon to Lowis, 10 January 1837, f. 251.

[84] NAI Foreign Political, 19 June 1837, No. 66: Lister to Government of India, 4 June 1837, ff. 1–3; NAI Foreign Political, 15 August 1838, No. 7: E. M. Gordon to Government of India, 31 July 1838, ff. 2–3.

[85] NAI Foreign Political, 19 June 1837, No. 66: Lister to Government of India, 04 June 1837, ff. 1–2.

[86] NAI Foreign Political, 21 November 1838, No. 104: Burnes to Jenkins, 03 October 1838, f. 513.

Burnes understood the Cacharis' violence to be characterised by excess. This quality simultaneously empowered the colonial state and seemed to threaten the message to the Nagas that the state was not just another tribe. Having extolled the martial qualities of the Cacharis and proposed that between 80 and 100 should be armed to fight the Nagas, Burnes insisted that a European officer accompany them as, left to their own devices, 'there is no knowing how far [they may] punish these savages'.[87] The Government of India authorised Burnes's proposal and ordered that the whole military party of 200 men should be formed of Cacharis rather than regular infantry troops. The great advantage of the Cacharis, according to the Government, was that they were 'accustomed to Hill and Jungle fighting under Gumbheer Sing and Govind Chunder', the rulers of Manipur and Cachar, respectively, whose reprisals against the Nagas some British officials had previously derided as barbaric.[88] As in Ricardo Roque's analysis of the Portuguese state in Timor, administrators at an edge of empire perceived that local forms and agents of violence were essential to instantiating colonial authority. At the Assam frontier, 'the foundations of colonial power were placed in the very zones of merging with the indigenous world that the Eurocentric viewpoint perceived as a source of weakness of the colonial establishment'.[89]

From the outset, the force of Cacharis under British leadership met with practical difficulties, including a shortage of transport labourers and the failure to combine with a party of Manipuris led by the British Political Agent in the Princely State. Colonial administrators nonetheless pronounced that the mission had succeeded in identifying the Angamis as the community behind the 'raids' into Cachar.[90] More importantly still, it established motives for the Angamis' actions: 'for plunder alone to obtain grain, cloth, conch shells, ornaments, slaves and scalps'.[91] Jenkins confidently pronounced that of these, the 'infamous trade in slaves ... [is] the chief cause of all the late commotions, the Nagas being incited to perpetual aggressions upon each other and their neighbours for the gain of the high prices given by the Bengalis for the captives'.[92] At a time of abolitionist zeal, categorising the Angamis' captives as slaves seemed to British officials to establish Naga violence as clearly distinct from their own.[93] Confident that the 'expedition' was righteous retribution against 'raids', the British planned another for the

---

[87] Ibid.
[88] NAI Foreign Political, 9 January 1839, No. 163: Government of India to Burnes, 9 January 1839, f. 462.
[89] Roque, *Headhunting*, p. 65.
[90] IOR/F/4/1832 (75911): Jenkins to Bigge, 18 December 1838, f. 36.
[91] NAI Foreign Political, 10 July 1839, No. 56: Jenkins to Government of India, 20 May 1839, f. 5.
[92] Ibid., f. 6.
[93] On the colonial assumption that 'slavery' formed an integral aspect of tribal societies in the northeast, see Sadan, *Kachin*, pp. 58–63.

following cold season. The officer in charge, E. R. Grange, was given open-ended instructions, empowering him in the event of being unable to apprehend the individual Angamis responsible for the forays into Cachar 'to lay hold of any other Nagas of the same Village as hostages, or to inflict such punishment as might be in his power'.[94]

This proposed display of force fell flat, however, as Grange felt in too weak a position 'to assume the high tone intended and to enforce the surrender of Captives and plundered property'.[95] Instead he had to be content with rather less spectacular displays, although ones in which violence was still present. The party's first contact with Angamis consisted of Grange firing shots to repel a small group that approached the British camp at night. Grange's meetings with Angami potentates were theatrical affairs, as he employed the well-established tactic of using technological devices as a means of overawing non-Europeans.[96] 'I showed them a watch and a telescope', Grange reported, 'and told them I could see all they did in their villages and after frightening [a chief] by shooting at a pumkin [sic.], gave him some presents and dismissed him'.[97] When he met the man who he supposed to be the leading Angami chief, Grange had to be content with concluding an oath in what he believed to be the Angami style, in which he held one end of a spear and the chief the other while the shaft was broken.[98] Grange and his superiors placed little faith in the ability of these improvised efforts to achieve the subjection of the Angamis. The interactions appeared close to meetings of equals, threatening to blur the distinction between state and tribe. As soon as the expedition concluded, senior officials assumed that another would be necessary and expressed confidence that the shortcomings were due to resolvable factors.[99]

Against the backdrop of further Angami incursions into North Cachar, plans were drawn up for a further expedition and the establishment of an outpost in the Angami hills. This was to be manned by a militia comprised not of Cacharis, after the Political Agent in Manipur raised concerns that they 'are all more or less at feud with different parties in the Hills', but by Shans – 'they being a hardy race'.[100] The instructions issued to Grange for this expedition claimed that 'hostile measures' were 'a last resort', but also anticipated that violence would be required to subjugate the men believed to be the major Angami chiefs, rendered 'Ikari' and 'Impoji' in colonial documents. It was

---

[94] IOR/F/4/1832 (75911): Political Letter from Government of India, 21 August 1839, f. 2.
[95] IOR/F/4/1832 (75911): Political Letter from Government of India, 22 January 1840, ff. 5–6.
[96] On the use of technology to intimidate and establish the supposed backwardness of non-Europeans, see Kennedy, *Last Blank Spaces*, p. 157; Mueggler, *Paper Road*, p. 58.
[97] IOR/F/4/1832 (75911): Grange to Bigge, undated, ff. 79–80.   [98] Ibid, ff. 84–85.
[99] IOR/F/4/1832 (75911): Jenkins to Government of India, Political Department, 20 May 1839, f. 65.
[100] IOR/F/4/1832 (75911): Burns to Government of India, Political Department, 15 February 1839, ff. 56–57.

even suggested that Grange might install new chiefs if he deposed them.[101] Once again, the reality bore little resemblance to these intentions. Hampered by transport difficulties and the failure to combine with a Manipuri detachment, and harried by a series of skirmishes en route to the village of the supposed Angami chiefs, Grange took to targetting houses and food stores as the people themselves 'fled, and the nature of that country prevent[ed] any extended search'.[102] As in Upper Sind, colonial forces in the Angami uplands struggled to combat tribal mobility in an environment that impeded established military tactics. They resorted instead to forms of indirect coercion that had substantial impacts on entire Naga communities as it did on whole Baloch tribes.

Despite the failure of the 1840 expedition, Francis Jenkins remained convinced that regular episodes of violence were essential to change Angami habits and enforce the border.[103] Other officials were less certain. George Gordon, who had previously acclaimed the impact of military actions, argued that repeated displays of violence were unlikely to affect the Angamis' 'behaviour'.[104] As with those who had previously doubted military expeditions as a means of instantiating state authority in the frontier uplands, Gordon questioned both their impact and their propriety. 'After all you have said to me with regard to burning [Naga villages] by the [Manipuris]', Gordon wrote to Jenkins, 'I did not expect that an Officer conducting an Expedition under your orders would have destroyed even a portion of a village'.[105] Gordon's proposal to differentiate colonial power from that of its rivals and subsidiaries involved permanently stationing an officer and military party at a post in the hills. Nonetheless, he was reluctant to completely do away with the power that the colonial state accrued through sporadic bursts of violence carried out at the behest of men on the spot. 'There may be extreme cases requiring exception', he claimed, in which officers should burn villages 'to make an example'.[106] Even with this tempering, Gordon's criticism provoked a firm rebuttal from Jenkins's deputy, Lieutenant Bigge: 'I am quite at a loss to define, on what grounds Capt. Gordon offers the remarks he does, sanctioned as such acts are by all the customs of the most civilized nations in the world'.[107] This debate over the permissibility of burning property and food stores in order to instantiate state power in frontier regions typified the ambivalent nature of atavistic colonial practices. The supposed value of these practices lay in the assumption that their barbarity had a particular resonance with tribal subjects; but this was

---

[101] NAI Foreign Political, 01 January 1840, No. 112: Bigge to Grange, 26 November 1839, ff. 8–11.
[102] NAI Foreign Political, 25 May 1840, No. 118: Grange to Bigge, 30 January 1840, ff. 21–22.
[103] NAI Foreign Political, 25 May 1840, No. 118: Jenkins to Bigge, 11 April 1840, ff. 27–28.
[104] NAI Foreign Political, 3 August 1840, No. 93: Gordon to Jenkins, 23 April 1840, ff. 13–14.
[105] Ibid, ff. 30–31.   [106] Ibid, f. 32.
[107] NAI Foreign Political, 3 August 1840, No. 93: Bigge to Jenkins, 20 June 1840, f. 66.

the very quality that had to be avoided for the colonial state to uphold its self-image as a civilising force.

The Government of India approved another expedition against the Angamis in early 1841. Violence at last forced Ikari and Impoji to submit, prompting Jenkins to reaffirm his belief in the communicative potential of such undertakings: 'these barbarians [have] been taught by such painful but wholesome experience the superiority of our arms'.[108] There were, however, signs of the instability of violence as a means of instantiating colonial power. Inhabitants of the large Angami village of Samaguting, which had been razed the previous year, fled when the military party approached. Interpreters employed by the British said that Angami chiefs who had assisted colonial forces the previous year had been abandoned by their followers and had been obliged to move to other villages.[109] This prompted doubts among colonial administrators, similar to their counterparts in Upper Sind at around the same time, over whether Angami chiefs had less traction than they had initially supposed.

Following the 1841 expedition, an outpost manned by a Shan militia was established in Dimapur, at the western outskirts of Naga territory. A year and a half later, Jenkins optimistically commented: '[the Nagas'] excessive dread of fire arms would I think deter them, even if so inclined from becoming our enemies'.[110] But in 1844 some Angami villages refused to pay the 'tribute' they had tendered since the establishment of the Shan militia, undertook a major incursion into Assam, and attacked the Dimapur post.[111] The colonial state's reprisals revived debates over the effectiveness of burning villages when their inhabitants had deserted in advance of the military party's arrival. The Government of India intervened, stating that 'these harsh measures of general and indiscriminate vengeance' were 'not justifiable' and resulted in 'what was to be expected – a spirit of deeper enmity ... and a system of retaliation ... which it may be difficult to put down'.[112] By this assessment, the form of colonial violence that had become standard in the region was too unstable to be deployed as a communicative device among the Angamis. There were also disagreements between colonial administrators and institutions over the merits of the Shan militiamen who formed the bulk of colonial parties. John Butler, who led the expedition of 1846, complained that they were 'given to opium, indolent, & lax in the performance of their duty', and proposed that they should

---

[108] NAI Foreign Political, 12 April 1841, No. 79: Jenkins to Government of India, 21 March 1841, f. 175.

[109] NAI Foreign Political, 22 March 1841, No. 92: Bigge to Jenkins, 30 January 1841, ff. 190–91.

[110] NAI Foreign Political, 14 December 1842, No. 162: Jenkins to I. T. Gordon, 11 November 1842, f. 214.

[111] NAI Foreign Political, 24 August 1844, No. 35: Sturt to Jenkins, 4 June 1844, ff. 55–56.

[112] NAI Foreign Political, 23 May 1845, No. 72: Government of India to Jenkins, 23 May 1845, ff. 1–2.

be replaced with 'young and efficient men from the Cacharee tribes'.[113] Butler's superiors agreed that the Shans were unruly but linked this to the very qualities that rendered them effective agents of colonial violence. Jenkins commented that the Shans 'are everywhere held in dread by the hill people which gives them a moral influence the same number of disciplined men might fail to obtain'.[114] The Government of India concurred: the Shans, 'though idle and wayward, and difficult to manage, have physical qualities which render them useful'.[115] British violence against the Nagas continued, then, to deploy strategies and personnel that could not be clearly distinguished from the violence it was ostensibly deployed to counteract.

Even at the level of actions undertaken and theories advanced by individual officers, frontier violence was prone to shifts and inconsistencies. Having previously extolled expeditions through the hills as the only means to communicate state power to Angamis, in 1846 Jenkins suddenly argued that these fleeting performances of power had merely 'led the Nagas to suppose that we cannot maintain a position in the hills'.[116] This change of heart by the leading administrator in the colonial northeast led to the establishment of a permanent military post manned by Shans during the cold season of 1846 to 1847. British administrators nonetheless expressed unease over the Shans' actions if left under their own officers, so instituted a lowlander named Bhog Chund as the colonial state's representative in the region and overseer of the militia.[117] John Butler remained cautious about the chances of establishing colonial authority, writing to Jenkins that 'the Angamee chiefs are powerless & we can hardly therefore say that they are responsible for the violence of the people'.[118] He also emphasised the lack of colonial infrastructure in the region. To get to Dimapur, the gateway to the Angami region, required a seventy-mile slog through 'dense forest jungle', a journey that allowed luggage carriers to desert in droves with complete impunity.[119] Bhog Chund, Butler suggested, had some hope of success, 'though for some years to come he may fail in suppressing [the Angamis'] exterminating feuds'.[120]

Angamis launched a large-scale attack on the post at Samaguting little more than two years after its establishment, killing Bhog Chund and thirteen sepoys

[113] NAI Foreign Political, 13 June 1846, No. 29: Butler to Jenkins, 17 January 1846, f. 10.
[114] NAI Foreign Political, 13 June 1846, No. 29: Jenkins to Government of India, 8 May 1846, f. 3.
[115] NAI Foreign Political, 23 May 1846, No. 32: Government of India to Jenkins, 23 May 1846, ff. 142–4.
[116] NAI Foreign Political, 10 September 1846, No. 17: Jenkins to Government of India, 19 August 1846, ff. 1–3.
[117] NAI Foreign Political, 24 April 1847, No. 37: Jenkins to Government of India, 23 March 1847, f. 213.
[118] NAI Foreign Political, 24 April 1847, No. 38: Butler to Jenkins, 10 February 1847, ff. 235–6.
[119] Ibid., ff. 218–24.   [120] Ibid., ff. 260–61.

and labourers.[121] British officials knew almost nothing about Bhog Chund's brief tenure. Uncertainty persisted over whether his death followed excessive interference in Angami affairs. Indeed, the hazy nature of the authority the colonial state vested in him meant that what constituted excessive interference was a matter of post facto debate. In the letter to the Government of India in which he reported his death, Jenkins attempted to institute a narrative in which Bhog Chund was 'zealous for [the Nagas'] improvement' and acted within the limits of his authority.[122] A large military party was dispatched to avenge Bhog Chund's 'murder', a decision that Jenkins justified with reference to the effectiveness of the Manipur state's violence, which he had elsewhere derided as barbarous.[123] The Governor-General informed Jenkins merely that he was 'willing to leave a very wide discretion in your hands as to the steps to be taken';[124] Jenkins in turn told the officer in charge that he 'must ... greatly be guided by his own discretion'.[125] This was a clear instance of the subcontracting of authority for deploying state violence that tended to lie at the core of frontier expeditions. But far from establishing the justice of colonial actions, the military party unearthed evidence that Bhog Chund had 'deceived the Nagas'. Jenkins changed tack once again, not only renouncing his previous support for Bhog Chund, but also stating that 'we cannot rely on Native management with a people so totally rude and independent as the Clans of Angami Nagas'.[126] Jenkins's wholesale reversal of opinion in this instance was yet another instance of the precarity and mutability of British assessments of the cycle of violence between the Angamis and colonial forces during the 1840s.

In 1850, the effective imposition of colonial authority among the Angami Nagas seemed to officials in Assam to be more distant than it had ten years earlier. The notion that the Angamis were intractably prone to violence became more prominent than it had been during the 1840s, when notions of 'improvement' provided a counterbalance. Jenkins came to believe that headhunting and 'blood feud[s]' had an 'overpowering' influence among Nagas.[127] He and other administrators also emphasised two other elements that contrasted with their initial understandings of the Nagas and their uplands. First, in place of the

---

[121] NAI Foreign Political, 17 November 1849, No. 156: Jenkins to Government of India, 14 August 1849, f. 225.

[122] Ibid.

[123] NAI Foreign Political, 17 November 1849, No. 169: Jenkins to Government of India, 30 October 1849, f. 256.

[124] NAI Foreign Political, 17 November 1849, No. 171: Government of India to Jenkins, 17 November 1849, f. 258.

[125] NAI Foreign Political, 22 December 1849, No. 102: Jenkins to Butler, 3 December 1849, ff. 10–11.

[126] NAI Foreign Political, 7 February 1851, No. 201: Jenkins to Government of India, 2 January 1851, f. 335.

[127] NAI Foreign Political, 7 June 1850, No. 142: Jenkins to Government of India, 25 April 1850, ff. 1–2.

presumption that there were chiefs and leading villages that exerted significant influence over the Angamis as a whole, they now tended to understand the community as 'completely democratic'.[128] Accordingly, there seemed no chance of enforcing colonial oversight by winning over particular individuals or villages by threats or inducements. Second, the British perceived the region as environmentally intractable, rather than a space that might be rendered controllable by building a system of roads and military posts.[129] These shifts underpinned a change of policy to 'non-interference'. The decision was not made in the upper echelons of the colonial state, nor did it result from assessments of imperial strategy. Rather, the evidence of British involvement with the Angamis presented by frontier officials suggested that violence was simply not communicating colonial power. Worse still, it seemed that the message was at times farcically misinterpreted: Angamis were responding with violence of their own rather than submission. Non-interference remained contentious among British officials during its fifteen-year span from 1851 to 1866. Despite the officially stated determination to cease interactions with upland communities south of the Brahmaputra, the expansion of tea gardens and continued Naga incursions meant the boundaries between Angami country and British Assam and Cachar continued to be amorphous.[130] In addition, a Naga complement to an already existing Kuki military levy was created in 1855, further blurring the limits of colonial authority. The rationale behind this measure was that Angamis were 'cruel and ruthless in their attacks and when flushed with victory commit many atrocities which it is painful to contemplate'.[131] Colonial dealings with the Angamis continued, albeit in a different form, to give rise to atavistic tensions of reliance on the very qualities that provoked criticism.

By the mid-1860s, frontier administrators' lurid tales of helplessness in the face of Naga violence piled up. Like the decision to implement the policy of non-interference, the move to end it was based on the representations of officials stationed at the fringes of empire. Especially striking was an extraordinary assessment of the fragile British position in the northeast by the Commissioner of Assam Henry Hopkinson in 1865. 'We are', he warned, 'on all sides surrounded in Assam by inflammable material, which may blaze out at any moment without previous warning'.[132] Hopkinson returned to the

[128]   Ibid., f. 3.
[129]   On road building, NAI Foreign Political, 23 May 1846, No. 30: Jenkins to Government of India, 11 April 1846, f. 81; on intractable environment, NAI Foreign Political, 17 November 1849, No. 160: Jenkins to Government of India, 19 October 1849, f. 239.
[130]   NAI Foreign Political, 5 May 1854, No. 64: Government of India to Government of Bengal, 29 April 1854, ff. 41–42; NAI Foreign Political, 19 January 1855, No. 129: Bengal Government, 'Note on the Angami Nagas', undated, ff. 58–59.
[131]   NAI Foreign Political, 14 April 1855, No. 26: Stewart to Bivar, 10 March 1855, f. 33.
[132]   NAI Foreign Political A, 07/1865, No. 49: Hopkinson to Bengal Government, 03 May 1865, f. 6.

well-worn option of deploying violence to establish state authority among the Angamis and thereby secure colonial territory — especially tea gardens — in Assam. He insisted that violence was the only language understood by not only Nagas but the 'utter savages' of the entire arc of northeast frontier.[133] To justify this renewed emphasis on violent state interference, Hopkinson constructed an animalistic tribal subject. He passed from musing on the impossibility of 'exterminat[ing] wild beasts' in the frontier tracts to the south of the Brahmaputra to claim that

the circumstances under which the Nagas and the Garrows, or even the Abors, live, are not so very dissimilar from the conditions under which wild animals exist, that we should expect to be able to control the one, when we frankly admit the impossibility of extirpating the other; the difficulty in the one case is really precisely that of the other.[134]

Along with similar cases in the northwest, this was an instance of the broader tendency of modern European empires to render colonial subjects that, in Achille Mbembe's words, 'belonged to the *sphere of objects* [and] could be destroyed, as one may kill an animal'.[135]

Configuring the upland communities of the northeast as animals that might be killed with impunity was of a piece with Hopkinson's insistence that among 'hill tribes . . . punishing the innocent with the guilty must generally be made a question of circumstances rather than principle'.[136] This was premised on an assessment of tribal structure and the environmental demands of the Assam frontier. In the 'state of anarchy' that prevailed among these communities, no one was fully innocent: 'by not intervening, [they] make themselves to some extent participators in the crime'.[137] Their form of violence was perfectly attuned to the 'country void of roads, void of supplies, . . . of interminable hills, of vast swamps covered with a dense forest'; and unlike for colonial forces, to the Nagas 'hill and swamp and forest are resources rather than obstacles'.[138] These features demanded a different reference point for colonial discipline. Hopkinson came up with the following: 'if certain of the children of Bloomsbury Parish School were in the habit of breaking off the noses of the statues when they visited the British

---

[133] NAI Foreign Political A, 07/1865, No. 51: Hopkinson to Bengal Government, 05 May 1865, f. 8.

[134] ASA, Bengal Government Papers, No. 305: Hopkinson to Bengal Government, 30 October 1865.

[135] Achille Mbembe, *On the Postcolony* (Berkeley, CA: University of California Press, 2001), p. 27 (emphasis in original).

[136] NAI Foreign Political, July 1865, No. 51: Hopkinson to Bengal Government, 5 May 1865, f. 9.

[137] Ibid.; ASA, Bengal Government Papers, No. 305: Hopkinson to Bengal Government, 30 October 1865.

[138] ASA, Bengal Government Papers, No. 305: Hopkinson to Bengal Government, 30 October 1865.

Museum, and the school refused to denounce the iconoclasts, the exclusion of the school from the institution would appear to be the most proper course to take'.[139] His analogy of upland communities and youths of central London was sufficient to persuade the Government of India to pronounce that 'in our dealing with a tribe, we ought on important occasions to deal with them as a body corporate'.[140] In this shift from non-interference to the perception that entire communities were legitimate targets of violence, there are parallels with Jon Wilson's reading of colonial utilitarianism emerging from a sense of estrangement among colonial officials in Bengal rather than confidence in liberal values.[141] Tribal responsibility was not premised on certainty that Naga tribes were coherent political units. Even Hopkinson acknowledged that there was not 'such a thing as a Naga aristocracy'.[142] He was concerned not with precise ethnographic description, but with establishing the necessary guilt of all those caught up in colonial violence. Tellingly, he did not specify whether he took the limits of the tribe to be at level of a sub-group within a village, an entire village, or the whole Angami population. As was the case with border making and knowledge production at India's frontiers, this colonial project emanated from indeterminacy rather than fixity.

The use of violence, including the destruction of villages and food stores, continued to be a key colonial strategy after the establishment of the Naga Hills District in 1866 (see Section 1.3). The District's founding Deputy Commissioner, Lieutenant Gregory, also ensured that the tradition of using uplanders as agents of colonial violence continued. The 'police force' at Samaguting, which also acted as a roving militia, 'should consist entirely of hill-men, Cacharies, Kookies, Garos, and Nepalese', he insisted.[143] The Government of India acquiesced, adding that 'when conciliation fails, punitive measures will not be shrunk from'.[144] Violence continued, however, to be a source of contention among British administrators. Even Hopkinson's advocacy of military actions against loosely defined collectives wavered. Towards the end of his tenure as Commissioner of Assam in 1873, he argued against a military response to headhunting by a community beyond the eastern limits of the Naga Hills District. The perpetrators, he envisaged, would flee from the colonial party, leaving it to burn down the village, 'and

---

[139] NAI Foreign Political, July 1865, No. 51: Hopkinson to Bengal Government, 5 May 1865, f. 9.
[140] NAI Foreign Political, July 1865, No. 53: Government of India to Bengal Government, 11 July 1865, f. 15.
[141] Wilson, *Domination*.
[142] NAI Foreign Political, July 1865, No. 51: Hopkinson to Bengal Government, 5 May 1865, f. 8.
[143] NAI Foreign Political A, December 1866, No. 137: Gregory, 'Memorandum', f. 14.
[144] ASA, Bengal Government Papers, No. 305: Government of India, Foreign Department, to Bengal Government, 8 June 1866.

what would be the use of that?'[145] More generally, he suggested, 'petty military expeditions ... very rare[ly] do any real, or anything like lasting good'.[146] According to Hopkinson, the central flaw in expeditions was that they failed to render themselves distinct from tribal violence in the minds of their target audience. 'When the Nagas commit an outrage and we send a party in the hills to avenge it, the whole transaction is in their eyes nothing but raid and counter-raid ... We must avoid raiding ourselves, that is, we must not have recourse to partial and desultory acts of warfare'.[147] By imagining Angamis describing British actions as 'raiding', Hopkinson revealed the failure of the Government of Bengal's expectation when founding the Naga Hills District that permanently stationing a colonial force at Samaguting would make state violence 'appear like punishment, and less like a reprisal in kind'.[148]

As the District expanded in both territorial expanse and colonial military presence during the closing decades of the nineteenth century, uncertainties about violence persisted. From 1884, there were intense debates among administrators regarding the merits of regular tours by a party of the district police led by the Deputy Commissioner to villages beyond direct administration at the shifting eastern edge of the District, which were held responsible for 'growing turbulence' in the region.[149] Although some officials believed these tours would inflame discontent and the Government of India initially refused to sanction them, they went ahead from 1885.[150] The term 'promenades', which the Deputy Commissioner R. B. McCabe attached to the tours, sanitised their use of significant violence against communities previously beyond colonial control. McCabe insisted that they 'put an end to ... murderous raids'.[151] When McCabe left his post in 1888, the former Chief Commissioner of Assam positioned him in an elite pantheon of tribal administration alongside 'the influence exerted by the greatest men in Anglo-Indian history over the Santhals, the Bhils and the tribes of the Derajat'.[152] Other colleagues derided McCabe's promenades. His successor as Deputy Commissioner argued that they had killed large numbers, and 'it is small wonder' that this engendered 'a savage revenge' against those who had

---

[145] ASA, Bengal Government Records, Nos. 26–30: Hopkinson to Bengal Government, 13 August 1873.
[146] Ibid.   [147] Ibid.
[148] NAI Foreign Political A, August 1866, No. 136: Bengal Government to Hopkinson, f. 1.
[149] NAI Foreign External A, October 1884, No. 389: Assam Chief Commissioner to Government of India, Foreign Department, 22 August 1884.
[150] NAI Foreign External A, October 1884, No. 391; NAI Foreign External A, May 1885, Nos. 175–81.
[151] NAI Foreign External A, July 1888, No. 122: McCabe to Chief Commissioner of Assam, 24 May 1888.
[152] Charles Elliott, quoted in Reid, *History*, p. 116.

assisted colonial forces.[153] The Chief Commissioner of Assam advanced a directly contradictory critique, contending that a combination of 'material difficulties' and 'views of morality as entertained by us' rendered the promenades ineffective. 'The most we can do', he opined, 'is to burn a village, and if, which rarely happens, the people resist, to shoot a few of them. But the burning of a village or the loss of a few members of the tribe are with them such very ordinary events that they make little impression'.[154] The apprehension that violence was futile was especially sharp when directed against Naga communities to the east, which practised shifting *jhuming* cultivation in contrast to the Angamis' terraced agriculture in fixed locations. Colonial military parties accordingly had fewer fixed objects to damage and destroy.

Variations on the long-established colonial tendency to oscillate between 'non-interference' and violence in the Naga Hills continued into the twentieth century.[155] Despite the substantial increase in material and human resources deployed against Nagas as the nineteenth century progressed, violence was still an unstable source of both power and concern for British officials. The irregular levies using steep paths to penetrate the forested hills sporadically during the late 1830s gave way to a police force able to navigate a burgeoning network of roads and outposts fifty years later. The environment of the Naga Hills was no longer seen as an insuperable obstacle to the deployment of colonial violence. There were, however, notable continuities across the period. State violence in this region did not emanate from a position of confidence and certainty. It was instead intended as a means of instantiating authority in situations in which officials lacked knowledge and believed that they faced major challenges from the structure of Naga society and the region's terrain. Furthermore, deploying violence to lay the foundations of colonial authority often failed in practice, generating resistance rather than instituting acceptance of colonial power. The shortcomings and inherent volatility of violence often vexed officials. Their changing assessments of its practical efficacy and moral propriety, coupled with mutable understandings of Naga communities and their upland environment, drove great fluctuations in how the colonial state operated in this region. But unease never consistently overcame what might be termed the allure of violence, which acted in conjunction with the administrators' frequent refusal to adhere to legal and geographical boundaries. These elements collectively rendered the frontier south of Assam a zone in which 'the distinction between war and peace did not avail'.[156]

---

[153] NAI Foreign External A, January 1889, No. 77: Porteous to Assam Chief Commissioner, 21 September 1888.
[154] NAI Foreign External A, January 1889, No. 76: Assam Chief Commissioner to Government of India, Foreign Department, 14 November 1888.
[155] Reid, *History*, pp. 129–31.
[156] Achille Mbembe, 'Necropolitics', trans. Libby Meintjes, *Public Culture*, 15, 1 (2003), pp. 11–40; here p. 25.

4.3 'Few Permanent Results': Military Expeditions on the Punjab Frontier, 1849–1901

The Punjab frontier presented British administrators with a sufficiently diverse array of ecological, sociological, and strategic imperatives to resist stable comprehension as a unified whole. Colonial militarisation in the region was heavier in key locales such as the Khyber Pass than at any other frontier but still endlessly debated. Along with portions of British Baluchistan, especially the garrison town of Quetta, from the 1860s telegraph and rail connected outposts abutting the Punjab frontier to centres of colonial power. Following Russian expansion into Central Asia during the mid- to late 1860s, the frontier was subject to increasingly intense scrutiny as an area of crucial strategic significance. This combination of plentiful attention and resources did not prevent colonial violence against frontier inhabitants from sharing many of the key features of violence in the Naga Hills and even the Upper Sind frontier of the 1840s. In particular, there were similar debates over whether violence was effective or justified. As the nineteenth century progressed, many officials became ever less confident that military violence had meaningful effects among 'democratic' Pashtun tribes inhabiting uplands ill-suited to conventional colonial military tactics. These doubts were not confined to men stationed at the frontier, but shared by those at the upper echelons of the colonial apparatus who took a peculiar degree of interest in the Punjab frontier. Especially telling was a refrain repeated by no fewer than three Viceroys – Lytton in 1877, Lansdowne in 1889, and Curzon in 1900: 'punitive expeditions have been frequent, but have been attended with very few permanent results'.[157] State violence on the Punjab frontier was frequently criticised but persistently reenacted, including with the authorisation of each of these three men. This section explores shifting colonial capacities and rationales for violence at the Punjab frontier, and how these incorporated the effects of persistent failure.

Military expeditions against unadministered Pashtuns were deployed regularly from the outset of British rule in Punjab. These ostensibly punished violence against revenue-paying colonial subjects, military personnel, and infrastructure, along with thefts of livestock and food. Roads designed to facilitate British military access to key locales, especially passes into Afghanistan, were particular targets at this stage. Some frontier administrators expressed a degree of sympathy with the 'fear and jealousy' these projects induced among Pashtuns 'well aware' that they enhanced the potential for future colonial interference.[158] Almost all, however, immediately believed that

---

[157] Lansdowne to Punjab Government, 17 October 1889, quoted in Curzon, 'Minute on Frontier Administration', 1900, MSS Eur F111/319, p. 5.

[158] NAI Foreign Secret, 22 March 1850, No. 49: George Lawrence to Campbell, 5 February 1850.

directing violence against communities with 'no common head' that could 'retire at will to their fastnesses' further into the uplands required special measures.[159] They marked immovable items – crops and buildings, 'especially Towers' – as prime targets, even though Governor-General Dalhousie insisted that these should be 'a last resort'.[160] They also configured the assumed Pashtun proclivity to violence as a resource as well as a threat: irregular parties of Pashtuns accompanied regular troops in many early expeditions, and in 1852 the Board of Administration advocated organising 'an active and efficient Police ... selected from the flower of the warlike population'.[161] By 1855, irregular forces outnumbered regular ones, and all frontier districts except Peshawar were policed almost exclusively by these locally raised levies.[162] Another key strategy was to take advantage of what the Board termed 'the scarcity of culturable land in the hills', and restrict Pashtuns from obtaining particular goods from British-governed territory.[163]

Whether these measures overcame the dual obstacles of 'democratic' tribal structures and the 'friction of terrain' remained a moot point.[164] In 1850, Charles Napier, the Commander-in-Chief overseeing military action against Afridis in the Kohat Pass region, extolled expeditions as 'teach[ing] the vast power of discipline, against which mountains and plains and rivers and jungles, all cease to be insuperable obstacles'.[165] Following another Afridi attack on an administered village, those stationed at the frontier were less convinced.[166] The region, one wrote, was 'a perfect network of broken rugged hills, and narrow vallies [sic.]', the people 'live principally in caves, not easily destroyed', and Afridi chiefs 'at best have little power over their people'.[167]

[159]   NAI Foreign Secret, 27 September 1850: Lumsden, Memorandum, 21 August 1850, f. 1275; NAI Foreign Secret 26 April 1850, No. 66: Punjab Board of Administration to Government of India, f. 3.

[160]   NAI Foreign Secret, 26 April 1850, No. 66: Punjab Board of Administration to Government of India, 27 March 1850, f. 3; No. 69: Government of India to Punjab Board of Administration, 13 April 1850, f. 6.

[161]   NAI Foreign Secret, 26 April 1850, No. 65: George Lawrence to Punjab Board of Administration, f. 3; NAI Foreign Secret, 30 April 1852, No. 75: Punjab Board of Administration to Government of India, Foreign Department, 18 March 1852, f. 4.

[162]   Richard Temple and R. H. Davies, *Report showing the relations of the British Government with the tribes on the North-West Frontier of the Punjab, from annexation in 1849 to the close of 1855; and continuation of the same to August 1864* (Lahore: Punjab Government Press, 1865), p. 60.

[163]   NAI Foreign Secret, 30 April 1852, No. 75: Punjab Board of Administration to Government of India, Foreign Department, 18 March 1852, f. 5.

[164]   On the 'friction of terrain', see Scott, *Art*.

[165]   NAI Foreign Secret, 22 March 1850, No. 43: Napier, 'General Orders', 16 February 1850, f. 264.

[166]   NAI Foreign Secret, 30 August 1850, Nos. 14–7.

[167]   NAI Foreign Secret, 27 September 1850: Lumsden, 'Memorandum', 21 August 1850, f. 1275; NAI Foreign Secret, 25 October 1850: Lumsden to Punjab Board of Administration, 18 September 1850, f. 9.

In 1855, the Secretary to the Punjab Government Richard Temple wrote the first significant summary and justification of colonial violence at the Punjab frontier. After outlining the sixteen military actions on a sufficient scale to be termed 'expeditions' that had taken place since annexation, Temple expounded general principles. Pashtuns, he claimed, were characterised by propensity to violence and absence of political structures. All communities beyond the administrative frontier of Punjab lacked anything 'approaching to government or civil institutions' and were 'thievish and predatory to the last degree'.[168] His 'fickle' tribal subject was a counterpoint to the colonial government as a model of 'civilised' consistency.[169] He insinuated that avoiding violence against such people was patently absurd, 'requir[ing] nothing less than a Chinese wall securely manned for 800 miles!'[170] Despite insisting that 'no servant of the British Government would dare to enter [independent tribal] country on any account whatever', Temple stated that the deployment of military parties 'prov[e] beyond doubt that the hills can be penetrated'.[171] He represented military violence as exceptional and sovereign-founding in Carl Schmitt's sense – an obliteration of the norm so that the norm could be instituted.[172] Just as at the outskirts of Sind and Assam, the boundary had to be violated in order for it to be imposed through the communicative power of violence. Temple's acclamation of the expeditions was based on precisely this notion that they were foundational moments for the institution of spatially delimited colonial sovereignty in Punjab: 'in almost every one of these cases the tribes behaved *badly before* and *well after* the expedition'.[173]

Temple also sought to justify military deployments against entire communities. He distinguished expeditions from 'civilised warfare' on the basis that

the enemy does *not* possess troops that stand to be attacked, *nor* defensible posts to be taken, *nor* innocent subjects to be spared. He has only rough hills to be penetrated, robber fastnesses to be scaled, and dwellings containing people, *all of them to a man concerned in hostilities. There is not a single man of them who is innocent.*[174]

By this reasoning, modes of violence that would have been illegitimate in colonial India were not only acceptable but necessary among difficult-to-access upland tribes with flat social structures and limited infrastructure to attack. Temple's colleagues widely shared this sentiment. In 1850, Governor-General Dalhousie assented to violence beyond the rules of ordinary warfare, on the basis that 'barbarous tribes . . . can understand no other punishment and feel &

---

[168] Temple and Davies, *Report*, pp. 62–63.   [169] Ibid., p. 65.   [170] Ibid., p. 70.
[171] Ibid., p. 66.   [172] Schmitt, *Concept*.
[173] Temple and Davies, *Report.*, p. 69 (emphases in the original).
[174] Ibid., pp. 67–68 (emphases in the original).

fear nothing less'.[175] The Board of Administration pronounced that directing violence against entire tribal groups was not only 'the principle of all international law', but 'in unison with the feelings, habits, and custom of all the Hill tribes themselves'.[176] The British frequently employed a lexicon of pedagogy in rationalising violence against Pashtuns. For example, in 1853 one member of the Government of India couched expeditions as 'teach[ing] them, in the only way understood by them', and wrote of the need for overwhelming military force 'that the lesson may be so taught as never to be forgotten'.[177] A year later, the officer overseeing the Kohat Pass Afridis also wrote of teaching 'the hard lesson' by 'punish[ing] to the extent of our power those who resist . . . again and again'.[178] Growing awareness among British administrators during the 1850s of the principle of hospitality that formed a central plank of *pashtunwali* reinforced their notion that collective punishment was necessary, educative, and just. In 1855, the Chief Commissioner of Punjab John Lawrence suggested 'a stern example' was necessary against communities in Kurram that 'not only appear to have withheld their cooperation against . . . robbers, but to have been actually instrumental in their escape'.[179] Five years later, his successor declared that the need for violence against collectives arose because Pashtuns 'make the cause of the murderers their own, and . . . thus prevent the possibility of distinction between the innocent and the guilty'.[180]

British officials in frontier districts during the decade following annexation were generally aware of the similarity between colonial frontier violence and that of the Sikh state that preceded it in Punjab. Unlike their counterparts in Assam however, most did not view this resemblance through a lens of atavism. One administrator's justification for burning crops and destroying villages – 'I do not think we can do better than follow [the Sikhs'] example' – typified this attitude.[181] But during the 1860s officials came increasingly to view military expeditions as problematic. R. H. Davies, who updated Temple's report in 1864, continued to insist that 'morally we have the fullest right . . . to chastise in their corporate capacity tribes who openly and habitually rob and murder our subjects or violate our territory'.[182] However, he largely replaced Temple's claims of the justice of expeditions with a focus solely on their efficacy. 'The

---

[175] NAI Foreign Secret, 26 April 1850, No. 69: Government of India to Punjab Board of Administration, 13 April 1850, f. 2.
[176] NAI Foreign Secret, 30 April 1852, No. 75: Punjab Board of Administration to Government of India, Foreign Department, 18 March 1852, ff. 1–2.
[177] NAI Foreign Secret, 26 August 1853, No. 74: J. Lowis, 'Minute', 10 August 1853, ff. 1–3.
[178] NAI Foreign Secret, 25 August 1854, No. 38: Coke to Edwardes, 17 July 1854, f. 34
[179] NAI Foreign Secret, 27 July 1855, No. 54: John Lawrence to Edwardes, 23 April 1855, f. 1453.
[180] NAI Foreign Political A, 30 March 1860, No. 7: Punjab Government to Government of India, Foreign Department, 3 February 1860, f. 42.
[181] NAI Foreign Secret, 26 April 1850, No. 67: George Lawrence to Punjab Board of Administration, 23 February 1850, f. 11.
[182] Temple and Davies, *Report*, p. 98.

question is, indeed, much less one moral right than of political expediency and military practicability ... The military success which in varying degrees has always attended expeditions ... [has] done much to subjugate the minds and compel the respect of the hill population'.[183] And he admitted that even the practical impact of violence was doubtful: 'politically the advantages to be obtained will always depend on the concomitant circumstances ... Success less distinguished might ... excite [frontier inhabitants] to continued rapine and resistance'.[184] Some administrators continued to advance sanguine assessments of the ability of military actions to shape tribal minds and master frontier terrain. In some cases, the two were seen to go hand-in-hand: one official noted in 1860 that by using explosives to construct a road through a narrow gorge, 'we have left [the Waziris] a permanent mark in their wild hills'.[185] But a more sceptical outlook began to compete with these narratives, emerging from the growing tendency during the late 1850s and early 1860s for colonial forces to become embroiled in prolonged and indeterminate cycles of violence with certain communities along the entire length of the Punjab frontier. The targets of state violence seemed less clear, with administrators becoming lost in the thickets of competing models of tribal social structure and responsibility.[186] The effects of state violence also appeared increasingly unstable, as liable to generate further resistance as to facilitate the colonial state's desired frontier arrangements.

Four expeditions between 1852 and 1891 in the Black Mountain region in the northern Punjab frontier typify the evolution of colonial violence against unadministered communities in this region. These were among the most substantial military undertakings in any Indian frontier in terms of the size of the parties involved. They took place against a particularly complicated sociological, political, and topographical backdrop. The area was inhabited not only by various long-established tribes of Pashtuns and 'Swatis' (who colonial administrators understood as a distinct group[187]) but also by the 'Hindustani Fanatics', a recently arrived Wahhabist group against which the colonial state waged a long-running campaign.[188] Colonial interference began with an act of official subversion in 1851. The head of the Punjab Government customs department travelled with a military patrol to the Agror Valley at the foot of the Black Mountain against the advice of his superiors.[189] All members of the

---

[183] Ibid.   [184] Ibid.
[185] NAI Foreign Political A, 30 March 1860, No. 7: James to Punjab Government, 26 January 1860, ff. 80–81.
[186] On the Waziris, for example, see NAI Foreign Political A, March 1862, No. 215.
[187] NAI Foreign Political A, December 1868, No. 82: Pollock to Punjab Government, 31 October 1868, f. 17.
[188] Hopkins, '"Hindustani Fanatics"'.
[189] *Frontier and Overseas Expeditions from India. Vol. I: Tribes North of the Kabul River* (Simla: Government Monotype Press, 1907), pp. 101–11.

party were killed in a region without any officially designated boundary. Assuming the complicity of an entire tribe, the Hassanzais, British administrators despatched a force that, following practices already established further south on the Punjab frontier, razed villages and destroyed grain stores.[190]

In the later 1860s, against the backdrop of Russian expansion into Central Asia, the colonial state sought to expand its presence at various frontier locales, including the Agror Valley at the base of the Black Mountain.[191] In 1868 there was an attack on the police post that constituted the primary colonial presence in Agror and a number of British-administered villages. Officials suspected the collusion of the Khan of Agror and gave credence to rumours of a 'general combination' of independent uplanders with Muslim inhabitants of Agror and the district of Hazara.[192] Leaflets written by the Deputy Commissioner and distributed in Agror and the adjacent uplands claimed that 'Government oppresses no one unless he is guilty of committing an outrage ... [and] calls to account and punishes only those who offend it'.[193] In practice, colonial violence was directed against whole communities, with a huge party of 14,000 regular troops operating alongside a force commanded by the Nawab of Amb, who controlled a portion of the hills beyond the colonial state's administrative boundary. The Punjab Government recognised the violence of the Nawab's men as a crucial element of British efforts to instantiate authority, noting with approval that 'a considerable number of the hostile tribes have been slain by his followers'.[194]

The expedition initially generated optimism among colonial administrators. Forgetting that this was the second expedition against communities of the Black Mountain, the Commissioner of Peshawar asserted that 'the result of a successful expedition is markedly and long-lastingly beneficial ... No tribe has hitherto required to be dealt with twice'.[195] Viceroy John Lawrence echoed this sentiment, stating that expeditions 'produced considerable effects and tended to a subsequent respect for our power and of our territories'.[196] For a brief period, it seemed to administrators that the military action of 1868 had successfully done more than just avenging a particular transgression. It was, in Walter Benjamin's terms, a form a violence that 'establishes a law far more than

---

[190] Temple and Davies, *Report*, pp. 4–6.
[191] NAI Foreign Political A, October 1868, No. 242: Johnstone to Punjab Government, 4 September 1868, ff. 13–14.
[192] NAI Foreign Political A, August 1871, Nos. 361–71.
[193] NAI Foreign Political A, December 1868, No. 74: Pollock, 'Proclamation to Trans-Indus Tribes generally', undated, f. 1.
[194] NAI Foreign Political, September 1868, No. 11: Punjab Government to Government of India, Foreign Department, 16 August 1868, f. 1.
[195] NAI Foreign Political A, October 1868, No. 226: Pollock to Punjab Government, 27 August 1868, f. 6.
[196] NAI Foreign Political A, October 1868, No. 460: Government of India, Military Department, to Lumsden, 10 October 1868, f. 2.

it punishes the infringement of a law that already exists'.[197] Sanguine British assessments soon dissipated, however, as communities around the Black Mountain frequently continued to pierce the proclaimed border in Agror. Colonial authorities instituted a form of martial law from late 1869, overseen by an officer invested with 'powers ... for repression and vengeance ... [that] will closely resemble the Lord Warden of the Scottish Marches of olden days', a formulation echoing Jacob's prescription for the Upper Sind frontier.[198] Although proclaimed as a short-term measure, it remained in force as sporadic attacks on villages in Agror continued through the early 1870s.[199]

The manifest inadequacy of violence as a means of instantiating stable sovereign territory in Agror caused the British consensus on its utility and propriety to fragment. The Government of India vetoed the Punjab Government's more radical suggestions concerning the authority of the military commander in Agror to perpetrate violence at 'the least appearance of robbery or raid'. While continuing to insist that tribal communities 'must be taught' that attacks on villages were 'acts of murder', the authorities in Calcutta began subtly to shift their appraisal of violence as a policy. Swift military reprisals for border violations '[have] not hitherto been effectual' and were 'not always just', they pronounced.[200] Looking beyond British India's 'independent' frontiers at a time of heightened strategic tensions, the Government of India also expressed concerns that violence in the Black Mountain region was having the wrong sort of communicative effect. 'These expeditions', it said, 'give occasion to our enemies to misrepresent our motives and spread false and alarming rumours regarding the internal peace of the empire. [They] are watched and discussed by Asiatic nations, and quoted as evidence that parts of India are still unsubjugated'.[201] The recently installed Viceroy Lord Mayo expressed these fears in even more vivid terms, invoking the spectre of atavism. 'Unlike our officers in Scinde, the Punjab authorities have devised no better means of dealing with [independent tribes] ... than by copying their own savage mode of warfare'.[202] Like Henry Hopkinson in Assam just three years later, Mayo's criticism called into question the distinction between colonial expeditions and tribal raids that Punjab officials continually reinscribed. British frontier administrators, Mayo suggested, had become too tribal in their attitude to violence, 'adopt[ing] what is doubtless the view taken by these mountaineers

---

[197] Benjamin, 'Critique', p. 243.
[198] NAI Foreign Political A, February 1870, No. 103: Hughes, Commanding Punjab Frontier Force, to Punjab Government, Military Department, 29 October 1869, f. 5.
[199] NAI Foreign Political A, February 1870, No. 103: Punjab Government, Military Department, to Hughes, [unreadable] January 1870, ff. 7–8.
[200] NAI Foreign Political A, February 1870, No. 107: Government of India, Foreign Department, to Punjab Government, 16 February 1870, f. 1.
[201] Ibid., ff. 2–3.
[202] NAI Foreign Political A, February 1870, Nos. 105–7: Viceroy's Memo, f. 2.

themselves of these affairs'.[203] By claiming that 'we are not always sure that we are punishing the right men' and objecting to the notion that 'killing people for the sake of prestige is morally right', Mayo implicitly advanced a more individualised tribal subject in place of the collectives targeted throughout the Punjab frontier over the preceding two decades.[204]

In the wake of the Viceroy's critique of colonial frontier violence, the Khan of Agror was restored and the force imposing martial law in the Valley reduced.[205] British officials in the region continued to express suspicions of the Khan's connivance in trans-border unrest, which carried on through the early 1870s, and repeatedly called for violence to be deployed against independent tribes.[206] The upper echelons of the British Indian administration, including successive Viceroys in the wake of Mayo's death at the hands of a Pashtun prisoner in the Andaman Islands in 1872, rebuffed these requests. The hitherto unquestioned notion that violence beyond the administrative border was a communicative instrument essential to founding colonial sovereignty in Agror was now contentious. In 1875, Mayo's successor Northbrook refused the Punjab Government permission to use violence against the Akazai community in the Black Mountain region. In doing so, he admitted the impossibility of ever having a fully secure border in the region given the indefensibility of villages within British-claimed territory high on the hillside. He also suggested that communicating state authority through violence was doomed to failure, as 'retaliatory expeditions create bad blood, and though they may strike terror for a short time, they leave a long account to be settled when opportunity occurs'.[207] Northbrook's wording was notably reminiscent of British descriptions of blood-feuds, which officials by this stage had established as a key tenet of *pashtunwali*.[208] The palpable ineffectiveness of state violence in the Black Mountain region led to diminishing confidence that it could be securely separated from its ostensible counterpoint. Expeditions came to seem to some administrators to be more like, and more likely to induce, tribal violence.

The Government of India's refusal to authorise violence in the Black Mountain area persisted despite a steady flow of reports of numerous small-scale border incursions. The demands of the local Deputy Commissioner F. D. Cunningham and the Punjab Government to send a military party beyond the administrative border became increasingly persistent in 1888 after a spate of boundary violations. Cunningham argued that he alone, as the man on the spot, could accurately determine tribal guilt, and sought powers essentially akin to those that John Jacob had wielded on the Upper Sind frontier. 'It is difficult,

[203] Ibid., f. 4.   [204] Ibid., f. 4.   [205] NAI Foreign Political A, December 1870, Nos. 545–7.
[206] NAI Foreign Political A, July 1871, Nos. 187–214.
[207] NAI Foreign Political A, December 1875, Nos. 103–38, Keep-With.
[208] Martin Sökefeld, 'Rumour and Politics on the Northern Frontier: The British, Pakhtun Wali and Yaghestan', *Modern Asian Studies*, 36, 2 (2002), pp. 299–340, here p. 304.

if not frequently impossible', Cunningham wrote in 1888, 'to sift through to the bottom [of] all the conflicting reports and statements about a raid . . . and it is nearly always impossible to secure such evidence against individuals as would convince a person merely reading the record'.[209] The Government of India was unconvinced by this critique of bureaucratic decision-making. The unrest, it insisted, was 'petty' rather than a sign of 'general hostility', and the 'inevitable result of the contact of civilization with barbarism'.[210] Abjuring the option of the military expedition was a means of demonstrating the colonial state's self-attributed distinctiveness from its tribal neighbours.

Three months later, Cunningham reported that two British officers accompanied by Gurkha troops – part of the force permanently stationed in Agror as part of the expansion of colonial military presence along the Punjab frontier during and after the Second Anglo-Afghan War – had been attacked on the Agror side of the Black Mountain. Cunningham's immediate superior, the Commissioner of Peshawar District W. G. Waterfield, continued to push against a violent response. The expedition of 1868 had, he contended, 'left nothing more behind it in the minds of those whom it was supposed to coerce, than a recollection of futility. We are still reaping the fruits thereof'.[211] A further consideration was the border's uncertain location on the Black Mountain. Although the colonial party had not crossed the crest of the mountain, which the British conceived was the border, Waterfield suggested that it could have strayed into 'what might perhaps be called neutral ground'. The boundary was 'still in some parts insecure' and was transgressed in myriad quotidian ways, with cattle grazing and 'often intimate relations' being maintained across the mountain ridge.[212] The Punjab Government concurred with Waterfield's assessment, affirming that the party was 'practically . . . out of the beat of our police and troops [in an area] less in our possession than in that of the Trans-border tribes in time of blockades or hostilities'.[213] Key personnel and institutions within the colonial administration came, then, to share the unadministered communities' conception of the Black Mountain boundary as hazy and zonal rather than crisp and linear. Nonetheless, the Punjab Government and the Government of India both authorised a large display of military force involving 8,000 colonial troops accompanied by 1,000 Kashmiris.[214] Unlike the confidence surrounding the expedition twenty years earlier, and despite its similar scale, the 1888 undertaking was a desperate

---

[209] IOR/L/PARL/2/284/1: Cunningham to Waterfield, 03 November 1887, p. 11.
[210] NAI Foreign Frontier A, April 1888, Keep-With 1; NAI Foreign Frontier A, June 1888, No. 50: Government of India, Foreign Department, to Punjab Government, 25 May 1888.
[211] IOR/L/PARL/2/284/1: Waterfield to Punjab Government, 12 July 1888, pp. 155–56.
[212] Ibid., p. 157.
[213] IOR/L/PARL/2/284/1: Punjab Government to Government of India, 30 July 1888, pp. 138–39.
[214] Ibid., p. 139; IOR/L/PARL/2/284/1: Viceroy to Secretary of State for India, 24 September 1888, p. 5.

lashing out by a state unable to instantiate stable sovereignty over a defined territory. More senior administrators did not share Cunningham's insistence that the expedition could 'enforc[e] on our neighbours ... respect for British property and British law'.[215] The Viceroy professed his hope – but not expectation – that violence 'may be kept within well defined limits' and anticipated the possibility that the expedition would induce rather than reduce resistance.[216] These doubts proved well founded. The force failed to achieve even its basic aim of securing the supposed ringleader of the attack, Hashim Ali Khan, and he continued to refuse to conclude any agreement with the colonial state.[217]

In the aftermath of the expedition, a new form of boundary making was implemented: 'the periodical march of troops along the border'.[218] Roads were constructed on the Black Mountain, which, similar to approximately contemporaneous undertakings in the Naga and Lushai Hills, were seen as key devices for projecting colonial power. Cunningham argued that unlike expeditions, which 'to these people [are] an earthquake which once in a hundred years shakes a city', regular appearances by soldiers would constitute the 'frequent signs of activity ... necessary to persuade the dwellers on the slope that there is a force within the mountain which may be dangerous'.[219] The first roads were constructed in 1890, partly by tribal labour. They served to exacerbate rather than resolve British dilemmas; Hassanzais and Akazais greeted the first appearance of colonial troops on the mountain ridge road in October 1890 not with deference but a barrage of rifle fire. The plan for regular marches was abandoned immediately despite Cunningham's plea that it was 'but the thin end of the wedge; if this cannot be driven in, it is difficult to see by what means to carry out the [remaining] roads'.[220] Many communities beyond the borders also considered the march to be the thin end of the wedge, but in the alternative sense that the roads were a violation that, if unopposed, would entrench boundary arrangements they deemed illegitimate.[221]

Yet another military party was deputed to compel the complete submission of the tribes and to complete the roads up to and along the mountain ridge.[222] Once again, this was launched out of a sense of desperation rather than in the expectation that it would serve to constitute a basis for a newly effective border or recognition of British sovereignty in Agror. The Commissioner of Peshawar

---

[215] IOR/L/PARL/2/284/1: Cunningham to Waterfield, 28 March 1888, p. 123.
[216] IOR/L/PARL/2/284/1: Viceroy to Secretary of State for India, 24 September 1888, p. 5.
[217] IOR/L/PARL/2/284/2: Ommanney to Punjab Government, 11 July 1889, p. 50.
[218] Ibid., p. 51.
[219] IOR/L/PARL/2/284/2: Cunningham to Ommanney, 20 September 1890, p. 69.
[220] Ibid., p. 68.   [221] Ibid., p. 75.
[222] IOR/L/PARL/2/284/2: Government of India to Punjab Government, 02 January 1891, p. 77.

Edward Ommanney, who initially had been more bullish than his predecessor Waterfield on the potential effects of colonial violence, opined that 'their punishment in 1888 was very severe; it would be difficult to say what more could have been done short of remaining in the country; their villages were burnt, fodder consumed, and country occupied, but on our departure, they return, rebuild their houses, till their lands, and, as now proved, are ready to oppose us again'.[223] Far from being penetrable and controllable by colonial infrastructure such as the roads, Ommanney represented the region as one of 'forest-clad mountain heights [that] enable [the inhabitants] to inflict loss with comparative impunity'.[224] This nexus of tribe and topography was one that seemed fundamentally resistant to the very form of colonial violence about to be launched.

As in 1888, the expedition substantially bore out these assumptions. Hashim Ali Khan eluded capture, and a settlement with the Hassanzais and Akazais lasted for only eighteen months before another incursion broke through the colonial state's border.[225] Thereafter, there were no major incidents until governmental responsibility for the Black Mountain region was removed from the Punjab Government with the creation of North-West Frontier Province in 1901. Some administrators acknowledged that this period of inaction did not vindicate the efficacy of violence as a tool for instantiating state authority. Thomas Holdich instead characterised it as serving to illustrate 'the extreme difficulty of administering a satisfactory thrashing to a mountain-bred people who have an open door behind them'.[226] As such, it was representative of the increasingly common complaint among officials throughout the Punjab frontier that the ability of uplanders to withdraw into an ungoverned hinterland militated against British efforts at coercion.

The four Black Mountain expeditions both moulded and reflected changing British attitudes towards, and capacities for, violence at the Punjab frontier. During the decade following the annexation of Punjab there was an unusual degree of unanimity among officials on the necessity, efficacy, and justice of deploying large military parties against frontier populations. From the 1860s onwards, dissenting voices within the colonial state became increasingly audible, even as the capacity for military interventions increased along with heightened strategic imperatives to secure India's northwest frontier. The final decades of the nineteenth century, in which expeditionary forces on the Punjab frontier were generally larger and supported by ever more developed

---

[223] IOR/L/PARL/2/284/2: Ommanney to Punjab Government, 29 January 1890, p. 72
[224] Ibid.
[225] *Frontier and Overseas Expeditions Vol. I*, pp. 188–89; NAI Foreign Frontier A, May 1892, No. 82: Cunningham to Punjab Government, 18 April 1892.
[226] Holdich, *Indian Borderland*, p. 233.

communications infrastructures, also witnessed increasingly sharp doubts over the legitimacy and impact of violence.

4.4   Conclusion: 'Exterminate All the Brutes'

The forms of violence directed against colonial subjects, soldiers, agriculture, and infrastructure differed across India's frontiers and changed over the course of the nineteenth century. Diverse environmental and social dynamics – factors in flux rather than fixed quantities – shaped when, how, and why communities fought. Many colonial administrators recognised this variety, and they were certainly forced to come up with responses to it. The violence they perpetrated against inhabitants of 'independent' regions also took distinctive forms. Forces, ranging from dozens of troops to thousands, were equipped with rifles in some cases and heavy artillery in others, and operated almost completely without central oversight in the 1840s but with rapid telegraphic connections by the century's end. Yet significant similarities ran through the multiple arenas and eras of colonial frontier violence. Most military actions employed at least some men drawn from peripheral communities supposed to share with those they attacked exceptional tendencies for violence. They also tended to try and turn tribal tactics back on the tribes. However devastating their immediate effects, military actions also generally failed to live up to the predictions and promises of those who authorised and directed them, especially in their longer-term impacts. In part because of these persistent and widespread shortcomings, among the most ubiquitous features of colonial frontier violence were debates over its efficacy and legitimacy. Imperial archives are replete with such uncertainty; critiques of British violence at India's frontiers remain necessary but are also nothing new. Administrators' writings on frontier violence often lacked any shared notion of what Ann Laura Stoler terms colonial 'common sense', resulting in 'stories retold in disquieted European voices, tangled by multiple meanings'.[227]

Acts and discourses of state violence at colonial India's frontiers partook in the core contradiction of modern European empire that Joseph Conrad identified in *Heart of Darkness*, between a self-image of 'august Benevolence' and an impulse to 'exterminate all the brutes'.[228] Many individual British administrators, and the colonial state at large, were unable to decide on the fundamental tenets of how supposedly independent frontier populations should be conceived of and controlled. Should frontier inhabitants be influenced through methods of engagement and consent or by fear of violence? Should they be

---

[227] Stoler, *Archival*, p. 234.
[228] Joseph Conrad, *Heart of Darkness* (London: Penguin, 1995 [1902]), pp. 83–84.

dealt with as individualised subjects with fully human capacities or as animalistic collectives? Could military force be a communicative tool to 'improve' tribal populations, or was it simply a means of punishing irredeemable violence? These indeterminacies fed into the unresolved question of whether the state's violence was distinct from that of tribes and local potentates, or risked rendering the state an atavistic mimic of the very people and practices the British derided as barbaric.

5 Administration

In October 1847, shortly after troops of the Sind Horse had slaughtered 600 Bugtis (see Section 4.1), one of the few chiefs to have avoided the massacre tendered his submission to the British official in charge of the adjacent district in Sind.[1] Islam Khan's community was suffering from the colonial state's redefinition and policing of the Upper Sind boundary. Previously porous, which was essential to their food supplies, the border was now closed under pains of death. Members of the civilian administration in Sind, including Oliver Goldney, the Collector and Magistrate of Shikarpur District who received Islam Khan, couched this submission in the colonial language of 'improvement'. Goldney avowed hopes that 'by a kind & conciliatory treatment', Islam Khan and his followers might be 'reclaim[ed] to settled and peaceful habits'.[2] This attempt to present the submission and the colonial state's response as beneficent was tendentious. By Goldney's account, Islam Khan requested that the remaining Bugtis be allowed and helped to settle in colonial Sind – a proposal that Goldney and his superiors in the Sind Government greeted positively. Whether or not Goldney in fact foisted the proposal on Islam Khan, it is evident that the latter was acting from a position of extreme weakness when he took up the option of moving his followers and those of two other chiefs from their long-standing home in the hills to the administered plains. His community, as the Sind Government admitted, had been reduced to mere 'remnants' by colonial violence. Harried by the threat of further military action, many people were on the verge of starvation.[3]

The placement of Bugtis in so-called 'colonies' located in Sind was less a paragon of liberal imperial policy than an episode in a longer saga of violent upheaval and displacement at the fringes of British rule. It also showed the coexistence of 'improvement' and extreme violence in the colonial state's

---

[1] MSA Political, 1847, Vol. 107: Merewether to Jacob, 2 October 1847, f. 35.
[2] NAI Foreign Secret, 28 April 1848, No. 6: Sind Government to Goldney, 2 November 1847, ff. 1143–4.
[3] Ibid.; Jacob stated that he was proceeding with a force to capture Islam Khan when the latter tendered his submission to Goldney: NAI Foreign Secret, 28 April 1848, No. 12: Jacob to Sind Government, 11 November 1847, ff. 1203–5.

repertoire. Extirpatory action premised on the characterisation of an entire community as an enemy, members of which could be killed with impunity, rapidly gave way to professed faith in the potential agricultural productivity and governability of sections of the same community. And despite the officials' suggestions that the colonies were an integral part of a process of 'pacification', the colonial state continued to coerce their inhabitants after they had been established in British India (see Section 5.1). These colonies, like others across India's frontiers, were located conceptually between idealistic social intervention and the concentration camps that infamously emerged during the era of high imperialism.[4] Like the case of uplanders in western India analysed by Sumit Guha, colonial claims to 'settle' frontier communities elided a more destructive set of interventions aimed at removing the possibility of resistance.[5] This chapter builds on recent work that sees violence and administrative techniques not as discrete repertoires founded upon mutually exclusive logics of repression and conciliation but as thoroughly entangled. Focusing on colonial constructions of 'fanaticism' at the northwest frontier and the 1867 Murderous Outrages Act in particular, Elizabeth Kolsky and Mark Condos have shown that state violence was enshrined in, rather than displaced by, legal codes.[6] The case studies that I examine indicate that purportedly pacific techniques of administration were bound up with violence at colonial India's frontiers from the very outset of British involvement with the people of these regions.

I also develop recent work by historians of northeast and northwest India in showing how British officials sought to bind frontier inhabitants by placing them beyond the bounds of 'normal' government but within the realm of colonial political economy. India's frontiers were not regions in which colonial administration was uniformly absent, but spaces in which particular forms of administration developed. In making this claim, I work with Benjamin Hopkins's concept of 'frontier governmentality', which describes state interventions that acted upon populations while keeping them outside forms of administration practised elsewhere in British India.[7] The Bugtis in the late 1840s were far from the only frontier community to find itself uncomfortably positioned within the legal, judicial, and fiscal spheres of the colonial state.

---

[4] On British concentration camps during the Second Anglo-Boer War, see Denis Judd and Keith Surridge, *The Boer War: A History*, 2nd ed. (London: I.B. Tauris, 2013), ch. 12. On the logic of colonial concentration camps, see Agamben, *Homo Sacer*, pp. 166–67.

[5] Guha, *Environment*, pp. 136–42. On comparable and approximately contemporaneous displacements in colonial Tasmania and the United States, see, respectively, Lyndall Ryan, *Tasmanian Aborigines: A History since 1803* (Sydney: Allen & Unwin, 2012), pp. 219–62; and Daniel Walker Howe, *What Hath God Wrought: The Transformation of America, 1815–1848* (New York, NY: Oxford University Press, 2007), pp. 346–57.

[6] Condos, 'Licence'; Condos, '"Fanaticism"'; Kolsky, 'Colonial'.

[7] Marsden and Hopkins, *Fragments*, p. 51; Hopkins, 'Frontier Crimes Regulation', pp. 370–71.

Along portions of the frontiers at both edges of the subcontinent, administrators devised various schemes of taxation, subsidies, and recruitment alongside new legal and judicial arrangements. As Lipokmar Dzüvichü has pointed out in the case of the Naga Hills, officials were concerned with the symbolism of these interventions, seeing them as tokens of submission to state authority from people at the hazy edges of empire.[8] Administrative innovations also had very real effects. Existing arrangements of trade, social precedence, and political relations were uprooted in some areas and substantially repurposed in others.[9] Previously flexible and dynamic forms of exchange and deference, such as *posa* (see Section 1.1), became fixed as the colonial state regularised, bureaucratised, and monetised them.[10] The past decade has seen historians investigate how officials deployed these techniques to discipline frontier communities by embedding social hierarchies – especially by empowering tribal chiefs – and rendering them dependent on the colonial state.

In this chapter, I show that although many of these undertakings were enormously disruptive for the targeted populations, they tended to be rooted in ambiguous logics and also failed to meet the expectations of the administrators who designed and implemented them. I nuance Hopkins's notion of a singular 'frontier governmentality' based on the treatment of frontier inhabitants as 'imperial objects' to be 'managed' rather than 'governed' like the 'colonial subjects' in British India proper.[11] The administrative schemes considered in this chapter were instead premised on slippages between conceiving of frontier peoples as 'objects' and 'subjects' in Hopkins's terms. Administrators projected some form of 'improvement' suggestive of subjecthood, but simultaneously suggested that frontier communities were essentially different from other colonised peoples in India and had to be managed as such. Persistent ambiguities and failures were significant not merely as tokens of the hazy and limited nature of colonial power, but because they provided openings for further administrative interventions and innovations. Officials used shortcomings and crises of impersonal, codified, and bureaucratised rule at India's frontiers to make the case for modes of government in which individuals retained wide-ranging, discretionary powers. Administrative failure and uncertainty were made into alibis for an alternative mode of conceiving space and self at the outskirts of empire. The conception that the both the frontier official and his counterpart the tribal chief should have substantial autonomy to govern in line with ideals of masculine

---

[8] Lipokmar Dzüvichü, 'Empire on Their Backs: Coolies in the Eastern Borderlands of the British Raj', *International Review of Social History*, 59 (2014), pp. 89–112.

[9] For an instance of uprooting, see Misra, 'Sovereignty'. For an instance of repurposing, see Kar, 'Nomadic Capital'.

[10] On the northwest, see Hopkins, 'Frontier Crimes Regulation', pp. 379–80; Marsden and Hopkins, *Fragments*, pp. 56–57.

[11] Hopkins, 'Frontier Crimes Regulation', p. 375.

heroism was a vital element of the peculiarity and variability of frontier administration.[12]

In this ideal of the 'frontier official' and in other respects, British interventions in northeast and northwest India shared substantial common ground.[13] Comparing material from administrative hotspots in both regions, I develop in this chapter two key contentions regarding the geography and chronology of frontier governmentality. First, I argue that major modes of frontier administration developed first at the outskirts of Assam and in Balochistan rather than the often-prioritised fringes of Punjab. Second, I suggest that there were two eras featuring distinct primary types of administrative schemes premised on subtly different logics. Sections 5.1 and 5.2 analyse the mid-nineteenth century, focusing on the colonial state's displacement of people from beyond the formal administrative limits of Sind and Assam and their relocation to colonies within fully governed British India. Administrators projected ambitious outcomes, such as the 'improvement' of entire tribes, while also conceiving of the colonies as prison camps and buffers against violence from other frontier dwellers. In practice, just like similar schemes that emerged later in the nineteenth century at the Punjab frontier, the colonies in Assam and Sind comprehensively failed to fulfil either aspect of these mixed intentions.[14]

Sections 5.3 and 5.4 turn to the period from the 1860s onwards and focus on Balochistan and the Naga Hills, respectively. These were vital regions of administrative experimentation in which state expansion was formalised but never fully normalised. Reflecting the different concerns and capacities of the colonial state in the later nineteenth century, this era saw the full-fledged emergence of forms of administration that were distinct from the tribal colonies. This shift was not a definitive rupture, nor was it rooted in a grand strategic move from 'close border' to 'forward policy'.[15] Although the notion of 'improving' frontier people never disappeared entirely, officials focused more on administering in line with what they couched as existing structures of authority and custom. This mode of frontier governmentality dealt with upland- and desert-dwelling populations as permanently distinct from their neighbours in the agrarian plains – closer to 'objects' than 'subjects'. Crucially, it generated internal variegation within administered frontier populations,

---

[12] On the growing significance of the physicality of British officials in India during the second half of the nineteenth century, see Elizabeth Collingham, *Imperial Bodies: The Physical Experience of the Raj, c.1800–1947* (Cambridge: Polity, 2001), pp. 118–25.

[13] My suggestion of the similarity of the northeast and northwest in administrative terms contrasts with that of Hopkins in 'Frontier Crimes Regulation', whose comparative material on the northeast is drawn primarily from Robb, 'Colonial State'.

[14] Mark Condos and Gavin Rand, 'Coercion and Conciliation at the Edge of Empire: State-Building and Its Limits in Waziristan, 1849–1914', *The Historical Journal*, 61, 3 (2018), pp. 695–718.

[15] For a recent interpretation that emphasises such a shift, see Tripodi, *Edge*.

creating frontiers within frontiers. It also privileged the discretionary authority of the individual officer in conjunction with the tribal chief, with only equivocal efforts to fix uniform administrative principles and the perpetuation of hinterlands that were open to largely personal rule by 'the man on the spot'.

5.1   'Strangers and Exiles': Tribal Colonies on the Upper Sind Frontier

When Oliver Goldney corralled the Bugtis into 'colonies' in Upper Sind, displacing apparently difficult-to-govern populations and ensnaring them within economic and legal structures was nothing new in colonial India. In formulating policy towards frontier inhabitants, the Commissioner of Sind explicitly drew on the example of the Bhils of western India.[16] Following the defeat of the Marathas in 1818, the colonial state deliberately targeted the Bhils' forest environs and forced them into unfamiliar socio-political relations through 'bribery, force, and intrigue'.[17] The Bhils were not, however, the direct precursor to the Bugti colonies. In March 1845, during military violence led by Charles Napier against the hill communities bordering Upper Sind, Goldney established a colony of Balochs in previously disused and recently irrigated land north of the town of Shikarpur in Upper Sind.[18] Goldney was at pains to emphasise his beneficence towards the 'settlers', with rent-free grants of land, investment in irrigation canals to enable the inhabitants to raise their own crops, and rations provided until these crops were sufficient to provide for the colony's population. He also extolled the success of the first crop and pronounced himself 'astonished at the good behaviour of these reclaimed robbers', ignoring existing Baloch traditions of irrigated agriculture.[19] These elements preempted the governmental logic at work in the Punjab Canal Colonies some forty years later, centring on paternalistic notions of the 'improvement' through the colonial state's investment and technical mastery.[20]

To an even greater extent than the later Canal Colonies, in which major disturbances broke out in 1907, the coercion and violence involved in the Baloch settlement repeatedly broke through officials' preferred discourse of mutually productive 'civilisation'.[21] Describing the process of founding the colony to his superiors in the Sind Government, Goldney termed its inhabitants 'prisoners', contradicting his insistence elsewhere that they had been located in

---

[16] MSA Political, 1852, Vol. 159: Frere to Governor of Bombay, 18 July 1851, ff. 27–28.
[17] Guha, *Environment*, pp. 130–81, quotation on p. 130.
[18] MSA Political, 1847, Vol. 107: Goldney to Sind Government, 25 October 1847, ff. 188–92.
[19] Ibid, ff. 190–2. On pre-colonial Baloch irrigation, see Gilmartin, *Blood*, pp. 28–40.
[20] Ali, *Punjab*.
[21] On this aspect of the Canal Colonies, see N. Gerald Barrier, 'The Punjab Disturbances of 1907: The Response of the British Government to Agrarian Unrest', *Modern Asian Studies*, 1, 4 (1967), pp. 353–83.

British-administered Sind as a condition of their 'surrender'.[22] In keeping with many dealings on the Sind frontier in the 1840s and those more generally in frontier India during the nineteenth century, the legal status of colonial inter-actions with these communities was indeterminate and specified only in retro-spect. Regardless of British categorisation, it was clear that the colonists had not moved of their own volition. Napier boasted to the Governor-General that colonial troops had 'deservedly plundered' the Balochs, taking 'almost everything ... except what was in possession of their women and children'.[23] The incarcerating function of the colony was clear in Napier's instructions to Goldney that although Balochs who came to join the settlement were not to be harmed, anyone 'attempting to regain the Hills must be treated as enemies'.[24] These orders insinuated that any attempt by Baloch colonists to return to their former homes would mean they would be classified as people that agents of the state could kill with impunity. The self-assigned authority of British officials to decide the colonists' juridical status played out in practical situations, too. Reviewing exceptions to the settled Balochs' generally 'good behaviour', Goldney categorised a 'barbarous murder' and an 'inroad' into Kachhi as 'grave crimes', but insisted that a series of attacks against a group of Bugtis also settled in British-governed Sind were 'not crimes but irregularities – more of a political and military character'.[25]

The Bugti colonisation of 1847 was, then, part of a broader process of intervention on the Upper Sind frontier in the decade following annexation, in which incarceration and paternalism intermingled.[26] Among the terms that Goldney presented to Islam Khan for his 'surrender' was that 'any Boogtie settlers quitting the settlement, if found by the Frontier Cavalry will be liable to seizure or to be slain'.[27] When the Sind Government objected to these refer-ences to violence in the terms of the surrender, Goldney defended them on the basis that Islam Khan's status as a '"free booter"' made 'some stringent threats' necessary. He also claimed that, regardless of the justness of the stipulation concerning the summary punishment of absconding settlers, having already agreed the terms with Islam Khan, 'any alteration ... will prove fatal to the permanency of the arrangements'.[28] The Sind Government backed the terms.

---

[22] MSA Political, 1847, Vol. 107: Goldney to Sind Government, 15 October 1847, ff. 183–84; Goldney to Sind Government, 25 October 1847, ff. 188–92.

[23] MSA Political, 1848, Vol. 147: Napier to Hardinge, 9 March 1845, ff. 14–15.

[24] MSA Political, 1847, Vol. 107: Napier to Goldney, 29 March 1845, f. 197.

[25] MSA Political, 1847, Vol. 107: Goldney to Sind Government, 25 October 1847, f. 192

[26] On the first decade of British rule in Sind, see Matthew A. Cook, 'After Annexation: Colonialism and Sindh during the 1840s' (unpublished doctoral thesis, Colombia University, 2007).

[27] NAI Foreign Secret, 28 April 1848, No. 12: Goldney to Sind Government, 08 November 1847, f. 1172.

[28] NAI Foreign Secret, 28 April 1848, No. 12: Goldney to Sind Government, 27 November 1847, ff. 1192–4.

As in many other cases, the ostensibly junior official successfully justified his appropriation of sovereign power by insisting that any contradiction of his decision would result in chaos.[29]

The threat of violence that hung over the relocated Bugtis was rarely alluded to in colonial correspondence, which instead focused on their supposed productivity. It was, however, evident in a sketch map that Goldney produced to illustrate the location of the colonies. The map showed the location of two new military posts, 'Shahdadpoor' and 'Byram', to the immediate northwest of the northernmost colony (Figure 5.1). These posts lay directly between the colony and Kachhi, the desert region that interposed between Upper Sind and the Bugtis' erstwhile homeland. Just as the heavily militarised border arrangements implemented by John Jacob had pushed the Bugtis and other communities to the brink of mass starvation over the preceding three years, so the same potential for state violence incarcerated Bugtis in Sind. Jacob attempted to justify these restrictions as an exercise in improvement: 'Permitting free intercourse between that part of the [Bugti] tribe lately become British subjects, and their lawless and predatory brethren will tend more than any thing to prevent the former from settling down in peaceful habits'.[30]

The operation of the colonies over the following five years showed that the threat of violence failed to meet British expectations. Goldney's successor in Shikarpur District complained in 1849, two years after the colonies' foundation, that the inhabitants' 'depredations were of such frequent occurrence that some degree of surveillance became necessary'.[31] By this stage, the Bugti colonies and the Baloch colony founded in 1845 in Lower Sind had been combined at the site of one of the original Bugti settlements in Larkhana in Upper Sind. Although the area of land cultivated by the collected colonists increased substantially from 1849 to 1852, the government continued to subsidise the settlement until, in 1852, approximately 785 of the 1,000 colonists chose to leave. British administrators allowed them to do so, having become increasingly convinced that the colony could not be made 'productive'.[32] Having given the lie to colonial assumptions that chiefs reliably spoke for entire Baloch communities, the thirty families that remained were no longer provided with assistance and were administered in line with the surrounding villagers. The reclamation project-cum-prison camp had ceased to exist within five years of its inception.

---

[29] NAI Foreign Secret, 28 April 1848, No. 12: Sind Government to Goldney, 4 December 1847, f. 1197.

[30] NAI Foreign Secret, 28 April 1848, No. 32: Jacob to Sind Government, 23 February 1848, f. 1311.

[31] MSA Political, 1853, Vol. 150: Frere to Governor of Bombay, 1 May 1853, ff. 255–56.

[32] Ibid., ff. 256–60.

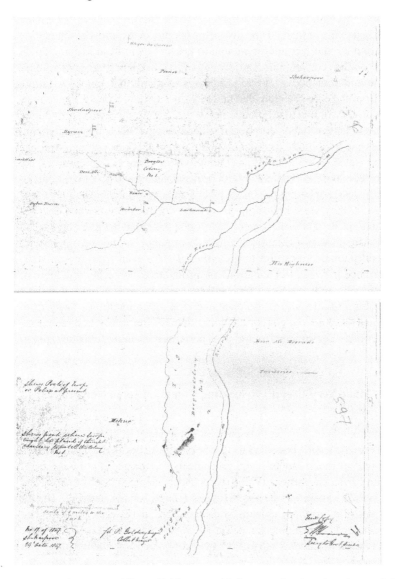

Figure 5.1 Oliver Goldney, untitled map showing locations of Bugti 'colonies' and troop positions (1847).[33]

Bartle Frere, the Commissioner of Sind, attributed the failure of the colony to its distance from the border and its being surrounded by established Sindhi

[33] MSA Political, 1847, Vol. 107, Goldney to Sind Government, 29 October 1847.

cultivators. This combination, he argued, made the Bugtis 'feel they were mere strangers and exiles, a marked and distrusted people, in the midst of temptation to thieve and be idle, yet not far enough to prevent them from keeping up all their old Border conventions and feelings, and becoming in consequence restless and dissatisfied'.[34] Frere's analysis implied that colony's failure resulted from the core principle that underlay its creation, namely, the deliberate isolation and continued differentiation of the colonists from the surrounding inhabitants in Upper Sind.[35] Although the conclusion of the colony experiment did not feature the bloody destruction that marked previous colonial dealings with many Baloch communities, its continuity with these violent episodes, the overlap of colonial motivations in both projects, and the dislocation it engendered were clearly apparent. When the Bugtis and other Balochs returned to the hills in 1852, they were hollowed out versions of the communities that had encountered the British forces trampling through their homelands on the road to southern Afghanistan a little over a decade previously, and were unable to provide substantial opposition to the colonial state even from the uplands. The difference between 'reclamation' as 'productive' subjects – the logic of 'pacification' – and mass extirpation frequently became elided at India's frontiers. Large-scale acts of violence and ripping communities away from their locales had a shared goal of denuding them of the ability to threaten the state, and on the Upper Sind frontier both policies contributed substantially to that end.

5.2   'Made Very Useful': Relocating Communities in Northeastern Assam

While intermittent expansion took place in the uplands to the south of Assam from the 1830s, the hills bounding the Brahmaputra Valley to the north and east were subject to more sporadic and piecemeal interference. Following early forays into particular portions of this region, such as interventions in *posa* and Richard Wilcox's route surveys (see Sections 1.1 and 2.1, respectively), British dealings with the northern uplands were few and far between until the late 1850s. Sustained colonial interference at the eastern fringes of lowland Assam, where the Patkai Mountains separated newly conquered colonial territory from Burma, began earlier. After the perceived threat of Burmese attacks subsided around the mid-1830s, tea production became the dominant feature of the British presence in Upper Assam.[36] During the 1830s, tea plantations

---

[34] Ibid., ff. 254–55.
[35] I concur with David Gilmartin's assessment that Frere's comment showed that the British sought to subvert tribal distinctiveness and identity through the colonies: Gilmartin, *Blood*, p. 42.
[36] Sharma, *Empire's Garden*.

encroached onto land occupied since the late eighteenth century by members of the Singpho community, despite colonial officials' acknowledgement of these areas as Singpho land in the previous decade. This was another instance of colonial interference provoking major resistance, culminating in 1843 in an uprising involving Singphos and members of other communities from both sides of the Patkai Range.[37] Even the Government of India acknowledged that the encroachment of tea gardens had been ill judged and constituted a major source of irritation among the Singphos.[38]

Discontent at the dislocating impact of the expansion of colonial military and capital among communities at the eastern fringes of Upper Assam had already been evident four years earlier. Members of various communities that administrators had previously considered to be disconnected attacked the British army outpost at Sadiya, at the extreme northeast of the Brahmaputra Valley.[39] The British response combined violence – destroying villages absented by their populations, who fled to the hills in advance – with the relocation of the Hkamti community that remained within reach of colonial forces. In the immediate aftermath of the attack on Sadiya, Francis Jenkins, the senior British official in Assam, neatly captured the imbrication of extirpation and exclusion in the multivalent comment that the Hkamtis' 'entire removal just now would be very satisfactory'.[40] While military violence harried those who fled to the hills, approximately nine hundred people who remained in the vicinity of Sadiya and tendered submission to colonial authorities were removed from their home villages and relocated in various parts of Lakhimpur District in Upper Assam.[41] This undertaking was predicated on spatial 'divide-and-rule'. Jenkins avowed that the 'Khamtis will be divided and settled in our districts where they will not be tempted into mischief by having assistance of kindred tribes at hand'. He added that 'they may eventually be made very useful, by taking advantages of their bravery and warlike temper and employing their services against the Duflahs'.[42] The Hkamtis' proven capacity for violence against the colonial state could, in other words, be turned to its advantage in perpetrating violence against other communities.

There is relatively little evidence in colonial archives of the subsequent activities of the relocated communities in Lakhimpur. That the British continued to see them as a distinct community is evident from a complaint by the District's Superintendent of Police in the early 1870s that Hkamtis 'seem to

---

[37] Sadan, *Kachin*, pp. 42–52.
[38] NAI Foreign Political, 12 August 1843, No. 106: Government of India to Jenkins, 12 August 1843, ff. 335–9.
[39] NAI Foreign Political, 20 February 1839, Nos. 105–12.
[40] NAI Foreign Political, 20 February 1839, No. 109: Jenkins to Government of India, 8 February 1839, f. 199.
[41] NAI Foreign Political, 10 July 1839, No. 61: Jenkins to Government of India, 14 June 1839, f. 4.
[42] Ibid., ff. 4–5.

take up land and place their villages wherever they please, without paying revenue of any kind, and with the utmost disregard of our guards' located around the northern administrative boundary.[43] There is more documentary evidence of British interference with those Hkamtis who remained in the vicinity of Sadiya after 1839. In a localised instance of what Kim Wagner diagnoses as 'the colonial culture of fear' in British India, officials over-compensated for having been taken by surprise by outbreak of unrest in 1843 by giving credence in the following years to a host of rumours of combinations among frontier communities.[44] In late 1843, administrators forced the Hkamtis to move a colony north of Sadiya, providing them with rent-free land for cultivation. The relocation had two avowed aims. By placing distance between the Hkamtis and the bulk of the Singpho population, it was supposed to reduce the threat of a combination of multiple communities against British forces. Simultaneously, the relocated Hkamtis were seen as a buffer between Assamese cultivators in eastern Upper Assam and the 'depredations of Mishmees or Singphos, who are occasionally in the habit of making inroads to carry off slaves and cattle'.[45] British administrators apparently harboured the hope that the Hkamtis rather than the taxed Assamese population would be the targets of violence from these surrounding communities. This was also the basis of a proposal in the early 1860s to relocate a portion of the Bugti community to the southern Punjab district of Dera Ghazi Khan. The officials who proposed the scheme rehearsed the notion that this would 'civilize the rude tribes'. But its primary appeal lay in the Bugtis' ability to 'form a good foil to the Murrees', another Baloch community, 'who will not be able to make any attack on British territory, except with the connivance of the Boogties, for whose good behaviour the portions of the Tribe residing in British territory will be security'.[46] Just as was the case with the Hkamtis a few decades earlier, the Bugtis were to act in a dual role as police and fodder against attacks from unadministered communities.

No sooner had administrative and military upheaval nullified the eastern edges of the Brahmaputra Valley as a troublesome frontier than the same colonial agents opened another problematic zone to the north of the Valley. Violent clashes occurred between Adis (known in colonial discourse as 'Abors') and a party of colonial troops led by Hamilton Vetch, the Political

---

[43] ASA, R011/S1/02: J. B. Goad, 'Report on Visit to the Abor and Mishmi Frontier during 1873–74'.

[44] Kim A. Wagner, '"Treading upon Fires": The "Mutiny"-Motif and Colonial Anxieties in British India', *Past and Present*, 218 (2013), pp. 159–97, here p. 162.

[45] NAI Foreign Political, 20 January 1844, No. 61: Jenkins to Government of India, 05 December 1843, ff. 1–5; No. 63: Vetch to Jenkins, 29 November 1843, ff. 15–16.

[46] NAI Foreign Political A, 06/1863, No. 123: Punjab Government to Government of India, 15 May 1863; No. 124: Dera Ghazi Khan Deputy Commissioner to Derajat Commissioner, 27 March 1863.

Agent in Upper Assam who ordered the repression and relocation of the Hkamtis and Singphos. In their aftermath, a missionary created a 'colony' of around eighty Adis was settled in the vicinity of the town of Dibrugarh on the Brahmaputra.[47] Although the colony was not established by administrators and did not have the same degree of violence in its formation or preservation as other resettlements of frontier groups, the state was complicit in its operation. In subsequent years, administrators used the settlers as a source of information on upland communities in the region.[48]

A little further to the east, the British resumed interfering with the Mishmi community in 1855, following a long hiatus since Wilcox's journeys in the region during the 1820s. After Mishmis killed two French missionaries, a colonial military party composed mostly of resettled Hkamtis entered the hills and captured Kowsa, the Mishmi chief supposed to be responsible, killing two of his sons in the process.[49] Although British officials acknowledged that Kowsa and his community had never owed allegiance to rulers of Assam, the Government of India directed that he would be tried in a Criminal Court 'such as would have been competent to try him for the Offence if it had been committed in British territory'.[50] During the trial, presided over by Edward Dalton, who later authored the *Descriptive Ethnology of Bengal* (see Section 3.4), Kowsa's legal representative argued that the Government of India had no jurisdiction over this community.[51] Although the court and officials at various levels of the colonial state refuted this claim, they had significant difficulty in justifying it. The Commissioner of Assam and the Government of India airily invoked 'the universal law of nations' and 'the rules of international law' in seeking to substantiate the colonial state's authority to try Kowsa.[52] This was a very different rationale to the one that Dalton employed as Magistrate. While he admitted that Kowsa's 'total ignorance of our laws' and the 'locality of the crime' were relevant factors that rendering the death penalty inappropriate, Dalton claimed that the 'premeditated, unprovoked, cold-blooded and cowardly' nature of the act justified British punishment.[53] The state's authority to try and punish Kowsa were not established in existing law, but hastily and

---

[47] ASA, pre-1874 Assam Commissioner files, No. 686: H. S. Bivar to Jenkins, 29 October 1858.

[48] Ibid.

[49] NAI Foreign Political, 18 May 1855, No. 41: Vetch to Bengal Government, Judicial Department, 28 March 1855, f. 320; No. 42: E. T. Dalton to Jenkins, 17 March 1855, f. 325.

[50] NAI Foreign Political, 18 May 1855, No. 41: Vetch to Government of Bengal, Judicial Department, 28 March 1855, ff. 320–21; No. 45: Government of India to Bengal Government, 16 May 1855, f. 339.

[51] NAI Foreign Political, 7 September 1855, No. 90: Vetch to Government of India, 26 July 1855, f. 227

[52] Ibid, ff. 228–29; NAI Foreign Political, 7 September 1855, No. 96: Government of India to Vetch, 4 September 1855, f. 253.

[53] NAI Foreign Political, 7 September 1855, No. 90: Vetch to Government of India, 26 July 1855, ff. 227–28.

variously justified during and after its execution. Kowsa was sentenced to transportation overseas for life, which might be seen as a particular application of the colonial logic of resettling frontier inhabitants.[54] Although dealing with an individual rather than an entire community, Kowsa's case shared with the earlier resettlements in the northeast the same arrogation by lower-level officials of discretionary and uneven sovereign rights over frontier areas and peoples. Especially when it came to moving frontier inhabitants, agents of the colonial state reworked administrative categories with impunity.

The relocations of communities at the northeast fringes of Assam from the 1830s to the 1850s shared much with those that took place in northern Sind from 1845. Both were driven by officials 'on the spot', and both involved severe dislocation that was preceded, and enforced, by violence. Their more extensive prior experience as cultivators meant that the Hkamtis were better suited to sedentary agriculture than the primarily pastoralist Bugtis. In both cases, though, colonial interventions deliberately shattered dynamic and thriving communities in an attempt to assimilate them to the twin ends of colonial security and political economy (irrigated agriculture in Upper Sind; tea plantations in Assam). The creation of colonies was a 'dramatic break' of the magnitude that Sanghamitra Misra shows also resulted from British interference in the political economy of the Garos in the uplands between northern Bengal and western Assam.[55] As in the case of the Bugtis, mass movements of people in Upper Assam achieved the primary colonial intention of exterminating these groups as political threats. This enabled the region to turn from a focal point of colonial anxieties in Assam to a space of intensive European capital.[56] The relocations also fit with contemporaneous dynamics in British India away from frontier regions. C. A. Bayly and Radhika Singha demonstrated that the period between the Company-State's defeat of the Marathas in 1818 and the 1857 Rebellion did not simply constitute a 'liberal moment', but featured numerous violent assertions of state authority. Rural rebellions were brutally suppressed and summary actions executed against perceived threats posed by itinerant communities, most notably *thagi*.[57] Forced relocations of frontier communities in the northeast and northwest can be seen as elements within this broader dynamic of British rule during the early to mid-nineteenth century.

The Punjab frontier was a latecomer to modes of resettling frontier communities already established at the fringes of Sind and Assam. Following grants of newly irrigated land to reward Pashtuns who had supported the British annexation of

---

[54] NAI Foreign Political, 7 September 1855, No. 96: Government of India to Vetch, 4 September 1855, f. 253.

[55] Misra, 'Sovereignty', pp. 348–49.   [56] Mackenzie, *History*, pp. 57–72.

[57] On rural rebellions, see C. A. Bayly, *Indian Society and the Making of the British Empire* (Cambridge: Cambridge University Press, 1988), ch. 4. On *thagi*, see Singha, *Despotism*, pp. 172–73.

Punjab in 1849, administrators devised a number of schemes targeting sections of previously unadministered communities during the 1860s. The plan to place Bugtis in Dera Ghazi Khan District was among the first.[58] The most sustained instance of resettlement in Punjab began two years later, with the gift of agricultural land and places in the frontier militia to a number of families in the Mahsud Waziri community. The Mahsuds were renowned among British officials for their unusual cohesion and winter migration into Punjab, which rendered the administrative border in the southern portion of the province particularly flimsy. The settlement scheme was predicated on the local Deputy Commissioner's sense of futility in his previous dealings with the Mahsuds, which he attributed to 'the fact that the tribe is too united and too strong to be dealt with as a whole'.[59] Like elsewhere in the northwest and northeast, a large military expedition in 1860 inflamed rather than quelled unrest among the Mahsuds.[60] Mahsud settlements in the 1860s and subsequent decades shared notable similarities in terms of intent and effects with earlier tribal colonies in Sind and Assam. As Mark Condos and Gavin Rand argue, the Waziri projects followed on from and were continuous with more overt deployments of state violence.[61] The colonies also clearly sought to create divisions within communities perceived to pose a genuine threat to colonial control in a particular border area. Like similar undertakings in Assam and Sind, they failed to live up to administrators' optimistic projections. The first Mahsud settlement was small, comprising approximately twenty families, and short lived. It did not induce more of the community to follow of their own volition. It also failed to produce the anticipated changes in tribal habits and customs that formed a core rationale for the venture: settlers continued to engage in activities such as camel theft.[62] Although further Mahsud colonies were created (and disbanded) until the end of the nineteenth century,[63] by this stage alternative forms of frontier administration had come to the fore in both the northeast and the northwest.

5.3   'Doing Nothing But Write-Write-Write': Irregular Administration at the Northeast Frontier

The era of high empire in the late nineteenth century is renowned for the extension of European sovereignty and administration into vast continental

[58] NAI Foreign Political A, June 1863, Nos. 123–5.
[59] NAI Foreign Political A, January 1866, No. 88: Dera Ismail Khan Deputy Commissioner to Derajat Commissioner, 8 August 1865, f. 5.
[60] NAI Foreign Political A, December 1860, Nos. 775–8; NAI Foreign Political A, March 1862, Nos. 276–93; NAI Foreign Political A, April 1866, No. 68: Derajat Commissioner to Punjab Government, 12 March 1866, f. 2.
[61] Condos and Rand, 'Coercion'.
[62] Andrew M. Roe, *Waging War in Waziristan: The British Struggle in the Land of Bin Laden, 1849–1947* (Lawrence, KS: University Press of Kansas, 2010), p. 69.
[63] NAI Foreign Political A, May 1877, Nos. 180–8; Condos and Rand, 'Coercion', pp. 705–11.

hinterlands.[64] The extension of colonial administration into particular sections of hitherto 'independent' Indian frontier regions was of a piece with this trend. There was no definitive beginning to formal administration in frontier locales, especially in the northeast. As discussed previously (Section 4.2), the western portion of the area inhabited by Naga communities was subject to short-lived administrative incursions in the 1840s, which came to an abrupt and violent end in the early 1850s. British forces occupied the Khasi and Jaintia Hills, forming the eastern section of the present-day Indian state of Meghalaya and widely considered by colonial officials to be part of the northeast frontier, from the mid-1830s. But until the 1860s, administration in this region was irregular even by the variable standards of British India. Even after Governor-General Dalhousie ordered in 1855 that the taxes levied in other Hill States be collected in Jaintia, no revenue was collected in the region.[65]

In 1860, British officials in the area finally imposed a fixed levy on each household. 'Within a few months', Alexander Mackenzie succinctly noted in his 1884 official history of the northeast frontier, 'the people were in open rebellion'.[66] While this outbreak was quickly repressed, confusion and resistance continued following the introduction that same year of income tax throughout British India. Officials in Assam were uncertain as to whether this ostensibly universal measure should be applied in the Khasi and Jaintia Hills, and the Government of India's orders were typically cryptic, leaving a great deal to the discretion of local agents. The result was inconsistency, as the income tax was not applied in the Khasi Hills, but some inhabitants of the Jaintia Hills were required to pay and resisted throughout 1862 and 1863. While the income tax was annulled in this region, the house tax remained and a form of limited administration was instituted involving a single British official with authority over a network of village representatives who had specified civil and criminal powers.[67] This trajectory of intermittent governmental interference followed by the violent implementation of limited forms of administration was repeated over the following decades in other upland areas to the south of the Assam Valley.

These schemes had two key features. The first was that state intrusion was limited in the legal sphere to what the British took to be severe crimes, such as murder and rebellion, and in the fiscal sphere to basic forms of taxation, generally a flat-rate annual house tax. Although often exaggerated claims of the mineral wealth these regions had not completely dissipated by the 1860s

---

[64] For example, Jürgen Osterhammel, *The Transformation of the World: A Global History of the Nineteenth Century*, trans. Patrick Camiller (Princeton, NJ: Princeton University Press, 2014), pp. 322–91; Belich, *Replenishing*.

[65] Mackenzie, *History*, pp. 217–41. On earlier dealings with the Khasi Hills, see Cederlöf, *Founding*, pp. 51–52.

[66] Mackenzie, *History*, pp. 240–41.   [67] Ibid., pp. 241–3.

from their peak around the turn of the nineteenth century,[68] financial motivations for expansion had declined since the years around the British annexation of Assam. Taxing frontier communities was understood primarily to be of symbolic, not monetary, value, denoting obedience rather than covering the cost of administration.[69] As one official wrote of the Garo community as early as 1847: 'it is better that the amount of tribute should be so trifling as to be always easily and willingly paid, as a return for the privilege of attending and benefitting by our Hauts or Markets, as well as in token of their submission'.[70] The second aspect of administration was its cumulative character across the uplands south of Assam. Officials frequently cited the imposition of taxation and criminal oversight in the Khasi and Jaintia Hills as a positive example for the extension of the same measures to the Garo Hills, Naga Hills, and Lushai Hills. In turn, these three areas were also mutually invoked in a circular discourse of expansion. In 1869, the Government of India proposed that the Lushai Hills copy the supposedly successful administrative structure of a single officer taking engagements from tribal chiefs and collecting a nominal tribute, which had been developed over the previous few years in the Garo and Naga Hills.[71] Four years later, the Government of Bengal pointed towards 'the Garo country, and to some extent even ... the Lushais' as proof that firmer control should be taken over the Naga Hills, a view echoed by the Chief Commissioner of Assam in 1877 when he wrote of the Garo Hills being the 'prototype' of the Naga Hills administration.[72] By the late 1870s, the Garo and Naga Hills regions were cited as an example for frontier tracts to the north of the Brahmaputra Valley.[73] The circularity of these exemplars was not only a product of administrative confusion. It also enabled officials to overlook the difficulties and violence of extending governmental structures. Examples of ostensibly successful expansion served to construct myths of what the Chief Commissioner of Assam termed 'advancement from turbulence and barbarism towards civilization and good government'.[74]

[68] See, for example, Lieutenant Williamson's claims of valuable resources in the Garo Hills following his tour in 1866, which formed the first part of the attempt to found British administration in the area: NAI Foreign Political A, June 1866, No. 56. On mineral interests such as limestone mining in the Khasi Hills, see Cederlöf, *Founding*, pp. 3–4; 51–52.

[69] On this point, see Dzüvichü, 'Empire', pp. 99–100.

[70] NAI Foreign Political, 17 July 1847, No. 23: Dalton to Jenkins, 12 June 1847, f. 18.

[71] NAI Foreign Political A, December 1869, No. 248: Government of India, Foreign Department to Bengal Government, 18 September 1869, f. 237.

[72] NAI Foreign Political A, July 1873, No. 469: Bengal Government to Government of India, Foreign Department, 14 June 1873, f. 3; ASA, 198, 117-D: Assam Chief Commissioner, Resolution, 14 June 1877.

[73] NAI Foreign Political A, June 1879, No. 319: Assam Chief Commissioner to Government of India, Foreign Department, 23 December 1878, f. 10.

[74] ASA, 198, 117-D: Assam Chief Commissioner, Resolution, 14 June 1877.

The extension of administration into upland areas of the northeast in fact entailed tumultuous upheavals and frequent reversals. The cycle of violence that characterised British interactions prior to the 1860s with the Garos in the western portion of present-day Meghalaya was broadly similar to state interference with the Nagas (see Section 4.2). British relations with Garos were longer running than those with Nagas, as the upland region inhabited by the latter bordered the northern reaches of the territory over which the British gained revenue-collecting powers when they obtained diwani status in Bengal in 1765.[75] From 1815, British administrators in northern Bengal became increasingly embroiled with Garos following violence between upland inhabitants and neighbouring, revenue-paying landowners (see introduction to Chapter 4). Having acknowledged that encroachments by zamindars prompted these outbreaks, in 1822 the Government of Bengal implemented a regulation that provided for the extension of British fiscal and judicial authority over Garo villages.[76] The regulation left substantial discretion to the colonial official 'on the spot'. The precise form of legal prescriptions was largely unstated, apart from the requirement that it was to be in keeping with custom, the determination of which was left to the local British administrator. In practice, the regulation had relatively little effect. There were few recorded colonial dealings in these uplands until 1836, when some Garos attacked revenue collectors. It transpired that this episode followed depredations by Company-State officials at frontier markets during the intervening period – another instance of colonial harassment preceding a frontier community's response.[77] During the decades that followed, inconsistent British attempts to levy taxes from, and administer justice in, some Garo villages met with responses ranging from refusal to open resistance.[78]

Throughout the mid-nineteenth century, most administrators believed that any attempt to extend more uniform administrative structures into the Hills would prove problematic. Pragmatic considerations and romantic notions of tribal isolation coalesced in Edward Dalton's claim in 1847 that it was inadvisable to 'increase the rate of tribute from clans so remotely situated as these are, their moral condition will not be improved by further interference with their independence, and ... it would be difficult to collect if objections were raised'.[79] These ideas also informed the colonial state's inactivity towards reports of slavery in the Garo Hills at this time.[80] Despite claiming that the 'extent to which slavery prevails amongst the Garrows [sic] may ... prove

---

[75] Cederlöf, *Founding*, pp. 53–5; Misra, *Becoming*, pp. 81–3.

[76] Simpson, 'Forgetting'; Mackenzie, *History*, pp. 245–51; Barooah, *David Scott*, pp. 40–62.

[77] Mackenzie, *History*, pp. 254–6.

[78] NAI Foreign Political, 2 September 1843, Nos. 124–6; NAI Foreign Political, 24 April 1847, Nos. 46–8.

[79] NAI Foreign Political, 17 July 1847, No. 23: Dalton to Jenkins, 12 June 1847, ff. 17–18.

[80] Reticence to intervene in 'slavery' had been a feature of British rule in Assam from the outset: on David Scott's attitude, see Barooah, *David Scott*, pp. 159–75.

a serious difficulty in raising these people to a higher state of civilization', Dalton advised that 'this subject should be approached with caution, [as] an over zealous abolitionist would likely raise an insurrection'.[81] To Dalton's practical objection, Francis Jenkins, the leading official in Assam, added a domestic British comparison with overtones of romanticism. 'It is probable', Jenkins wrote, 'that though we call the followers of the great Chiefs slaves they are no more so than were the followers of the Scottish Highland Chiefs'.[82] These debates suggest that British officials did not adopt a uniform strategy in response to labour systems they understood as 'slavery' among the frontier tribes of the northeast. In contrast to heavy-handed interventions among the Singphos at the opposite end of the Assam Valley during the 1830s,[83] the case of the Garos shows caution and an acknowledgement on the part of British officials that 'slavery' covered diverse practices.

As was the case in the Naga Hills at the same time, the intensification of administrative interference the Garo Hills in the 1860s was not a single, decisive event. In both cases the British undertook a creeping advance, with villages brought under state control one by one. Administrators set great stock by the supposedly voluntary nature of the 'submission' of villages, although, as with relocations of frontier communities, they were imbued with the threat or reality of state violence. The first agreements between Garo communities and Captain Williamson, the officer posted to the region in late 1866 to extend and enact British administration, came in the wake of a bout of violence in which troops had razed two villages to the ground.[84] Many Garos remained independent of colonial authority into the early 1870s, when further violence brought about its extension into the remainder of the region. An annual house tax of eight annas was enforced as part of the terms of surrender to the military party that marched through the previously independent portion of the Hills.[85] The Government of Bengal glossed the advent of administration in the Garo Hills as an act of 'remarkable service' conducted in a 'bloodless manner' by Williamson alone.[86] The reductive version of the beginnings of sustained state involvement in the region found a visual counterpart in Robert Woodthorpe's sketch depicting the orderly submission of Garo chiefs to Williamson (Figure 3.7). These were localised attempts to draw 'a secret

[81] NAI Foreign Political, 17 July 1847, No. 23: Dalton to Jenkins, 12 June 1847, f. 45.
[82] NAI Foreign Political, 17 July 1847, No. 22: Jenkins to Government of India, Foreign Department, 25 June 1847, f. 5.
[83] Sadan, *Kachin*, pp. 59–80.
[84] NAI Foreign Political A, June 1866, No. 56: Lt. Williamson to Assam Chief Commissioner, undated.
[85] IOR/L/P&S/6/99, Political Letter No. 65 of 1873: Haughton to Bengal Government, 26 December 1872, ff. 741L.
[86] IOR/L/P&S/6/99, Political Letter No. 65 of 1873: Bengal Government to Government of India, Foreign Department, 1 March 1873, f. 746.

veil' over 'the beginnings of government', as Edmund Burke famously prescribed in opening the impeachment of Warren Hastings in 1788.[87]

The colonial state's repeated inability to deal with disruptions largely of its own agents' making at its territorial fringes was a major impulse to administrative expansion. In the case of the Garos, officials were unable to comprehend or manage the nuanced trade and revenue arrangements that connected zamindars in British Bengal to ostensibly independent communities. After the destructive expedition of 1866, Williamson admitted that the primary cause of the Garos' unrest had been a blockade against their villages instituted by a local zamindar after they refused to pay revenue.[88] In the case of the Naga Hills, the colonial state proved unable to manage the ever-shifting boundary between European-owned tea gardens and Naga communities. The notion that the disputes and skirmishes connected with what the Commissioner of Assam Henry Hopkinson termed 'the great tea interest' could not be managed from governed Assam was a key impulse of administrative expansion into the region during the 1860s and 1870s.[89] The twin borderland pressures of expanding tea gardens and resistance to zamindars' demands were not new at this time, but officials assigned increased importance to them. There was, in fact, a substantial reconceptualisation of the space of the Brahmaputra Valley and the surrounding hill ranges. For the preceding twenty years or so agents of the colonial state in Assam had focused on measures to solidify its rule and raise agricultural productivity (and therefore its revenue) in the lowlands. But in the mid-1860s, there suddenly emerged a notion that conditions in frontier regions fundamentally imperilled colonial interests in the valley. Lower-level officials echoed Hopkinson's sentiment that 'we are on all sides surrounded in Assam by inflammable material' (see Section 4.2).[90] The younger John Butler, for example, concurred with the assessment of one of his contemporaries that Assam was 'all frontier'.[91]

The renewed ideational significance attached to the frontier was not a simple by-product of particular events. Nor can it be explained as a direct consequence of strategic developments or specific actions on the part of the frontier communities. Hopkinson expanded on his characterisation of the frontiers of Assam as 'inflammable material' by admitting that 'there is no greater chance of its igniting now than there is at all times'.[92] Although he cited recent Naga border

---

[87] Burke, quoted in Dirks, *Scandal*, p. 167.

[88] NAI Foreign Political A, June 1866, No. 56, f. 5.

[89] Quotation from NAI Foreign Political A, July 1873, No. 473: Assam Chief Commissioner to Bengal Government, Judicial Department, 11 March 1873, f. 3.

[90] NAI Foreign Political A, July 1865, No. 49: Hopkinson to Bengal Government, 3 May 1865, f. 6.

[91] IOR/L/P&S/7/6, Political Letter No. 213 of 1875: Butler to Assam Chief Commissioner, 30 April 1875, f. 587.

[92] NAI Foreign Political A, July 1865, No. 49: Hopkinson to Bengal Government, 3 May 1865, f. 6.

incursions to evidence his fears, he made clear that these were unexceptional and that his core concern was a tribal attack on an unprecedented scale. 'Our assumption of security', he opined, 'has no better foundation than the fact that so large a body of Nagas or Abors has never yet come down into the plains against us ... I cannot regard it as a contingency at all beyond the limits of ordinary calculation that they should project a descent into our territory on a scale that might do us an amount of mischief I do not like to think of'.[93] This reimagining of Assam's frontier seemed to demand administrative expansion into the Naga, Garo, and Lushai Hills. It resulted from the intersection of various factors: anxieties over the fragility of colonial rule in the wake of the Rebellion of 1857 to 1858; weariness at repeated border skirmishes with communities along the fringes of the Brahmaputra Valley; and frustrations at the ineffectuality of the colonial state's methods of influencing frontier populations. By no means least among the impulses to administrative expansion was excitement at the opportunities that the extension of government into frontier regions afforded, especially the provision of substantial executive power in individual officials.

The desire to open out spaces of non-regulation administration was encapsulated in Thomas Lewin's famous formulation regarding the Chittagong and Lushai Hills: 'What is wanted here is not measures but a man ... not a mere cog in the great wheel of Government'.[94] Finding new pastures for a domineering form of personal rule was especially pressing in the northeast in the 1860s, as by this time administration in the lowland areas of Assam had become normalised, with the revenue system firmly established and governmental structures set in place. Regional administrators actively promoted the idea of a distinct form of frontier government. For instance, Richard Keatinge, Chief Commissioner during the mid-1870s, celebrated the eastwards expansion of the Naga Hills District in terms of masculine vigour, claiming that 'the idea that, when injured, we content ourselves with writing despatches, that we are only fit for riding on horses and elephants, and cannot penetrate their hills, is exploded'.[95] Peter Robb's claim that the extension of colonial administration into the Naga Hills was part of a liberal shift towards implementing normalised government and pursuing developmentalist goals underplays the persistence of attempts to maintain frontiers as distinct administrative spaces.[96] Officials dismissed attempts to implement taxation beyond the flat-rate house tax or to exercise more intensive judicial administration among upland populations as poorly suited to the social and economic structures of these communities. These limited administrative structures resulted from officials' aspiration to

---

[93] Ibid.   [94] Lewin, *Hill Tracts*, p. 118.
[95] IOR/L/P&S/7/6, Political Letter No. 213 of 1875: Assam Chief Commissioner to Government of India, Foreign Department, 7 July 1875, f. 573.
[96] Robb, 'Colonial State'.

maintain zones of irregular, heroic government. Fixed legal and fiscal precepts ran counter to the exercise of discretionary power by individual officials every bit as much as immutable linear boundaries. Governing in accordance with strictly codified principles ran the risk, administrators argued, of emasculating colonial personnel in frontier regions and reducing them to the degenerated figures of derision that Hopkinson feared they had already become among unadministered populations, 'doing nothing but write–write–write!'[97]

Such concerns were apparent from the inception of the Naga Hills District in 1866, in which the application of regulation laws that operated elsewhere in British India was felt to be inadmissible. The loudest calls to do away with fixed legal principles came from those most intimately involved with the District. Lieutenant Gregory, the official deputed to establish British administration in the Hills, couched his suggestions for the powers to be vested in him in the form of a quotation of an earlier Superintendent of Cachar District, who had previously held responsibility for relations with Angami Nagas. The Deputy Commissioner of the Naga Hills District should be allowed 'to decide … without reference to regulation, law, forms, or practice, all disputes and other matters connected with these rude mountaineers that may be submitted to him … No interference on the part of the Bengal Police or Ministerial Officers should, on any account, be permitted'.[98] Gregory's stated rationale for constituting the Naga Hills as a legally anomalous space was that 'the trammels of regulation laws … [are] not the sort of justice that satisfies these wild and ignorant people'.[99] Presented as pragmatic – legal difference as response to racial-cultural difference – the supposition of this particular form of otherness fitted officials' desire to maintain frontiers as areas of governmental distinctiveness. The argument proved sufficient to convince the Commissioner of Assam, and the Bengal Government added only minor amendments: the Deputy Commissioner 'should follow the spirit of [the Code of Criminal Procedure] as closely as possible', judicial sentences would be appealable to the Bengal Judicial Commissioner, and all death penalty verdicts would require the Judicial Commissioner's confirmation.[100] The almost total lack of formalised legal structures was a key element in subcontracting sovereignty to 'men on the spot', a key feature of administration in the Naga Hills just as it was in state violence across the Subcontinent's frontiers.

Gregory's proposal also touched upon labour requirements imposed on governed Nagas, another crucial element of the peculiar form of frontier

---

[97] NAI Foreign Political A, July 1873, No. 476: Hopkinson to Bengal Government, Judicial Department, 22 March 1873, f. 5.
[98] NAI Foreign Political A, December 1866, No. 137: Gregory, 'Memorandum', f. 22.
[99] Ibid.
[100] NAI Foreign Political A, December 1866, No. 139: Bengal Government to Hopkinson, 29 October 1866, f. 30.

administration in the northeast. Gregory proposed that each man in Samaguting, initially the only village in the Naga Hills District, should be obliged to pay a house tax and undertake eight days of labour annually as a token of submission to British rule.[101] A similar system of compulsory labour had been instituted in the Garo Hills, and in both areas it proved to be a substantial and repeated irritant. These were instances in which the shallowness of frontier administration interplayed with ill-conceived elements of interference that provoked resistance. Unlike the house tax, the demand for labour was not merely a symbolic token of submission. It was also intended to construct the infrastructure, especially roads, that would enable the state to penetrate upland regions.[102] The frequent demands for labour underlay tensions between British officials and frontier communities that frequently flared into outbreaks of violence, threatening the very instantiation of authority the practice was supposed to facilitate.[103] In addition, labour shortages hampered numerous road-building projects and survey and military parties, a striking indication of the colonial state's administrative limitations in frontier areas.

The inclusion of ever more Naga villages within the formal sphere of colonial government quickly assumed proportions that clearly exceeded the original rationale to prevent incursions into cultivated lowland areas. The Government of India's eventual capitulation in the late 1870s to the administrative expansion urged by its junior officials in the Naga Hills indicated how the principles underpinning government in the region had changed fundamentally over the preceding decade. The Government agreed that 'a more definite policy ought to be adopted in our dealings with these tribes. Such a policy would necessarily look beyond our immediate needs and interests, and could not be confined to questions of the best system for protecting our own settled districts, and the villages in the Naga Hills which have submitted to our authority'.[104] The Assam Government also forwarded a radically altered rationale for administration, claiming the colonial state was 'bound by our duties as a great civilized power, by considerations of prestige, all through the Naga Hills'.[105]

Despite this shift in motivations and justifications, the actual form of administration in the Naga Hills District remained 'no more than the rudimentary

[101] NAI Foreign Political A, December 1866, No. 137: Gregory, 'Memorandum', f. 18.
[102] Dzuvichu, 'Roads'.
[103] For instances of enforced labour prompting resistance in the Naga Hills in 1874 and 1886–7 respectively, see NAI Foreign Political A, December 1874, No. 273: Butler to Keatinge, 30 May 1874, f. 6; Reid, *History*, pp. 109–10. For an instance in the Garo Hills in 1881–2, see Mackenzie, *History*, pp. 266–67.
[104] IOR/L/P&S/7/19, Political Letter No. 211 of 1878: Government of India to Assam Chief Commissioner, 20 July 1878, f. 1184.
[105] NAI Foreign Political A, July 1874, No. 40: Assam Chief Commissioner to Government of India, Foreign Department, 16 April 1874, f. 2.

functions of Government ... protecting [Nagas] from raid, and receiving some taxes, and ... keep[ing] out the Manipuris from the whole district'.[106] The central element of administration remained the enforcement of a house tax as a symbol of acceptance of subjecthood, summed up by the Deputy Commissioner in 1879 in the following terms: 'A savage who pays revenue considers himself a British subject bound to carry out all orders given him, while a savage who does not pay revenue considers himself independent, and free to obey orders or not as he chooses'.[107] Beyond the tax, labour demands, and a summary form of justice delivered – often outside of the District's boundaries – by the Deputy Commissioner, governmental interventions were few and sporadic. Occasional efforts aimed at Nagas' welfare, including vaccinations in areas with outbreaks of smallpox and the advent of schools, had a limited effect, not least because most officials considered education to come under the purview of missionaries rather than the colonial state.[108]

There were two important exceptions to British administrators' reticence to intervene in Naga social structures. The first, instigated in 1868, was to assemble at the seat of colonial power in the Hill District 'delegates' from major villages further to the east. Although the initial hope that these representatives would broker peace between their clans failed to transpire, officials in Naga Hills quickly repurposed them as 'most useful ... go-between[s] of the clans they represent and the Deputy Commissioner'.[109] John Butler referred to them as 'Dobashas' (interpreters) but acknowledged that their role was multifarious, including accompanying him on 'tours' through and beyond the District, and informing him of 'what is going on in the interior'.[110] This system remained in place throughout colonial rule in the Hills and the role continued to expand to meet the needs of the Deputy Commissioner, eventually encompassing occasional police functions and collecting ethnographic information.[111]

---

[106] IOR/L/P&S/7/19, Political Letter No. 211 of 1878: Government of India to Assam Chief Commissioner, 20 July 1878, f. 1184.

[107] NAI Foreign Political A, January 1880, No. 507: Assam Chief Commissioner to Government of India, Foreign Department, 19 August 1879.

[108] On vaccinations, see ASA, 43, 117-D: Maxwell, Naga Hills Political Officer, to Assam Chief Commissioner, 25 May 1878; on the importance of schools, see NAI Foreign Political A, December 1866, No. 137: Gregory, 'Memorandum', f. 17; NAI Foreign Political A, January 1880, No. 509: G. H. Damant, Naga Hills Political Officer, to Assam Chief Commissioner, 21 February 1879.

[109] NAI Foreign Political A, December 1870, No. 29: A. H. James, Assistant Commissioner i/c Naga Hills, to Assam Commissioner, 9 September 1870, f. 2.

[110] NAI Foreign Political A, June 1872, No. 512, ff. 1–2: Butler to Assam Commissioner, 1 May 1872; *Report on the Administration of the Province of Assam for the years 1874–75 and 1875–76* (Shillong: Assam Secretariat Press, 1877), pp. 17–18.

[111] J. P. Mills, quoted in Reid, *History*, p. 160.

The second exception, which only began in 1882, was the institution in some villages of headmen – initially termed *lambardars* but later known as *gaonburras* – appointed by the Deputy Commissioner.[112] This represented a partial return to the policy of dealing with Angami chiefs employed during the abortive British expansion of the 1840s. The strategy had comprehensively failed then, and, when the Naga Hills District was instituted in 1866, frontier officials believed it was not worth repeating. Gregory spoke out against providing subsidies to chiefs, as 'there is no guarantee that any engagement made by them would be ratified by their clans over which they have as little social or political power as a Captain of Volunteers over his company of parade'.[113] The lack of sway of Naga – especially Angami – headmen was repeated to the point of cliché during the 1870s,[114] although they continued to be conduits of communication for colonial administrators. If anything, as the significance of the 'khel' rather than the village in Naga society became clearer to the British (see Section 3.4), they perceived the headman's sphere of influence to be diminished still further.[115] The colonial institution of village headmen from 1882 therefore constituted a significant departure. The headmen were assigned elements of the limited form of administration the British had implemented in the District, assessing the house tax in exchange for 20 per cent of the revenue collected and distributing the labour demand among households.[116] The innovation undoubtedly promised to introduce an unprecedented form of social hierarchy within the villages to which it applied. However, the intention of the Chief Commissioner of Assam that the headmen would 'control and guide the villagers', bringing about a basic change in their 'democratic and independent habits' was not realised to any great extent.[117] In 1921, J. H. Hutton noted that although the Deputy Commissioner formally appointed Angami *gaonburras*, this was 'more or less on the nomination of the clan'. Their authority was so limited, Hutton claimed, that 'more often than not they are compelled to disgorge for the benefit of their clan [their] commission on their collection of house tax'.[118] The impact of these British innovations on Naga social structures was significantly less pronounced than that of the forms of chiefly authority instigated in Balochistan during the same era (see Section 5.4).

While they targeted larger populations and expanding areas, some colonial administrative interventions in frontiers of the northeast became shallower as

---

[112] NAI Foreign Political A, January 1882, Nos. 134–7; Dzuvichu, 'Roads', p. 490.
[113] Gregory, quoted in ASA Bengal Government Papers, No. 305: Hopkinson to Bengal Government, 30 October 1865.
[114] For instance, Woodthorpe, 'Wild Tribes Part I', p. 68.
[115] IOR/L/P&S/7/19, Political Letter No. 211 of 1878: Assam Chief Commissioner to Government of India, Foreign Department, ff. 1193–94.
[116] Dzuvichu, 'Empire', pp. 108–9.   [117] Elliott, quoted in Robb, 'Colonial State', p. 261.
[118] J. H. Hutton, *The Angami Nagas: With Some Notes on Neighbouring Tribes* (London: Macmillan and Co., 1921), p. 143.

the nineteenth century progressed.[119] For instance, there was an aggressive colonial campaign against 'slavery' among the Singphos and Hkamtis in the 1830s, an expression both of the abolitionism that pervaded the British imperial world at the time and of a liberal interventionist moment in colonial Indian government.[120] Such interference was not replicated in the Garo Hills during the late 1840s, and a cautious approach to the issue was also evident in the Naga Hills District. In the early 1870s, Hopkinson suggested that 'the slavery of the Khamptis [sic] and Singphos ... is not that of the savage hill-tribes' like the Nagas. The former, he claimed, had been 'more elaborate and highly organised' than that of the communities of both the northern and southern upland fringes of the Brahmaputra Valley.[121] The Government of Bengal envisaged that the eastward extension of the administered Naga Hills would entail the prohibition of 'raiding, cutting, and slave-dealing propensities', but Hopkinson's scepticism towards active intervention ultimately won out.[122] Although in 1886 a temporary Deputy Commissioner of the Naga Hills District ordered Ao Naga chiefs to cease 'slavery' on pains of punishment,[123] his successor followed a less invasive policy of allowing the practice to disappear slowly by not enforcing the slaveowners' rights.[124] Active state intervention concerning slavery among Ao communities was limited to preventing the subjection of new slaves and the killing of children born to female slaves.[125]

Administrators' fear of inducing resistance and awareness of the limited capacity of the state to effect change to supposedly ingrained social structures undoubtedly generated reticence to intervene. However, entwined with calculations of what could be done were notions of what should be done. Uniform administrative schemes seemed to many officials to run the risk of curtailing their freedom of action, reducing them to implementers of schemes that had been devised and already applied elsewhere. Their belief that frontier regions

---

[119] This goes against Peter Robb's contention that the early 1880s was 'an important new beginning' in the normalisation of colonial government in the Naga Hills: Robb, 'Colonial State', p. 256.

[120] On anti-slavery sentiment and humanitarianism in the British Empire, see Alan Lester, *Imperial Networks: Creating Identities in Nineteenth-Century South Africa and Britain* (London: Routledge, 2001); Seymour Drescher, *Abolition: A History of Slavery and Antislavery* (Cambridge: Cambridge University Press, 2009). On liberal interventionism in British India, see Metcalf, *Ideologies*, pp. 28–43.

[121] NAI Foreign Political A, July 1873, No. 504: Hopkinson to Bengal Government, 30 April 1873, f. 21.

[122] NAI Foreign Political A, July 1873, No. 469: Bengal Government to Government of India, Foreign Department, 14 June 1873, f. 3.

[123] NAI Foreign External A, August 1886, No. 212: Greer, Naga Hills Officiating Deputy Commissioner to Assam Chief Commissioner, 12 June 1886.

[124] NAI Foreign External A, February 1890, No. 156: A. Porteous, Naga Hills Deputy Commissioner to Chief Commissioner, 8 March 1889.

[125] NAI Foreign External A, February 1890, No. 157: Assam Chief Commissioner to Porteous, 27 March 1889.

could not be administered in the same fashion as the rest of British India was a manifestation of their desire to maintain regions of independent action. As was the case with schemes to relocate communities at the fringes of British India, efforts to impose new socio-political relations within these regions tended to fail on their own terms but to cause substantial dislocation among their target populations. Although constantly concerned by their own limitations among frontier terrains and peoples, officials at all levels of the colonial state were prone to spectacularly ill-considered administrative interventions and impositions, many of which provoked powerful reactions. The late nineteenth century in British India was not merely an interlude of growing state power and administrative entrenchment between the incessant rebellions of the first half of the nineteenth century and the rise of nationalism in the early twentieth century.[126] Rather, the interplay of indeterminacies and violence involved in colonial expansion were pushed to the territorial margins.

5.4   'A Rough Half-Subdued Country': Administering Balochistan, 1877–1900

> [Sandeman's] very considerable administrative capacities were best seen in a rough half-subdued country where he could have his own way, choose his own methods, and bring into full play his special faculty of influence over Asiatics. For laws, financial rules, and official regulations generally he had no predilection.   Alfred Lyall, 1891.[127]

In March 1876, Robert Sandeman returned from the hills to the north of Kalat having spent the preceding four months of his mission accompanied by approximately 2,000 administered and 'independent' Baloch men.[128] That Sandeman's was not a conventional diplomatic mission was evident from his repeated stretching of already loose official orders, culminating in an outright refusal to obey his immediate superior's instruction to abort the mission. That same month, the Governor of Bombay Bartle Frere claimed that British officials 'dealt with Khelat as far as possible as we would with Belgium or Switzerland'.[129] Sandeman's actions, celebrated in contemporary press accounts of 'his daring ride to Khelat' as the heroic work of a petty monarch,[130] gave the lie to Frere's suggestion of normalised diplomacy.[131]

---

[126] Bayly, *Indian Society*, pp. 136–78.   [127] Lyall, quoted in Thornton, *Sandeman*, p. 291.

[128] Bruce, *Forward Policy*, pp. 56–60.

[129] IOR/L/P&S/18/A12: Bartle Frere, 'Memorandum – Sind and Punjab Frontier Systems', 22 March 1876, p. 6.

[130] The *Pioneer*, quoted in Bruce, *Forward Policy*, pp. 227–28.

[131] Benjamin Hopkins also points out the distinction between British actions in Balochistan and 'the modern Westphalian model of statehood': Marsden and Hopkins, *Fragments*, p. 51.

Even the Military Secretary of the Government of India, Henry Norman, recognised this discrepancy: 'whether we take the cutting up of six hundred Bugtees in 1847 or [the Commissioner of Sind] Sir W. Merewether's argument for dethroning the Khan of Khelat, which I personally heard in Calcutta in 1875, I can conceive no policy less like that which we should adopt towards a European power than that which has [prevailed] in Sind'.[132] As in the Naga Hills, the expansion and formalisation of the colonial state's interference in Balochistan did not lead to uniform and bureaucratised government but to a fragmented region governed as a series of variously exceptional spaces and populations.

Christian Tripodi's recent analysis of British administration in Balochistan understands the state's limited penetration as a deliberately benign, 'light touch' administration acting in harmony with tribal society.[133] In doing so, it essentially repeats the narrative of pragmatic paternalism popularised by Richard Bruce and other late nineteenth-century hagiographers of Sandeman, and first constructed by Sandeman himself. The determination of Sandeman and his underlings to administer through their own discretionary interventions led to the configuration of governmental spaces in Balochistan as areas of individual authority. Tripodi's suggestion that 'Sandeman was trying engineer a form of administration that could run itself, that is, indirect rule' requires rethinking.[134] Sandeman was, in fact, trying to engineer a form of administration that could not run without the charismatic presence of the frontier official, that is, personal rule.

The application of this brand of administration in Balochistan was in line with the Government of India's expectations. A month after Sandeman was made Agent to the Governor-General, the Viceroy Lord Lytton wrote of Balochistan: 'It is by the everyday acts of earnest, upright English gentlemen that lasting influence must be obtained, not by spasmodic demonstrations, nor any sudden and temporary influence purchased by money and payments'.[135] Notwithstanding the widespread use of payments to tribal potentates (and Sandeman's Scottish rather than English roots), Lytton's comments serve to indicate that personal rule was not simply a matter of low-level transgressions of orders. It was instead the result of the Government of India knowingly subcontracting sovereignty to frontier administrators. Contemporary officials recognised and sometimes bemoaned Sandeman's exceptional status. A. A. Munro, who briefly oversaw his dealings beyond the administrative

---

[132] NAI Foreign Political A, February 1878, Nos. 149–56, Keep-With, ff. 12–13.

[133] Tripodi, *Edge*, p. 58; Hopkins provides a more nuanced account, although he suggests that Sandeman 'facilitated the convergence of interests between the tribesmen and the colonial state': *Fragments*, p. 57.

[134] Tripodi, *Edge*, p. 59.

[135] Lytton to Lord Salisbury, 23 March 1877, quoted in Thornton, *Sandeman*, pp. 94–95.

boundary in 1876,[136] opined that Sandeman's 'personal influence over the tribes' and 'personal idiosyncracies [*sic.*] are often valuable doubtless' in establishing colonial authority, but that these elements could work against 'our object ... to simplify and consolidate [so] that those who succeed the executive inaugurators of the policy may have no difficulty in following suit'.[137] Subsequent developments bore out Munro's concerns. Sandeman and his successors clung jealously to personal rule, meaning that the value of hazily defined qualities such as 'special experience and aptitude' became axioms of colonial administration in the region.[138]

These foundational principles of personal rule in Balochistan remained after it became formally incorporated into British India in 1887. Government in the region shared with administered areas of upland northeast India an avowed aversion to bureaucratic principles and celebration of masculine physicality. 'Strong powers of physical endurance' were prerequisite, according to Sandeman's biographer, along with 'a minimum of desk work'.[139] The primary justification of this form of administration took the form of rose-tinted references to officers on the Upper Sind and Punjab frontier in the 1840s and the early 1850s.[140] In 1874, the retired Political Superintendent of the Upper Sind Frontier Henry Green echoed his still-active successors' fears of emasculation via a celebration of John Jacob's methods of the 1840s. 'While the school formed by Jacob of *men*, who, while gaining experience prided themselves on setting all difficulties at defiance, and who took a pleasure in exposure and hard work', Green wrote, '[the Balochistan frontier] has now become a nursery for squalling children, and an asylum for worn-out men'.[141] The forms of personal rule that underpinned colonial administration in Balochistan should be understood against the backdrop of the valorisation of earlier frontier governance and the notion that normalised processes of government constituted a form of degeneration from these halcyon days.[142]

The colonial state officially disavowed that it exercised formal control in Balochistan until 1887, despite intruding into growing portions of the region during the preceding two decades. Long-running confusions among officials located at a distance from the southern Punjab and northern Sind frontier over

---

[136] Munro, the Commissioner of Derajat Division in Punjab, took over from Merewether, the Commissioner of Sind, after the Government of India ruled against the latter's decision to recall Sandeman from his mission into Balochistan from November 1875 to March 1876—a recall that Sandeman ignored. See IOR/L/P&S/7/7, Political Letter No. 6 of 1876.

[137] IOR/L/P&S/7/8: Political Letter No. 64, Enclosure No. 39: Munro to Punjab Government, 12 February 1876, f. 252.

[138] Thornton, *Sandeman*, p. 190.   [139] Ibid.   [140] Ibid.

[141] IOR/L/P&S/7/1, Political Letter No. 13 of 1875: Green to Secretary of State for India, 23 October 1874, f. 432 (emphasis in original).

[142] On related fears of 'degeneration' in the late nineteenth century, see Daniel Pick, *Faces of Degeneration: A European Disorder, c.1848-c.1918* (Cambridge: Cambridge University Press, 1989).

the activities of their underlings 'on the spot' were partly responsible for the misleading official account of the beginnings of British administration. For instance, the Bombay Government had pronounced in 1869 that intervening between the Khan of Kalat and his subjects would 'lead to very mischievous results'.[143] This assessment came a year after Sandeman bypassed the Kalat state altogether and extended direct colonial funding to the powerful Marri community in northern Balochistan in exchange for service of some of its members in a militia.[144] Sandeman's agreement with Marri and Bugti chiefs, authorised by the Government of India nine months later, included the employment of five men of each community in the Punjab Government's frontier militia.[145] 'Tribal service' expanded to a total of thirty-one men following the Mithankot Conference in 1871, when the Government of India officially handed control over the northern Baloch communities to Sandeman and provided a sizeable budget for what it termed 'the subsidizing plan'.[146]

Employing members of frontier communities in colonial military parties had a notable regional precursor in the form of John Jacob's irregular levies. Sandeman himself cited Jacob's schemes in attempting to justify enhanced payments to the Marris in 1875, despite having claimed eight years earlier that service was an 'entirely ... experimental measure'.[147] Officials in Sind and Punjab also couched the engagement of Balochs as an extension of schemes employed in Punjab since annexation.[148] One administrator even suggested that tribal service in Punjab was predicated on the colonial government's continuation of the Sikh government's methods of frontier administration, which '[left] much to be effected through the political management of border tribes'.[149] These arrangements in the northwest also shared significant

---

[143] NAI Foreign Political A, September 1869, No. 63: Bombay Government to Merewether, 3 August 1869, f. 1.

[144] NAI Foreign Political A, June 1868, No. 83: Sandeman to Munro, 11 September 1867, ff. 3–7.

[145] Ibid, ff. 5–6; NAI Foreign Political A, June 1868, No. 84: Government of India, Foreign Department, to Punjab Government, 9 June 1868, f. 1.

[146] NAI Foreign Political A, April 1874, No. 93: Sind Commissioner to Government of India, Foreign Department, 8 February 1874, f. 2; IOR/L/P&S/7/1, Political Letter No. 13 of 1875, Enclosure No. 28: F. Loch, Upper Sind Frontier Superintendent, to Merewether, 20 November 1874, f. 501.

[147] This is largely ignored in existing works: for example, Tripodi, *Edge*, pp. 56–9. NAI Foreign Political A, November 1875, No. 276: Sandeman to Merewether, 29 May 1875, f. 5; NAI Foreign Political A, June 1868, No. 83: Sandeman to Munro, 11 September 1867, f. 6.

[148] NAI Foreign Political A, April 1874, No. 93: Merewether to Government of India, Foreign Department, 8 February 1874, f. 2; IOR/L/P&S/7/1, Political Letter No. 13 of 1875, Enclosure No. 28: Loch to Merewether, 20 November 1874, f. 501. For examples of earlier payments to frontier communities and employment by the colonial state, see NAI Foreign Secret, 26 April 1850, No. 66: Punjab Board of Administration to Government of India, 27 March 1850, ff. 1–2; Foreign Political A, 02/1861, No. 47: Peshawar Commissioner to Government of Punjab, 26 January 1861.

[149] NAI Foreign Political A, October 1874, No. 169A: Derajat Commissioner to Punjab Government, 23 April 1874, f. 258.

similarities with interventions at Assam frontier, where the use of levies had been a feature of British interventions in frontier communities since the 1830s.[150] Relative to the supposedly 'democratic' Pashtuns and communities of the upland northeast, administrators widely held that Balochs were unusually suited to such arrangements because they had firmly established and effective chiefs who could raise and control levies. Colonial ethnography and administration marched in lockstep on this issue. Ralph Hughes-Buller's influential 1901 census report (see Section 3.6) claimed that the fundamental basis of chiefly authority in Baloch tribes was that 'before the advent of the British [authority, they] . . . were continually on the war-path', meaning they – unlike Pashtuns – were 'organised and officered expressly for offence'.[151] By this reckoning, British levies were merely updates of an existing structure rather than an alien imposition. It is notable that attempts from the late 1880s to extend the system of payments and levies to Waziris rested on a sociological claim. The 'democratic character' of Pashtuns, Sandeman's protégé Richard Bruce argued, 'is exceptional and of recent growth, and is in large measure due to our dealing direct with men who had no hereditary standing, and on lines quite opposed to their own tribal customs and procedure'.[152] Instituting colonial authority through Waziri chiefs rested on the contention that Pashtuns were more like Balochs than previous British accounts and actions had supposed. While the policy in Waziristan failed to vindicate Bruce's claims (see also Section 1.7), colonial patronage and financial support entrenched and enhanced Baloch chiefs' authority.[153]

The Treaty of Mastung concluded in 1876 by Sandeman, the Khan of Kalat, and leading Brahui potentates expanded British administrative interference in Balochistan beyond the existing combination of payments and levies. It formally constituted the Government of India as the final referee in cases of disputes between the Khan and his Sirdars and provided for British troops to be located in Quetta and connected to Sind by railway line and telegraph wire. The extension in the 1870s and 1880s of courthouses, legal codes, and communications infrastructure partially integrated some parts of Balochistan, especially Quetta, into British India.[154] The official creation of British Baluchistan

---

[150] On the deployment of Singphos in military ventures north of the Brahmaputra, see ASA, pre-1874 files, Assam Commissioner No. 686: Bivar to Hopkinson, 23 February 1862.

[151] Hughes-Buller, *1901 Baluchistan Census Report*, p. 129.

[152] Bruce, *Forward*, p. 167. NAI Foreign Secret E, July 1890, No. 115: Bruce, 'Memorandum', 6 November 1889.

[153] I draw here on Gilmartin's idea of 'an emerging British vision of themselves as patrons of a tribal social order' in Balochistan: Gilmartin, *Blood*, p. 65.

[154] For an account emphasising the impact of the railways, see Scholz, *Nomadism*, pp. 109–10. On the immediate extension of the telegraph system, see NAI Foreign Political A, November 1878, No. 161: Quarter-Master General to Government of India, Military Department, 20 April 1877, f. 1.

in 1887 accelerated this trend, with eight new courts constructed (bringing the total to twenty-five) and the adoption of a legal code partly comprising regulations made originally for the Punjab and Burma frontiers.[155] But other areas remained for forms of Sandeman to exercise his preferred forms of personal administration, unbound by legal codification and rapid communication technologies. The Zhob Valley in the north of Balochistan was one such region (see Section 1.4), and Sandeman and his colleagues also undertook numerous tours beyond British Baluchistan's administrative limits to bring an ever-greater territory under their sway.

The sparsely populated deserts to the west and south of Kalat stretching to the limits of Persian authority provided rich pickings for these men. Since the 1860s, this region British interest in this region had been bound up with attempts to lay telegraph cables as part of the route from London to India. Telegraphic expansion resulted in the permanent stationing of a British agent in the port city of Gwadar, an outpost east of Persia that was subject to the sovereignty of the Sultan of Muscat.[156] There was no intention to extend colonial administration to these regions, beyond the occasional involvement of the Political Agent at Gwadar in the affairs of communities in Makran when these affected telegraph hardware.[157] Sandeman initiated expansion in 1883, leading a military party to the Naushirwani community on the pretense that it had opposed the Khanate of Kalat.[158] After reasserting sovereignty – nominally of Kalat, but really his own – over the Naushirwanis, Sandeman journeyed beyond the southwestern limits of Kalat's effective authority to Gwadar. In discussions with the British Political Agent there, Sandeman made it clear that despite no previous suggestion to this effect, he considered Gwadar part of Balochistan and therefore under his orders.[159]

The tour reiterated both Sandeman's obsession with expanding the field of his discretionary power and his tendency to administer in the loosest possible fashion. During a whirlwind three-day stay, he enacted his self-arrogated authority by reversing the Political Agent's policy of demanding 'indemnity' payments from communities in Makran that committed acts of aggression towards inhabitants of Gwadar.[160] He justified these actions by claiming their

---

[155] Thornton, *Sandeman*, pp. 204–9.

[156] On the telegraph in this area, see Deep Kanta Lahiri Choudhury, *Telegraphic Imperialism: Crisis and Panic in the Indian Empire, c.1830–1920* (Basingstoke: Palgrave Macmillan, 2010), pp. 89–94.

[157] NAI Foreign Political A, June 1884, No. 480: Sandeman to Government of India, 25 March 1884.

[158] Thornton, *Sandeman*, pp. 180–2.

[159] NAI Foreign Political A, June 1884, No. 536: E. Mockler, Political Agent in Gwadar, 'Memorandum', undated.

[160] NAI Foreign Political A, June 1884, No. 480: Sandeman to Government of India, 25 March 1884.

similarity to British policy on the Punjab frontier 'for the last forty years' and suggesting that harsher treatment would induce the communities to flee to Persia.[161] In fact, the measures were consistent with Sandeman's brand of personal administration. He placed particular emphasis on convening and chairing jirgas or 'darbars' of tribal potentates, having already developed this system among northern Balochs.[162] These meetings placed Sandeman symbolically and practically at the centre of an informal system of colonial administration in the outlying portions of Balochistan. As members of the Government of India pointedly commented, in these settings he avoided oversight from distant superiors by being 'out of the reach of telegrams' and 'giv[ing] us as little information on any subject as he can'.[163] Arrayed around him were potentates representing whole communities, whose status was bolstered as a result.[164] The symbiosis of chiefly and personal authority in Sandeman's Balochistan was neatly summarised in Richard Bruce's claim that 'Beluch Tumandars and jirgas ... [are] essential parts in the tribal machine, which requires specially trained officers for its successful working'.[165]

The arrangements that Sandeman concluded at the jirgas on his 1883 tour met with disapproval from his superiors in the Government of India.[166] They also continued to cause problems for his successors more than a decade later, as communities used the concessions they secured to refuse later revenue demands.[167] The chaos and condemnation did not prevent Sandeman from enacting similar arrangements on subsequent trips to the western outskirts of Balochistan. Most notable was his tour to this region in 1891, during which he pressed the Government of India to authorise the extension of a particular 'kind of civil administration', consisting of 'a European officer posted on the spot, and with a sufficient escort of regular troops to ensure his authority being respected'.[168] Although his recommendation was refused, Sandeman's tours in 1883 and 1891 enacted perfunctory judicial and fiscal administration beyond the limits of formal colonial authority.[169] In this respect, despite being less regular, they performed

---

[161] Ibid.
[162] On the importance of jirgas to Sandeman's administration, see Marsden and Hopkins, *Fragments*, p. 57.
[163] NAI Foreign Political A, June 1883, Nos. 306–24, Keep-With, notes by J. W. R. and A. H. M.
[164] Titus, 'Honor', pp. 672–73.   [165] Bruce, *Forward*, p. 110.
[166] NAI Foreign Political A, June 1884, No. 580: Government of India, Foreign Department, to Sandeman, 16 June 1884.
[167] NAI Foreign Secret E, August 1894, No. 278: H. Ramsey, S. E. Baluchistan Political Agent, to J. Browne, Baluchistan Agent to Governor-General, 17 February 1894.
[168] NAI Foreign External A, April 1891, No. 45: Sandeman to Government of India, Foreign Department, 12 January 1891; NAI Foreign External A, October 1891, No. 79: Sandeman to Government of India, Foreign Department, 22 April 1891.
[169] It also took two full years—until after Sandeman's death in 1892—for the Government of India's order for colonial troops to be withdrawn from Makran to be executed: *Administration Report of the Baluchistan Agency for 1892–93* (Calcutta: Government Press, 1893), p. 9.

similar functions to the military 'promenades' undertaken beyond formal colonial jurisdiction in the Naga Hills during the same period (see Section 4.2).

Under Sandeman, the sub-Agencies of Thal Chotiali and Quetta-Pishin at the core of British Baluchistan were governed differently to the outlying regions of Makran, Zhob, and Las Bela. Administration reports for the former acclaimed as 'civilising' influences the rapid extension of railway and telegraph networks and the advent, on a more modest scale, of civil dispensaries, vaccination schemes, and sanitation infrastructure.[170] In addition, officials wrote in soaring terms of the progress of aspects of normalised government, such as the implementation of fixed land revenue demands and a legal code specific to Balochistan.[171] The best indicator of colonial administrative intrusion was not fanciful assessments from officials, however, but the resistance that resulted. There were persistent '*ghazi*' attacks.[172] In response, administrators expanded military recruitment programmes brokered through individually mediated agreements with tribal chiefs.[173] By 1887 around 2,000 men had been formed into levies for policing Balochistan and the northern border with Waziristan.[174] In Richard Bruce's words, 'the tribal leaders ... and the tribal levies [became] the backbone of a frontier officer's political arrangements'.[175]

Exceptions abounded in the legal and fiscal spheres. The justice system was a patchwork of colonial courts, local potentates, village councils, and arbitrators. In Zhob, for instance, the Political Agent 'deemed [it] expedient to settle the great bulk of disputes which occur more according to the customs of the people, or, as they call it, "politically"'.[176] Despite the advent of a legal code specific to British Baluchistan following the creation of the Chief Commissionership, various alternatives continued to be applied to different cases based on local evaluations of expediency.[177] Land revenue across the sub-Agencies of British Baluchistan was collected according to an array of different systems, which were repeatedly revised.[178] Focusing on the detail of administration in the areas of Balochistan over which the British exercised

[170] *Administration Report of the Baluchistan Agency for 1887–88* (Calcutta: Government Press, 1890), pp. 19–20.

[171] Ibid, p. 32.

[172] NAI Foreign Political A, September 1887, Nos. 229–64; *Administration Report of the Baluchistan Agency for 1890–91* (Calcutta: Government Press, 1892), p. 126. On *ghazi*, see Condos, '"Fanaticism"'; Kolsky, 'Colonial'.

[173] NAI Foreign Political A, September 1887, No. 261: Foreign Secretary to Oliver St. John, Officiating Baluchistan Agent to the Governor-General, 6 August 1887.

[174] *Administration Report of the Baluchistan Agency for 1888–89* (Calcutta: Government Press, 1891), p. 16; *Administration Report of the Baluchistan Agency for 1891–92* (Calcutta: Government Press, 1892), p. 113; IOR/V/23/326: *Administration Report 1892–93*, p. 7; the number in tribal levies is taken from Thornton, Sandeman, pp. 188–90.

[175] Bruce, *Forward*, p. 125.   [176] *Administration Report 1890–91*, p. 119.

[177] For example, *Administration Report 1891–92*, pp. 106–7.

[178] *Administration Report 1890–91*, p. 7; *Administration Report 1891–92*, p. 9.

most direct control indicates that the proclaimed normalisation of government was, in reality, little more than a veneer.

Through a nexus of tribal chiefs and roving British officials, the colonial state's interventions in Balochistan during the late nineteenth century were more substantial than in any other frontier region, including the Naga Hills. However, administration remained patchy and personal rather than uniform and systematic. By the turn of the twentieth century, Balochistan was divided into four distinct regions: British Baluchistan, Agency territories, native states, and tribal areas. Between and within these spatial categories, administrative arrangements were manifold and fluctuating. State penetration was intermittent, with elements of fiscal and legal fixity implemented unevenly and often subject to resistance from local inhabitants. The boundaries between administrative regions in Balochistan remained hazy and prone to frequent alterations.[179] These arrangements were indicative of British officials' determination to retain exceptional spaces even after state expansion had been formalised. Through undertakings such as the dispensation of summary justice at hastily convened jirgas in Makran, tours to delineate sovereign boundaries in Seistan, and variable judicial proceedings in the Zhob Valley, Sandeman and his underlings created frontiers within frontiers, exceptions within exceptions.

5.5   Conclusion: Fashioning Fractals

It might be said that the only aspect of administration in Balochistan that was fixed was the provision of spatially differentiated and discretionary powers for officials 'on the spot'. The year before the formal advent of British Baluchistan, Sandeman (referring to himself in the third person) stated in the Agency's administration report that 'the Agent of the Governor-General has practically taken the place of the Khan as head of the Baloch confederation ... and his mandate naturally commands a great deal more respect and obedience than did ever that of His Highness'.[180] In short, Sandeman positioned himself as the absolute monarch of a region that remained closer to a subsidiary kingdom than a province of British India. The hostility to bureaucracy and normalisation in British Baluchistan was also evident in other schemes of frontier administration in the late nineteenth century. The Political Agencies encompassing patches of the Punjab frontier tapped into the same core principles of tribal recruitment, hazy legal codes, and wide-ranging discretionary authority for officials.[181]

---

[179] Scholz, *Nomadism*, pp. 102–4.
[180] Baluchistan Agency Administration Report, 1886, quoted in Thornton, *Sandeman*, p. 178.
[181] Tripodi, *Edge*, pp. 16–17. On the Gilgit Agency, see Algernon Durand, *The Making of a Frontier: Five Years' Experiences and Adventures in Gilgit, Hunza, Nagar, Chitral, and the Eastern Hindu Kush* (London: John Murray, 1899). On the Khyber Agency, see Warburton, *Eighteen Years*.

As this chapter has shown, colonial interventions encompassed larger frontier populations and became increasingly formalised from the 1860s onwards. These interventions took various forms, from the incorporation of Balochistan and uplands south of Assam into administered British India, to the advent of legal codes targeting ostensibly 'independent' frontier communities. As highlighted in recent work analysing the 1867 Murderous Outrages Act and 1872 Frontier Crimes Regulation as acts of 'lawfare' – control by 'coercive use of legal means' – the latter was especially prevalent along the northwest frontier.[182] Whether limited to the legal sphere or involving broader governmental powers, this synchronous burst of administrative expansion common to northeast and northwest sought to open up new spaces of extreme executive power vested primarily in officials 'on the spot'.

Its progenitors and supporters construed this mode of frontier administration as an escape from the stultifying norms of high imperial bureaucratic government. Among its core principles was the internal variegation of frontier space and population. British laws, taxes, subsidies, recruitment, tours, and punishments constructed frontiers as distinct from normally governed British India; but they also fragmented frontiers, dividing them into innumerable differently governed sub-sections. Mandy Sadan has suggested that the hyper-fragmented social landscape of Kachins from Yunnan to Assam can best be described through the concept of fractals – complexity that does not reduce even at the local scale.[183] At India's frontiers, British officials did not so much suffer from fractal complexity as actively work to create it. Fracturing the frontier into ever-smaller portions was of a piece with a particular persona of the heroic administrator – the lone man immersed in a specific locality and responding instinctively rather than following standardised instructions.

The high imperial version of frontier governmentality represented a subtle but significant shift from that earlier in the nineteenth century. The prominent discourse of 'improvement' that had sat uneasily alongside the violently punitive logic of the 'colonies' and relocations of frontier communities waned, without ever disappearing entirely.[184] Although destructive and subject to significant resistance, the taxes, laws, and recruitment systems that extended over greater numbers of frontier peoples in the later nineteenth century were avowedly limited versions of 'normal' government elsewhere in colonial India and left much to the discretion of individual administrators. Through them, British rule over portions of India's frontiers was formalised but not normalised.

---

[182] The term 'lawfare' and its definition come from John Comaroff, 'Colonialism, Culture, and Law: A Foreword', *Law and Social Inquiry*, 26, 2 (2001), pp. 305–14, here p. 306; quoted in Kolsky, 'Colonial', p. 1244. See also Condos, 'Licence', pp. 485–8.

[183] Sadan, *Kachin*, pp. 20–4.   [184] On this shift in Balochistan, see Gilmartin, *Blood*, pp. 63–5.

Conclusion
The Significance of the Frontier in British India

'On the Outskirts of Empire'

George Curzon didn't quite know what to make of the idea that British India's frontiers were becoming fixed and mastered. Borderlines and borderlands substantially defined Curzon's time as Viceroy from 1899 to 1905, as they did the careers of many less storied contemporaries in the era of high empire. Curzon's 'personal experience' of the fractured and fractious landscapes and communities of Central Asia and India's northwest frontier began with a private trip to the region as a twenty-nine year old in 1888 and 1889.[1] His obsession with empire's edges remained when he returned to the subcontinent as Viceroy – with profound practical consequences. He substantially designed and oversaw the creation of the North-West Frontier Province, carved out of Punjab in 1901. Riding roughshod over a host of complaints from regional administrators, he ensured the Province came under the direct supervision of the Viceroy, thereby making himself a kind of frontiersman-at-a-distance.[2] In justifying this reorganisation, Curzon emphasised 'the special talents that are required for the Frontier' and claimed that these were fundamentally inimical to the virtues of normal administration.[3] His masterminding of the notoriously bloody 'expedition' to Lhasa in 1903 to 1904 and the ill-conceived partition of Bengal shortly before his resignation were wholly in keeping with Curzon's penchant – shared with many agents of high empire – for making and breaking boundaries.[4]

When invited to deliver the prestigious Romanes lecture at Oxford University two years after his departure from India, Curzon chose to speak

---

[1] Curzon, *Frontiers*, p. 4. Curzon's account of this trip, undertaken while he was a British Member of Parliament, was withdrawn from publication when he was appointed Viceroy, and was published only recently: George Curzon, *On the Indian Frontier*, ed. Dhara Anjaria (Karachi: Oxford University Press, 2012). For the manuscript of this text, see MSS Eur F111/119.

[2] MSS Eur F111/319: Curzon, 'Minute on Frontier Administration', 1900. For the complaints of the Punjab Government, see *Report on the Administration of the North-West Frontier Province* (Simla: Punjab Government Press, 1901); David Gilmour, *Curzon: Imperial Statesman 1859–1925* (London: John Murray, 1994), pp. 197–98.

[3] Curzon, 'Minute on Frontier Administration', f. 25.

[4] Gilmour, *Curzon*, pp. 271–7, 287–91, 321–4.

about 'Frontiers'. His interest was theoretical as well as practical, engaging the field of geopolitics that was emerging at that time within the rapidly changing discipline of geography.[5] He devoted the majority of his lecture to establishing frontiers as an object of 'scientific' analysis. Despite being 'the chief anxiety of nearly every Foreign Office in the civilized world', Curzon argued that frontiers had hitherto lacked the systematic thinking that they warranted.[6] Tapping into a well-established discourse of 'natural' and 'artificial' boundaries, he constructed an exhaustively (and, for his audience, perhaps exhaustingly) detailed framework of categories and sub-categories to fill this scholarly void.[7] His was an evolutionary narrative of frontiers, marshalling historical material to tell a tale of how 'the primitive forms, except where resting upon indestructible natural features, have nearly everywhere been replaced by boundaries, the more scientific character of which ... is undoubtedly a preventative of misunderstanding, a check to territorial cupidity, and an agency of peace'.[8] According to this way of thinking, British preponderance on the global stage went hand-in-hand with frontiers as scientific objects: high empire and perfectible boundaries were mutually reinforcing aspects of an increasingly uniform and stable modern world.[9]

Towards the end of his paper, however, Curzon's line of argument shifted.[10] Having extolled the progressive tendency and global similarity of frontiers, he abruptly claimed that

it would be futile to assert that an exact Science of Frontiers has been or is ever likely to be evolved: for no one law can possibly apply to all nations or peoples, to all Governments, all territories, or all climates. The evolution of Frontiers is perhaps an art rather than a science, so plastic and malleable are its forms and manifestations.[11]

From this point in the lecture, Curzon conceptualised frontiers as a thoroughly distinct type of object to that which he had laboriously established. His transition involved a turn to a distinct intellectual lineage – away from 'natural frontier' discourse with a long pedigree in European thought and

---

[5] Gerry Kearns, *Geopolitics and Empire: The Legacy of Halford Mackinder* (Oxford: Oxford University Press, 2009); Agnew, *Geopolitics*.

[6] Curzon, *Frontiers*, pp. 3–4.

[7] On the history of the concept of 'natural borders', see J. J. Fall, 'Artificial States? On the Enduring Myth of Natural Frontiers', *Political Geography*, 29 (2010), pp. 140–7.

[8] Curzon, *Frontiers*, p. 48.

[9] A pair of articles published in the late 1880s made clear Curzon's belief that British leadership was essential to proper boundaries and that Russia in particular could not be trusted to implement 'scientific' frontiers. Curzon, '"Scientific Frontier"'; George N. Curzon, 'The Fluctuating Frontier of Russia in Asia', *The Nineteenth Century: A Monthly Review*, 144 (1889), pp. 267–83.

[10] Historians who have examined Curzon's lecture have tended not to examine this shift. For example, Gardner, 'Moving Watersheds'; Condos and Rand, 'Conciliation', p. 713.

[11] Curzon, *Frontiers*, p. 53.

towards the new world of scholarship on the American frontier.[12] Earlier in the lecture, Curzon had alluded briefly to the United States as an example of an 'artificial frontier' that was necessarily unfixed because of its lack of correspondence to geographical features. It would, he argued, inevitably and properly cease to exist in accordance with a scientifically comprehensible evolutionary process in which weak frontiers were sifted out and only the strong and 'natural' remained. At this late stage of the lecture, he turned to Frederick Jackson Turner's 1893 paper 'The Significance of the Frontier in American History' and put forward a completely different argument.[13] The frontier that he had disparaged as a temporary aberration became the source of the United States' greatness. Following Turner, Curzon proclaimed that 'the entire [American] nation' was 'purified and united in its search for the Frontier'.[14] *This* American frontier was, he insisted, directly relevant to high imperial Britain:

On a widely different arena, but amid kindred travail, the British Empire may be seen shaping the British character, while the British character is building the British Empire. There, too, on the manifold Frontiers of dominions, now amid the gaunt highlands of the Indian border, or the eternal snows of the Himalayas, now on the parched sands of Persia and Arabia, now in the equatorial swamps and forests of Africa, in an incessant struggle with nature and man, has found a corresponding discipline for men of our stock.[15]

In this rendering, frontiers remained globally distributed objects. But their significance lay in their being perpetually open and mutable zones defined by challenging embodied experiences, rather than precise lines to be determined and permanently settled by distant enquiry. It was 'on the outskirts of Empire', Curzon avowed, 'where the machine is relatively impotent and the individual is strong, [that there] is to be found an ennobling and invigorating stimulus for our youth, saving them alike from the corroding ease and morbid excitements of Western civilization'.[16] 'The Frontiers of Empire' were the space of national and racial salvation. And, as Curzon was at pains to emphasise in the penultimate sentence of his lecture, they were not yet fully fixed objects of scientific knowledge brought within the pale of an enervating civilisation but 'continue to beckon'.[17] Britain's imperial frontiers, in Curzon's rendering, had to remain spaces of excess, imagination, and threat, in which conquests were never fully assured.

---

[12] On European 'natural frontier' discourse, see Sahlins, *Boundaries*; Lucien Febvre, '*Frontière*: The Word and the Concept', trans. K. Folka, in Peter Burke (ed.), *A New Kind of History: From the Writings of Febvre* (London: Routledge and Kegan Paul, 1973), pp. 208–18.
[13] For Curzon's annotated copies of Turner's articles, see MSS Eur F112/633. Frederick Jackson Turner, 'The Significance of the Frontier in American History', *Annual Report of the American Historical Association*, 9 (1893), pp. 197–227.
[14] Curzon, *Frontiers*, p. 53.   [15] Ibid., p. 55.   [16] Ibid., pp. 56–57.   [17] Ibid., p. 57.

'The Invisible Shadow'

The deeply ambivalent concept of frontiers in Curzon's 1907 lecture tells us much about their significance to agents of empire in British India around the turn of the twentieth century. In this era, frontiers were conceived of as spaces of tension between closure – in the form of clearly delineated borders, normalised and bureaucratised administration, and authoritative knowledge of people and space – and openness – in the form of spatial, epistemic, and administrative indeterminacy. Historians examining frontiers across the globe during the decades either side of 1900 have tended to focus on closure, suggesting that this period saw the final partition of the world by Euro-American settlement, knowledge, and government.[18] This model works better for settler colonies and the borderlands of North America than for British India.[19] It is tempting to construe the designation of new administrative zones – capped with North-West Frontier Province in 1901 and the North-East Frontier Tracts a decade later[20] – and the related delineation of international boundaries (see Section 1.7) as the closure of frontiers in the colonial subcontinent. The junction of British and Russian surveying in Central Asia's high Pamirs in 1895 and the long-awaited final 'discovery' of the route and main features of the Tsangpo-Brahmaputra River in 1914 might be seen as cartographic counterparts in northwest and northeast, respectively.[21]

This reading overlooks not only ongoing challenges to colonial schemes by frontier terrain and inhabitants, but also that that many British personnel engaged at India's frontiers sought to subvert the very processes of closure in which they were actively complicit. Building on Antoinette Burton's contention that 'empire was made – as in, constituted by – the very trouble its efforts and practices provoked', we might say that at India's frontiers agents of empire generated and revelled in such trouble rather than merely suffering it.[22] Administrators periodically railed against fixed borderlines and legal codes, surveyors sometimes disputed the value of maps, ethnographers frequently doubted the possibility of meaningful visual and written representations, and

---

[18] For example, Adelman and Aron, 'Borderlands'; Osterhammel, *Transformation*, pp. 322–91; William O'Reilly, 'Frederick Jackson Turner's Frontier Thesis, Orientalism, and the Austrian *Militärgrenze*', *Journal of Austrian-American History*, 2, 1 (2018), pp. 1–30.

[19] On North American borderlands around the turn of the twentieth century, see Readman, Radding, and Bryant, 'Introduction', here pp. 5–7; Hämäläinen, *Comanche*, pp. 321–41. On British settler colonies, see Belich, *Replenishing*.

[20] On the definition of the North-East Frontier Tracts, see NAI Foreign External A, 04/1915, Nos. 4–10.

[21] On the Pamirs survey, see Holdich, *Indian Borderland*, pp. 284–313; Strahan, *General Report 1894–95*, pp. 89–90. On the Tsangpo-Brahmaputra, see Arupjyoti Saikia, *The Unquiet River: A Biography of the Brahmaputra* (Delhi: Oxford University Press, 2019).

[22] Antoinette Burton, *The Trouble with Empire: Challenges to Modern British Imperialism* (Oxford: Oxford University Press, 2015), p. 11.

soldiers on occasion acknowledged the farcical nature of frontier violence. These colonial personnel often went to extraordinary lengths to maintain some degree of openness at frontiers, seeing this as bound up in their masculine, national, and racial identities.[23] Curzon alluded to the entanglement of frontier making and active self-fashioning when he spoke of 'our twentieth century Marcher Lords', for whom 'the breath of the Frontier has entered their nostrils and infused their being'.[24] Like Thomas Lewin, considered at the very start of this book, many engaged in 'on-the-spot' frontier work shared Curzon's conviction in the necessity and value of becoming a frontiersman and changing oneself in the act of engaging frontier terrain and peoples. They insisted on constructing India's frontiers as exceptional and elusive spaces, performing their own versions of Curzon's swerve late in his lecture away from apparently inexorable processes of incorporating and stabilising peripheral regions. To many of those engaged in imagining and enacting British India's frontiers, complete closure would constitute not the final validation of imperial rule and their own roles but the point at which these self-destructed.

Of course, frontiers were not only zones of self-fashioning for the small cadre of British personnel stationed at empire's edges. Just as the frontier was significant for the officials, institutions, and materials that comprised British India, so colonialism was hugely significant for India's frontier. British activities and imaginaries had substantial effects in terms of rendering frontier inhabitants and spaces exceptional relative to the rest of the subcontinent. Their impact has persisted: tensions between intervention and withdrawal, 'development' and violence, and spatial definition and haziness continued to dominate state engagements with these regions into the postcolonial era.[25] In understanding the destructive effects of British interventions, this book has shown that it is vital to view colonial power as fragmented and fractious. Frontier-making projects were heterogeneous from the outset: agents of empire did not think with one mind, and ambiguities went all the way down, with individual officials often split between contradictory logics. The terrain and peoples of India's frontiers further 'disturbed' colonial projects, causing some to fail and others to be substantially reshaped.[26] The outskirts of empire came to be considered key locales of surveying and ethnography even as – and in part precisely because – they defied extant ways of understanding spatial and human diversity. They similarly resisted conventional means of setting boundaries,

---

[23] On the anxieties feeding cultures of race and masculinity in late nineteenth-century Europe, see for example, Patrick Brantlinger, *Rule of Darkness: British Literature and Imperialism, 1830–1914* (Ithaca, NY: Cornell University Press, 1988), pp. 227–54; Pick, *Faces*.

[24] Curzon, *Frontiers*, p. 56.

[25] On these lasting effects in the northeast, see Baruah, *Durable Disorder*; in the northwest, see Akbar Ahmed, *The Thistle and the Drone: How America's War on Terror Became a Global War on Tribal Islam* (New Delhi: HarperCollins, 2013).

[26] Driver, 'Distance'.

establishing state sovereignty, and governing populations. As in the case of the field sciences, these administrative challenges were productive for agents of empire, justifying repeated re-engagements with frontier locales and validating new methods rooted in heroic ideals.

Ranging across the nineteenth century, this book has shown that processes of knowing and governing people and space did not dissolve dissensus and resolve variation over time. Quite the opposite: colonial interventions constituted India's frontiers as zones in which these qualities were permanently locked in. The notion that these were 'other spaces', resistant to methods practised elsewhere in the Subcontinent and requiring distinctive types of knowledge and government, became ever more embedded as the nineteenth century progressed. Although British engagements with these areas intensified from the mid-1860s onwards, these projects became, in some important respects, less ambitious. Whereas colonial personnel of the mid-nineteenth century tended to act in accordance with the idea that frontiers could be altered and understood, their successors operated more on the basis that these spaces and populations were insurmountably distinctive and elusive. As such, frontiers were to many agents of empire disruptive but also enormously significant – spaces of salvation and excess in an imperial world that seemed ever more regulated and stultifying. British India's frontier was 'the invisible shadow' cast by, but functioning in opposition to, the forms of fixing, settling, and normalising that epitomised high imperial space, science, and power.[27]

---

[27] Heidegger conceives of 'the invisible shadow' as 'a space withdrawn from representation', projected by, yet undercutting, man's capacity to 'calculate completely' in the 'modern age': 'Age', pp. 134–6.

Bibliography

Archival Collections

Assam State Archives, Dispur (ASA)
  Assam Administration Reports
  Assam Commissioner Papers
  Bengal Government Papers
  Irregular Reports on Frontier Affairs
  Maps Collection
British Library, London, India Office Records (IOR)
  Additional Manuscripts Collection (Add MSS)
    Ripon Papers
  Board of Control Collections (F/4)
  Correspondence with India (E/4)
  Drawing Collection
    Postans Album (WD485)
  European Manuscripts (MSS Eur)
    Curzon Papers (F111, F112)
    Durand Papers (D727)
    Jenkins Papers (F257)
    Pearse Papers (E417)
    Risley Papers (E295)
    Thomas Papers (F171)
    Younghusband Papers (F197)
  Frontier Operations Reports (L/PARL/2/284)
  Irregular Official Reports (V/27)
  Maps (X)
  Provincial Administration Reports (V/10)
  Photo Collections (Photo)
    Bailey (Photo 1083)
    Bellew (Photo 50/1)
    Bourne and Shepherd (Photo 576)
    Burke (Photo 487, Photo 1054)
    Burke and Baker (Photo 6)
    Holmes (Photo 627)
    Macnabb (Photo 752/12)
    Montgomerie (Photo 25)

Tanner (Photo 143)
Political and Secret Department (L/P&S)
Proceedings of Provincial/Presidency Governments (P)
Selections from the Records of the Government of India (V/23)
Survey of India Annual Reports (V/24)
Cambridge University Library, Cambridge (CUL)
Maps Collection
Centre of South Asian Studies, Cambridge (CSAS)
Macgregor Collection
Stewart Collection
Maharashtra State Archives, Mumbai (MSA)
Political Department Files
National Archives of India, New Delhi (NAI)
Cartographic Section
Historical Maps of the Survey of India
Dehra Dun Volumes
Foreign Department
External Consultations
Political Consultations
Secret Consultations
Secret Supplement
Military Department
Pitt Rivers Museum, Oxford (PRM)
Woodthorpe Collection
Hutton Collection
Mills Collection
Punjab State Archives, Chandigarh (PSA)
Foreign Department Files
Royal Anthropological Institute, London (RAI)
Council Minutes
Godden Papers (MS 39, MS 40, MS 156)
Woodthorpe Papers (MS 442)
Royal Geographical Society, London (RGS)
Holdich Paintings (X610)
Walker Papers (JWA)
Younghusband Papers (CB7, GFY)
Senate House Library, London
Lewin Papers (811-II)
United Services Institute, New Delhi (USI)

Primary Published Works

Anon, 'Report of the Board: Mission to Asam', *The Baptist Missionary Magazine*, 22 (1841), p. 192
Anon, *General Report on the Administration of the Punjab for the Years 1849–50 and 1850–51* (Lahore: Punjab Government Press, 1851)

Anon, *Frontier and Overseas Expeditions from India*, four vols. (Simla: Government Monotype Press, 1907–1910)

Anon, *The Imperial Gazetteer of India Vol. XXVI: Atlas* (Oxford: Clarendon Press, 1909)

An Officer [John Butler], *A Sketch of Assam with Some Account of the Hill Tribes* (London: Smith, Elder and Co., 1847)

Allen, B. C., *Census of India, 1901. Volume IV. Assam. Part I. Report* (Shillong: Assam Secretariat, 1902)

Andrew, W. P., *Our Scientific Frontier* (London: W.H. Allen & Co., 1880)

Baines, J. A., *General Report on the Census of India, 1891* (London: Eyre and Spottiswoode, 1893)

Barton, William, *India's North-West Frontier* (London: John Murray, 1939)

Bigge, H. 'Despatch from Lieut. H. Bigge, Assistant Agent, Detached to the Naga Hills, to Capt. Jenkins, Agent Governor General, N.E. Frontier, Communicated from the Political Secretariat of India to the Secretary to the Asiatic Society', *Journal of the Asiatic Society of Bengal*, 110 (1841), pp. 129–36

Brodie, Capt., 'Narrative of a Tour over That Part of the Naga Hills Lying between the Diko and Dyang River', *Journal of the Asiatic Society of Bengal*, 168 (1845) pp. 828–44

Browne Wood, Mr., 'Extracts from a Report of a Journey into the Naga Hills in 1844', *Journal of the Asiatic Society of Bengal*, no.154 (1844), pp. 771–85

Bruce, C. G., *Twenty Years in the Himalaya* (London: Edward Arnold, 1910)

Bruce, Richard Isaac, *The Forward Policy and Its Results, or Thirty-Five Years' Work Amongst the Tribes on Our North-Western Frontier of India* (London: Longmans, Green, and Co., 1900)

Burnes, Alexander, *Travels into Bokhara; Being an Account of a Journey from India to Cabool, Tartary, and Persia* (London: John Murray, 1834)

Burnes, Alexander, 'On the Siah-posh Kaffirs with Specimens of Their Language and Costume', *Journal of the Asiatic Society of Bengal*, 7 (1838), pp. 325–33

Burnes, Alexander, *Cabool: A Personal Narrative of a Journey to, and Residence in that City in the Years 1836, 7, and 8* (London: Carey and Hart, 1843)

Butler, John, 'Rough Notes on the Angami Nagas', *Journal of the Asiatic Society of Bengal*, 44 (1875), pp. 307–46

Butler, John, *Volume I: Tour Diary of the Deputy Commissioner, Naga Hills. 1870* (Shillong: Assam Government Press, 1942)

Churchill, Winston Spencer, *The Story of the Malakand Field Force: An Episode of Frontier War* (London: Longmans, Green, and Co., 1899)

Conrad, Joseph, *Heart of Darkness* (London: Penguin, 1995 [1902])

Crooke, W., *Natives of Northern India* (London: Archibald Constable, 1907)

Crooke, W., 'The Stability of Caste and Tribal Groups in India', *The Journal of the Royal Anthropological Institute of Great Britain and Ireland*, 44 (1914), pp. 270–80

Curzon, George N., 'The "Scientific Frontier": An Accomplished Fact', *The Nineteenth Century: A Monthly Review*, 136 (1888), pp. 901–17

Curzon, George N., 'The Fluctuating Frontier of Russia in Asia', *The Nineteenth Century: A Monthly Review*, 144 (1889), pp. 267–83

Curzon of Kedleston, Lord G., *The Romanes Lecture 1907: Frontiers* (Oxford: Clarendon, 1907)

Curzon of Kedleston, Lord G., *On the Indian Frontier*, (ed.), Dhara Anjaria (Karachi: Oxford University Press, 2012)

Dacosta, John, *A Scientific Frontier; or, the Danger of a Russian Invasion of India* (London: W.H. Allen & Co., 1891)

Dalton, Edward Tuite, *Descriptive Ethnology of Bengal* (Calcutta: Office of the Superintendent of Government Printing, 1872)

Dames, M. Longworth, *A Text Book of the Balochi Language, Consisting of Miscellaneous Stories, Legends, Poems, and Balochi-English Vocabulary* (Lahore: Government Press, 1891)

Durand, Algernon, *The Making of a Frontier: Five years' Experiences and Adventures in Gilgit, Hunza, Nagar, Chitral, and the Eastern Hindu Kush* (London: John Murray, 1899)

Edwardes, Herbert, *A Year on the Punjab Frontier, in 1848–49* (London: Richard Bentley, 1851)

Elphinstone, Mountstuart, *An Account of the Kingdom of Caubul, and its Dependencies, in Persia, Tartary, and India* (London: Longman, Hurst, Rees, Orme, and Brown, 1815)

Elphinstone, Mountstuart, *An Account of the Kingdom of Caubul, and its Dependencies, in Persia, Tartary, and India*, 3rd ed. (London: Richard Bentley, 1839)

Forster, George, *A Journey from Bengal to England* (Calcutta, 1790)

Gait, E. A., *Census of India, 1891. Assam. Vol. I—Report* (Shillong: Assam Secretariat Printing Office, 1892)

Gait, E. A., *Census of India, 1911. Volume I. India. Part I—Report* (Calcutta: Government Press, 1913)

Godden, Gertrude M., 'Naga and Other Frontier Tribes of North-East India', *The Journal of the Anthropological Institute of Great Britain and Ireland*, 26 (1897), pp. 161–201

Godden, Gertrude M., 'Naga and Other Frontier Tribes of North-East India (continued)', *The Journal of the Anthropological Institute of Great Britain and Ireland*, 27 (1898), pp. 2–51

Grange, E. R., 'Extracts from the Narrative of an Expedition into the Naga Territory of Assam', *Journal of the Asiatic Society*, 90 (1839), pp. 445–70

Grange, E. R., 'Extracts from the Journal of an Expedition into the Naga Hills on the Assam Frontier', *Journal of the Asiatic Society*, 106 (1840), pp. 947–66

Griffith, William, 'Journal of a Visit to the Mishmee Hills in Assam', *Journal of the Asiatic Society of Bengal*, 65 (1837), pp. 325–41

Griffith, William, *Journal of Travels in Assam, Burma, Bootan, Affghanistan and the Neighbouring Countries* (Calcutta: Bishop's College Press, 1847)

Gurdon, P. R. T., *The Khasis*, 2nd ed. (London: Macmillan & Co., 1914)

Hanna, H. B., *India's Scientific Frontier: Where Is It? What Is It?* (London, Westminster: Archibald Constable and Company, 1895)

Hasrat, Bikrama Jit (ed.), *The Punjab Papers: Selections from the private papers of Lord Auckland, Lord Ellenborough, Viscount Hardinge, and the Marquis of Dalhousie, 1836–1849, on the Sikhs* (Hoshiarpur: V.V. Research Institute, 1970)

Hobson, J. A., *Imperialism: A Study* (Ann Arbor, MI: University of Michigan Press, 1965)

Hodgson, B. H., *On the Aborigines of India. Essay the First; on the Kooch, Bodo and Dhimal tribes* (Calcutta: Baptist Mission Press, 1847)

Hodgson, B. H., 'On the Aborigines of the Eastern Frontier', *Journal of the Asiatic Society of Bengal*, 18 (1849), pp. 967–75

Hodgson, B. H., 'Aborigines of the North East Frontier', *Journal of the Asiatic Society of Bengal*, 19 (1850), pp. 309–16

Holdich, T. H., 'Obituary: Major-General R.G. Woodthorpe, C.B., R.E.', *The Geographical Journal*, 12, 2 (1898), pp. 195–201

Holdich, T. H., 'The Use of Practical Geography Illustrated by Recent Frontier Operations', *The Geographical Journal*, 13, 5 (1899), pp. 465–77

Holdich, T. H., 'The Arab Tribes of Our Indian Frontier', *The Journal of the Anthropological Institute of Great Britain and Ireland*, 29, 1/2 (1899), pp. 10–20

Holdich, Thomas H., *The Indian Borderland 1880–1900* (London: Methuen, 1901)

H[oldich], T. H., 'Report of the Indian Survey Committee, 1904–1905', *The Geographical Journal*, 27, 4 (1906), pp. 392–5

Holdich, Thomas H., *Political Frontiers and Boundary Making* (London: Macmillan, 1916)

Howell, Evelyn, *Mizh: A Monograph on Government's Relations with the Mahsud Tribe* (Karachi: Oxford University Press, 1979 [1931])

Hughes-Buller, R., *Census of India—1901. Volume V. Baluchistan. Part I—Report* (Bombay: Times of India Press, 1902)

Hunter, W. W., *Our Indian Musalmans: Are They Bound in Conscience to Rebel Against the Queen?* (London: Trübner & Company, 1871)

Hutton, J. H., *The Angami Nagas: With Some Notes on Neighbouring Tribes* (London: Macmillan and Co., 1921)

Hutton, J. H., 'The Significance of Head-Hunting in Assam', *The Journal of the Royal Anthropological Institute of Great Britain and Ireland*, 58 (1928), pp. 399–408

Ibbetson, Denzil, *Panjab Castes* (Lahore: Government Press, 1916)

Leech, Robert, 'Brief History of Kalat, Brought Down to the Deposition and Death of Mehrab Khan, Braho-ee', *Journal of the Asiatic Society of Bengal*, 12 (1843), pp. 473–512

Leitner, G. W., 'Siah Posh Kafirs', *The Journal of the Anthropological Institute of Great Britain and Ireland*, 3 (1874), pp. 341–69

Lewin, T. H., *The Hill Tracts of Chittagong and the Dwellers Therein; With Comparative Vocabularies of the Hill Dialects* (Calcutta: Bengal Printing Company, 1869)

Lewin, T. H., *A Fly on the Wheel, or How I Helped to Govern India* (London: W.H. Allen & Co., 1885)

Lockhart, W. S. A. and R. G. Woodthorpe, *The Gilgit Mission 1885–86* (London: Eyre and Spottiswoode, 1889)

Macgregor, Charles Metcalfe, *Wanderings in Balochistan* (London: W.H. Allen & Co., 1882)

Mackenzie, Alexander, *History of the Relations of the Government with the Hill Tribes of the North-East Frontier of Bengal* (Calcutta: Home Department Press, 1884)

Markham, Clements R., *A Memoir on the Indian Surveys*, 2nd ed. (London: W.H. Allen and Co., 1878)

Masson, Charles, *Narrative of a Journey to Kalat, Including an Account of the Insurrection at that Place in 1840; and a Memoir on Eastern Balochistan* (London: Richard Bentley, 1843)

Maynard, F. P. (ed.), *Letters on the Baluch-Afghan Boundary Commission of 1896* (Calcutta: Baptist Missionary Press, 1896)

McCosh, J., 'Account of the Mountain Tribes on the Extreme N.E. Frontier of Bengal', *Journal of the Asiatic Society of Bengal*, no.52 (1836), pp. 193–208

M'Cosh, John, *Topography of Assam* (Calcutta: Bengal Military Orphan Press, 1837)

McLennan, John F., *Primitive Marriage: An Inquiry into the Origin of the Form of Capture in Marriage Ceremonies* (Edinburgh: Adam and Charles Black, 1865)

Mills, J. P., 'Certain Aspects of Naga Culture', *The Journal of the Royal Anthropological Institute of Great Britain and Ireland*, 56 (1926), pp. 27–35

Neufville, John Bryan, 'On the Geography and Population of Assam', *Asiatic Researches*, 16 (1828), pp. 331–52

Oliver, Edward E., *Across the Border or Pathan and Biloch* (London: Chapman and Hall, 1890)

Orwell, George, *Shooting an Elephant and Other Essays* (London: Penguin, 2003)

Peale, S. E., 'The Nagas and Neighbouring Tribes', *The Journal of the Anthropological Institute of Great Britain and Ireland*, 3 (1874), pp. 476–81

Pelly, Lewis (ed.), *The Views and Opinions of Brigadier-General John Jacob, C.B.*, 2nd ed. (London: Smith, Elder & Co., 1858)

Pemberton, R. B., *The Eastern Frontier of India* (Calcutta: J.B. Tassin, 1835)

Postans, J. [Thomas], 'Report on Upper Sindh and the Eastern Portion of Cutchee, with a Memorandum on the Beloochee and Other Tribes of Upper Sinde and Cutchee, and a Map of Part of the Country Referred to', *Journal of the Asiatic Society of Bengal*, 12 (1843), pp. 23–44

Postans, Thomas, *Personal Observations on Sindh* (London: Longman, Brown, Green, and Longmans, 1843)

Postans, T., 'On the Biluchi Tribes Inhabiting Sindh in the Lower Valley of the Indus and Cutchi', *Journal of the Ethnological Society of London*, 1 (1848), pp. 103–26

Pottinger, Henry, *Travels in Beloochistan and Sinde* (London: Longman, Hurst, Rees, Orme, and Brown, 1816)

Prichard, James Cowles, *Researches Into the Physical History of Man* (London: John and Arthur Arch, 1813)

Prichard, James Cowles, *Researches Into the Physical History of Mankind*, 3rd ed. in five vols. (London: Sherwood, Gilbert, and Piper, 1836–1847)

Raverty, H. G., *A grammar of the Pukhto, Pushto, or language of the Afghans* (Calcutta: Baptist Mission Press, 1855)

Raverty, H. G., 'Notes on Kafiristan', *Journal of the Asiatic Society of Bengal*, 28 (1859), pp. 317–68

Reid, Robert, *History of the Frontier Areas Bordering On Assam from 1883–1941* (Shillong: Assam Government Press, 1942)

Risley, H. H., *The Tribes and Castes of Bengal. Ethnographic Glossary, Volume I* (Calcutta: Bengal Secretariat Press, 1891)

Risley, H. H., *The Tribes and Castes of Bengal. Ethnographic Glossary, Volume II* (Calcutta: Bengal Secretariat Press, 1891)

Risley, H. H. and E. A. Gait, *Census of India, 1901. Volume I. India. Part I—Report* (Calcutta: Government Press, 1903)

Risley, Herbert, *The People of India* (Calcutta and Simla: Thacker, Spink & Co.; London: W. Thacker & Co., 1908)

Risley, Herbert, 'Presidential Address. The Methods of Ethnography', *The Journal of the Royal Anthropological of Great Britain and Ireland*, 41 (1911), pp. 8–19

Risley, Herbert, *The People of India*, 2nd ed., W. Crooke (ed.) (Calcutta and Simla: Thacker, Spink & Co.; London:W. Thacker & Co., 1915)

Robertson, George Scott, *The Kafirs of the Hindu-Kush* (London: Lawrence & Bullen, 1896)

Robinson, William, *A Descriptive Account of Asam* (Calcutta: Ostell and Lepage, 1841)

Robinson, William, 'Notes on the Languages Spoken by the Various Tribes Inhabiting the Valley of Asam and Its Mountain Confines', *Journal of the Asiatic Society of Bengal*, 27 (1849), pp. 183–237, 310–49

Rose, Archibald, 'Chinese Frontiers of India', *The Geographical Journal*, 39, 3 (1912), pp. 193–218

Scott, J. G., *Burma: From the Earliest Times to the Present Day* (London: T. Fisher Unwin, 1924)

Shakespear, J., *The Lushei Kuki Clans* (London: Macmillan and Co., 1912)

Tanner, H. C. B., 'Our Present Knowledge of the Himalayas', *Proceedings of the Royal Geographical Society and Monthly Record of Geography*, 13, 7 (1891), pp. 403–23

Tate, G. P., *The Frontiers of Baluchistan: Travels on the Borders of Persia and Afghanistan* (London: Witherby & Co., 1909)

Temple, R. H., *Report showing the relations of the British Government with the tribes on the North-West Frontier of the Punjab, from Annexation in 1849 to the Close of 1855* (Lahore: Punjab Government Press, 1856)

Temple, Richard and R. H. Davies, *Report showing the relations of the British Government with the tribes on the North-West Frontier of the Punjab, from Annexation in 1849 to the Close of 1855; and Continuation of the Same to August 1864* (Lahore: Punjab Government Press, 1865)

Thorburn, S. S., *Bannu; or Our Afghan Frontier* (London: Trübner & Co., 1876)

Thornton, Thomas Henry, *Colonel Sir Robert Sandeman: His Life and Work on Our Indian Frontier* (London: John Murray, 1895)

Tucker, A. L. P., *Sir Robert G. Sandeman: Peaceful Conqueror of Baluchistan* (New York: Macmillan, 1921)

Turner, Frederick Jackson, 'The Significance of the Frontier in American History', *Annual Report of the American Historical Association*, 9 (1893), pp. 197–227

Waddell, L. A., 'The Tribes of the Brahmaputra Valley:—A Contribution on Their Physical Types and Affinities', *Journal of the Asiatic Society of Bengal*, 69, pt. 3 (1900), pp. 1–127

Walker, J. T., 'On the Methods of Determining Heights in the Trigonometrical Survey of India', *Memoirs of the Royal Astronomical Society*, 33 (1863–4), pp. 103–14

Walker, J. T., 'Four Years' Journeyings Through Great Tibet, by One of the Trans-Himalayan Explorers of the Survey of India', *Proceedings of the Royal Geographical Society and Monthly Record of Geography*, 7, 2 (1885), pp. 65–92

Warburton, Robert, *Eighteen Years in the Khyber: 1879–1898* (London: John Murray, 1900)

Watson, J. Forbes and John William Kaye, *The People of India. A Series of Photographic Illustrations, with Descriptive Letterpress, on the Races and Tribes of Hindustan*, 8 vols. (London: India Museum, 1868–1875)

White, Adam *Memoir of the late David Scott, Esq. Agent to the Governor-General, on the North-East Frontier of Bengal* (Calcutta: Baptist Mission, 1832)

Wilcox, R., 'Memoir of a Survey of Asam and the Neighbouring Countries, executed in 1825–6-7-8', *Asiatic Researches*, 17 (1832), pp. 314–469

Wilson, H. H., *Documents Illustrative of the Burmese War. With an Introductory Sketch of the Events of the War, and an Appendix* (Calcutta: Government Gazette Press, 1827)

Woodthorpe, R. G., *The Lushai Expedition* (London: Hurst and Blackett, 1873)

Woodthorpe, R. G., 'Notes on the Wild Tribes Inhabiting the So-Called Naga Hills, on Our North-East Frontier of India. Part I', *The Journal of the Anthropological Institute of Great Britain and Ireland*, 11 (1882), pp. 56–73

Woodthorpe, R. G., 'Notes on the Wild Tribes Inhabiting the So-Called Naga Hills, on Our North-East Frontier of India. Part II', *The Journal of the Anthropological Institute of Great Britain and Ireland*, 11 (1882), pp. 196–214

Woodthorpe, R. G., 'Explorations on the Chindwin River, Upper Burma', *Proceedings of the Royal Geographical Society and Monthly Record of Geography*, 11, 1 (1889), pp. 197–216

Woodthorpe, R. G., 'The Country of the Shans', *The Geographical Journal*, 7, 6 (1896), pp. 577–600

Woodthorpe, R. G., 'Some Account of the Shans and Hill Tribes on the State of the Mekong', *Journal of the Anthropological Institute of Great Britain and Ireland*, 26 (1897), pp. 13–28

Wylly, H. C., *From the Black Mountain to Waziristan* (London: Macmillan, 1912)

Younghusband, F. E., *Report of a Mission to the Northern Frontier of Kashmir in 1889* (Calcutta: Government of India Press, 1890)

Younghusband, F. E., 'Chitral, Hunza, and the Hindu Kush', *The Geographical Journal*, 5, 5 (1895), pp. 409–26

Younghusband, Francis, *Kashmir* (London: Adam and Charles Black, 1909)

Secondary Published Works

Adelman, Jeremy and Stephen Aron, 'From Borderlands to Borders: Empires, Nation-States, and the Peoples in between in North American History', *American Historical Review*, 104, 3 (1999), pp. 814–41

Agamben, Giorgio, *Homo Sacer: Sovereign Power and Bare Life*, trans. Daniel Heller-Roazen (Stanford, CA: Stanford University Press, 1998)

Agnew, John, *Geopolitics: Re-visioning world politics*, 2nd ed. (London: Routledge, 2003)

Agnew, John, 'Borders on the Mind: Re-framing Border Thinking', *Ethics & Global Politics*, 1, 4 (2008), pp. 175–91

Agnew, John, 'The Hobbesian Excuse: Where Is Sovereignty and Why Does It Matter?', in Saul Takahashi (ed.), *Human Rights, Human Security, and State Security: The Intersection* (Santa Barbara, CA: Praeger, 2014), pp. 119–36

Ahmed, Akbar, *The Thistle and the Drone: How America's War on Terror Became a Global War on Tribal Islam* (New Delhi: HarperCollins, 2013)

Ali, Imran, *The Punjab under Imperialism, 1885–1947* (Princeton, NJ: Princeton University Press, 1988)

Amrith, Sunil, *Unruly Waters: How Mountain Rivers and Monsoons Have Shaped South Asia's History* (London: Allen Lane, 2018)

Anderson, Clare, 'Oscar Mallitte's Andaman Photographs, 1857–8', *History Workshop Journal*, 67 (2009), pp. 152–72

Appadurai, Arjun, 'Number in the Colonial Imagination', in Carol A. Breckenridge and Peter van der Veer (eds.), *Orientalism and the Postcolonial Predicament* (Philadelphia, PA: University of Pennsylvania Press, 1993), pp. 314–40

Arendt, Hannah, *The Origins of Totalitarianism*, 3rd ed. (London: George Allen & Unwin, 1967)

Arnold, David, *The Tropics and the Traveling Gaze: India, Landscape, and Science 1800–1856* (Delhi: Permanent Black, 2005)

Asad, Talal, 'Introduction', in Talal, Asad, (ed.), *Anthropology and the Colonial Encounter* (Atlantic Highlands, NJ: Humanities Press, 1973), pp. 9–19

Azoulay, Ariella, *The Civil Contract of Photography* (New York, NY: Zone Books, 2008)

Ballantyne, Tony, *Orientalism and Race: Aryanism in the British Empire* (Basingstoke: Palgrave Macmillan, 2002)

Barooah, Nirode K., *David Scott in North-East India, 1802–1831: A Study in British Paternalism* (New Delhi: Munshram Manoharlal, 1970)

Barrier, N. Gerald, 'The Punjab Disturbances of 1907: The Response of the British Government to Agrarian Unrest', *Modern Asian Studies*, 1, 4 (1967), pp. 353–83

Baruah, Sanjib, *Durable Disorder: Understanding the Politics of Northeast India* (New Delhi: Oxford University Press, 2005)

Basalla, George, 'The Spread of Western Science', *Science*, 156, 3775 (1967), pp. 611–22

Bates, Crispin, 'Race, Caste, and Tribe in Central India: The Early Origins of Indian Anthropometry', in Peter Robb (ed.), *The Concept of Race in South Asia* (Delhi: Oxford University Press, 1995), pp. 219–59

Bayly, C. A., *Indian Society and the Making of the British Empire* (Cambridge: Cambridge University Press, 1988)

Bayly, C. A., 'From Company to Crown. Nineteenth-Century India and Its Visual Representation', in id (ed.), *The Raj: India and the British 1600–1947* (London: National Portrait Gallery, 1990), pp. 130–40

Bayly, C. A., *Empire and Information: Intelligence Gathering and Social Communication in India, 1780–1870* (Cambridge: Cambridge University Press, 1996)

Bayly, C. A., *The Birth of the Modern World: 1870–1914* (Oxford: Blackwell, 2004)

Bayly, Susan, *Caste, Society and Politics in India from the Eighteenth Century to the Modern Age* (Cambridge: Cambridge University Press, 1999)

Bayly, Martin, *Taming the Imperial Imagination: Colonial Knowledge, International Relations, and the Anglo-Afghan Encounter, 1808–1878* (Cambridge: Cambridge University Press, 2016)

Belich, James, *Replenishing the Earth: The Settler Revolution and the Rise of the Anglo-World, 1783–1939* (Oxford: Oxford University Press, 2009)

Benjamin, Walter, 'Critique of Violence', in M. Bullock and M. W, Jennings (eds.), *Selected Writings* (Cambridge, MA: Harvard University Press, 1996)

Benton, Lauren, *A Search for Sovereignty: Law and Geography in European Empires, 1400–1900* (Cambridge: Cambridge University Press, 2010)

Berg, E. and H. van Houtum (eds.), *Routing Borders between Territories, Discourses and Practices* (Aldershot: Ashgate, 2003)

Bergmann, Christoph, 'Confluent Territories and Overlapping Sovereignties: Britain's Nineteenth-Century Indian Empire in the Kumaon Himalaya', *Journal of Historical Geography*, 51 (2016), pp. 88–98

Beverley, Eric Lewis, 'Frontier as Resource: Law, Crime, and Sovereignty on the Margins of Empire', *Comparative Studies in Society and History*, 55, 2 (2013), pp. 241–72

Bhadra, Gautam, 'Two Frontier Uprisings in Mughal India', in Ranajit Guha (ed.), *Subaltern Studies II: Writings on South Asian History and Society* (Delhi: Oxford University Press, 1983, pp. 43–59

Bourguet, Marie-Noëlle, Christian Licoppe and H. Otto Sibum (eds.), *Instruments, Travel and Science: Itineraries of Precision from the Seventeenth to the Twentieth Century* (London: Routledge, 2002)

Bourguet, Marie-Noëlle, 'A Portable World: The Notebooks of European Travellers (Eighteenth to Nineteenth Centuries)', *Intellectual History Review*, 20, 3 (2010), pp. 377–400

Brantlinger, Patrick, *Rule of Darkness: British Literature and Imperialism, 1830–1914* (Ithaca, NY: Cornell University Press, 1988)

Breckenridge, Keith, 'No Will to Know: The Rise and Fall of African Civil Registration in Twentieth-Century South Africa', *Proceedings of the British Academy*, 182 (2012), pp. 357–83

Breckenridge, Keith, *Biometric State: The Global Politics of Identification and Surveillance in South Africa, 1850 to the Present* (Cambridge: Cambridge University Press, 2014)

Burnett, D. Graham, *Masters of All They Surveyed: Exploration, Geography, and a British El Dorado* (Chicago and London: University of Chicago Press, 2000)

Burton, Antoinette, *The Trouble With Empire: Challenges to Modern British Imperialism* (Oxford: Oxford University Press, 2015)

Cannon, Garland, *The Life and Mind of Oriental Jones: Sir William Jones, the Father of Modern Linguistics* (Cambridge: Cambridge University Press, 1990)

Cederlöf, Gunnel, 'Fixed Boundaries, Fluid Landscapes: British Expansion into Northern East Bengal in the 1820s', *Indian Economic and Social History Review*, 46, 4 (2009), pp. 513–40

Cederlöf, Gunnel, *Founding an Empire on India's North-Eastern Frontiers, 1790–1840: Climate, Commerce, Polity* (New Delhi: Oxford University Press, 2014)

Chakrabarti, Pratik, *Western Science in Modern India: Metropolitan Methods, Colonial Practices* (New Delhi: Permanent Black, 2004)

Chakrabarty, Dipesh, *Provincializing Europe: Postcolonial Thought and Historical Difference*, 2nd ed. (Princeton, NJ: Princeton University Press, 2008)

Chartier, Roger, *The Order of Books: Readers, Authors, and Libraries in Europe between the Fourteenth and Eighteenth Centuries*, trans. Lydia G. Cochrane (London: Polity, 1994)

Chatterjee, Partha, *The Nation and Its Fragments: Colonial and Postcolonial Histories* (Princeton, NJ: Princeton University Press, 1993)

Choudhury, Deep Kanta Lahiri, *Telegraphic Imperialism: Crisis and Panic in the Indian Empire, c.1830–1920* (Basingstoke: Palgrave Macmillan, 2010)

Clayton, Daniel W., *Islands of Truth: The Imperial Fashioning of Vancouver Island* (Vancouver: UBC Press, 1999)

Cohn, Bernard S., *An anthropologist among the Historians and Other Essays* (Delhi: Oxford University Press, 1987)

Cohn, Bernard S., *Colonialism and Its Forms of Knowledge: The British in India* (Princeton, NJ: Princeton University Press, 1996)

Collingham, Elizabeth, *Imperial Bodies: The Physical Experience of the Raj, c.1800–1947* (Cambridge: Polity, 2001)

Comaroff, John, 'Colonialism, Culture, and Law: A Foreword', *Law and Social Inquiry*, 26, 2 (2001), pp. 305–14

Condos, Mark, 'Licence to Kill: The Murderous Outrages Act and the Rule of Law in Colonial India, 1867–1925', *Modern Asian Studies*, 50, 2 (2016), pp. 479–517

Condos, Mark, '"Fanaticism" and the Politics of Resistance along the North-West Frontier of British India', *Comparative Studies in Society and History*, 58, 3 (2016), pp. 717–45

Condos, Mark and Gavin Rand, 'Coercion and Conciliation at the Edge of Empire: State-building and Its limits in Waziristan, 1849–1914', *The Historical Journal*, 61, 3 (2018), pp. 695–718

Daston, Lorraine and Peter Galison, *Objectivity* (New York: Zone Books, 2007)

de Certeau, Michel, *The Practice of Everyday Life*, trans. Steven Rendall (Berkeley, CA: University of California, 1984)

Delano-Smith, Catherine, 'Milieus of Mobility: Itineraries, Route Maps, and Road Maps', in James R. Akerman (ed.), *Cartographies of Travel and Navigation* (Chicago, IL: University of Chicago Press, 2006), pp. 16–68

Dewan, Janet, 'Delineating Antiquities and Remarkable Tribes: Photography for the Bombay and Madras Governments 1855–70', *History of Photography*, 16, 4 (1992), pp. 302–17

Dirks, Nicholas B., *Castes of Mind: Colonialism and the Making of Modern India* (Princeton, NJ: Princeton University Press, 2001)

Dirks, Nicholas B., 'Annals of the Archives: Ethnographic Notes on the Sources of History', in Brian Axel (ed.), *From the Margins: Historical Anthropology and Its Futures* (Durham, NC: Duke University Press, 2002), pp. 47–65

Dirks, Nicholas B., *The Scandal of Empire: India and the Creation of Imperial Britain* (Cambridge, MA: Harvard University Press, 2006)

Dodge, Martin and Chris Perkins, 'Reflecting on J.B. Harley's Influence and What He Missed in "Deconstructing the Map"', *Cartographica*, 50, 1 (2015), pp. 37–40

Dodge, Toby, *Inventing Iraq: The Failure of Nation Building and a History Denied* (London: Hurst, 2003)

Drayton, Richard, 'Where Does the World Historian Write From? Objectivity, Moral Conscience and the Past and Present of Imperialism', *Journal of Contemporary History*, 46, 3 (2011), pp. 671–85

Drescher, Seymour, *Abolition: A History of Slavery and Antislavery* (Cambridge: Cambridge University Press, 2009)

Dritsas, Lawrence, 'Expeditionary Science: Conflicts of Method in Mid-Nineteenth-Century Geographical Discovery', in Charles W. J. Withers and David N. Livingstone (eds.), *Geographies of Nineteenth-Century Science* (Chicago and London: University of Chicago Press, 2011), pp. 255–78

Driver, Felix, *Geography Militant: Cultures of Exploration and Empire* (Oxford: Blackwell, 2001)

Driver, Felix, 'Distance and Disturbance: Travel, Exploration and Knowledge in the Nineteenth Century', *Transactions of the Royal Historical Society*, Sixth Series, 14 (2004), pp. 73–92

Driver, Felix, 'Hidden Histories Made Visible? Reflection on a Geographical Exhibition', *Transactions of the Institute of British Geographers*, 38 (2013), pp. 420–35

Dunn, Richard, 'North by Northwest? Experimental Instruments and Instruments of Experiment', in Fraser MacDonald and Charles W. J. Withers (eds.), *Geography, Technology and Instruments of Exploration* (Farnham: Ashgate, 2015), pp. 57–76

Dzuvichu, Lipokmar, 'Roads and the Raj: The Politics of Road Building in Colonial Naga Hills, 1860s–1910s', *The Indian Economic and Social History Review*, 50, 4 (2013), pp. 473–94

Dzüvichü, Lipokmar, 'Empire on Their Backs: Coolies in the Eastern Borderlands of the British Raj', *International Review of Social History*, 59 (2014), pp. 89–112

Edney, Matthew H., *Mapping an Empire: The Geographical Construction of British India, 1765–1843* (Chicago, IL: University of Chicago Press, 1997)

Edney, Matthew H., 'Bringing India to Hand: Mapping an Empire, Denying Space', in Felicity Nussbaum (ed.), *The Global Eighteenth Century* (Baltimore, MD: John Hopkins University Press, 2003), pp. 65–78

Edney, Matthew H., 'The Irony of Imperial Mapping', in James R. Akerman (ed.), *The Imperial Map: Cartography and the Mastery of Empire* (Chicago, IL: University of Chicago Press, 2009), pp. 11–45

Edwards, David B., 'Mad Mullahs and Englishmen: Discourse in the Colonial Encounter', *Comparative Studies in Society and History*, 31, 4 (1989), pp. 649–70.

Edwards, Elizabeth, 'Science Visualized: E.H. Man in the Andaman Islands', in *id* (ed.), *Anthropology and Photography 1860–1920* (New Haven and London: Yale University Press, 1992), pp. 108–21

Edwards, Elizabeth, *Raw Histories: Photographs, Anthropology and Museums* (Oxford and New York: Berg, 2001)

Edwards, Elizabeth, 'Tracing Photography', in Marcus Banks and Jay Ruby (eds.), *Made to Be Seen: Perspectives on the History of Visual Anthropology* (Chicago, IL: University of Chicago Press, 2011), pp. 159–89

Edwards, Elizabeth, 'Anthropology and Photography: A Long History of Knowledge and Affect', *Photographies*, 8, 3 (2015), pp. 235–52

Elden, Stuart, 'Land, Terrain, Territory', *Progress in Human Geography*, 34, 6 (2010), pp. 799–817

Elden, Stuart, *The Birth of Territory* (Chicago, IL: University of Chicago Press, 2013)

Elliott, J. G., *The Frontier 1839–1947: The Story of the North-West Frontier of India* (London: Cassell, 1968)

Elshakry, Marwa, 'When Science Became Western: Historiographical Reflections', *Isis*, 101, 1 (2010), pp. 98–109

Fabian, Johannes, *Out of Our Minds: Reason and Madness in the Exploration of Central Africa* (Berkeley, CA: University of California Press, 2000)

Falconer, John, 'Photography in Nineteenth-Century India', in C. A. Bayly (ed.), *The Raj: India and the British 1600–1947* (London: National Portrait Gallery, 1990), pp. 264–77

Falconer, John, '"A Pure Labor of Love": A Publishing History of *The People of India*', in Eleanor M. Hight and Gary D. Sampson (eds.), *Colonialist Photography: Imag(in) ing race and place* (London: Routledge, 2002), pp. 51–83

Fall, J. J., 'Artificial States? On the Enduring Myth of Natural Frontiers', *Political Geography*, 29 (2010), pp. 140–7

Febvre, Lucien, '*Frontière*: The Word and the Concept', trans. K. Folka, in Peter Burke (ed.), *A New Kind of History: From the writings of Febvre* (London: Routledge and Kegan Paul, 1973), pp. 208–18

Fleetwood, Lachlan, '"No Former Travellers Having Attained Such a Height on the Earth's Surface": Instruments, Inscriptions, and Bodies in the Himalaya, 1800–1830', *History of Science*, 56, 1 (2018), pp. 3–34

Foliard, Daniel, *Dislocating the Orient: British maps and the making of the Middle East, 1854–1921* (Chicago, IL: University of Chicago Press, 2017)

Foucault, Michel, 'Of Other Spaces', trans. Jay Miskowiec, *Diacritics*, 16, 1 (1986), pp. 22–7

Foucault, Michel, *The Hermeneutics of the Subject: Lectures at the College de France, 1981–1982*, (ed.), Frédéric Gros, trans. Graham Burchell (New York, NY: Picador, 2005)

Fuoli, Francesca, 'Incorporating North-western Afghanistan into the British Empire: Experiments in Indirect Rule through the Making of an Imperial Frontier, 1884–87', *Afghanistan*, 1, 1 (2018), pp. 4–25

Gaenszle, Martin, 'Brian Hodgson as Ethnographer and Ethnologist', in David M. Waterhouse (ed.), *The Origins of Himalayan Studies: Brian Houghton Hodgson in Nepal and Darjeeling 1820–1858* (Abingdon: Routledge, 2004), pp. 206–26

Galbraith, John S., 'The "Turbulent Frontier" as a Factor in British Expansion', *Comparative Studies in History and Society*, 2, 2 (1960), pp. 150–68

Gardner, Kyle, 'Moving Watersheds, Borderless Maps, and Imperial Geography in India's Northwestern Frontier', *The Historical Journal*, 62, 1 (2019), pp. 149–70

Gilmartin, David, *Blood and Water: The Indus River Basin in Modern History* (Oakland, CA: University of California Press, 2015)

Gilmour, David, *Curzon: Imperial Statesman 1859–1925* (London: John Murray, 1994)

Gregory, Derek, *Geographical Imaginations* (Oxford: Blackwell, 1994)

Grewal, J. S., *The Sikhs of Punjab*, 2nd ed. (Cambridge: Cambridge University Press, 2008)

Guha, Ranajit, *A Rule of Property for Bengal*, 2nd ed. (New Delhi: Orient Longman, 1981)

Guha, Ranajit, *Elementary Aspects of Peasant Insurgency in Colonial India* (Durham, NC: Duke University Press, 1999)

Guha, Sumit, *Environment and Ethnicity in India: 1200–1991* (Cambridge: Cambridge University Press, 2006)

Guite, Jangkhomang, 'Civilisation and Its Malcontents: The Politics of Kuki Raid in Nineteenth Century Northeast India', *The Indian Economic and Social History Review*, 48, 3 (2011), pp. 339–76

Guyot-Rechard, Bérénice, *Shadow States: India, China and the Himalayas, 1910–1962* (Cambridge: Cambridge University Press, 2017)

Hämäläinen, Pekka, *The Comanche Empire* (New Haven, CT: Yale University Press, 2008)

Hämäläinen, Pekka, 'What's in a Concept? The Kinetic Empire of the Comanches', *History and Theory*, 52 (2013), pp. 81–90

Hansen, Peter H., *The Summits of Modern Man: Mountaineering after the Enlightenment* (Cambridge, MA: Harvard University Press, 2013)

Harley, J. B., *The New Nature of Maps: Essays in the History of Cartography*, ed. Paul Laxton (Baltimore, MD: Johns Hopkins University Press, 2001)

Harrison, Mark, 'Science and the British Empire', *Isis*, 96, 1 (2005), pp. 56–63

Heathcote, T. A., *Balochistan, the British and the Great Game: The Struggle for the Bolan Pass, Gateway to India* (London: Hurst, 2016)

Heidegger, Martin, 'The Age of the World Picture', in *The Question Concerning Technology and Other Essays*, trans. William Lovitt (New York, NY: Harper, 1977), pp. 115–54

Heuman, Gad, *'The Killing Time': The Morant Bay Rebellion in Jamaica* (London: Macmillan, 1994)

Hevia, James L., 'The Photography Complex: Exposing Boxer-Era China (1900–1901), Making Civilisation', in Rosalind C. Morris, (ed.), *Photographies East: The camera and its histories in East and Southeast Asia* (Durham, NC: Duke University Press, 2009), pp. 79–119

Hevia, James, *The Imperial Security State: British Colonial Knowledge and Empire-Building in Asia* (Cambridge: Cambridge University Press, 2012)

Hevly, Bruce, 'The Heroic Science of Glacier Motion', *Osiris*, 11 (1996), pp. 66–86

Honour, Hugh, *Romanticism* (New York, NY: Westview, 1979)

Hopkins, Benjamin D., 'The Bounds of Identity: The Goldsmid Mission and the Delineation of the Perso-Afghan Border in the Nineteenth Century', *Journal of Global History*, 2 (2007), pp. 233–54

Hopkins, Benjamin D., *The Making of Modern Afghanistan* (Basingstoke: Palgrave Macmillan, 2008)

Hopkins, Benjamin D., 'A History of the "Hindustani Fanatics" on the Frontier', in id and Magnus Marsden (eds.), *Beyond Swat: History, Society and Economy along the Afghanistan-Pakistan Frontier* (New York, NY: Columbia University Press, 2013), pp. 39–49

Hopkins, Benjamin D., 'The Frontier Crimes Regulation and Frontier Governmentality', *Journal of Asian Studies*, 74, 2 (2015), pp. 369–89

Hopwood, Nick, *Haeckel's Embryos: Images, Evolution, and Fraud* (Chicago, IL: University of Chicago Press, 2015)

Howe, Daniel Walker, *What Hath God Wrought: The Transformation of America, 1815–1848* (New York, NY: Oxford University Press, 2007)

Hull, Matthew S., *Government of Paper: The Materiality of Bureaucracy in Urban Pakistan* (Berkeley, CA: University of California Press, 2012)

Hussain, Nasser, *The Jurisprudence of Emergency: Colonialism and the Rule of Law* (Ann Arbor, MI: University of Michigan Press, 2003)

Ingold, Tim, *Lines: A brief history* (London: Routledge, 2007)

Jacobs, Julian, Alan Macfarlane, Sarah Harrison, and Anita Herle, *The Nagas: Society, Culture and the Colonial Encounter*, 2nd ed. (London: Edition Hansjörg Mayer, 2012)

Jasanoff, Maya, *Edge of Empire: Lives, Culture, and Conquest in the East, 1750–1850* (London: Vintage, 2006)

Jauss, Hans Robert, *Toward an Aesthetics of Reception*, trans. Timothy Bahti (Minneapolis, MN: University of Minnesota Press, 1982)

Jay, Martin and Sumathi Ramaswamy, 'Section I: The Imperial Optic', in id (eds.), *Empires of Vision: A Reader* (Durham, NC: Duke University Press, 2014), pp. 23–43

Jay, Martin, 'Conclusion. A Parting Glance: Empire and Visuality', in id and Sumathi Ramaswamy (eds.), *Empires of Vision: A Reader* (Durham, NC: Duke University Press, 2014), pp. 609–20

Jones, Reece, 'Spaces of Refusal: Rethinking Sovereign Power and Resistance at the Border', *Annals of the Association of American Geographers*, 102, 3 (2011), pp. 685–99

Judd, Denis and Keith Surridge, *The Boer War: A history*, 2nd ed. (London: I.B. Tauris, 2013)

Kar, Bodhisattva, 'When Was the Postcolonial? A History of Policing Impossible Lines', in Sanjib Baruah (ed.), *Beyond Counter-Insurgency: Breaking the Impasse in Northeast India* (New Delhi: Oxford University Press, 2009), pp. 49–77

Kar, Bodhisattva, 'Nomadic Capital and Speculative Tribes: A Culture of Contracts in the Northeastern Frontier of British India', *The Indian Economic and Social History Review*, 53, 1 (2016), pp. 41–67

Kearns, Gerry *Geopolitics and Empire: The Legacy of Halford Mackinder* (Oxford: Oxford University Press, 2009)

Keighren, Innes M., Charles W. J. Withers, and Bill Bell, *Travels into Print: Exploration, Writing, and Publishing with John Murray, 1773–1859* (Chicago, IL: University of Chicago Press, 2015)

Kennedy, Dane, *The Last Blank Spaces: Exploring Africa and Australia* (Cambridge, MA: Harvard University Press, 2013)

Khan, Omar, *From Kashmir to Kabul: The Photographs of John Burke and William Baker, 1860–1900* (Munich: Prestel, 2002)

Kitchin, Rob, Chris Perkins, and Martin Dodge, 'Thinking about Maps', in id (eds.), *Rethinking Maps* (Abingdon: Routledge, 2009), pp. 1–25

Kolsky, Elizabeth, *Colonial Justice in British India* (Cambridge, Cambridge University Press, 2010)

Kolsky, Elizabeth, 'The Colonial Rule of Law and the Legal Regime of Exception: Frontier "Fanaticism" and State Violence in British India', *American Historical Review*, 120, 4 (2015), pp. 1218–46

Kostal, R. W., *A Jurisprudence of Power: Victorian Empire and the Rule of Law* (Oxford: Oxford University Press, 2005)

Kuklick, Henrika, *The Savage Within: The Social History of British Anthropology, 1885–1945* (Cambridge: Cambridge University Press, 1991)

Lambert, David, *Mastering the Niger: James MacQueen's African Geography and the Struggle over Atlantic Slavery* (Chicago, IL: University of Chicago Press, 2013)

Lambrick, H. T., *John Jacob of Jacobabad* (London: Cassell, 1960)

Latour, Bruno, *Science In Action: How to Follow Scientists and Engineers through Society*, trans. (Cambridge, MA: Harvard University Press, 1987)

Latour, Bruno, *We Have Never Been Modern*, trans. Catherine Porter (Cambridge, MA: Harvard University Press, 1993)

Layton, Simon, 'Discourses of Piracy in an Age of Revolutions', *Itinerario*, 35, 2 (2011), pp. 81–97

Layton, S. H., 'Hydras and Leviathans in the Indian Ocean World', *International Journal of Maritime History*, 25 (2013), pp. 213–25

Leake, Elisabeth, *The Defiant Border: The Afghan-Pakistan Borderlands in the Era of Decolonization, 1936–1965* (Cambridge: Cambridge University Press, 2017)

Legg, Stephen, *Spaces of Colonialism: Delhi's Urban Governmentalities* (Oxford: Blackwell, 2007)

Leonard, Zak, 'Colonial Ethnography on India's North-west Frontier, 1850–1910', *The Historical Journal*, 59, 1 (2016), pp. 175–96

Lester, Alan, *Imperial Networks: Creating Identities in Nineteenth-Century South Africa and Britain* (London: Routledge, 2001)

Lindholm, Charles, *Frontier Perspectives: Essays in Comparative Anthropology* (Karachi: Oxford University Press, 1996)

Longkumer, Arkotong, '"Along Kingdom's Highway": The Proliferation of Christianity, Education, and Print amongst the Nagas in Northeast India', *Contemporary South Asia*, 27 (2019), pp. 160–78

Ludden, David, 'Investing in Nature around Sylhet: An Excursion into Geographical History', *Economic and Political Weekly*, 29 November 2003, pp. 5080–8

Ludden, David, 'The First Boundary of Bangladesh on Sylhet's Northern Frontiers', *Journal of the Asiatic Society of Bangladesh*, 48, 1 (2003), pp. 1–54

Ludden, David, 'The Process of Empire: Frontiers and Borderlands', in P. F. Bang and C. A. Bayly (eds.), *Tributary Empires in Global History* (London: Palgrave Macmillan, 2011), pp. 132–50

MacDonald, Fraser and Charles W. J. Withers (eds.), *Geography, Technology and Instruments of Exploration* (Farnham: Ashgate, 2015)

Maier, Charles S., 'Transformations of Territoriality: 1600–2000', in Gunilla Budde, Sebastian Conrad and Oliver Janz (eds.), *Transnationale Geschichte: Themen, Tendenzen und Theorien* (Göttingen: Vandenhoeck & Ruprecht, 2006), pp. 32–55

Majeed, Javed, *Colonialism and Knowledge in Grierson's Linguistic Survey of India* (Abingdon: Routledge, 2019)

Majeed, Javed, *Nation and Region in Grierson's Linguistic Survey of India* (London: Routledge, 2019)

Mandler, Peter, *Return from the Natives: How Margaret Mead won the Second World War and lost the Cold War* (New Haven, CT: Yale University Press, 2013)

Marsden, Magnus and Benjamin D. Hopkins, *Fragments of the Afghan Frontier* (London: Hurst, 2011)

Massey, Doreen, *For Space* (London: Sage, 2005)

Mathur, Nayanika, *Paper Tiger: Law, Bureaucracy and the Developmental State in Himalayan India* (Cambridge: Cambridge University Press, 2015)

Mbembe, Achille, *On the Postcolony* (Berkeley, CA: University of California Press, 2001)

Mbembe, Achille, 'Necropolitics', trans. Libby Meintjes, *Public Culture*, 15, 1 (2003), pp. 11–40

Metcalf, Thomas R., *Ideologies of the Raj* (Cambridge: Cambridge University Press, 1998)

Michael, Bernardo A., 'Making Territory Visible: The Revenue Surveys of Colonial South Asia', *Imago Mundi*, 59, 1 (2007), pp. 78–95

Michael, Bernardo A., *Statemaking and Territory in South Asia: Lessons from the Anglo-Gorkha War (1814–1816)* (London: Anthem Press, 2012)

Misra, Sanghamitra, *Becoming a Borderland: The Politics of Space and Identity in Colonial Northeastern India* (New Delhi: Routledge, 2011)

Misra, Sanghamitra, 'The Sovereignty of Political Economy: The Garos in a Pre-conquest and Early Conquest Era', *The Indian Economic and Social History Review*, 55, 3 (2018), pp. 345–87

Mitchell, Timothy, 'The World As Exhibition', *Comparative Studies in Society and History*, 31, 2 (1989), pp. 217–36

Mitchell, Timothy, *Rule of Experts: Egypt, Techno-Politics, Modernity* (Berkeley, CA: University of California Press, 2002)

Morrison, A. S., *Russian Rule in Samarkand 1868–1910: A Comparison with British India* (Oxford: Oxford University Press, 2008)

Mueggler, Erik, *The Paper Road: Archive and Experience in the Botanical Expedition of West China and Tibet* (Berkeley, CA: University of California Press, 2011)

Mukherjee, Rudrangshu, *Awadh in Revolt 1857–1858: A Study of Popular Resistance* (Delhi: Oxford University Press, 1984)

Myint-U, Thant, *The Making of Modern Burma* (Cambridge: Cambridge University Press, 2001)

Nichols, Robert, *Settling the Frontier: Land, Law, and Society in the Peshawar Valley, 1500–1900* (Karachi: Oxford University Press, 2001)

Nietzsche, Friedrich, *The Birth of Tragedy and Other Writings*, (ed.), Raymond Geuss and Ronald Speirs, trans. Ronald Speirs (Cambridge: Cambridge University Press, 1999)

Noelle, Christine, *State and Tribe in Nineteenth-Century Afghanistan: The Reign of Amir Dost Muhammad Khan (1826–1863)* (Richmond, VA: Curzon, 1997)

O'Reilly, William, 'Frederick Jackson Turner's Frontier Thesis, Orientalism, and the Austrian Militärgrenze', *Journal of Austrian-American History*, 2, 1 (2018), pp. 1–30

Ortner, Sherry B., 'Resistance and the Problem of Ethnographic Refusal', *Comparative Studies in Society and History*, 37, 1 (1995), pp. 173–93

Osterhammel, Jürgen, *The Transformation of the World: A Global History of the Nineteenth Century*, trans. Patrick Camiller (Princeton, NJ: Princeton University Press, 2014)

Pachuau, Joy L. K. and Willem van Schendel, *The Camera as Witness: A Social History of Mizoram, Northeast India* (Delhi: Cambridge University Press, 2015)

Parker, Noel, Nick Vaughan-Williams, et al, 'Lines in the Sand? Towards an Agenda for Critical Border Studies', *Geopolitics*, 14, 3 (2009), pp. 582–7

Phillimore, R. H., *Historical Records of the Survey of India. Volume V. 1844 to 1861: Andrew Waugh* (Dehra Dun: Survey of India, 1968)

Phillips, Eoin, 'Instrumenting Order: Longitude, Seamen and Astronomers, 1770–1805', in Fraser MacDonald and Charles W. J. Withers (eds.), *Geography, Technology and Instruments of Exploration* (Farnham: Ashgate, 2015), pp. 37–56

Pick, Daniel, *Faces of Degeneration: A European Disorder, c.1848-c.1918* (Cambridge: Cambridge University Press, 1989)

Piliavsky, Anastasia, 'The "Criminal Tribe" in India before the British', *Comparative Studies in Society and History*, 57, 2 (2015), pp. 323–54

Pinch, William, 'Same Difference in India and Europe', *History and Theory*, 38, 3 (1999), pp. 389–407

Pinney, Christopher, 'Colonial Anthropology in the "Laboratory of Mankind"', in C. A. Bayly (ed.), *The Raj: India and the British 1600–1947* (London: National Portrait Gallery, 1990), pp. 252–63

Pinney, Christopher, *Camera Indica: The Social Life of Indian Photographs* (London: Reaktion Books, 1997)

Pinney, Christopher, *The Coming of Photography in India* (London: British Library, 2008)

Poleykett, Branwyn, 'Pasteurian Tropical Medicine and Colonial Scientific Vision', *Subjectivity*, 10, 2 (2017), pp. 190–203

Poskett, James, *Materials of the Mind: Phrenology, Race, and the Global History of Science, 1815–1920* (Chicago, IL: University of Chicago Press, 2019)

Prakash, Gyan, *Another Reason: Science and the Imagination of Modern India* (Princeton, NJ: Princeton University Press, 1999)

Pratt, Mary Louise, *Imperial Eyes: Travel Writing and Transculturation* (London: Routledge, 1992)

Qureshi, Sadiah, *Peoples on Parade: Exhibitions, Empire, and Anthropology in Nineteenth-Century Britain* (Chicago, IL: University of Chicago Press, 2011)

Rae, Eugene, Catherine Souch and Charles W. J. Withers, '"Instruments in the Hands of Others": The Life and Liveliness of Instruments of British Geographical Exploration, c.1860–c.1930', in Fraser MacDonald and Charles W. J. Withers (eds.), *Geography, Technology and Instruments of Exploration* (Farnham: Ashgate, 2015), pp. 139–60

Raj, Kapil, *Relocating Modern Science: Circulation and the Construction of Knowledge in South Asia and Europe, 1650–1900* (Basingstoke: Palgrave Macmillan, 2007)

Raj, Kapil, 'Mapping Knowledge Go-Betweens in Calcutta, 1770–1820', in Simon Schaffer, Lissa Roberts, Kapil Raj, and James Delbourgo (eds.), *The Brokered World: Go-Betweens and Global Intelligence, 1770–1820* (Sagamore Beach, FL: Watson, 2009), pp. 105–50

Raj, Kapil, 'Beyond Postcolonialism ... and Postpositivism: Circulation and the Global History of Science', *Isis*, 104, 2 (2013), pp. 337–47

Ramaswamy, Sumathi, *The Lost Land of Lemuria: Fabulous Geographies, Catastrophic Histories* (Berkeley, CA: University of California Press, 2004)

Readman, Paul, Cynthia Radding, and Chad Bryant, 'Introduction: Borderlands in a Global Perspective', in id (eds.), *Borderlands in World History, 1700–1914* (Basingstoke: Palgrave Macmillan, 2014), pp. 1–23

Robb, Peter, 'The Colonial State and Constructions of Indian Identity: An Example on the Northeast Frontier in the 1880s', *Modern Asian Studies*, 31, 2 (1997), pp. 245–83

Roe, Andrew M., *Waging War in Waziristan: The British Struggle in the Land of Bin Laden, 1849–1947* (Lawrence, KS: University Press of Kansas, 2010)

Rood, Daniel, 'Toward a Global Labor History of Science', in Patrick Manning and Daniel Rood (eds.), *Global Scientific Practice in an Age of Revolution, 1750–1850* (Pittsburgh, PA: University of Pittsburgh Press, 2016), pp. 255–74

Roque, Ricardo, *Headhunting and Colonialism: Anthropology and the Circulation of Human Skulls in the Portuguese Empire, 1870–1930* (Basingstoke: Palgrave Macmillan, 2010)

Rose-Redwood, Reuben (ed.), 'Deconstructing the Map: 25 Years On', special issue *of Cartographica*, 50, 1 (2015)

Ryan, James R., *Picturing Empire: Photography and the Visualization of the British Empire* (London: Reaktion Books, 1997)

Ryan, Lyndall, *Tasmanian Aborigines: A History Since 1803* (Sydney: Allen & Unwin, 2012)

Sadan, Mandy, *Being and Becoming Kachin: Histories Beyond the State in the Borderworlds of Burma* (Oxford: Oxford University Press, 2013)

Safier, Neil, *Measuring the New World: Enlightenment Science and South America* (Chicago, IL: University of Chicago Press, 2008)

Sahlins, Peter, *Boundaries: The Making of France and Spain in the Pyrenees* (Berkeley, CA: University of California Press, 1989).

Saikia, Arupjyoti, *The Unquiet River: A Biography of the Brahmaputra* (Delhi: Oxford University Press, 2019)

Sampson, Gary D., 'The Success of Samuel Bourne in India', *History of Photography*, 16, 4 (1992), pp. 336–47

Satia, Priya, *Spies in Arabia: The Great War and the Cultural Foundations of Britain's Covert Empire* (Oxford: Oxford University Press, 2008)

Schaffer, Simon, *From Physics to Anthropology—and Back Again* (Cambridge: Prickly Pear, 1994)

Schaffer, Simon, 'Late Victorian Metrology and Its Instrumentation: A Manufactory of Ohms', in Mario Biagioli (ed.), *The Science Studies Reader* (London: Routledge, 1999), pp. 457–78

Schaffer, Simon, Lissa Roberts, Kapil Raj, and James Delbourgo (eds.), *The Brokered World: Go-Betweens and Global Intelligence, 1770–1820* (Sagamore Beach, FL: Watson, 2009).

Schaffer, Simon, 'Easily Cracked: Scientific Instruments in States of Disrepair', *Isis*, 102, 4 (2011), pp. 706–17

Schmitt, Carl, *The* Nomos *of the Earth in the International Law of the* Jus Publicum Europaeum, trans. G. L. Ulmen (New York, NY: Telos Press, 2003 [1950])

Schmitt, Carl, *The Concept of the Political*, trans. George Schwab (Chicago, IL: University of Chicago Press, 2007 [1932])

Scholz, Fred, *Nomadism and Colonialism: A Hundred Years of Baluchistan, 1872–1972*, trans. Hugh van Skyhawk (Oxford: Oxford University Press, 2002 [1974])

Scott, James C., *Seeing Like A State: How Certain Scheme to Improve the Human Condition Have Failed* (New Haven, CT: Yale University Press, 1998)

Scott, James C., *The Art of Not Being Governed: An Anarchist History of Upland Southeast Asia* (New Haven, CT: Yale University Press, 2009)

Secord, James A., 'Knowledge in Transit', *Isis*, 95, 4 (2004), pp. 654–72

Sen, Anandaroop, 'The Law of Emptiness: Episodes from Lushai and Chin Hills (1890–98)', in Neeladri Bhattacharya and Joy L. K. Pachuau (eds.), *Landscape, Culture, and Belonging: Writing the History of Northeast India* (Cambridge: Cambridge University Press, 2019), pp.207–36

Sen, Satadru, *Savagery and Colonialism in the Indian Ocean: Power, Pleasure and the Andaman Islanders* (Abingdon: Routledge, 2010)

Sera-Shriar, Efram, *The Making of British Anthropology, 1813–1871* (London: Pickering & Chatto, 2013)

Sharma, Aradhana and Akhil Gupta, 'Introduction: Rethinking Theories of the State in an Age of Globalization', in id (eds.), *The Anthropology of the State: A Reader* (Oxford: Blackwell, 2006), pp. 1–41

Sharma, Jayeeta, 'Making Garden, Erasing Jungle: The Tea Enterprise in Colonial Assam', in Deepak Kumar, Vinita Damodaran and Rohan D'Souza (eds.), *The British Empire and the Natural World: Environmental Encounters in South Asia* (Oxford: Oxford University Press, 2010), pp. 119–41

Sharma, Jayeeta, *Empire's Garden: Assam and the Making of India* (Durham and London: Duke University Press, 2011)

Sherman, Taylor C., *State Violence and Punishment in India* (London: Routledge, 2010)

Simpson, Thomas, '"Clean Out of the Map": Knowing and Doubting Space at India's High Imperial Frontiers', *History of Science*, 55, 1 (2017), pp. 3–36

Simpson, Thomas, 'A Fragmented Gaze: Depictions of Frontier Tribes and the Beginnings of Colonial Anthropology', in Marcus Banks and Annamaria Motrescu-Mayes (eds.), *Visual Histories of South Asia* (New Delhi: Primus, 2018), pp. 73–92

Simpson, Thomas, 'Historicizing Humans in Colonial India', in Efram Sera-Shriar (ed.), *Historicizing Humans: Deep Time, Evolution and Race in Nineteenth-century British Sciences* (Pittsburgh, PA: University of Pittsburgh Press, 2018), pp. 113–37

Simpson, Thomas, 'Forgetting like a State in Colonial North-east India', in Shah Mahmoud Hanifi (ed.), *Mountstuart Elphinstone in South Asia: Pioneer of British colonial rule* (London: Hurst, 2019), pp. 223–47.

Singha, Radhika, *A Despotism of Law: Crime and Justice in Early Colonial India* (Delhi: Oxford University Press, 1998)

Sinha, Mrinalini, *Colonial Masculinity: The Manly Englishman and the Effeminate Bengali* (Manchester: Manchester University Press, 1995)

Sivaramakrishnan, K., 'British Imperium and Forested Zones of Anomaly in Bengal, 1767–1833', *The Indian Economic and Social History Review*, 33, 3 (1996), pp. 243–82

Sivasundaram, Sujit, 'Sciences and the Global: On Methods, Questions, and Theory', *Isis*, 101, 1 (2010), pp. 146–58

Skaria, Ajay, *Hybrid Histories: Forests, Frontiers and Wildness in Western India* (Delhi: Oxford University Press, 1999)

Sökefeld, Martin, 'Rumour and Politics on the Northern Frontier: The British, Pakhtun Wali and Yaghestan', *Modern Asian Studies*, 36, 2 (2002), pp. 299–340

Stocking Jr., George W., 'The Ethnographer's Magic: Fieldwork in British Anthropology from Tylor to Malinowski', in id (ed.), *Observers Observed: Essays on Ethnographic Fieldwork* (Madison, WI: University of Wisconsin Press, 1983), pp. 70–120

Stocking Jr., George W., *Victorian Anthropology* (New York, NY: Maxwell Macmillan, 1987)

Stocking Jr., George W., *After Tylor: British Social Anthropology, 1888–1951* (London: Athlone, 1996)

Stokes, Eric, *The Peasant and the Raj: Studies in Agrarian Society and Peasant Rebellion in Colonial India* (Cambridge: Cambridge University Press, 1978)

Stoler, Ann Laura, *Along the Archival Grain: Epistemic Anxieties and Colonial Common Sense* (Princeton, NJ: Princeton University Press, 2009)

Stoler, Ann Laura, 'Colonial Aphasia: Race and Disabled Histories in France', *Public Culture*, 23, 1 (2011), pp. 121–56

Swidler, Nina, 'Kalat: The Political Economy of a Tribal Chiefdom', *American Ethnologist*, 19, 3 (1992), pp. 553–70

Tagg, John, *The Burden of Representation: Essays on Photographies and Histories* (Basingstoke: Macmillan Education, 1988)

Tilley, Helen, *Africa as a Living Laboratory: Empire, Development, and the Problem of Scientific Knowledge, 1870–1950* (Chicago, IL: University of Chicago Press, 2011)

Titus, Paul, 'Honor the Baloch, Buy the Pushtun: Stereotypes, Social Organization and History in Western Pakistan', *Modern Asian Studies*, 32, 3 (1998), pp. 657–87

Trautmann, Thomas R., *Aryans and British India* (Berkeley, CA: University of California Press, 1997)

Travers, Robert, *Ideology and Empire in Eighteenth-Century India: The British in Bengal* (Cambridge: Cambridge University Press, 2007)

Tripodi, Christian, *Edge of Empire: The British Political Officer and Tribal Administration on the North-West Frontier 1877–1947* (London: Ashgate, 2011)

Twyman, Michael, 'The Illustration Revolution', in David McKitterick (ed.), *The Cambridge History of the Book in Britain. Volume VI: 1830–1914* (Cambridge: Cambridge University Press, 2009), pp. 117–43

Urry, James, '"Notes and Queries on Anthropology" and the Development of Field Methods in British Anthropology, 1870–1920', *Proceedings of the Royal Anthropological Institute of Great Britain and Ireland* (1972), pp. 45–57

van Driem, George, 'Hodgson's Tibeto-Burman and Tibeto-Burman Today', in David M. Waterhouse (ed.), *The Origins of Himalayan Studies: Brian Houghton Hodgson in Nepal and Darjeeling 1820–1858* (Abingdon: Routledge, 2004), pp. 227–48

von Brescius, Moritz, *German Science in the Age of Empire: Enterprise, Opportunity and the Schlagintweit Brothers* (Cambridge: Cambridge University Press, 2018)

von Stockhausen, Alban, *Imag(in)ing the Nagas: The Pictorial Ethnography of Hans-Eberhard Kauffmann and Christoph von Furer-Haimendorf* (Stuttgart: Arnoldische Art Publishers, 2014)

von Stockhausen, Alban, 'Naga: Lineages of a Term', in Neeladri Bhattacharya and Joy L. K. Pachuau (eds.), *Landscape, Culture, and Belonging: Writing the History of Northeast India* (Cambridge: Cambridge University Press, 2019), pp. 131–50

Wagner, Kim A., '"Treading upon Fires": The "Mutiny"-Motif and Colonial Anxieties in British India', *Past and Present*, 218 (2013), pp. 159–97

Walker, Andrew, *The Legend of the Golden Boat: Regulation, Trade and Traders in the Borderlands of Laos, Thailand, China and Burma* (Richmond, VA: Curzon, 1999)

Walker, Andrew, 'Borders in Motion on the Upper-Mekong: Siam and France in the 1890s', in Yves Goudineau and Michel Lorrillard (eds.), *Recherches nouvelles sur le Laos* (Vientiane, Paris: École française d'Extrême-Orient, 2008), pp. 183–208

Walker, Andrew, 'Conclusion: Are the Mekong Frontiers Sites of Exception?', in Martin Gainsborough (ed.), *On the Borders of State Power: Frontiers in the Greater Mekong Sub-Region* (London, New York: Routledge, 2009), pp. 101–11

Waller, Derek, *The Pundits: British Exploration of Tibet and Central Asia* (Lexington, KY: The University Press of Kentucky, 1990)

Whitehead, John, *Thangliena: The Life of T.H. Lewin* (Gartmore: Kiscadale, 1992)

Wilson, Jon, *The Domination of Strangers: Modern Governance in Eastern India, 1780–1835* (Basingstoke: Palgrave Macmillan, 2008)

Wilson, Jon, 'How Modernity Arrived to Godavari', *Modern Asian Studies*, 51, 2 (2017), pp. 399–431

Wilson, Thomas M. and Hastings Donnan (eds.). *Border Identities: Nation and State at International Frontiers* (Cambridge: Cambridge University Press, 1998)

Wise, M. Norton (ed.), *The Values of Precision* (Princeton, NJ: Princeton University Press, 1995)

Withers, Charles W. J., *Geography and Science in Britain, 1831–1939: A Study of the British Association for the Advancement of Science* (Manchester: Manchester University Press, 2010)

Yapp, Malcolm, *Strategies of British India: Britain, Iran, and Afghanistan, 1798–1850* (Oxford: Clarendon Press, 1980)

Yusoff, Kathryn, 'Climates of Sight: Mistaken Visibilities, Mirages and "Seeing Beyond" in Antarctica', in Denis Cosgrove and Veronica della Dora (eds.), *High Places: Cultural Geographies of Mountains, Ice and Science* (London: I.B. Tauris, 2009), pp. 48–63

Zou, David Vumlallian and M. Satish Kumar, 'Mapping a Colonial Borderland: Objectifying the Geo-Body of India's Northeast', *The Journal of Asian Studies*, 70, 1 (2011), pp. 141–70

Unpublished Thesis

Cook, Matthew A., 'After Annexation: Colonialism and Sindh during the 1840s' (unpublished doctoral thesis, Colombia University, 2007)

Online Articles

Columbia University, 'Afghans' images www.columbia.edu/itc/mealac/pritchett/00rou tesdata/1800_1899/northwest/afghans/afghans.html

'Behali Killings: Assam Registers Case Against 12', *Times of India*, 14/02/2014

Index